Lecture Notes in Computer Science   8362

Commenced Publication in 1973
Founding and Former Series Editors:
Gerhard Goos, Juris Hartmanis, and Jan van Leeuwen

Michalis Faloutsos
Aleksandar Kuzmanovic (Eds.)

Passive and Active Measurement

15th International Conference, PAM 2014
Los Angeles, CA, USA, March 10-11, 2014
Proceedings

 Springer

Volume Editors

Michalis Faloutsos
University of New Mexico
Computer Science Department
Engineering Building II, Albuquerque, NM 87131, USA
E-mail: michalis@cs.unm.edu

Aleksandar Kuzmanovic
Northwestern University
EECS Department
2145 Sheridan Road, Evanston, IL 60208, USA
E-mail: akuzma@northwestern.edu

ISSN 0302-9743   e-ISSN 1611-3349
ISBN 978-3-319-04917-5   e-ISBN 978-3-319-04918-2
DOI 10.1007/978-3-319-04918-2
Springer Cham Heidelberg New York Dordrecht London

Library of Congress Control Number: 2014930886

LNCS Sublibrary: SL 5 – Computer Communication Networks
and Telecommunications

Typesetting: Camera-ready by author, data conversion by Scientific Publishing Services, Chennai, India

Printed on acid-free paper

Springer is part of Springer Science+Business Media (www.springer.com)

Preface

Welcome to the proceedings of the 2014 Passive and Active Measurement (PAM) Conference. The event, which was held in Los Angeles this year, focused on research in and the practice of Internet measurements. This was the 15th PAM. Following its genesis in 2000, the conference has maintained a strong workshop feel, providing an opportunity for the presentation of innovative and early work, with lively discussion and active participation from attendees.

In 2012 the conference broadened its scope, reflecting the widening uses of network measurement and analysis methods. The aim was to facilitate the understanding of the expanding role that measurement techniques play as they become building blocks for a variety of networking environments, application profiling, and cross-layer analysis. In 2014 we continued with this wider scope, although we did not neglect PAM's core topics.

PAM 2014 attracted 76 submissions. The papers came from academia and industry from around the world. It was especially pleasing to see the global nature of submissions.

The Technical Program Committee was chosen from a group of experts in Internet measurement, drawing on past contributors to PAM including distinguished academic and industrial researchers, but also with a group of first-time members. Additionally, we aimed to have a strong global representation on the committee, and achieved this with members from around the world.

The final program of 24 papers was selected after each submission was carefully reviewed by at least three members of the Program Committee (PC), at least one of whom rated themselves as knowledgeable with regard to the content of the paper. We were delighted with the quality of reviews – they were careful, insightful, and paid attention to detail. The reviews were followed by an extensive discussion phase. PAM has traditionally avoided a large PC meeting and the difficulties it creates for a global PC and instead uses on-line discussions. This year, these were impressively robust: Reviewers provided more than 350 comments on papers, some almost as detailed as the reviews themselves. Most of the final papers were then shepherded by PC members.

This year's conference also continued the selection criteria related to reproducible research, which was established in 2013. It is our belief that one of the most pressing issues in the field of Internet measurement research is the fact that many papers report on data sets that are never disclosed. Hence, PAM strongly encourages the authors to publish their data sets.

In addition, the PC selected seven papers to appear as posters at the conference, and these are included in this volume as extended abstracts. The final program included papers on a wide range of measurement topics, and included authors from 13 countries and five continents. Our most sincere thanks go to the PC members for their diligence and care in reviewing, discussing, and shepherding the papers that appear here, and to Marcel Flores for organizing and maintaining the HotCRP site for us.

We are also most grateful to the Steering Committee, Jelena Mirkovic, who was the local chair, and Jedidiah Crandall who served as the publicity chair. We hope that you enjoy the papers in these proceedings.

March 2014   Aleksandar Kuzmanovic
                                                         Michalis Faloutsos

Organization

Organizing Committee

Conference Chair

Michalis Faloutsos   The University of New Mexico, USA

Program Chair

Aleksandar Kuzmanovic   Northwestern University, USA

Local Chair

Jelena Mirkovic   USC Information Sciences Institute

Publicity Chair

Jedidiah Crandall   The University of New Mexico, USA

Steering Committee

Fabio Ricciato	University of Salento, Italy
George Riley	Georgia Institute of Technology, USA
Ian Graham	Endace, New Zealand
Neil Spring	University of Maryland, USA
Nevil Brownlee	The University of Auckland, New Zealand
Nina Taft	Technicolor Palo Alto Research Center, USA
Matthew Roughan	University of Adelaide, Australia
Rocky K. C. Chang	The Hong Kong Polytechnic University

Program Committee

Alan Mislove	Northeastern University, USA
Alberto Dainotti	CAIDA, USA
Arun Venkataramani	UMass, USA
Bernhard Ager	ETH Zurich, Switzerland
Bin Liu	Tsinghua University, China
Bruce Maggs	Akamai and Duke University, USA
Constantine Dovrolis	Georgia Tech, USA
David Choffnes	Northeastern University, USA
Dmitri Logiunov	Texas A&M, USA
Fernando Silveira	Technicolor, USA
Gabor Vattay	Eotvos Larand University, Hungary
Han Song	Narus Inc, USA

Jelena Mirkovic   ISI, USA
Marios Iliofotou   Narus Inc., USA
Mark Allman   ICSI, USA
Matthew Luckie   CAIDA, USA
Michael Rabinovich   Case Western Reserve University, USA
Minaxi Gupta   Indiana University, USA
Myungjin Lee   University of Edinburgh, UK
Neil Spring   University of Maryland, USA
Paul Barford   Wisconsin Madison, USA
Rade Stanojevic   Telefónica, Spain
Sergey Gorinsky   IMDEA, Spain
Thomas Karagiannis   Microsoft, UK
Xenofontas Dimitropoulos   ETH Zurich, Switzerland
Youngseok Lee   CNU, Korea
Zhichun Li   NEC Labs, USA
Zhi-Li Zhang   University of Minnesota, USA

Sponsoring Institutions

University of New Mexico, USA

Table of Contents

Performance Measurement

Protocol And Application Behavior

Characterization of Network Behavior

Network Security and Privacy

Poster Abstracts

RadioProphet: Intelligent Radio Resource Deallocation for Cellular Networks

Junxian Huang[1], Feng Qian[2], Z. Morley Mao[3],
Subhabrata Sen[2], and Oliver Spatscheck[2]

[1] Google Inc.
[2] AT&T Labs – Research
[3] University of Michigan

Abstract. Traditionally, radio resources are released in cellular networks by statically configured inactivity timers, causing substantial resource inefficiencies. We propose a novel system **RadioProphet** (**RP**), which dynamically and intelligently determines in real time when to deallocate radio resources by predicting the network idle time based on traffic history. We evaluate **RP** using 7-month-long real-world cellular traces. Properly configured, **RP** correctly predicts 85.9% of idle time instances and achieves radio energy savings of 59.1% at the cost of 91.0% of signaling overhead, outperforming existing proposals. We also implement and evaluate **RP** on real Android devices, demonstrating its negligible runtime overhead.

1 Introduction

Cellular networks employ a specific radio resource management policy distinguishing them from wired and Wi-Fi networks. Previous studies [5][10][8] have shown that in cellular networks, the origin of low resource efficiency comes from the way resources are *released*. To avoid high signaling load, radio resources are only released after an idle time (also known as the "tail time" or T_{tail}) controlled by statically configured inactivity timers. During the tail time, energy is essentially wasted by the radio interface.

Without knowing when network traffic will occur, long tail timer settings (*e.g.,* 11.6 seconds configured by an LTE network [8]) are essentially a conservative way to ensure low signaling overhead, which is known to be a bottleneck for cellular networks. Given that application behaviors are not random, using a statically configured timer is clearly suboptimal. A smaller static timer value helps reduce radio energy, but is not an option due to the risk of overloading cellular networks caused by signaling load increase.

An attractive alternative is to configure the timer dynamically — adaptively performing radio resource release signaled by the handset by monitoring the traffic and accommodating different traffic patterns. But the key challenge is determining when to release resources, which essentially comes down to accurate and efficient *prediction of the idle time period*. Clearly, the best time to do so is when the handset is about to experience a long idle time period, otherwise the incurred resource allocation overhead (*i.e.,* signaling load) might be unacceptably high. Therefore, accurate and efficient prediction of the idle time period is a critical prerequisite for dynamic timer schemes.

This paper proposes **RadioProphet** (**RP**), a practical system running on a handset that makes dynamic decisions to deallocate radio resources based on accurate and efficient prediction of network idle times. It makes the following contributions.

M. Faloutsos and A. Kuzmanovic (Eds.): PAM 2014, LNCS 8362, pp. 1–11, 2014.

First, **RP** utilizes standard online machine learning (ML) algorithms to accurately predict the network idle time, and performs resource deallocation only when the idle time is sufficiently long. We explored various ML algorithms and prediction models with tunable parameters, with the main contribution of using a measurement-driven approach to find robust and easy-to-measure features, whose complex interaction with the network idle time can be automatically discovered by the ML algorithms. The model is validated using seven-month-long traces collected from real users (§5).

Second, we implement **RP** on a real Android smartphone to demonstrate its negligible energy and CPU overhead. In contrast, all previous proposals [10][4][7] only perform trace-driven simulation. To reduce the runtime overhead, **RP** strategically performs *binary* prediction (*i.e.,* whether the idle time is short or long) at the granularity of a traffic *burst* consisting of a packet train sent or received in a batch. Compared to fine-grained prediction of the precise value of packet inter-arrival time, our proposed approach is much more efficient while yielding similar optimization results.

Third, we overcome critical limitations of previously proposed approaches, *i.e.,* RadioJockey [4] and MakeIdle / MakeActive [7] are only applicable to background applications without user interaction, with the ideal usage scenario of RadioJockey for a single application only. With multiple concurrent applications, it suffers from low prediction accuracy with increased overhead. In contrast, **RP** is specifically designed for both foreground and background traffic. Since its prediction is based on the aggregate traffic of all apps, **RP** incurs no additional overhead for supporting concurrent apps.

Fourth, we conduct comprehensive measurement of **RP** using real-world smartphone traces (7 months from 20 users). The overall prediction accuracy is 85.9%. **RP** achieves radio energy saving by 59.1%, at the cost of 91.0% additional signaling overhead in LTE networks, significantly outperforming previous proposals. To achieve the same energy saving, the additional signaling overheads incurred by MakeIdle [7] and naïve fast dormancy [1] are 305% and 215%, respectively. The maximal energy saving achieved by RadioJockey [4] is only 27% since it is only applicable to background traffic.

Paper Organization. We provide sufficient background in §2 before giving an overview of the **RadioProphet** (**RP**) system in §3. We detail how we select relevant features for idle time prediction in §4, and then systematically evaluate **RP** in §5. In §6, we describe related work before concluding the paper.

2   Background

In cellular networks, there is a radio resource control (RRC) state machine that determines radio resource usage based on application traffic patterns, affecting device energy consumption and user experience. Conceptually similar RRC state machines exist in different types of cellular networks from 2G to 4G LTE. In 3G UMTS networks, there are usually three RRC states [11]: idle, low-power state, and high-power state. In 4G LTE networks, there are only two RRC states: idle and active [8]. Note that **RP** works for any type of RRC state machine with fast dormancy (described soon) support.

State Transitions. There are two types of state transitions. State promotions switch from a low-power state to a high-power state. They are triggered by user data transmission in either direction. State demotions go in the reverse direction, usually triggered by inactivity timers configured by the radio access network (RAN). For example, for a commercial LTE network [8], at the active state, the RAN resets the timer to a constant threshold T_{tail}=11.6 seconds whenever it observes any data frame. If there is no user data transmission for T_{tail} seconds, the timer expires and the state is demoted to idle. Similar timers exist in 3G networks (e.g., 12 seconds [11]).

State promotions incur long "ramp-up" delays of up to several seconds during which tens of control messages are exchanged between the handset and the RAN for resource allocation. Excessive state promotions increase the signaling overhead at the RAN and degrade user experience, especially for short data transfers [3][10]. On the other hand, state demotions incur *tail times* (T_{tail}) causing waste of radio resources and handset energy [5]. During the tail time, no data is transferred but the handset radio power is much higher than that at the idle state (e.g., 1060mW vs 11mW for LTE [8]).

Fast Dormancy. Why are tail times necessary? First, the overhead of resource allocation (i.e., state promotions) is high and tail times prevent frequent allocation and deallocation of radio resources. Second, the RAN has no easy way of predicting the network idle time of a handset, so it conservatively appends a tail to every network usage period. This naturally gives rise to the idea of letting the handset actively request for immediate resource release. Based on this intuition, a feature called Fast Dormancy has been included in 3GPP since Release 7 [1][2]. It allows a handset to send a control message to the RAN to immediately demote the RRC state to idle (or a hibernating state) without experiencing the tail time. Fast dormancy is supported by many handsets [2]. It can dramatically reduce the radio resource and the handset energy usage with the potential penalty of increased signaling load when used aggressively [3][10].

3   The RadioProphet (RP) System

The static tail times are the root cause of low resource efficiency in cellular networks. RP leverages fast dormancy to dynamically determine when to release radio resources.

Challenge 1: trading off between resource saving and signaling load. The best time to perform resource deallocation is when the handset is about to experience a long idle time period t. If t is longer than the tail time, deallocating resources immediately saves resources without any penalty of signaling load (i.e., state promotions). Otherwise, doing so incurs an additional state promotion. Balancing such a critical tradeoff requires predicting the idle time between data transfers so that fast dormancy is only invoked when the idle time is sufficiently long.

Challenge 2: handling both foreground and background traffic. Idle time prediction is particularly difficult for applications involving user interactions. Previous systems, such as RadioJockey [4] and MakeActive [7], simply avoid this by only handling traffic generated by applications running in the background.

Challenge 3: trading off between prediction accuracy and system performance. RP is a service running on a handset with limited computational capabilities and more importantly, limited battery life. So we need to minimize the overhead without sacrificing much of the prediction accuracy.

To address **Challenge 1**, we establish a novel machine-learning-based framework for idle time prediction. Besides measuring the effectiveness and efficiency of a wide-range of ML algorithms, our key contribution is addressing the hard problem of selecting discriminating features that are relevant to idle time prediction. Based on extensive measurement, we find that strategically using a few simple features (*e.g.*, packet direction and size) leads to high prediction accuracy (§4). To address **Challenge 2**, we designed a general prediction framework that works for the aggregated (possibly concurrent) traffic containing both foreground and background traffic. In contrast, previous systems such as RadioJockey have the ideal usage case for a single app. Further, we leverage the screen status [9], which indicates whether a user is interacting with the device, to customize the prediction for screen-on and off traffic. Such a novel approach can better balance the aforementioned tradeoff between resource saving and signaling load. To address **Challenge 3**, RP performs *binary* prediction at the granularity of a traffic *burst* consisting of a train of packets. In other words, we find that the knowledge of whether the inter-burst time (**IBT**) is short or long (determined by a threshold) is already accurate enough for guiding the resource deallocation. Such an approach is much more efficient while yielding similar accuracy compared to the expensive approach of predicting the precise value of packet inter-arrival time.

RP consists of three components: a traffic monitor, an **IBT** prediction module, and a Fast Dormancy (FD) scheduler. The monitor inspects network traffic (only examines packet headers) and extracts lightweight features for each burst in an online manner. The features are then fed into the **IBT** prediction module, which trains models to predict the **IBT** for the current burst. Then, the FD scheduler makes decision on whether to invoke fast dormancy based on the **IBT** prediction result.

For **IBT** prediction, we formulate the traffic pattern as follows. The traffic is a sequence of packets $\{P_i\}(1 \le i \le n)$ in both directions. Let the timestamp of P_i be t_i. Using a burst threshold **BT**, the packets are grouped into *bursts*, *i.e.*, $\{P_p, P_{p+1}, ..., P_q\}$ belongs to a burst B if and only if: (1) $t_{k+1} - t_k \le$ **BT** for $\forall k \in \{p, ..., q - 1\}$, (2) $t_{q+1} - t_q >$ **BT**, and (3) $t_p - t_{p-1} >$ **BT**. We define the inter-burst time **IBT** of burst B to be the time gap following this burst, *i.e.*, $t_{q+1} - t_q$. We use a short **IBT** threshold called **SBT** to classify an **IBT**, *i.e.*, if **IBT** $\le$ **SBT**, the burst is *short*, otherwise, it is *long*.

The **IBT** prediction module trains a model based on historical traffic information, which consists of an array of bursts $\{B_1, ..., B_m\}$. Each B_i is a vector $(f_1, f_2, ..., f_t, ibt_i)$ where $\{f_1, ..., f_t\}$ is the list of features of B_i and ibt_i is the **IBT** following burst B_i observed by the traffic monitor. Whenever there is an idle time of **BT**, *i.e.*, a new bust appears, the prediction process starts. The feature vector of the current burst $\{f_1, ..., f_t\}$ is generated and fed to the prediction module, which predicts whether the **IBT** following the current burst is short or long. If short, no change is made and the handset stays in the tail, since a packet is likely to appear soon. Otherwise, the FD scheduler invokes fast dormancy to save energy. The prediction model is customized for each handset, and is dynamically updated to adapt to the recent traffic pattern.

4 Feature Selection

We describe the measurement dataset before studying the feature selection in §4.2.

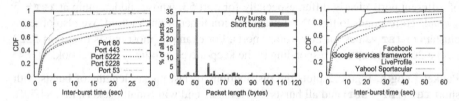

Fig. 1. IBT distributions of bursts whose last packets have specific port numbers

Fig. 2. Distributions of bursts grouped by packet length of the last packet

Fig. 3. IBT distributions of bursts whose last packets are associated with specific apps

4.1 The UMICH Dataset

The measurement data used in this study, which we call the UMICH dataset, is collected from 20 students at University of Michigan for seven months. The students were given Motorola Atrix (11 of them) or Samsung Galaxy S smartphones (9 of them) running Android. Our custom data collection software continuously runs in the background and collects three types of data. (1) Packet traces (only headers are used in this study). (2) The process name responsible for sending or receiving each packet. (3) Other system information such as screen status. Over the seven months (May to Dec 2011) we collected 152 GB data. Although both cellular and Wi-Fi traces were collected, in this study, we only use cellular traces, which contribute to 57.8% of the total traffic volume.

4.2 Measurement Driven Feature Selection for Burst Classification

We use a measurement-driven approach to derive features for the prediction model by analyzing the correlation between various features and the **IBT**. First, to predict whether an **IBT** is short or long, we look at the burst *right before* the **IBT**, since we observe that the correlations between the **IBT** and earlier bursts' features are much weaker. Second, the features are extracted from the *last three* packets of a burst. This is because in most cases, bursts are small (53% of bursts consist of no more than 3 packets), and even for large bursts, we can usually tell their nature based on the last three packets, *e.g.,* TCP three-way handshake. Third, we only inspect packet headers since examining payload incurs much higher overhead and also because traffic is increasingly being encrypted.

The lightweight features of the last three packets[1] used by **RP** are listed below: (1) packet direction, (2) server port number, (3) packet length (including header), (4) protocol field in IP header, (5) TCP flags field in TCP header (0 if not TCP), and (6) application name associated with the packet. These features are selected empirically so that they are most relevant to **IBT** based on our measurement. We show three features below as examples. We start our analysis with **BT** =1s and **SBT** =3s. Later we explore how different **BT** and **SBT** settings affect our results in a quantitative manner (§5.4).

Port Number. Figure 1 shows **IBT** distributions of the top 5 ports ordered from top to bottom in the legend, *e.g.,* 80 is the most popular port, across all users. **IBT** distributions

---

[1] If a burst contains less than three packets, all features for the missing packet(s) have a value of 0.

of different ports clearly differ, especially for port 53, whose sudden jump at **IBT** = 5 seconds corresponds to the DNS retransmission timeout on Android. We also observe clusters of **IBT** values for many other ports. For example, most bursts over port 5222 have a 20-second **IBT** corresponding to the keep-alive periodicity of Facebook.

Packet Length. Figure 2 plots the distributions of last packet lengths of bursts with short **IBT** (**IBT** < **SBT**) and all bursts. Most bursts end with small packets, *i.e.*, 84.59% have their last packets ≤ 100 bytes, as a large packet is typically in the middle of a burst. We observe high correlation for a few packet lengths values. For example, for 121 bytes, 93.04% bursts have short **IBT**s. The machine learning algorithms could automatically discover these rules for prediction.

Applications. In Figure 3, the legend shows the sorted list of apps contributing the largest amount of bursts with Facebook ranked at top 1. The differences in **IBT** values are clear across apps. We also observe that for some apps, their periodic transfer behaviors contribute to clusters of specific **IBT** values, *e.g.*, Facebook and LiveProfile. The application information can be very efficiently obtained (*e.g.*, on Android [11]).

5   Implementation and Evaluation

5.1   Implementation

Trace-Driven Evaluation. We implement simulators of **RP**, MakeIdle [7], and Radio-Jockey [4] on a desktop (3.16 GHz Xeon CPU with 16GB memory) using Matlab. They work with an RRC state machine simulator (§5.2). We use them to evaluate the accuracy and resource savings of **RP** under various configurations (§5.3, §5.4), as well as to compare **RP** with other optimization techniques (§5.5), using the UMICH trace.

Implementation on Real Android Phone. We also implement the full **RP** system on a Samsung Galaxy S3 phone running Android 4.0.4 to evaluate its running overhead (§5.6). A modified TcpDump program is used as the traffic monitor. The IBT prediction module is implemented as a native Android application running in the background.

5.2   Evaluation Methodology

We use three metrics to evaluate **RP**: prediction accuracy, saved radio energy, and increased signaling load. The accuracy is defined as the number of bursts whose immediate **IBT** (short or long) are correctly predicted divided by the total number of bursts in the input trace. The radio energy, denoted as E, is the energy consumed by the handset radio interface. It is one of the most significant components for the overall energy usage of a handset, along with screen and CPU energy [11]. We build an RRC state machine simulator, which takes as input a packet trace and employs the LTE radio energy model derived in our previous work [8] to calculate E (using a UMTS model [11] yields qualitatively similar results). The signaling load, denoted as S, is quantified by the number of state promotions, each incurring a fixed number of signaling messages [4]. S is also computed by the RRC state machine simulator.

Assume when a specific user trace is evaluated without any optimization performed (no fast dormancy), E and S are calculated to be E_d and S_d, respectively. When **RP**

Table 1. Impact of α, β on the prediction accuracy (`PerUserDynamic` model)

α =	100	500	1000	2000	5000
$\beta = 1$	81.5%	83.7%	**84.2%**	82.4%	80.2%
$\beta = 2$	80.1%	81.4%	82.9%	82.0%	80.0%
$\beta = 5$	79.8%	80.9%	81.4%	81.0%	79.3%
$\beta = 10$	79.4%	80.0%	80.9%	80.0%	79.0%
$\beta = 20$	78.9%	79.6%	80.2%	79.5%	78.7%

Table 2. Summary of prediction models

Name	Description	Accuracy
PerUser Dynamic	Use most recent α bursts of a user to predict next β bursts for that user	84.2%
PerUser Static	Use a fixed set of n bursts of a user to train a fixed model for that user	80.8%
AllUser Static	Use a fixed set of k bursts of all users train a fixed model for all users	77.5%

is used, the resulting E and S become E' and S', respectively. We define $\Delta(E) = (E_d - E')/E_d$ and $\Delta(S) = (S' - S_d)/S_d$ (usually both are positive). They correspond to the reduction of the radio energy and the increase of the signaling load brought by RP, respectively. RP's goal is to maximize $\Delta(E)$ while minimizing $\Delta(S)$.

5.3 Prediction Model Comparison

In RP, we use recent traffic information of a user to train a model, denoted as `PerUserDynamic`. Specifically, for each user, the most recent α bursts are used to predict the next β bursts. We study the impact of α, β in Table 1, using the Ensemble Bagging [6] learning algorithm as an example (number of trees set to 20). If α is too small, there is not enough training data for learning; if α is too large, the user is more likely to switch to new applications that generate different traffic patterns so previously learned rules may not be useful. Based on Table 1, we choose $\alpha = 1000$ and $\beta = 1$ that maximize the accuracy. In practice, α and β could also be dynamically adjusted.

Table 2 compares the `PerUserDynamic` model with two other models, `PerUserStatic` (a fixed model for each user) and `AllUserStatic` (a fixed model for all 20 users). For fair comparison, we use the same ML algorithm (Ensemble Bagging) as used in Table 1. We set $\alpha = 1000$ and $\beta = 1$ for the `PerUserDynamic` model as discussed previously, and use $n = 10,000$ for `PerUserStatic` and $k = 10,000$ for `AllUserStatic` (n and k defined in Table 2). Similar to Table 1, n and k are empirically selected to yield good prediction accuracies. We observe that `PerUserDynamic` has higher prediction accuracy than the other two models, suggesting that it is necessary to have a dynamic model for each user whose traffic pattern may be different from others.

5.4 Selecting Burst Thresholds

We study the impact of BT and SBT (previous evaluations use BT =1s and SBT =3s). In Table 3, S_0 to S_4 correspond to representative (BT, SBT) pairs. We find that aggressively using a short SBT (S_1) can significantly increase $\Delta(S)$. Among all settings, S_4 yields the highest $\Delta(E)/(1 + \Delta(S))$ value (the average radio energy saving per unit of signaling load). It quantifies how well the balance between $\Delta(E)$ and $\Delta(S)$ is handled.

As mentioned in §3, configuring screen-on and off settings differently may yield better optimization results, as screen-off traffic is usually generated by background apps without user interaction, leading to statistically longer IBT. Therefore a more aggressive

Table 3. Impact of **BT** and **IBT** (Classification Tree with **PerUserDynamic** model, α=1000, β=1)

Settings (unit: sec)	Accuracy	$\Delta(E)$	$\Delta(S)$	$\frac{\Delta(E)}{(1+\Delta(S))}$
S_0 **BT**: 1 **SBT**: 3	82.65%	52.10%	101.64%	0.26
S_1 **BT**: 1 **SBT**: 2	84.80%	56.69%	158.99%	0.22
S_2 **BT**: 1 **SBT**: 4	81.94%	49.07%	83.34%	0.27
S_3 **BT**: 0.5 **SBT**: 3	84.71%	53.74%	100.36%	0.27
S_4 **BT**: 1.5 **SBT**: 3	85.39%	58.85%	93.75%	0.30
S_5 **BT**: 1/1.5 off/on **SBT**: 2.5/3 off/on	85.88%	59.07%	91.01%	0.31

Table 4. Performance and accuracy of different ML algorithms

ML Algorithm	Prediction time (Training time)	Accuracy
Naïve Bayes	2.5 ms 6.4 ms	76.1%
Classification Tree	5.9 ms 136.9 ms	85.9%
Ensemble Bagging	106.6 ms 626.1 ms	87.4%

setting (smaller **BT** and **SBT**) can be applied to screen-off traffic without incurring much signaling overhead. In Table 3, S_5 is such a screen-aware setting. Compared with S_4, S_5 saves more energy with less signaling overhead incurred. In fact, S_5 achieves results comparable to the optimal scenario to be shown in Table 5. This also indicates that dynamically changing **BT** and **SBT** can help improve the effectiveness of **RP**.

5.5 Comparing Fast Dormancy Based Resource Optimization Approaches

Table 5 compares various optimization techniques using the UMICH dataset.

Basic fast dormancy. We set T_{tail} to a fixed value smaller than its original value.

RadioJockey [4] uses system calls to predict the end-of-session (EOS) for background app without user interaction, with the ideal usage scenario for a single app. Given that we do not have system call traces in our dataset, we make two assumptions in our simulation: (1) we use end-of-burst to approximate end-of-session, (2) RadioJockey has high prediction accuracies (90% and 100%) for both single and concurrent apps (although in reality, it performs worse when concurrent apps exist). A key limitation of RadioJockey is it does not handle foreground traffic and only works when the screen is idle (see §6), so we only apply RadioJockey to screen-off traffic[2].

MakeIdle [7] computes a wait time T_{wait} that maximizes the energy saving if T_{tail} is set to T_{wait} for the previous M packets, it then applies this T_{wait} for the next N packets. The range we search for the optimal T_{wait} is $[0.5, 11.5]$ seconds, as suggested by the authors. Since no recommendations have been made for the values of M and N, we empirically select different combinations of (M, N) pairs.

RadioProphet : we explore three off-the-shelf machine learning algorithms with the **PerUserDynamic** model (α=1000 and β=1): Naïve Bayes, Classification Tree, and Ensemble Bagging. Their performance and accuracy are summarized in Table 4[3].

We now discuss the results in Table 5. "Fast dormancy 1s" is an aggressive approach incurring unacceptable signaling overhead. "Fast dormancy 3s" reduces $\Delta(S)$ with less energy saving as expected. For both approaches, their $\Delta(E)/(1 + \Delta(S))$ values

---

[2] We configured short screen timeout for the 20 phones so screen-off is good approximation for screen-idle.

[3] The performance numbers in Table 4 correspond to the execution time of the scripts written in Matlab on desktop. Our real implementation on the S3 smartphone uses C++ so it is much more efficient (§5.6).

Table 5. Comparison of optimization approaches. For **RP**, we use the **PerUserDynamic** model (α=1000, β=1) with setting S_5 in Table 3. RadioJockey is only applicable to screen-off traffic.

Name	Description & Configuration	$\Delta(E)$	$\Delta(S)$	$\frac{\Delta(E)}{(1+\Delta(S))}$
Basic Fast dormancy 1s	Invoke fast dormancy after 1s idle time	62.7%	214.9%	0.20
Basic Fast dormancy 3s	Invoke fast dormancy after 3s idle time	40.9%	95.8%	0.21
RadioJockey Assuming 100% accuracy	RadioJockey applied to only screen-off traffic	30.1%	51.7%	0.20 (screen-off)
RadioJockey Assuming 90% accuracy	RadioJockey applied to only screen-off traffic	27.2%	52.0%	0.18 (screen-off)
MakeIdle M:1000, N:100	MakeIdle: based on previous M packets, predict next N packets	64.9%	305.2%	0.16
MakeIdle M:10, N:10	MakeIdle: based on previous M packets, predict next N packets	44.9%	195.2%	0.15
RP: Naïve Bayes	Naïve Bayes classification with *mvmn*: multivariate multinomial distribution	53.0%	107.9%	0.25
RP: Classification Tree	Binary decision tree for classification	59.1%	91.0%	0.31
RP: Ensemble Bagging	Method: *Bag*; type: classification weak leaner: decision tree; # of trees: 20	59.3%	90.2%	0.31
RP: Optimal	Predict all **IBT**s correctly	59.8%	85.4%	0.32

(the average radio energy saving per unit of signaling load) are low due to a lack of adaptation to dynamic traffic patterns.

For RadioJockey, by assuming the prediction accuracy for each background app to be 90%, it saves 27.2% of radio energy with 52% of signaling load, which can be slightly improved when the accuracy increases to 100%. The overall saving is lower than that of **RP** because RadioJockey does not handle foreground traffic usually triggered by user interaction (§6). For MakeIdle, we use two representative (M, N) settings. In both cases, the incurred signaling load is prohibitive, since MakeIdle does not consider the very important signaling load metric in its optimization framework.

For **RP**, in the optimal case assuming 100% prediction accuracy, it saves 59.8% of radio energy with 85.4% of signaling load incurred. The signaling load is not zero, because for **IBT**s smaller than T_{tail} but larger than **SBT**, even if the prediction is correct, invoking fast dormancy would still incur an extra state promotion. This is inherent for any fast dormancy based optimization technique. Among the three machine learning algorithms, Ensemble Bagging achieves the best results, likely due to its usage of multiple submodels to avoid overfitting. However, as shown in Table 4, its runtime overhead is very high. The Classification Tree approach achieves similar optimization results with much lower runtime overhead. The $\Delta(E)/(1 + \Delta(S))$ metric indicates that **RP** outperforms other approaches in balancing $\Delta(E)$ and $\Delta(S)$.

5.6 Running Overhead on Real Phone

We implement the **RadioProphet** system on Android as discussed in §5.1, in order to demonstrate its practicality on today's smartphones. We breakdown its runtime overhead into three components: (1) traffic monitoring and feature extraction, (2) model training and prediction, and (3) fast dormancy invocation. We found invoking fast dormancy incurs negligible overhead. We therefore focus on (1) and (2) below.

Traffic Monitoring and Feature Selection. Unlike RadioJockey requiring system call instrumentation, RP only needs to monitor packet traces, which is also needed by RadioJockey. On the S3 smartphone, our traffic monitor incurs no more than 1% of CPU overhead for parsing packet headers and generating burst features, although the overhead is much lower when the throughput is low (*e.g.*, less than 200 kbps). The additional power to run the data collector is less than 17mW most of the time. In contrast, the LTE radio power is at least 1000 mW [8].

Model Training and Prediction: Our implementation on S3 uses the Classification Tree model that balances between accuracy and performance (Table 4). We measure the average model training time to be 200ms and the average prediction time to be 0.1ms. Its incurred power overhead is always negligible (less than 10 mW).

6   Related Work and Concluding Remarks

We compare RP with three representative adaptive resource deallocation proposals.

TOP [10] leverages fast dormancy to eliminate the tail. It assumes each individual application can predict an imminent long IBT with reasonable accuracy, and fast dormancy is only invoked when the aggregate prediction across all concurrent apps is long enough. TOP provides the prediction framework, but it does not solve the challenging prediction problem itself, which is the key focus of RP.

MakeIdle [7] uses packet timing to calculate the optimal idle time before invoking fast dormancy, in order to maximize the radio energy saving. However, MakeIdle considers minimizing radio energy as the only objective, leading to unacceptably high signaling overhead shown in Table 5. It leaves the job of reducing the signaling load to another algorithm called **MakeActive** [7] that changes the traffic pattern by shifting packets. MakeActive does not work with foreground traffic that is usually delay-sensitive, and even for background traffic, there is no guarantee that it does not affect user experience. In contrast, RP does not rely on changing traffic patterns and it works with both foreground and background traffic. It can in fact coexist with traffic shaping based optimization techniques such as MakeActive and TailEnder [5].

RadioJockey [4] uses program execution traces to predict the end of communication spurts and invoke fast dormancy when necessary. It however has several limitations. (1) It needs heavy instrumentation *i.e.*, requiring complete system call traces in addition to packet traces, while RP only examines packet header information. (2) RadioJockey only works for background app without user interaction, since "predicting EOS events for foreground applications turns out to be challenging since user interactions can trigger network communications at any point in time" [4]. (3) RadioJockey treats different apps separately and does not predict start-of-session, hence when concurrent apps exist, the prediction accuracy would be affected. In contrast, RP introduces a general, lightweight, and effective framework that naturally optimizes concurrent traffic from both foreground and background apps. RP achieves even better optimization results for all traffic than RadioJockey does for only background traffic (Table 5).

To conclude, we propose a novel, practical, and effective system called **RadioProphet** that intelligently predicts long idle period using off-the-shelf machine learning algorithms, and deallocate resources based on **IBT** prediction for cellular networks. Using 7-month data collected from 20 real users, we show that **RP** outperforms existing proposals in balancing the key tradeoff between resource saving and signaling load. We present the first implementation of adaptive resource deallocation using fast dormancy, demonstrating the feasibility of **RP** on real smartphones. We believe **RP** is an important step towards application-aware energy and resource optimization in wireless networks.

Acknowledgements. This research was supported in part by the National Science Foundation under grants CNS-1039657, CNS-1059372 and CNS-0964545.

References

1. UE "Fast Dormancy" behavior. 3GPP discussion and decision notes R2-075251 (2007)
2. Configuration of fast dormancy in release 8. 3GPP discussion notes RP-090960 (2009)
3. System Impact of Poor Proprietary Fast Dormancy. 3GPP discussion and decision notes RP-090941 (2009)
4. Athivarapu, P., Bhagwan, R., Guha, S., Navda, V., Ramjee, R., Arora, D., Padmanabhan, V., Varghese, G.: RadioJockey: Mining Program Execution to Optimize Cellular Radio Usage. In: MobiCom (2012)
5. Balasubramanian, N., Balasubramanian, A., Venkataramani, A.: Energy Consumption in Mobile Phones: A Measurement Study and Implications for Network Applications. In: IMC (2009)
6. Breiman, L.: Bagging Predictor. Machine Learning 24(2) (1996)
7. Deng, S., Balakrishnan, H.: Traffic-Aware Techniques to Reduce 3G/LTE Wireless Energy Consumption. In: CoNEXT (2012)
8. Huang, J., Qian, F., Gerber, A., Mao, Z.M., Sen, S., Spatscheck, O.: A Close Examination of Performance and Power Characteristics of 4G LTE Networks. In: MobiSys (2012)
9. Huang, J., Qian, F., Mao, Z.M., Sen, S., Spatscheck, O.: Screen-Off Traffic Characterization and Optimization in 3G/4G Networks. In: Proc. ACM SIGCOMM IMC (2012)
10. Qian, F., Wang, Z., Gerber, A., Mao, Z.M., Sen, S., Spatscheck, O.: TOP: Tail Optimization Protocol for Cellular Radio Resource Allocation. In: Proc. ICNP (2010)
11. Qian, F., Wang, Z., Gerber, A., Mao, Z.M., Sen, S., Spatscheck, O.: Profiling Resource Usage for Mobile Applications: a Cross-layer Approach. In: MobiSys (2011)

Mobile Network Performance from User Devices: A Longitudinal, Multidimensional Analysis

Ashkan Nikravesh[1], David R. Choffnes[2], Ethan Katz-Bassett[3],
Z. Morley Mao[1], and Matt Welsh[4]

[1] University of Michigan
[2] Northeastern University
[3] University of Southern California
[4] Google Inc.

Abstract. In the cellular environment, operators, researchers and end users have poor visibility into network performance for devices. Improving visibility is challenging because this performance depends factors that include carrier, access technology, signal strength, geographic location and time. Addressing this requires longitudinal, continuous and large-scale measurements from a diverse set of mobile devices and networks.

This paper takes a first look at cellular network performance from this perspective, using 17 months of data collected from devices located throughout the world. We show that (i) there is significant variance in key performance metrics both within and across carriers; (ii) this variance is at best only partially explained by regional and time-of-day patterns; (iii) the stability of network performance varies substantially among carriers. Further, we use the dataset to diagnose the causes behind observed performance problems and identify additional measurements that will improve our ability to reason about mobile network behavior.

1 Introduction

Cellular networks are the fastest growing, most popular and least understood Internet systems. A particularly difficult challenge in this environment is capturing a view of network performance that is representative of conditions at end user devices. A number of factors frustrate our ability to capture this view. For instance, carriers enforce different policies depending on the traffic types or geographic/social characteristics of different locations such as population [1, 2], causing user perceived performance to differ from advertised performance for access technologies. Other environmental factors have a significant impact on performance, including device model [3], mobility [4], network load [2], packet size [5, 6] and MAC-layer scheduling [4].

To account for various factors impacting Internet performance in mobile networks, we need pervasive network monitoring that samples a variety of devices across carriers, access technologies, locations and over time. This work takes a first look at such a view using data collected from controlled measurement experiments in 144 carriers during 17 months, comprising 11 cellular network technologies. We use this data to identify the patterns, trends, anomalies, and evolution of cellular networks' performance.

This study demonstrates that characterizing and understanding the performance in today's cellular networks is far from trivial. We find that all carriers exhibit significant

M. Faloutsos and A. Kuzmanovic (Eds.): PAM 2014, LNCS 8362, pp. 12–22, 2014.

variance in end-to-end performance in terms of latency and throughput. To explain this variance, we investigate geographic and temporal properties of network performance. While we find that these properties account for some differences in performance, importantly we observe that performance is inherently unstable, with some carriers providing relatively more or less predictable performance. Last, we identify alternative sources of variance in performance that include routing and signal strength. An important open question is how to design a measurement platform that allows us to understand reasons behind most observed performance differences.

This paper differs from previous related work in that our study is longitudinal, continuous, pervasive and gathered from mobile devices using controlled experiments. In contrast, some related work [7–9] passively collected network traffic from cellular network infrastructure, using one month of data or less. These studies tend to be limited to a single carrier, hampering our ability to conduct meaningful comparisons across carriers. Other work collected network performance data at mobile devices [10, 1, 11], but did not use controlled experiments to capture a continuous view of performance.

Roadmap. We describe our methodology and dataset in §2, then present our findings regarding network performance across different network technologies, carriers, locations, and times in §3.1, §3.2, and §3.3 respectively. Then we study the root causes for performance degradation in §3.4. We discuss related work in §4 and conclude in §5.

2 Methodology and Dataset

This paper studies cellular network performance using a broad longitudinal view of network behavior impacting user-perceived performance. To this end, we consider HTTP GET throughput, round trip time latency from ping, and DNS lookup time as end-to-end performance metrics. In addition to gathering raw performance data, we annotate our measurements with path information gathered from traceroute, the identify of the device's carrier, its cellular network technology, signal strength, location and timestamp.

We focus on performance from mobile devices to Google, a large, popular content provider. We argue that Google is an ideal target for network measurements because it is highly available and well provisioned, making it easier to isolate network performance to cell networks vs. Google's network. Focusing on these measurements, we identify the performance impact of carrier, network technology, location and time. To reason about the root cause behind performance changes, we use path information, DNS mappings and signal strength readings.

Our data is collected by two Android apps using a nearly identical codebase, Speedometer and Mobiperf.[1] Speedometer is an internal Android app developed by Google and deployed on hundreds of volunteer devices, mainly owned by Google employees. As such, the bulk of our dataset[2] is biased toward locations where Google employees live and work. Speedometer collected the following measurements from 2011-10 to 2013-2 (17 months): 6.6M ping RTTs to www.google.com (each sample consists of 10 consecutive probes), 1.7M HTTP GETs to measure TCP throughput

---

[1] http://www.mobiperf.com/

[2] This dataset is publicly available at
https://storage.cloud.google.com/speedometer

Table 1. Number of Measurement and Carriers for the Network Technologies

	HSPA	HSDPA	UMTS	EDGE	GPRS	LTE	EVDO	eHRPD	1xRTT
# of Measurements	439K	2326K	563K	506K	58K	1460K	2183K	301K	68K
# of Carriers	50	111	96	85	48	7	8	2	3

using a 224KB file hosted on a Google server, 0.4M UDP burst samples for measuring packet loss rate, 0.8M DNS resolutions of google.com, and 0.8M traceroute (without hop RTTs) from 144 carriers and 9 network technologies. The dataset includes ≈ 4-5 measurements per minute. Each measurement is annotated with device model, coarse-grained location information (k-anonymized latitude and longitude), timestamp, carrier, and network type.[3] All users consented to participate in the measurement study; the anonymization process is explained in the dataset's README file. Because of anonymization, the number of users who participated in data collection is unknown.

We augment the Speedometer dataset with 11 months of data collected by Mobiperf. Mobiperf conducts a superset of measurements in Speedometer, and notably adds signal strength information. The number of measurements collected by Mobiperf for each task ranges from 17K (HTTP GET) to 58K (ping RTT test) from 71 carriers. We use Mobiperf data to study the impact of signal strength on measurement results. Table 1 shows the number of measurements collected from the most frequently seen 9 network technologies (ordered by peak speed) for both GSM and CDMA technologies in the combined datasets.

3 Data Analysis

3.1 Performance across Carriers

This section investigates the performance of five access technologies for each of several carriers. Our goal is to understand how observed performance matches with expectations across access technologies, and how variable this performance is across carriers. In Fig. 1, we plot percentile distributions (P5, P25, median, P75, and P95) of the latency and throughput of 9 carriers from Asia, America, Europe, and Australia. We select these carriers based on their geographic locations and relatively large data sample sizes. One of the key observations is that performance varies significantly across carriers and access technologies; further, the range of values is also relatively large.

For carriers that have high latency, we use traceroute data to investigate if the cause is inefficient routes to Google [12]. However, approximately half of the carriers such as SFR (French Carrier) and Swisscom have direct peering points with Google, making this unlikely to be the cause for high latency.

For carriers such as AT&T, T-Mobile US, and Airtel (India), we observe high variability in latency. In the following subsections, we investigate whether this is explained by regional differences, time-of-day effects and/or other factors.

Surprisingly, we do not observe significant latency differences across access technologies for some carriers. For example, the latency of UMTS, HSDPA, and HSPA

---

[3] https://github.com/Mobiperf/Speedometer

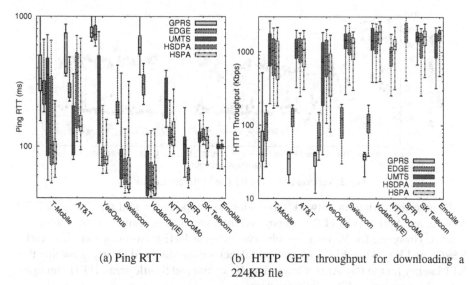

(a) Ping RTT

(b) HTTP GET throughput for downloading a 224KB file

Fig. 1. Throughput and latency across access technology and carriers

in Emobile (Ireland), SK Telecom (Korea), and Swisscom are almost equal. Users in these networks may not see noticeable differences in performance for delay-sensitive applications when upgrading to newer technologies.

In Fig. 1b, we plot HTTP throughput for downloading a 224KB file from a Google domain. Compared to ping RTT, the difference between the throughput of carriers is relatively smaller, indicating that the high variability in ping RTTs is often amortized over the duration of a transfer.

Note that the throughput for UMTS, HSDPA, and HSPA are almost identical. This occurs because the flow size is not sufficiently large to saturate the link for high-capacity technologies. This indicates a need for better low-cost techniques to estimate available capacity in such networks [13]. However, the figure shows significant performance difference between GPRS/EDGE and other access technologies.

We observe that lower latency is generally correlated with higher HTTP GET throughput, but this depends on the carrier. We quantify this using the correlation coefficient between HTTP throughput and ping RTT for specific carrier and network type. The strongest correlation coefficient observed was for Verizon LTE users with -0.53 and lowest was -0.01 for T-Mobile HSDPA users, using one-hour buckets.

Having observed significant differences in performance within and between carriers, we now investigate some of the potential factors behind this variability.

3.2 Performance across different Locations

We now investigate the impact of geography on network performance. We focus on four major US carriers in three US regions where our dataset is densest (New York, Seattle, and Bay Area). Each of these carriers exhibits different topologies (Internet egress, Google ingress and ASes between) in different regions, potentially leading to performance differences in each region.

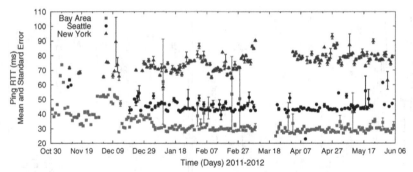

Fig. 2. Verizon LTE Ping RTT in Different Locations

Despite the variety in network topologies, we surprisingly find that for AT&T, T-Mobile, and Sprint, both of the latency and throughput were similar in these three locations. However, for Verizon, we observe different LTE performance in New York, Seattle, and Bay Area. Fig. 2 plots these latencies over time, and clearly show that the RTT latency for the Bay Area is lower than New York and Seattle areas. HTTP throughput in these regions exhibit similar patterns.

We use DNS data in the Seattle area and observe that 97% of DNS requests for google.com resolve to an IP for a server in the Los Angeles area instead of Seattle, in part explaining the gap in latency between the two regions. For the NY area, our measurements did not provide enough geographic information to understand whether increased latency was due to path inefficiencies.

The key takeaway from this section is that geography alone doesn't explain the variance in performance observed in the previous section; however, for one carrier (Verizon), it explains some of it. Further, we observe that each region experiences changes in performance independently – the correlation of performance across regions for each carrier is negligibly small. Last, when correlating ping RTT and HTTP GET throughput within each region, we find higher correlations than carrier-wide correlations presented in the previous section. This further suggests that performance is affected by location.

3.3 Performance over Time

We now analyze how performance depends on time – both in terms of time-of-day effects and the stability of measurement performance over time. These properties allow us to identify when to measure the network (*e.g.,* during known busy hours) and when *not* to measure (*e.g.,* at ten minute intervals), thus allowing us to efficiently allocate the limited measurement resources that users provide.

Time-of-Day and Long-Term Trends. Fig. 3 plots HTTP throughput for four major carriers in the US. As expected, throughput decreases (and variance tends to increase) during the busy hours for mobile usage (8AM to 7PM), likely due to higher load on the network. Interestingly, different carriers experience minimum throughput at different times. T-Mobile and AT&T reach their minimum throughput at 1PM and 5PM, respectively; Sprint experiences minimum performance at 9PM and Verizon, two troughs occur at 8AM and 9PM. Last, these carriers experience different relative variations in

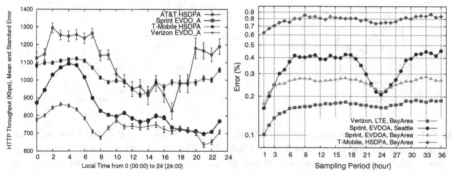

Fig. 3. Time of day pattern of HTTP throughput

Fig. 4. Weighted Moving Average Error (Median Ping RTT, $W = 2$)

performance during busy hours: AT&T and Sprint throughput drops by approximately a third during busy hours while Verizon drops by 25%, and T-Mobile by 16%.

Next, we investigate the long-term performance trends over the duration of our study, allowing us to tell if new cellular technologies and infrastructure are keeping pace with increased mobile Internet usage. Specifically, we look at the change in throughput and latency of carriers through time over consecutive days for each network technology they support in different areas. We did not observe improvement; despite technology upgrades, performance is highly variable over time and there is no statistically significant change during the observation period.

Stability of Performance. The predictability and stability of network performance are important not only for users, who are often frustrated more by variations in performance than the average value, but also for determining how and when to conduct measurements for future experiments. In this section, we compute stability using a weighted moving average and autocorrelation.

First, we group the data into 1-hour buckets (to obtain a sufficiently large sample size). Then for each bucket, we use either the median or 5th percentile latency. We compute the moving average error for different window sizes and sampling periods.

We compute the moving average error as follows: for a window size W, we predict the next data point on that series by computing moving average for the previous consecutive W points. For each W and sampling period (e.g., every N hours for $N = 1, 2, 3, \ldots$), we compute the average over different offsets.

Fig. 4 plots the average error for all data points with windows size of 2 and different sampling periods for median ping RTT (results with larger window sizes of 3, 4, and 5 are similar). We observe that prediction accuracy varies significantly by carrier, with Verizon and Sprint in the Bay Area being relatively predictable, and T-Mobile and Sprint in Seattle being relatively unpredictable. Also, for all of these carriers, prediction accuracy is best when looking at the most recent data (one hour sampling period) and error tends to increase with longer durations, with the exception of 24hr (day) and 168hrs (week) sampling periods, which are local minima. The results from autocorrelation are similar.

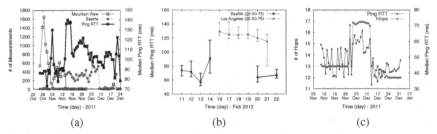

Fig. 5. Performance Degradation in: (a)T-Mobile HSDPA network in Bay Area due to server selection flapping from Bay Area to Seattle (b)T-Mobile HSDPA network in Seattle due to change in ingress point of transit AS between T-Mobile and Google (c) Verizon LTE network in Bay Area

These predictability results indicate that despite the large overall variance in cellular network performance, there are regions and time scales over which performance is relatively predictable, depending on the carrier. Importantly, we can use this information to inform the design of measurement system that uses prediction to minimize probes that would provide redundant results. For instance, if we subsample every other value (*i.e.,* 50% sampling rate) in the Verizon LTE ping data in the Bay Area (which has the lowest error in the full sample), the distribution of latencies is nearly identical.

3.4 Performance Degradation: Root Causes

We now use our measurements to identify the reasons for persistent performance degradation observed in consecutive days. We focus on cases where the issue affects both ping RTT and HTTP throughput.

Inefficient Paths. A reason for performance degradation is inefficient paths. Zarifis et al [14] provide a detailed taxonomy and analysis of path inflation in mobile networks; here we focus on their time evolution and constrain our analysis to only those cases where both latency and throughput were impacted.

For example, we observe an increase in ping RTT in T-Mobile's Bay Area HSDPA network from Nov 12, 2011 to Dec 10, 2011. Using DNS lookups, we find that clients previously sent to Mountain View were being sent to Seattle, with the additional delay explained by path inflation (Fig. 5a). After Dec 10, clients are again directed toward Mountain View.

We also observed a high-latency event for T-Mobile's Seattle HSDPA network in Seattle (Fig. 5b). Prior to the event, traceroutes indicate that traffic from T-Mobile ingresses into Level 3 in Seattle, then enters Google's network. After Feb 15, traffic from these subscribers ingressed into Level 3 at a peering point in Los Angeles before entering Google's network. After Feb 20, routing returns back to its previous state (ingress and egress point in Seattle area) and the median RTT decreases to its previous value, strongly implying that the change in performance was due to the topology change.

In Fig. 5c, we observe that ping RTT and the number of traceroute hops increases for Verizon LTE users in the Bay Area. Previously, clients were sent to a Google frontend in the Bay Area; after the change clients are sent to the same Google ingress point, but then traffic is sent to a frontend in Seattle (leading to $\approx 30\%$ higher latency).

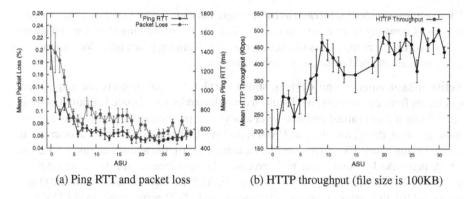

(a) Ping RTT and packet loss   (b) HTTP throughput (file size is 100KB)

Fig. 6. Impact of signal strength on latency, packet loss, and throughput

In this section we show that fixed-line inefficiencies can significantly impact the performance of LTE and HSDPA networks. For these newer technologies, since the RTT is lower, the impact of inefficient routes is even relatively higher (around 80% increase in the RTT of T-Mobile HSDPA in Seattle).

Signal Strength. It is well known that weak signal strength reduces channel efficiency for wireless communication; therefore, it is important to account for this when interpreting measurements. Using Mobiperf clients, we gather network measurements annotated with the signal strength, in Arbitrary Strength Units (ASUs),[4] reported during the probes and determine the impact of signal strength on performance.

Fig. 6 shows how three performance metrics vary with ASU values for AT&T HSDPA users in Seattle. The figures indicate high packet loss, latency and low throughput for ASU values between 0 and 8 (confirming the results in [15]); at larger ASU values that increase in signal strength has less impact on performance. These results indicate that accounting for signal strength is critically important for properly interpreting measurement results. For example, when measuring a carrier's capacity, it is important to do such tests in regions with high signal strength.

4 Related Work

Many previous studies attempt to improve our visibility into and understanding of mobile network performance. We can broadly characterize them according to *what* type of network performance they measured, *where* they conducted measurements and *how* they performed measurements. In this work, we are the first to use controlled, active measurement experiments to continuously monitor end-to-end network performance seen from mobile devices, across more than 100 carriers during a period of 17 months. Previous work differs as follows.

---

[4] Android shows zero signal bar for the ASU values between 0 and 2 and full signal bars when ASU value is more than 12.

Passive measurements, infrastructure, single carrier. Several studies focus on passive measurements from inside mobile carriers [7–9]. While important for debugging the infrastructure components of latency, the view from such locations does not necessarily indicate the performance on mobile devices.

Active measurements, end devices, single carrier. Several projects use active measurements from end devices, but focus on a single carrier for a limited duration of time, often doing a fine-grained and low-level analysis of performance. In [5], authors measured goodput, delay, and jitter of HSDPA and WCDMA networks from an operator in Finland using active measurements from a laptop. In [6], the authors compare LTE and HSPA networks by conducting high precision latency measurements for an operator in Austria. In [16, 4, 17, 18], authors studied the TCP performance in CDMA2000 networks. In[16], the authors investigate the steady-state TCP performance over CDMA 1x EV-DO downlink/uplink with the active measurement of long-lived TCP connections at the end-points for a Korean operator. [18, 4] conducted a cross-layer measurement of transport, physical and MAC layer parameters. [18] characterizes the wireless scheduler in a commercial CDMA2000 network and its impact on TCP performance by performing end-to-end experiments and sending UDP and TCP packets.

Active measurements, end devices, several carriers.: Similar to the previous examples, several studies also include comparisons across multiple carriers. In [19], by investigating the performance of three Norwegian operator and conducting active measurements from end-to-end devices, they studied the impact of the packet size on the minimal one-way delay for the uplink in 3G mobile networks. In [11], by performing active measurements for more than 6 months from 90 voting locations and by measuring the round trip delay of three network operator in Norway, they found the operator-specific network design and configurations as the most important factor for delays. In [2], by measuring data throughput, latency, and video and voice calls handling capacities, they compared the 3G performance of three carriers in Hong Kong under saturated conditions by conducting measurements at 170 sites in four months.

Active measurements, end devices, pervasive. Most closely related to our work is [1] and [3]. Both projects gather active measurements from apps running on mobile devices; however, they all rely on user-generated tests. In contrast our work uses controlled experiments to schedule measurements independent of user activity. This enables a more continuous view of performance in mobile networks.

5   Conclusion

This paper took a first look at end-to-end performance as seen from mobile devices, using a dataset of scheduled network measurements spanning more than 100 carriers over 17 months. We find that there are significant performance differences across carriers, access technologies, geographic regions and over time; however, we emphasize that these variations themselves are not uniform, making network performance difficult to diagnose. Using supplemental measurements such as DNS lookups and traceroutes, we identified the reasons behind persistent performance problems. Further, we examined the stability of network performance, which can help inform efficient scheduling of future network measurements. Overall, we find that performance in cell networks is not improving on average, suggesting the need for more monitoring and diagnosis. As part of our future work, we are investigating how to automatically detect persistent performance problems in real time, gather additional network measurements to explain them and provide this information to carriers and end users automatically.

Acknowledgements. We thank our shepherd Han Song and anonymous reviewers for their valuable comments. This research was supported in part by the National Science Foundation under grants CNS-1039657, CNS-1059372 and CNS-0964545, as well as by the NSF/CRA CI Fellowship and a Google Research Award.

References

1. Sommers, J., Barford, P.: Cell vs. WiFi: on the performance of metro area mobile connections. In: Proc. ACM SIGCOMM IMC (2012)
2. Tan, W.L., Lam, F., Lau, W.C.: An Empirical Study on 3G Network Capacity and Performance. In: Proc. IEEE INFOCOM (2007)
3. Huang, J., Xu, Q., Tiwana, B., Mao, Z.M., Zhang, M., Bahl, P.: Anatomizing application performance differences on smartphones. In: Proc. ACM MOBISYS (2010)
4. Liu, X., Sridharan, A., Machiraju, S., Seshadri, M., Zang, H.: Experiences in a 3G network: interplay between the wireless channel and applications. In: Proc. ACM MOBICOM (2008)
5. Jurvansuu, M., Prokkola, J., Hanski, M., Perala, P.: HSDPA Performance in Live Networks. In: IEEE ICC (2007)
6. Laner, M., Svoboda, P., Romirer-Maierhofer, P., Nikaein, N., Ricciato, F., Rupp, M.: A comparison between one-way delays in operating HSPA and LTE networks. In: Proc. WINMEE (2012)
7. Vacirca, F., Ricciato, F., Pilz, R.: Large-Scale RTT Measurements from an Operational UMTS/GPRS Network. In: WICON (2005)
8. Laner, M., Svoboda, P., Hasenleithner, E., Rupp, M.: Dissecting 3G Uplink Delay by Measuring in an Operational HSPA Network. In: Spring, N., Riley, G.F. (eds.) PAM 2011. LNCS, vol. 6579, pp. 52–61. Springer, Heidelberg (2011)
9. Romirer-Maierhofer, P., Ricciato, F., D'Alconzo, A., Franzan, R., Karner, W.: Network-Wide Measurements of TCP RTT in 3G. In: Papadopouli, M., Owezarski, P., Pras, A. (eds.) TMA 2009. LNCS, vol. 5537, pp. 17–25. Springer, Heidelberg (2009)
10. Deshpande, P., Hou, X., Das, S.R.: Performance Comparison of 3G and Metro-Scale WiFi for Vehicular Network Access. In: Proc. ACM SIGCOMM IMC (2010)
11. Elmokashfi, A., Kvalbein, A., Xiang, J., Evensen, K.R.: Characterizing delays in norwegian 3G networks. In: Taft, N., Ricciato, F. (eds.) PAM 2012. LNCS, vol. 7192, pp. 136–146. Springer, Heidelberg (2012)
12. Zheng, H., Lua, E.K., Pias, M., Griffin, T.G.: Internet routing policies and round-trip-times. In: Dovrolis, C. (ed.) PAM 2005. LNCS, vol. 3431, pp. 236–250. Springer, Heidelberg (2005)
13. Huang, J., Qian, F., Guo, Y., Zhou, Y., Xu, Q., Mao, Z.M., Sen, S., Spatscheck, O.: An in-depth study of lte: Effect of network protocol and application behavior on performance. In: Proc. ACM SIGCOMM (2013)
14. Zarifis, K., Flach, T., Nori, S., Choffnes, D., Govindan, R., Katz-Bassett, E., Mao, Z.M., Welsh, M.: Diagnosing path inflation of mobile client traffic. In: Faloutsos, M., Kuzmanovic, A. (eds.) PAM 2014. LNCS, vol. 8362, pp. 21–30. Springer, Heidelberg (2014)

15. Schulman, A., Navday, V., Ramjeey, R., Spring, N., Deshpandez, P., Grunewald, C., Padman-abhany, K.J.V.N.: Bartendr: A practical approach to energy-aware cellular data scheduling. In: Proc. ACM MOBICOM (2010)
16. Lee, Y.: Measured TCP Performance in CDMA 1x EV-DO Network. In: Proc. PAM (2006)
17. Claypool, M., Kinicki, R., Lee, W., Li, M., Ratner, G.: Characterization by Measurement of a CDMA 1x EVDO Network. In: Proc. WICON (2006)
18. Mattar, K., Sridharan, A., Zang, H., Matta, I., Bestavros, A.: TCP over CDMA2000 net-works: A cross-layer measurement study. In: Uhlig, S., Papagiannaki, K., Bonaventure, O. (eds.) PAM 2007. LNCS, vol. 4427, pp. 94–104. Springer, Heidelberg (2007)
19. Arlos, P., Fiedler, M.: Influence of the Packet Size on the One-Way Delay in 3G Networks. In: Krishnamurthy, A., Plattner, B. (eds.) PAM 2010. LNCS, vol. 6032, pp. 61–70. Springer, Heidelberg (2010)

Diagnosing Path Inflation of Mobile Client Traffic

Kyriakos Zarifis[1], Tobias Flach[1], Srikanth Nori[1], David Choffnes[2],
Ramesh Govindan[1], Ethan Katz-Bassett[1], Z. Morley Mao[3], and Matt Welsh[4]

[1] University of Southern California, Los Angeles, CA 90089, USA
{kyriakos,flach,snori,ramesh,ethan.kb}@usc.edu
[2] Northeastern University, Boston, MA 02115, USA
choffnes@ccs.neu.edu
[3] University of Michigan, Ann Arbor, MI 48109, USA
zmao@umich.edu
[4] Google Inc., Mountain View, CA 94043, USA
mdw@google.com

Abstract. As mobile Internet becomes more popular, carriers and content providers must engineer their topologies, routing configurations, and server deployments to maintain good performance for users of mobile devices. Understanding the impact of Internet topology and routing on mobile users requires broad, longitudinal network measurements conducted from mobile devices. In this work, we are the first to use such a view to quantify and understand the causes of geographically circuitous routes from mobile clients using 1.5 years of measurements from devices on 4 US carriers. We identify the key elements that can affect the Internet routes taken by traffic from mobile users (client location, server locations, carrier topology, carrier/content-provider peering). We then develop a methodology to diagnose the specific cause for inflated routes. Although we observe that the evolution of some carrier networks improves performance in some regions, we also observe many clients - even in major metropolitan areas - that continue to take geographically circuitous routes to content providers, due to limitations in the current topologies.

1 Introduction

As mobile Internet becomes more popular, carriers and content providers must engineer their topologies, routing configurations, and server deployments to maintain good performance for users of mobile devices. A key challenge is that performance changes over space and time, as users move with their devices and providers evolve their topologies. Thus, understanding the impact of Internet topology and routing on mobile users requires broad, longitudinal network measurements from mobile devices.

In this work, we are the first to identify and quantify the performance impact of several causes for inflated Internet routes taken by mobile clients, based on a dataset of 901,000 measurements gathered from mobile devices during 18 months. In particular, we isolate cases in which the distance traveled along a network path is significantly longer than the direct geodesic distance between endpoints. Our analysis focuses on performance with respect to Google, a large, popular content provider that peers widely with ISPs and hosts servers in many locations worldwide. This rich connectivity allows

M. Faloutsos and A. Kuzmanovic (Eds.): PAM 2014, LNCS 8362, pp. 23–33, 2014.

us to expose the topology of carrier networks as well as inefficiencies in current routing. We constrain our analysis to devices located in the US, where our dataset is densest.

Our key results are as follows. First, we find that path inflation is endemic: in the last quarter of 2011 (Q4 2011), we observe substantial path inflation in at least 47% of measurements from devices, covering three out of four major US carriers. While the average fraction of samples experiencing path inflation dropped over the subsequent year, we find that one fifth of our samples continue to exhibit inflation. Second, we classify root causes for path inflation and develop an algorithm for identifying them. Specifically, we identify whether the root cause is due to the mobile carrier's topology, the peering between the carrier and Google, and/or the mapping of mobile clients to Google servers. Third, we characterize the impact of this path inflation on network latencies, which are important for interactive workloads typical in the mobile environment. We show that the impact on end-to-end latency varies significantly depending on the carrier and device location, and that it changes over time as topologies evolve. We estimate that additional propagation delay can range from at least 5-50ms, which is significant for service providers [4]. We show that addressing the source of inflation can reduce download times by hundreds of milliseconds. We argue that it will become increasingly important to optimize routing as last-mile delays in mobile networks improve and the relative impact of inflation becomes larger. Last, we make our dataset publicly available and provide an online tool for visualizing our network performance data.

2 Background and Related Work

Background. As Internet-connected mobile devices proliferate, we need to understand factors affecting Internet service performance from mobile devices. In this paper, we focus on two factors: the carrier topology, and the routing choices and peering arrangements that mobile carriers and service providers use to provide access to the Internet.

The device's carrier network can have multiple Internet *ingress points* — locations where the carrier's access network connects to the Internet. The carrier's network may also connect with a Web service provider at a *peering point* — a location where these two networks exchange traffic and routes. The *Domain Name System (DNS) resolvers* from (generally) the carrier and the service provider combine to direct the client to a server for the service by resolving the name of the service to a server IP address.

Idealized Operation. This paper focuses on Google as the service provider. To understand how mobile devices access Google's services, we make the following assumptions about how Google maps clients to servers to minimize latency. First, Google has globally distributed servers, forming a network that peers with Internet service provider networks widely and densely [2,5]. Second, Google uses DNS to direct clients (in our case, mobile devices) to topologically nearby servers. Last, Google can accurately map mobile clients to their DNS resolvers [6]. Since its network's rich infrastructure aims at reducing client latency, Google is an excellent case study to understand how carrier topology and routing choices align with Google's efforts to improve client performance.

We use Fig. 1 to illustrate the ideal case of a mobile device connecting to a Google server. A mobile device uses DNS to look up www.google.com. Google's resolver

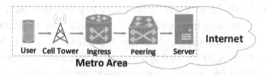

Fig. 1. Optimal routing for mobile clients

returns an optimal Google destination based on a resolver-server mapping. Traffic from the device traverses the carrier's access network, entering the Internet through an ingress point. Ideally, this ingress point is near the mobile device's location. The traffic enters Google's network through a nearby peering point and is routed to the server.

In this paper, we identify significant deviations from this idealized behavior. Specifically, we are interested in *metro-level path inflation* [10], where traffic from a mobile client to a Google server exits the metropolitan (henceforth metro) area even though Google has a presence there. This metro-level inflation impacts performance by increasing latency.

Example Inflation. Carrier topology determines where traffic from mobile hosts enters the carrier network. Prior work has suggested that mobile carriers have relatively few ingress points [11]. Therefore, traffic from a client in the Los Angeles area may enter the Internet in San Francisco because the carrier does not have an ingress in Los Angeles. If the destination service has a server in Los Angeles, the topology can add significant latency compared to having an ingress in LA. Routing configurations and peering arrangements can also cause path inflation. As providers move services to servers located closer to clients, the location where carriers peer with a provider's network may significantly affect performance. For instance, if a carrier has ingress points in Seattle and San Francisco, but peers with a provider only in San Francisco, it may route Seattle traffic to San Francisco even if the provider has a presence in Seattle.

Related Work. Research showed 10 years ago that interdomain routes suffer from path inflation particularly due to infrastructure limitations like peering points only at select locations, but also due to routing policies [8]. In recent work, researchers investigated reasons for suboptimal performance of clients of Google's CDN, showing that clients in the same geographical area can experience much different latencies to Google's servers [4,12]. Cellular networks present new challenges and opportunities for studying path inflation. One study demonstrates differences in metro-area mobile performance but does not investigate the root causes [7]. Other work shows that routing over suboptimal paths due to lack of nearby ingress points causes a 45% increase in RTT latency because of the additional distance traveled, compared to idealized routing [1]. We show how topologies and path inflation have evolved, and that ingress point location is only one of several factors that can affect performance.

3   Dataset

Data Collected. Our data consists of network measurements (ping, traceroute, HTTP GET, UDP bursts and DNS lookups) issued from Speedometer, an internal Android app developed by Google and deployed on thousands of volunteer devices. Speedometer conducts approximately 20-25 measurements every five minutes, as long as the device has sufficient remaining battery life (80%) and is connected to a cellular network.[1]

Our analysis focuses on measurements toward Google servers including 310K traceroutes, 300K pings and 350K DNS lookups issued in three three-month periods (2011 Q4, 2012 Q2 and Q4). We focus on measurements issued by devices in the US, where the majority of users is located, with a particular density of measurements in areas with large Google offices. All users running the app have consented to sharing collected data in an anonymized form.[2] Some fields are stripped (e.g. device IP addresses, IDs), others are replaced by hash values (e.g. HTTP URLs). Location data is anonymized to the center of a region that contains at least 1000 users and is larger than $1\ km^2$.

The above measurements are part of a dataset that we published to a Google Cloud Storage bucket and released under the Creative Commons Zero license[3]. We also provide *Mobile Performance Maps*, a visualization tool to navigate parts of the dataset, understand network performance and supplement the analysis in this paper: http://mpm.cs.usc.edu.

Finding Ingress Points. In order to identify locations of ingress points, for each carrier, we graphed the topology of routes from mobile devices to Google, as revealed by the traceroutes in our dataset. We observe that traceroutes from clients in the same regions tend to follow similar paths. We used the DNS names of routers in those paths to identify the location of hops at which they enter the public Internet. In general, the traceroutes form well-defined structures, starting with private or unresolvable addresses, where all measurements from a given region reach the Internet in a single, resolvable location, generally a point of presence of the carrier's backbone network. We define this location as the ingress point.

Finding Peering Points. To infer peering locations between the carriers and Google, we identified for each path the last hop before entering Google's network, and the first hop inside it (identified by an IP address from Google's blocks). Using location hints in the hostnames of those hop pairs, we infer peering locations for each carrier [9]. In cases where the carrier does not peer with Google (*i.e.,* sends traffic through a transit AS), we use the ingress to Google's network as the inferred peering location.

4   A Taxonomy of Inflated Routes

Types of Path Inflation. Table 1 shows, for traceroutes in our dataset from the four largest mobile carriers in the US, the fraction of routes that incurred a metro-level path inflation.

For three of the four carriers, *more than half of all traceoutes to Google* experienced a metro-level deviation in Q4 2011. Further, nearly *all* measurements from AT&T customers traversed inflated paths to Google. Note that these results are biased toward locations of users in our dataset and are not intended to be generalized. Nevertheless, at a high-level, this table shows that metro-level deviations occur in routes from the four

---

[1] The app source is available at: https://github.com/Mobiperf/Speedometer

[2] Google's privacy and legal teams reviewed and approved data anonymization and release.

[3] http://commondatastorage.googleapis.com/speedometer/README.txt

Table 1. Fraction of traceroutes from major US carriers that show metro-level inflation

	AT&T	Sprint	T-Mobile	Verizon
Q4 2011	0.98	0.10	0.65	0.47
Q2 2012	0.98	0.21	0.25	0.15
Q4 2012	0.00	0.21	0.20	0.38

major carriers, even though Google deploys servers around the world to serve nearby clients [4]. However, we also observe that the fraction of paths experiencing metro-level inflation decreases significantly over the subsequent 12 months. As we will show, we can directly link some of these improvements to the topological expansion of carriers.

In the rest of the paper, we examine path inflation to understand its causes and to explore what measures carriers have adopted to reduce or eliminate it. We begin by characterizing the different types of metro-level inflations we see in our dataset. We split the end-to-end path into three logical parts: client to carrier ingress point (Carrier Access), carrier ingress point to service provider ingress point (Interdomain), and service provider ingress point to destination server (Provider Backbone). Then we define the following observed traffic patterns of inflated routes:

Carrier Access Inflation. Traffic from a client in metro area **L** (Local) enters the Internet in metro area **R** (Remote), and is directed to a Google server in **R**.

Interdomain Inflation. Traffic from a client in area **L** enters the carrier's backbone in **L**, then enters Google's network in area **R** and is directed to a Google server there.

Carrier Access-Interdomain Inflation. Traffic from a client in metro area **L** enters the carrier's backbone in metro area **R**, then enters Google's network back in area **L** and is directed to a Google server there.

Provider Backbone Inflation. Traffic from a client in area **L** enters the carrier's backbone and Google's network in area **L**, but is directed to a Google server in a different area **R**. In all cases, Google servers are known to exist in both metro areas **L** and **R**.

Possible Causes of Path Inflation. If a carrier lacks sufficient ingress points from its cellular network to the Internet, it can cause *Carrier Access Inflation*. For example, if a carrier has no Internet ingress points in metro area **L**, it must send the traffic from **L** to another area **R** (Fig. 2, user B). If a carrier's access network ingresses into the Internet in metro-area **L**, a lack of peering between the mobile carrier and Google in metro-area **L** causes traffic to leave the metro area, resulting in *Interdomain Inflation* (Fig. 2, user C). If a carrier has too few ingresses and lacks peering near its ingresses, we may observe *Carrier Access-Interdomain Inflation*. In this case a carrier, lacking ingress in area **L**, hauls traffic to a remote area **R**, where it lacks peering with Google. A peering point exists in area **L**, so traffic returns there to enter Google's network. Though a provider like Google has servers in most major metropolitan areas, it can still experience *Provider Backbone Inflation* if either Google or the mobile carrier groups together clients in diverse regions when making routing decisions. In this case, Google directs at least some of the clients to distant servers. Google may also route a fraction of traffic long distances across its backbone for measurement or other purposes.

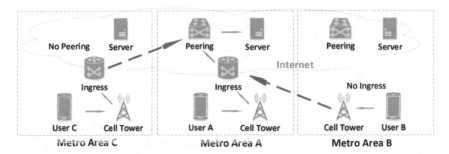

Fig. 2. Different ways a client can be directed to a server. User A is the ideal case, where the traffic never leaves a geographical area. User B and C's traffic suffers path inflation, due to lack of ingress point and peering point respectively.

Identifying Root Causes. We run one or more of the following checks, depending on the inflated part(s) of the path, to perform root cause analysis (illustrated in Fig. 3).

Examining Carrier Access Inflation. For inflated carrier access paths, we determine whether the problem is the lack of an available nearby ingress point. To do so, we examine the first public IP addresses for other traceroutes issued by clients of the same carrier in the same area. If none of those addesses are in the client's metro area, we conclude there is a **lack of available local ingress**.

Examining Interdomain Inflation. For paths inflated between the carrier ingress point and the ingress to Google's network, we determine whether it is due to a lack of peering near the carrier's ingress point. We check whether any traceroutes from the same carrier enter Google's network in that metro area, implying that a local peering exists. If no such traceroutes exist, we infer a **lack of local peering**.

Examining Provider Backbone Inflation. For paths inflated inside Google's network, we check for inefficient mappings of clients to servers. We look for groups of clients from different metro areas all getting directed to servers at either one or the other area for some period, possibly flapping between the two areas over time. If we observe that behavior, we infer **inefficient client/resolver clustering**.

A small number of traceroutes ($< 2\%$) experienced inflated paths but did not fit any of the above root causes. These could be explained by load balancing, persistent incorrect mapping of a client to a resolver/server, or a response to network outages.

5   Results

We first present examples of the three dominant root causes for metro-level inflation. We then show aggregate results from our inflation analysis, its potential impact on latency, and the evolution of causes of path inflation over time.

Case Studies. For each root cause, we now present one example. For each example, we describe what the traceroutes show, what the diagnosis was, and note the estimated performance hit, ranging from 7-72% extra propagation delay. We constrain our analysis to the period between late 2011 and mid 2012, where the dataset is sufficiently dense.

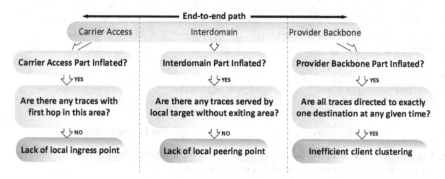

Fig. 3. Root cause analysis for metro-level inflation

Lack of ingress point. We observe that all traceroutes to Google from AT&T clients in the NYC area enter the public Internet via an ingress point in Chicago. Thus, Google directs these New York clients to a server in the Chicago area, even though it is not the server geographically closest to the clients. These Chicago servers are approximately 1074km further from the clients than the New York servers are, leading to an expected minimum additional round-trip latency of 16ms (7% overhead) [3].

Lack of peering. We observe AT&T peering with Google near San Francisco (SF),[4] but not near Los Angeles (LA) or Seattle. Therefore, Google directs clients in those two areas to servers in SF rather than in their local metros. While our data in these regions become sparse after mid 2012, we verified that this inflation persists for clients from LA in Q2 2013. The observed median RTT for Seattle users served by servers in SF is 90ms. Since those servers are 1089km farther away from the servers nearest to the Seattle users, they experience a delay inflation of at least 16ms (21%). As a result, loading even a simple website like the Google homepage requires an additional 160ms.

Coarse client-server mapping granularity or Inefficient client/resolver clustering. We observe a behavior for Verizon clients that suggests that Google is jointly directing clients in Seattle and SF. At any given time, traffic from both areas was directed towards the same Google servers, either in the Seattle or in the SF area, therefore exhibiting suboptimal performance for some distant clients. Figure 4 illustrates this behavior over a 2-month period. Normally, users served by servers in their metro area observe a median RTT of 22ms and 45ms for SF and Seattle respectively. However, when users in one area served by servers in the other area (indicated by the filled pattern in the figure), the additional 1089km one-way distance adds an extra 16ms delay (an overhead of 72% and 35% for SF and Seattle users respectively).

Inflation Breakdown by Root Cause. In this section, we show aggregated statistics of some of the observed anomalies that cause performance degradation. We focus on Q4 2011 and on AT&T and Verizon Wireless, the period and carriers for which the dataset is the densest. We also focus on three large metropolitan areas that were populated enough to generate significant data (SF, New York and Seattle). Google servers exist in all three areas. For all measurements issued from those areas, we quantify the fraction

---

[4] For the granularity of our analysis, we treat all locations in the Bay Area as equivalent.

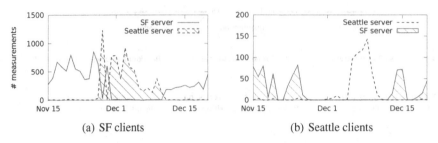

(a) SF clients   (b) Seattle clients

Fig. 4. Server selection flapping due to coarse client-server mapping. Dashed areas denote measurements where the client was directed to a remote server.

Table 2. Overall results for two carriers for 2011 Q4. The table shows what fraction of all traceroutes from clients in three different locations presented a deviation, cause of the deviation (I = Ingress, P = Peering, D = DNS/clustering), extra distance traveled (round-trip), extra round trip time (RTT), and extra page load time (PLT) when accessing the Google homepage.

	Closest Server	Count	Fraction Inflated	I	P	D	Extra Dst. (km)	Extra RTT (ms)	Extra PLT (ms)
AT&T	SF	7759	1.00	x	x		4200	31.5	315
	Seattle	303	1.00		x		2106	15.8	158
	NYC	2720	1.00	x			2148	16.1	161
Verizon	SF	20528	0.30			x	2178	16.3	163
	Seattle	2435	0.33			x	1974	14.8	148
	NYC	7029	0.98				694	5.2	52

of metro-level inflations and determine the root cause. We believe that the path inflation observed in those areas implies probable inflation in less-populated regions.

Table 2 shows aggregate results for the three regions. For each case, it includes the extra round-trip distance traveled as well as a loose lower bound of the additional delay incurred by traveling that distance, based on the speed of data through fiber [3]. We observed inflated routes from all regions for both carriers. Most of the traceroutes from Verizon clients in the NYC area went to servers near Washington, D.C., but we were unable to discern the exact cause. This represents a small geographic detour and may not impact performance in practice. Verizon clients from the Seattle and SF metro were routed together, possibly as a result of using the same DNS resolvers, as described in our case study above. For all traces from AT&T clients in the NYC area, the first public AT&T hop is in Chicago, indicating a lack of a closer ingress point. AT&T clients from the SF area were all served by a nearby Google server. However, traffic went from SF to Seattle before returning to the server in SF. In the traceroutes, the first public IP address was always from an AT&T router in Seattle, suggesting a lack of an ingress point near SF, and increasing the RTT by at least 31ms for all traffic. This behavior progressively disappeared in early 2012, with the observed appearance of an AT&T ingress point in the SF area. An informal discussion with the carrier confirms initial deployment of this ingress in 2011. Note that traceroutes from clients in Seattle were also routed to Google targets in the SF area. Though Seattle traffic reached a local ingress, AT&T routed it to SF before handing it to Google's network, indicating a lack of peering in Seattle and explaining why traffic from SF clients returned to SF after detouring to Seattle.

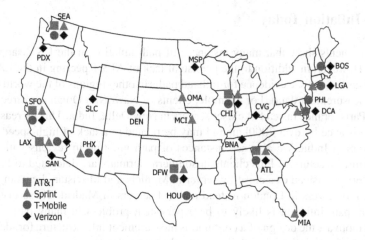

Fig. 5. Observed ingress points for major US carriers. Locations are labeled with airport codes belonging to the ingress metro area.

Evolution of Root Causes. As suggested above, carriers' topologies have evolved over time. Since our dataset is skewed towards some regions, we cannot enumerate the complete evolution of carrier topology and routing configuration, but can provide insight into why we see fewer path inflation instances over time for some carriers.

Ingress Points. Figure 5 maps the observed ingress points at the end of 2011. While our dataset is limited, we can see indications of improvement. An earlier study [11] found 4-6 ingress points per carrier, whereas our results indicate that some carriers doubled this figure. This expansion opens up the possibility of much more direct routes from clients to services. Additionally, we noticed the appearance of AT&T ingresses in SF and LA, and of at least one Sprint ingress point in LA during the measurement period.

Peering points. Table 3 summarizes the peering points that we observe. In 2011, most traceroutes from Sprint users in LA are directed to Google servers in Texas or SF. In measurements from Q2 2012, we observed an additional peering point between Sprint and Google near LA. Around the same time, we observe that Google started directing Sprint's LA clients to LA servers.

Table 3. Observed peering locations between carriers and Google. Locations are identified by airport codes belonging to the metro area.

Carrier	Peering locations (2011 Q4)	(2012 Q2)	(2012 Q4)
AT&T	CHI, DFW, HOU, MSP, PDX, SAT, SFO	+ ATL, CMH	+ DEN
Sprint	ASH, ATL, CHI, DFW, LGA, SEA, SFO	+ LAX	
T-Mobile	DCA, DFW, LAX, LGA, MSP, SEA, SFO	+ MIL	+ MIA
Verizon	ATL, CHI, DAL, DCA, DFW, HOU, LAX, SCL, SEA, SFO		+ ASH, MIA

6   Path Inflation Today

Our measurements show that many instances of path inflation in the US disappeared over time. However, in addition to the persistent lack of AT&T peering in the LA area mentioned earlier, we see evidence for inflated paths in other regions of the world (from Q3 2013 measurement data). For example, clients of Nawras in Oman are directed to servers in Paris, France instead of closer servers in New Delhi, India. This increases the round trip distance by over 7000km, and may be related to a lack of high-speed paths to the servers in India. We also see instances of path inflation in regions with well-developed infrastructure. E-Plus clients in southern Germany are delegated to Paris or Hamburg servers instead of a close-by server in Munich, and Movistar clients in Spain are directed to servers in London instead of local servers in Madrid. These instances suggest that path inflation is likely to be a persistent problem in many parts of the globe, and motivate the design of a continuous measurement infrastructure for identifying instances of path inflation, and diagnosing their root causes.

7   Conclusions

This paper took a first look into diagnosing path inflation for mobile client traffic, using a large collection of longitudinal measurements gathered by smartphones located in diverse regions and carrier networks. We provided a taxonomy of causes for path inflation, identified the reasons behind observed cases, and quantified their impact. We found that a lack of carrier ingress points or provider peering points can cause lengthy detours, but, in general, routes improve as carrier and provider topologies evolve. Our dataset is publicly available at http://mpm.cs.usc.edu and our ongoing work includes developing techniques for automatic detection of evolving topology issues.

References

1. Dong, W., Ge, Z., Lee, S.: 3G Meets the Internet: Understanding the Performance of Hierarchical Routing in 3G Networks. In: ITC (2011)
2. Gill, P., Arlitt, M., Li, Z., Mahanti, A.: The Flattening Internet Topology: Natural Evolution, Unsightly Barnacles or Contrived Collapse? In: Claypool, M., Uhlig, S. (eds.) PAM 2008. LNCS, vol. 4979, pp. 1–10. Springer, Heidelberg (2008)
3. Katz-Bassett, E., John, J.P., Krishnamurthy, A., Wetherall, D., Anderson, T., Chawathe, Y.: Towards IP geolocation using delay and topology measurements. In: IMC (2006)
4. Krishnan, R., Madhyastha, H.V., Srinivasan, S., Jain, S., Krishnamurthy, A., Anderson, T., Gao, J.: Moving Beyond End-to-End Path Information to Optimize CDN Performance. In: IMC (2009)
5. Labovitz, C., Iekel-Johnson, S., McPherson, D., Oberheide, J., Jahanian, F.: Internet inter-domain traffic. In: SIGCOMM (2010)
6. Mao, Z.M., Cranor, C.D., Douglis, F., Rabinovich, M., Spatscheck, O., Wang, J.: A Precise and Efficient Evaluation of the Proximity Between Web Clients and Their Local DNS Servers. In: USENIX ATC (2002)
7. Sommers, J., Barford, P.: Cell vs. WiFi: on the performance of metro area mobile connections. In: IMC (2012)

8. Spring, N.T., Mahajan, R., Anderson, T.E.: The causes of path inflation. In: SIGCOMM (2003)
9. Spring, N.T., Mahajan, R., Wetherall, D., Anderson, T.E.: Measuring ISP topologies with Rocketfuel. IEEE/ACM Trans. Netw. 12(1) (2004)
10. Tangmunarunkit, H., Govindan, R., Shenker, S., Estrin, D.: The Impact of Routing Policy on Internet Paths. In: INFOCOM (2001)
11. Xu, Q., Huang, J., Wang, Z., Qian, F., Gerber, A., Mao, Z.M.: Cellular data network infrastructure characterization and implication on mobile content placement. In: SIGMETRICS (2011)
12. Zhu, Y., Helsley, B., Rexford, J., Siganporia, A., Srinivasan, S.: LatLong: Diagnosing Wide-Area Latency Changes for CDNs. IEEE TNSM 9(3) (2012)

An End-to-End Measurement Study
of Modern Cellular Data Networks

Yin Xu, Zixiao Wang, Wai Kay Leong, and Ben Leong

Department of Computer Science, National University of Singapore
{xuyin,zixiao,waikay,benleong}@comp.nus.edu.sg

Abstract. With the significant increase in cellular data usage, it is critical to better understand the characteristics and behavior of cellular data networks. With both laboratory experiments and crowd-sourcing measurements, we investigated the characteristics of the cellular data networks for the three mobile ISPs in Singapore. We found that i) the transmitted packets tend to arrive in bursts; ii) there can be large variations in the instantaneous throughput over a short period of time; iii) large separate downlink buffers are typically deployed, which can cause high latency when the throughput is low; and iv) the networks typically implement some form of fair queuing policy.

1 Introduction

Cellular data networks are carrying an increasing amount of traffic with their ubiquitous deployments and their data rates have increased significantly in recent years [1]. However, networks such as HSPA and LTE have very different link-layer protocols from wired and WiFi networks. It is thus important to have a better understanding of the characteristics and behavior of cellular data networks.

In this paper, we investigate and measure the characteristics of the cellular data networks for the three ISPs in Singapore with experiments in the laboratory as well as with crowd-sourced data from real mobile subscribers. The latter was obtained using our custom Android application that was used by real users over a 5-month period from April to August 2013. From our results, we make the following observations on the cellular data networks investigated: i) transmitted packets tend to arrive in bursts; ii) there can be large variations in the instantaneous throughput over a short period of time, even when the mobile device is stationary; iii) large separate downlink buffers are typically deployed in mobile ISPs, which can cause high latency when the throughput is low; and iv) mobile ISPs typically implement some form of fair queuing policy.

Our findings confirm that cellular data networks behave differently from conventional wired and WiFi networks, and our results suggest that more can be done to optimize protocol performance in existing cellular data networks. For example, the fair scheduling in such networks might effectively eliminate the need for congestion control if the cellular link is the bottleneck link. We also found that different ISPs and devices use different buffer configurations and queuing policies.

M. Faloutsos and A. Kuzmanovic (Eds.): PAM 2014, LNCS 8362, pp. 34–45, 2014.

2 Related Work

A number of existing works have measured commercial cellular data networks. One common finding is that the throughput and latency in such networks vary significantly [9,13]. Other works have focused on measuring and characterizing the one-way delay of 3G/HSPA networks [4,7]. Winstein et al. also mentioned in passing that packet arrivals on LTE links do not follow an observable isochronicity [16]. Jiang et al. measured the buffers of 3G/4G networks for the four largest U.S. carriers as well as the largest ISP in Korea using TCP and examined the bufferbloat problem [6]. Our work extends their work by investigating the buffer sizes and queuing policies of mobile ISPs, and we found some surprising differences among the three local ISPs. Aggarwal et al. discussed the fairness of 3G networks and found that the fairness of TCP is adversely affected by a mismatch between the congestion control algorithm and the network's scheduling mechanism [3]. A recent study also showed various interesting effects of network protocols and application behaviors on the performance of LTE networks [5].

3 Methodology

In this section, we describe our measurement study methodology. Our experiments were conducted on the cellular data networks of the three local ISPs in Singapore, which we anonymize as A, B and C. Some measurements were taken in our laboratory at the National University of Singapore, while the rest were crowd-sourced with the assistance of real users using their personal mobile devices. For the laboratory experiments, we purchased 3G/LTE cellular data plans from each ISP and took measurements with different models of smartphones and USB modems. The LTE data plans were backward-compatible with the older HSPA and HSPA+ networks and allowed us to also access these older networks and use non-LTE-enabled mobile devices.

To obtain crowd-sourced measurements, we developed and published a measurement application, *ISPCheck* [2], on the Android Play Store. To date, it has about 50 installations and the data presented in this paper was obtained over a 5-month period from April to August 2013. During this period, 6,048 sets of experiments from 23 different users were collected, with 2,301 sets for HSPA networks and 3,747 sets for the faster HSPA+ networks. We did not include the data for LTE networks because we had relatively little data for these networks, since the LTE networks in Singapore are relatively new and the majority of subscribers have not yet upgraded to LTE.

In our experiments, the measured UDP throughput was never lower than the measured TCP throughput. This suggests that the local ISPs do not throttle UDP flows, unlike the ISPs for other countries [15]. As such, we decided to use UDP flows in all our experiments because UDP provides us with full control over the packet size and sending rate. Also, unless otherwise stated, the packet size for our experiments was 1,420 bytes (including IP headers), since we found that this was the default MTU negotiated by TCP connections in the local networks. For the experiments conducted in the laboratory, we synchronized the clock of the mobile phones to that of our server by pinging the phone over a USB connection with our server. By using pings with RTTs that are less than 2 ms, we were able to synchronize the clocks to within 1 ms accuracy.

This allows us to count the packets in flight and determine the exact one-way delay in our measurements precisely. While `tcpdump` was used to log the packets in our laboratory experiments, we could not use it in ISPCheck because it requires root access to the device. So ISPCheck simply logs packet traces at the application layer. All of our results are available online[1].

4   Packet Flow Measurement

In this section, we investigate the packet flow characteristics of cellular data networks. In particular, we demonstrate that the arrival pattern of cellular data packets is bursty, and it is thus necessary to take this pattern into account when we try to estimate the instantaneous throughput for cellular data networks. Finally, we investigate how the instantaneous throughput of cellular data networks varies over time and find that it can vary by as much as two orders of magnitude within a 10-min interval.

4.1   Burstiness of Packet Arrival

In cellular data networks, packets are typically segmented and transmitted over several frames in the network link and then reconstructed at the receiver. Such networks also incorporate an ARQ mechanism that automatically retransmits erroneous frames, and this can cause packets to be delayed or reordered. To investigate the effect of the link layer protocols on the reception pattern of IP packets, we saturated the mobile link by sending UDP packets from our server to a mobile device at a rate that is higher than the receiving rate. A HTC Desire (HSPA-only) phone was used to measure existing HSPA networks and a Samsung Galaxy S4 phone was used to measure existing HSPA+ and LTE networks. We cannot use the Galaxy S4 to measure HSPA networks because it would always connect to existing HSPA+ networks by default.

One key observation is that packets tend to arrive in bursts. In Fig. 1, we plot the inter-packet arrival times of a representative trace from one of our experiments. We can clearly see that packets tend to arrive in clusters at 10 ms intervals, and that within each cluster, most packets tend to arrive within 1 ms of one another. In Fig. 2, we plot the cumulative distribution of the inter-packet arrival times for 5 traces for networks with different data rates. From these results, we can see that packet arrival is bursty at 10 ms intervals in HSPA networks and at 4 ms in the faster HSPA+ and LTE networks.

In Fig. 3(a), we plot the cumulative distribution of the inter-packet arrival times for the crowd-sourced data collected with ISPCheck. In total, the data set consisted of more than 1 million downstream packets and over 400,000 upstream packets. Again, we can see that the packets arrive in distinct bands even when the packet traces are recorded at the application layer. We consider packets that arrive within 1 ms of each other to constitute a burst, and plot the cumulative distribution of burst sizes in Fig. 3(b). We can see that the majority of downstream packets arrive in bursts. This is likely because the downlink of cellular data networks allows for the parallel transmission of frames which could result in multiple packets being reconstructed at the same time at the receiver.

---

[1] Our data set is currently available at `http://www.opennat.com/ispcheck`

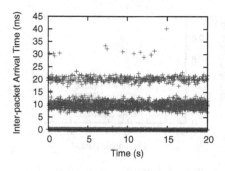

Fig. 1. Trace of the inter-packet arrival time of a downstream UDP flow for ISP C's HSPA network

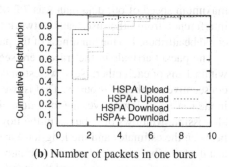

Fig. 2. Cumulative distribution of the inter-packet arrival times for ISP C

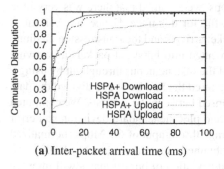

(a) Inter-packet arrival time (ms)   **(b)** Number of packets in one burst

Fig. 3. Inter-packet arrival times and number of packets in one burst for *ISPCheck*

The arrival of packets at distinct intervals of either 10 ms or 4 ms is likely due to the polling duty cycle of the radio driver in the mobile devices, but we were not able to verify this from the available hardware specifications. We noticed that older (and slower) phones like the HTC Desire had a longer interval of 10 ms, while the newer Galaxy S4 has an interval of only 4 ms. To ascertain that this was independent of the kernel tick interval, we performed the same experiments over a 802.11g WiFi network, and confirmed that there was no distinct banding of packets.

4.2 Measuring Instantaneous Throughput

Our observation of bursty packet arrivals suggests that traditional bandwidth measurement techniques using packet pairs [11] or packet trains [12] will not work well for cellular data networks. In order to obtain a reasonably good estimate of the instantaneous throughput, we would likely have to observe at least two bursts worth of packets, but even that might not be sufficient because of the coarse granularity of the clock.

To investigate the effect of bursty packet arrival on instantaneous throughput estimation, we initiated a large number of saturating downstream UDP flows (each 30 s long) over a period of time, until we found a trace where the flow seemed to be stable. Since this flow achieved an average throughput of 6.9 Mbps over the entire period, and the

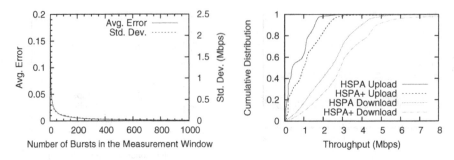

Fig. 4. The accuracy of throughput estimation with different window

Fig. 5. Plot of cumulative distribution of the throughput for data from *ISPCheck*

maximum speed of our data plan was 7.2 Mbps, we assumed that there was very little interference from other users and network traffic for this trace. Hence, any variations could be attributed to the burstiness of the packet arrivals and the transmission medium.

The packet arrivals in the trace were segmented into bursts of packets all arriving within 1 ms of each other. Next, we estimated the instantaneous throughput by using a consecutive number of n bursts. That is, we ignored the first burst and divided the data in the last $n - 1$ bursts over the total time elapsed between the n bursts. We computed all possible windows of n-bursts in the flow and plot the standard deviation and error between the estimates and the long-term average throughput of 6.9 Mbps (normalized against 6.9 Mbps) in Fig. 4 for the estimates obtained as n varies from 2 to 1,000.

As expected, the accuracy and the standard deviation of our estimates will improve if we use a larger number of bursts. However, it is not feasible to use too much data because doing so is not only costly, it might cause the measurement to take too long and the resulting instantaneous measurement might not be too meaningful. Our results in Fig. 4 suggest that using 50 bursts of packets achieves a reasonable trade-off between accuracy and data required. This translates to about 100 KB and 300 KB of data respectively, or at least 400 ms and 325 ms respectively in terms of time, for measuring the upstream and downstream throughputs of 2 Mbps upstream/7.2 Mbps downstream HSPA networks.

4.3   Variations in Mobile Data Network Throughput

We now present our findings on the variations in the networks that we investigated. In Fig. 5, we plot the cumulative distribution of the crowd-sourced data obtained from ISPCheck. As expected, HSPA+ networks are generally faster than HSPA networks. While HSPA+ can in principle achieve speeds higher than 7.2 Mbps, we rarely found speeds higher than that because most of the local data plans have a maximum rate limit of 7.2 Mbps. Overall, we see significant asymmetry in the upstream and downstream data rates and also that the actual throughput achieved by the local subscribers can vary significantly from a few Kbps to several Mbps.

To understand temporal variation, we initiated a 10-min long UDP flow in the HSPA+ network of ISP C and maintained a constant number of packets in flight to keep the

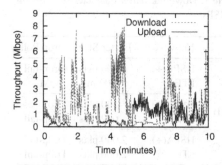

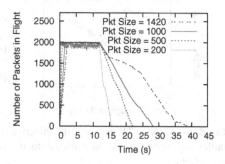

Fig. 6. The huge variation of the download and upload throughput for ISP C's HSPA+ network

Fig. 7. The number of packets in flight for downloads with different packet size for ISP C's HSPA network

buffer filled and ensure that the cellular link is always busy. We estimated the instantaneous throughput over the entire period using windows of 50 bursts of packets, as discussed in Section 4.1. We plot the estimated instantaneous throughput for both an upstream flow and a downstream flow in Fig. 6. We can see that not only does the throughput change fairly quickly, it also varies by as much as over two orders of magnitude several times within a 10-min interval. This corroborates the claims of previous work [13,16] and may lead to significant degradation in TCP and HTTP performance [5].

5   Buffer and Queuing Policy

This section highlights our measurements of the buffer configurations on both ends of the cellular data networks and our investigation into the queuing policies.

Downlink Buffer Size. We estimate the buffer size by sending UDP packets at a rate higher than the receiving rate, which causes the buffer to fill over time with packets and eventually overflow. We can accurately determine the number of outstanding packets in the network, or packets in flight, by synchronizing the clock of our mobile phones to that of the server. Finally, we can estimate the buffer size by subtracting the measured bandwidth-delay product from the total packets in flight. Interestingly, we found that instead of being conventionally sized in bytes, the downstream buffers at the ISPs are sized in packets. In these experiments, we vary the size of the packets from 200 to 1,420 bytes. We could not use packets smaller than 200 bytes because our receiving devices and tcpdump are not able to process such small packets fast enough when we try to saturate the networks to measure the buffer size.

Fig. 7 shows the plot of packets in flight against time for one of our experiments using different packet sizes over ISP C's HSPA network. We can see that the number of packets in flight plateaus at the same value for different packet sizes. In this instance, the bandwidth delay product was small ($\approx$ 50 packets), and so we deduced that the buffer size was fixed at about 2,000 packets. We observed similar behavior in the downstream buffers for all the networks studied, with the exception of ISP A's LTE network.

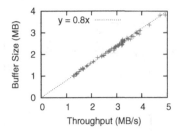

Fig. 8. In ISP A's LTE network, the effective buffer size seems to be proportional to the throughput.

Table 1. Downlink buffer characteristics for local ISPs

ISP	Network	Buffer Size	Drop Policy
ISP A	HSPA(+)	4,000 pkts	Drop-tail
	LTE	($\leq$ 800 ms)	AQM
ISP B	HSPA(+)	400 pkts	Drop-head
	LTE	600 pkts	Drop-tail
ISP C	HSPA(+)	2,000 pkts	Drop-tail
	LTE	2,000 pkts	Drop-tail

The downstream buffer for ISP A's LTE network behaved quite differently from the rest. As shown in Fig. 8, the buffer size seems to be a linear function of the throughput (c.f. $y = 0.8x$). In other words, the size of the buffer appears to vary proportionally to the throughput in a way that keeps the maximum queuing delay constant at 800 ms. We suspect that ISP A might have implemented a Codel-like [10] AQM mechanism in their network, i.e., packets are timestamped when they arrive, and checked at the head of the queue. Packets that spent more than 800 ms in the buffer would be dropped. While there is certainly an absolute limit of the buffer in terms of physical memory space, we were not able to exceed that even when we sent packets at the maximum supported data rate. A summary of the estimated buffer sizes for all three local ISPs is shown in Table 1.

Overall, we observed that the downstream buffers for most of the ISP networks are fairly large. Because the variation in the throughput can be very large, it is possible on occasion for the latency to become very high when throughput is too low to drain the buffer fast enough [6]. By controlling the maximum time that a packet can spend in the buffer (like in ISP A's LTE network), the maximum latency can however be kept at a stable value (about 800 ms for ISP A's LTE network) independent of the throughput.

Drop Policy. We also investigated the drop policy of the various ISPs by studying the traces of the packet losses and found that a drop-tail policy was implemented in all the networks except for ISP B's HSPA(+) and ISP A's LTE network. We repeated our experiments several times with different parameter settings and at different physical locations, and consistently obtained the results summarized in Table 1.

We explain how we inferred the drop policies with the following examples: in Fig. 9(a), we plot the number of packets sent, packets lost and packets in flight over time for ISP C's HSPA(+) network, and in Fig. 9(b), we plot a corresponding trace for ISP B's HSPA(+) network. Because the traces are analyzed offline, we could determine the lost packets by observing that they were sent but never received. However, we cannot determine precisely when the packet losses happened. Hence, the "Lost" line in our graphs refers to the time when the lost packets were sent and not when they were actually dropped. We see in Fig. 9(a), that for ISP C's network, packet losses only occur to packets sent after time $t = 5$. This also coincides with the start of a plateau in the number of packets in flight because we exclude known lost packets when plotting the number of packets in flight. Thus, we can infer that Fig. 9(a) suggests a drop-tail

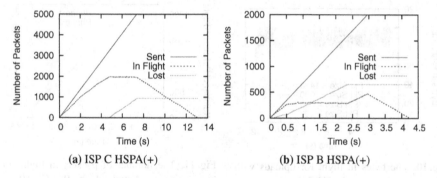

Fig. 9. Trace of the packets sent, lost and in flight in a UDP downstream flow

queue, where the buffer is fully saturated around time $t = 5$ and newly sent packets are dropped until no more packets are sent at time $t = 7.2$ and the buffer starts to empty.

In contrast, Fig. 9(b) paints a very different picture for ISP B's network. We see that packet losses start to occur very early in the trace and stop after time $t = 2.4$, i.e., there were no losses for the final batch of 400 packets sent after time $t = 2.4$. This suggests a drop-head queuing policy. In addition, the packets in flight plateaus at a lower value before increasing to a peak from time $t = 2.4$ to $t = 3$. The explanation for this observation is that the line for packets in flight excludes the lost packets even though for a drop-head queue, they would have occupied space in the buffer before they get dropped at the head of the queue. Thus, our estimate of the packets in flight is an underestimate of the actual value while packets are dropped at the head of the buffer. From time $t = 2.4$ to $t = 3$, the older packets in the buffer are still being dropped but no new packet are lost. Hence, the proportion of packets dropped decreases, which explains why our estimate of the packets in flight gradually increases to the true value at $t = 3$.

Uplink Buffer Size. The uplink buffer is at the radio interface of the mobile device, and for all the mobile phones we tested, the buffer is sized in terms of bytes rather than number of packets like the downlink buffer. In Fig. 10, we plot the bytes in flight over time for the experiments carried out on a HTC Desire phone. We see that the number of bytes in flight remained constant for different packet sizes. On the other hand, the Huawei USB modems we tested had buffers that were sized in terms of number of packets. Our results are summarized in Table 2.

Another interesting finding is that the newer Samsung Galaxy S3 LTE and Galaxy S4 phones seem to buffer packets in the kernel (which is sized in packets), in addition to the regular buffer in the radio interface (which is sized in bytes). Our measurement application was blocked from sending UDP packets once there were about 200 packets in the kernel buffer. This behavior was unexpected because we do not typically expect UDP packet transmissions to be blocked and indeed, this was not observed in the older Android phones. It is plausible that the phone manufacturers have come to realize that because the uplink bandwidth can sometimes be very low, not blocking UDP transmissions would likely cause packets to be dropped even before the phone can get a chance to transmit them, and thus have modified the kernel to implement blocking even for

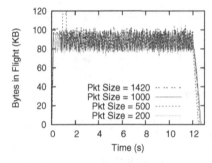

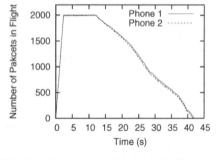

Fig. 10. The bytes in flight for uploads with different packet sizes for HTC Desire

Fig. 11. The number of packets in flight for two concurrent downloads for ISP C's HSPA network

Table 2. The radio interface buffer size of different devices

Device Type	Model	Network	Buffer Size
Android Phone	HTC Desire	HSPA	64 KB
	Galaxy Nexus	HSPA+	1.5 MB
	Galaxy S3 LTE[†]	HSPA+	200 KB
		LTE	400 KB
	Galaxy S4[†]	HSPA+	200 KB
		LTE	400 KB
USB Modem	Huawei E3131	HSPA+	300 pkts
	Huawei E3276	LTE	1,000 pkts

[†]These devices have additional buffering of 1,000 packets in the kernel.

UDP transmissions. To further investigate this phenomenon, we tethered the phone to a desktop computer via USB and used the desktop as the packet source, instead of an Android application. By running tcpdump on the USB and the radio interfaces of the phone, we can directly observe the flow of packets through the phone. In these experiments, we found that the buffering in the kernel was 1,000 packets for both the Galaxy S3 LTE and S4. There was no evidence that packets were buffered in the kernel for the other Android phone models that we investigated.

Separate Downlink Buffers. Winstein et al. claimed that ISPs implement a separate downlink buffer for each device in a cellular data network [16]. To verify this claim, we performed an experiment where we started saturating UDP flows to two mobile phones concurrently connected to the same radio cell. If there was a common buffer, we will likely see differences as the packets for the two flows jostle for a place in the common buffer. Instead, in Fig. 11, we can see that the packets in flight reach the same and constant value for both phones, indicating that it is unlikely for the buffer to be shared between the devices. We observed the same behavior for all the three ISPs.

Queuing Policy and Fairness. To investigate if the ISPs implement a fair scheduling algorithm such as Round Robin, Maximum C/I and Proportional Fair as specified in [14], we ran the following experiment: using two mobile phones connected to the

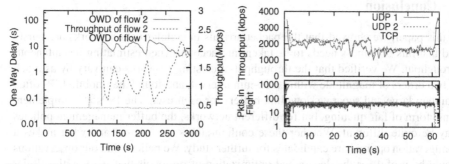

Fig. 12. Comparison of delay-sensitive flow and high-throughput flow for ISP C's HSPA network

Fig. 13. The throughput and packets in flight of three downlink flows for ISP C's HSPA network

same cell with the same signal strength, we sent a UDP flow to one of the phones at the constant rate of one 50-byte packet every 10 ms. After 2 min, we started a saturating UDP flow to the other phone using 1,420-byte packets and saturated the buffer by maintaining 1,000 packets in flight. The first flow mimics a low-throughput, delay-sensitive application, while the second mimics a high-throughput application. In Fig. 12, we plot the downstream one-way delay (OWD) of both flows together with the throughput of the second saturating UDP flow. If the queuing policy were FIFO, we would expect that since flow 2 saturates the buffer, the one-way delay for flow 1 would greatly increase. Instead, our results show that the delay of flow 1 remains low and stable throughout.

To investigate if the scheduling policy was fair among devices, we designed another experiment using three HTC Desire mobile phones connected to the same cell with similar signal strength. A downstream flow was initiated to each phone: i) a UDP flow that maintains 1,420 KB of data in flight, ii) a UDP flow that maintains 64 KB of data in flight, and iii) a TCP flow whose maximum receiver window was set at 64 KB. In Fig. 13, we plot the throughput of all three flows with the number of packets in flight. It turns out that the throughput is fairly distributed among the three devices, independent of the number of packets in their buffer. We repeated this experiment for the HSPA(+) networks of all three local ISPs and found similar results.

We make several observations from the results of our experiments. First, all the ISPs clearly implement some form of fair queuing and unlike in the core Internet, UDP and TCP traffic seem to be treated equally by our local mobile ISPs. While we could observe this behavior end-to-end, we could not determine if the fairness was enforced at the MAC layer or within the network. Second, having more data in flight may not help increase throughput because flows are effectively separated and do not compete for the same buffer space at a cellular base station. Instead, if the throughput is low, saturating the buffer will only result in increased latency. Third, since the fairness among connected mobile devices is enforced by a scheduling policy, congestion control at the transport layer (i.e. TCP) may not be necessary across a cellular link. This suggests that if the cellular link is the bottleneck link, which is common in the older HSPA networks, an end-to-end approach to congestion control may be possible [16]. Also, it is possible for an end-to-end flow to be split at the gateway of the cellular data network and a more efficient protocol can be used on the cellular link [17,8].

6 Conclusion

In this paper, we showed that the packet arrivals in cellular data networks are bursty and that this burstiness needs to be taken into account when estimating instantaneous throughput. We verified that the throughput of existing networks can vary by as much as two orders of magnitude within a 10-min interval, and found that mobile ISPs often maintain large and separate downlink buffers for each user. The ISPs also implement some form of fair queuing, but for different networks, the buffer management policies may be quite different. Whether these configurations are optimal and what makes a configuration optimal are candidates for further study. We believe that our observations would be useful for the design and optimization of protocols that work with cellular data networks.

Acknowledgment. This research was carried out at the SeSaMe Centre. It is supported by the Singapore NRF under its IRC@SG Funding Initiative and administered by the IDMPO.

References

1. Cisco Visual Networking Index: Global Mobile Data Traffic Forecast Update (2012-2017)
2. ISPCheck, https://play.google.com/store/apps/details?id=com.ispcheck
3. Aggarwal, V., Jana, R., Ramakrishnan, K., Pang, J., Shankaranarayanan, N.K.: Characterizing Fairness for 3G Wireless Networks. In: Proceedings of LANMAN 2011 (October 2011)
4. Elmokashfi, A., Kvalbein, A., Xiang, J., Evensen, K.R.: Characterizing Delays in Norwegian 3G Networks. In: Taft, N., Ricciato, F. (eds.) PAM 2012. LNCS, vol. 7192, pp. 136–146. Springer, Heidelberg (2012)
5. Huang, J., Qian, F., Guo, Y., Zhou, Y., Xu, Q., Mao, Z.M., Sen, S., Spatscheck, O.: An In-depth Study of LTE: Effect of Network Protocol and Application Behavior on Performance. In: Proceedings of SIGCOMM 2013 (August 2013)
6. Jiang, H., Wang, Y., Lee, K., Rhee, I.: Tackling Bufferbloat in 3G/4G Networks. In: Proceedings of IMC 2012 (November 2012)
7. Laner, M., Svoboda, P., Hasenleithner, E., Rupp, M.: Dissecting 3G Uplink Delay by Measuring in an Operational HSPA Network. In: Spring, N., Riley, G.F. (eds.) PAM 2011. LNCS, vol. 6579, pp. 52–61. Springer, Heidelberg (2011)
8. Leong, W.K., Xu, Y., Leong, B., Wang, Z.: Mitigating Egregious ACK Delays in Cellular Data Networks by Eliminating TCP ACK Clocking. In: Proceedings of ICNP 2013 (October 2013)
9. Liu, X., Sridharan, A., Machiraju, S., Seshadri, M., Zang, H.: Experiences in a 3G Network: Interplay Between the Wireless Channel and Applications. In: Proceedings of MobiCom 2008 (September 2008)
10. Nichols, K., Jacobson, V.: Controlling Queue Delay. Queue 10(5), 20:20–20:34 (2012)
11. Paxson, V.: End-to-end Internet Packet Dynamics. In: Proceedings of SIGCOMM 1997 (September 1997)
12. Ribeiro, V.J., Riedi, R.H., Baraniuk, R.G., Navratil, J., Cottrell, L.: pathChirp: Efficient Available Bandwidth Estimation for Network Paths. In: Proceedings of PAM 2003 (April 2003)
13. Tan, W.L., Lam, F., Lau, W.C.: An Empirical Study on the Capacity and Performance of 3G Networks. IEEE Transactions on Mobile Computing 7(6), 737–750 (2008)

14. Tapia, P., Liu, J., Karimli, Y., Feuerstein, M.J.: HSPA Performance and Evolution: A Practical Perspective. Wiley (2009)
15. Tso, F.P., Teng, J., Jia, W., Xuan, D.: Mobility: A Double-Edged Sword for HSPA Networks. In: Proceedings of MobiHoc 2010 (September 2010)
16. Winstein, K., Sivaraman, A., Balakrishnan, H.: Stochastic Forecasts Achieve High Throughput and Low Delay over Cellular Networks. In: Proceedings of NSDI 2013 (October 2013)
17. Xu, Y., Leong, W.K., Leong, B., Razeen, A.: Dynamic Regulation of Mobile 3G/HSPA Uplink Buffer with Receiver-Side Flow Control. In: Proceedings of ICNP 2012 (October 2012)

A Second Look at Detecting Third-Party Addresses in Traceroute Traces with the IP Timestamp Option

Matthew Luckie and kc claffy

CAIDA, UC San Diego, USA
{mjl,kc}@caida.org

Abstract. Artifacts in traceroute measurement output can lead to false inferences of AS-level links and paths when used to deduce AS topology. One traceroute artifact is caused by routers that respond to traceroute probes with a source address not in the path towards the destination, i.e. an off-path address. The most well-known traceroute artifact, the third-party address, is caused by off-path addresses that map to ASes not in the corresponding BGP path. In PAM 2013, Marchetta *et al.* proposed a technique to detect off-path addresses in traceroute paths [14]. Their technique assumed that a router IP address reported in a traceroute path towards a destination was off-path if, in a subsequent probe towards the same destination, the router did not insert a timestamp into a pre-specified timestamp option in the probe's IP header. However, no standard precisely defines how routers should handle the pre-specified timestamp option, and implementations are inconsistent. Marchetta *et al.* claimed that most IP addresses in a traceroute path are off-path, and that consecutive off-path addresses are common. They reported no validation of their results. We cross-validate their approach with a first-principles approach, rooted in the assumption that subnets between connected routers are often /30 or /31 because routers are often connected with point-to-point links. We infer if an address in a traceroute path corresponds to the interface on a router that received the packet (the in-bound interface) by attempting to infer if its /30 or /31 subnet mate is an alias of the previous hop. We traceroute from 8 Ark monitors to 80K randomly chosen destinations, and find that most observed addresses are configured on the in-bound interface on a point-to-point link connecting two routers, i.e. are on-path. Because the technique from [14] reports 70.9%–74.9% of these addresses as being off-path, we conclude it is not reliable at inferring which addresses are off-path or third-party.

1 Introduction

The AS-level view of the Internet afforded by public BGP data is severely limited by a well-known visibility issue: peer-to-peer links between ASes are observable only if one of the ASes or their downstream customer provides a public view [15], which few ASes do. Traffic data collected at IXPs [2], although typically proprietary, can reveal many AS peering links established at the IXP. IXP

M. Faloutsos and A. Kuzmanovic (Eds.): PAM 2014, LNCS 8362, pp. 46–55, 2014.

route-servers used to establish multilateral peering [6] may also support a query interface that reveals peering activity at the IXP. But many important peerings are established bilaterally using the IXP fabric, or at private exchange points, so traceroute retains an important role in uncovering AS-level topology [4].

Using traceroute to infer AS links and paths involves many recognized challenges [9,16,20]. Inferring AS paths from traceroute IP paths relies on an accurate AS inference for each IP address in traceroute, i.e. an IP2AS mapping. The most widely used IP2AS mapping technique is to associate each IP address in a path with the origin AS in a BGP path for the longest matching prefix. However, real-world practices such as (1) operators not announcing IP prefixes used to number their routers, (2) multiple ASes announcing the same prefix, and (3) organizations which own multiple ASes announcing different prefixes with different ASNs, all complicate IP2AS mapping. A further complication is routers which respond to traceroute probes using an *off-path* address; i.e. an address that does not represent the path through the router that the packet would have taken towards the destination. Off-path addresses are derived when (1) a router sets the source address of ICMP response packets to the outgoing interface used to send the response packet, and (2) that interface is not the in-bound or out-bound interface the router would have used to receive or transmit the packet if the router had forwarded the packet. A *third-party* address is an off-path address that resolves to a third-party AS that is not in the corresponding BGP path.

There has been considerable debate about the prevalence of third-party addresses. In PAM 2003, Hyun *et al.* [9] reported that third-party addresses were rare, often observed close to the destination probed, and caused by multi-homing and stale configurations. In PAM 2010, Zhang *et al.* [20] reported that the majority of false links in AS topology data derived from traceroute were due to third-party addresses. In PAM 2013, Marchetta *et al.* [14] proposed a technique to detect third-party addresses in traceroute paths using the pre-specified IP timestamp option. This option allows a host to request a timestamped response from a specific IP address (i.e., the associated router) in the path. RFC 791 [17] does not describe precisely how to implement this option, in particular whether the IP packet must actually traverse the IP interface configured with the pre-specified IP address in order to trigger the timestamp recording.

Figure 1 illustrates the technique from [14]. Using the same notation as Sherry *et al.* [18], a probe to destination G that requests B, C, D, and E include timestamps is denoted as G|BCDE. The technique from [14] assumes the behavior of a router with address B can be inferred from the response to an ICMP echo probe B|BBBB. If B embeds between one and three timestamps in the ICMP echo packet, [14] infers that the router embeds timestamps as the packet arrives or departs on the interface with address B; if B embeds four timestamps, [14] infers the router with B will insert timestamps regardless of the interface it arrived or departed from and therefore B cannot be classified as an on-path or off-path address. The technique from [14] also cannot classify routers that embed zero timestamps, remove the option, or do not reply to the ICMP probe. Because only destinations that quote the IP options in ICMP responses can be

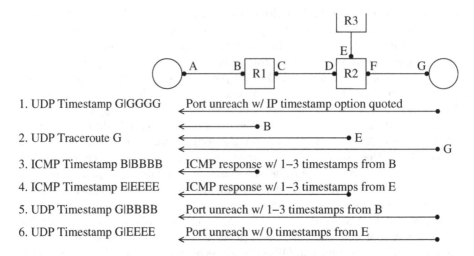

Fig. 1. Using pre-specified IP timestamps to infer third party addresses with the technique described in [14]. If G returns probes with the IP timestamp option quoted (1), then [14] evaluates the traceroute path B-E-G (2) for third-party addresses. First, [14] determines if routers will set timestamps for their IP address when a packet is sent directly to them (3, 4). For the routers that set 1-3 timestamps (i.e. set timestamps when the packet arrives and/or departs), [14] sends probes to the destination which also request those interfaces to embed a timestamp. [14] infers interface B is on-path because it does embed a timestamp (5), and infers E is a third-party address because it does not (6). However, RFC791 [17] is under-specified and it is not safe to assume E is a third-party address because it did not insert a timestamp.

evaluated for third-party addresses, the first step shown in figure 1 is to ensure a destination will respond to probes containing IP options and also quote the IP option in responses. The technique from [14] uses UDP probes for traceroute (step 2) and determining whether or not an address is on-path or off-path (steps 5, 6) because G quotes the timestamp option as the option was when G received the packet. Therefore, if B is observed in a traceroute path to G, and B embeds 1-3 timestamps to a probe G|BBBB, then the technique from [14] infers the interface with B is on-path toward G; if no timestamps are embedded by B then B is inferred by [14] to be off-path and could lead to a third-party address.

Marchetta *et al.* used their technique to estimate the prevalence of third-party IP addresses in traceroute paths. They used 53 PlanetLab nodes to obtain 12M traces towards 327K destinations among 14K ASes. They reported that most classified IP addresses in their data are off-path, and that consecutive off-path addresses are common [14]; Hyun *et al.* considered this to be a remote possibility. Further, they inferred that 17% of AS links in their dataset were inferred using third-party addresses. However, they reported no validation of their results. We revisit the effectiveness of their technique by attempting to determine which addresses in a traceroute path are likely to be the in-bound interface and thus on-path, and then examining the classification made using the technique from [14] for these in-bound interfaces. We find most in-bound interfaces are incorrectly classified by the technique from [14] to be off-path. Further, most addresses observed in our traceroute paths are assigned by operators to the in-bound interface. We believe that the results reported in [14] are not robust because their technique is unreliable; RFC791 under-specifies how the option should be implemented and there is considerable heterogeneity in how it is implemented.

2   Method and Data

In this section we describe the method and data collected to evaluate the utility of pre-specified timestamps for inferring third party addresses. Our cross-validation of [14] involves two steps. First, we infer which addresses in a traceroute path represent the in-bound interface on the router receiving the packet, and therefore are not off-path addresses. Then, we evaluate the classification made by the technique from [14] using the pre-specified timestamp IP option for the interfaces we infer to be in-bound interfaces.

We use the *prefixscan* method implemented in scamper and described in [12] to infer which addresses in a traceroute path are the in-bound address on a router. An address B is the in-bound interface of a router in a traceroute path if we find an alias A' of the address A returned for the previous hop and A' is a /31 or /30 mate of B, i.e. the link between A and B is a point-to-point (pt2pt) link. The prefixscan method infers A and A' are aliases if (1) the IPIDs in responses to five alternating probes sent one second apart monotonically increase and differ by no more than 5,000, or (2) probes to A and A' elicit responses with a common source address. The first technique is a pairwise comparison similar to Ally [19], and the second is the Mercator technique [7]. A threshold of 5,000 allows aliases to be inferred for routers with fast moving IPID counters and has a 7.6% chance of falsely inferring aliases, in the worst case, between two routers with fast moving but overlapping counters.

Because we may falsely infer aliases when two independent counters happen to overlap when we probe them [5], or when two routers randomly generated IPID values that happened to fall within the threshold, we probe A and A' six further times approximately ten minutes apart, with five probes per round. We do not classify a link as pt2pt if any of these subsequent probes do not solicit a monotonically increasing sequence or if the IPID distance falls outside of the threshold. For each hop in a traceroute path, we prefixscan with ICMP-echo, TCP-ack, and UDP probes (in that order) to maximize our potential to infer pt2pt links. We use this ordering because in previous cross-validation efforts, we found this order to produce the most accurate inferences [13]. We believe our pt2pt inferences are robust because other researchers have previously validated IPID-based alias inferences [19,5,10].

Table 1 lists the eight CAIDA Archipelago (Ark) vantage points (VPs) we use for our study. We chose the eight VPs that were operational on 2 September 2013 that also provide a complete BGP view publicly. We chose these VPs because we could also evaluate traceroute-inferred and BGP-observed AS path

Table 1. To support future study of traceroute and BGP incongruities, we chose for
our measurement study 8 Ark VPs that also provide a complete BGP view publicly

Ark VP	Hosting Network (AS)	Public BGP view (peer IP)
ams3-nl	RIPE NCC (3333)	RIPE rrc00 (193.0.0.56)
gva-ch	IP-Max SA (25091)	RIPE rrc04 (192.65.185.244)
nrt-jp	APAN (7660)	Routeviews 2 (203.181.248.168)
per-au	AARnet (7575)	Routeviews ISC (198.32.176.177)
sin-sg	DCS1 Pte Ltd (37989)	RIPE rrc00 (203.123.48.6)
syd-au	AARnet (7575)	Routeviews ISC (198.32.176.177)
sql-us	ISC (1280)	RIPE rrc14 (198.32.176.3)
zrh2-ch	Kantonsschule Zug (34288)	RIPE rrc12 (80.81.194.119)

incongruities on pt2pt links, shedding further light on how incongruities from
on-path addresses arise in practice. We leave this analysis for future work and
invite the research community to study this problem further using these VPs.

From each VP, we randomly chose 10,000 destinations that quoted a probe's
IP options in an ICMP destination unreachable message; these destinations were
useful because they quote the IP options (step 1 in figure 1). Each VP randomly
selected a different set of destinations to probe. To maximize our chances of
selecting useful destinations, we selected the 2.5M of the 14.5M addresses in
the ISI hitlist [1] with a score of at least 80 (where 99 represents an address
that has always responded to ISI's ICMP echo probes [8]). Despite selecting
destinations that were generally responsive to ping, we found that only 15.1% to
18.8% (depending on the VP) responded and echoed the pre-specified timestamp
option; i.e. we tried between 53K and 66K addresses to obtain 10,000 useful
destinations. Of the destinations that were not useful because we did not receive
a response with a quote of the IP options, only 3.5% to 5.9% did not quote the
timestamp option; another 94.1% to 96.5% of them did not respond at all. When
we probed the same destinations without the timestamp option, 36.4% to 36.8%
responded, implying that including a timestamp option in a UDP probe reduced
the fraction of responsive destinations by at least half.

Overall, we obtained 80,004 traces containing 150,188 IP addresses, inferring
197,335 IP-level links between 7,401 ASes. Many IP interfaces are observed from
multiple VPs; in our dataset, we observed 28.0% of interfaces (IP addresses) from
at least two VPs even though we only used eight VPs total. We received responses
to ICMP B|BBBB probes from 119,594 interfaces. For the 30,594 (25.6%) inter-
faces for which we received responses to ICMP B|BBBB probes from more than
one VP, all VPs observed the same timestamp behavior except for 538 interfaces
(1.8%). 324 of these (60.2%) were in one AS, suggesting routers in our data
behaved the same regardless of probing location for ICMP B|BBBB probes. For
each VP, the technique from [14] classified between 42.5% and 47.3% of interfaces in our data as appearing as on-path or off-path because they responded
with 1-3 timestamps when we probed them with ICMP B|BBBB packets. In
total, 77,348 of the 150,188 (51.5%) interfaces observed in our data embedded
1-3 timestamps when we probed them with ICMP B|BBBB probes.

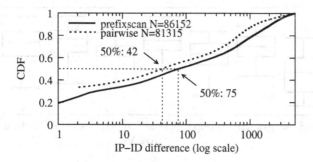

Fig. 2. IPID differences between inferred aliases A and A′. The smaller the difference, the more likely the alias inference is reliable. In our pairwise measurements, we rejected 4,837 initial pt2pt link inferences because either the IPIDs did not monotonically increase, or the counters increased too fast to reliably infer aliases. Of the 81K links remaining, 33% of the IPID values were strictly incremented between alias pairs.

We resolved the IP-level links to AS-level links using the longest matching prefix observed by peers at RouteViews; 31K (15.8%) have addresses that map to two different ASes (are inter-AS links), 153K (77.8%) have addresses that map to a single AS (are links internal to an AS), and 13K (6.4%) have addresses that are either not announced publicly, or whose longest matching prefix is originated by multiple ASes. In total, we infer 10,175 AS-level links from these traces. Of the 197,335 IP-level links, we inferred a /30 or /31 link for 86,152 links with an initial prefixscan; our followup pairwise measurements discarded 5K links because the returned IPID sequence did not meet our requirements, leaving us with 81,315 pt2pt links. Figure 2 shows the IPID differences where aliases were inferred between A and A′. The solid line corresponds to the initial prefixscan measurement that inferred a /30 or /31 mate A′ as an alias of A; we plotted the maximum IPID difference between any two samples in the sequence of five probes. 50% of the samples had a maximum difference of 75. The dashed line corresponds to the subsequent pairwise measurements; for each inferred alias, we plotted the minimum IPID difference between responses from the same probed address; i.e. the alias' IPID had to fit within the two IPID values. 50% of the samples had a minimum difference of 42, and 33.2% had a minimum difference of 2; in these latter cases the IPID of the alias fell immediately between a monotonic sequence. We therefore believe most of our pt2pt inferences are robust.

3   Results

In this section, we focus on addresses in traceroute paths that we inferred to be the address of the in-bound interface on a router and visited across a pt2pt link (i.e. were on-path). Of the 197,335 IP-level links, we inferred 81,315 (41.2%) to be pt2pt. Figure 3 plots the distribution of the fraction of in-bound interfaces in traceroutes observed by each VP. In our data, we inferred that more than half

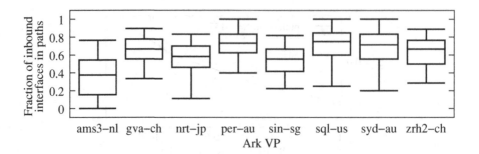

Fig. 3. Distribution of the fraction of in-bound interfaces observed by each VP at the 2nd, 25th, 50th, 75th, and 98th percentiles. For 7 of the 8 VPs, more than half of the interfaces in paths represent the in-bound interface for at least half of their traceroutes.

Table 2. Consistency of timestamps embedded by interfaces that we infer to be the in-bound interface on a pt2pt link. Between 70.9% and 74.6% of interfaces do not insert a timestamp despite being on-path. Between 1.0% and 1.5% of interfaces behaved differently depending on the destination probed (mixed column).

VP	1-3 TS (on-path)	Zero TS (off-path)	4 TS (juniper)	mixed
ams3-nl	1631 (26.1%)	4550 (72.8%)	1 (0%)	64 (1.0%)
gva-ch	1678 (26.4%)	4600 (72.3%)	0 (0%)	83 (1.3%)
nrt-jp	1543 (27.6%)	3958 (70.9%)	1 (0%)	84 (1.5%)
per-au	1547 (24.8%)	4610 (73.8%)	2 (0%)	89 (1.4%)
sin-sg	1649 (25.8%)	4657 (72.9%)	0 (0%)	80 (1.3%)
sql-us	1583 (24.8%)	4698 (73.7%)	1 (0%)	90 (1.4%)
syd-au	1524 (24.0%)	4731 (74.6%)	0 (0%)	91 (1.4%)
zrh2-ch	1404 (26.1%)	3900 (72.5%)	0 (0%)	74 (1.4%)

of the interfaces in each path were the in-bound interface for at least half of the VP's traceroutes for 7 of the 8 VPs. This is a lower bound on the actual fraction of in-bound interfaces for these VPs because some routers do not respond to our prefixscan probes that we use to infer pt2pt links. In particular, many paths from the Ark node in Amsterdam (ams3-nl) traverse AS7018 (AT&T), but none of AT&T's routers will respond to probes.

We next examine the classification made using the technique from [14] for the addresses we inferred to represent the in-bound interface on the router for paths that traversed a pt2pt link. Of the 77,348 interfaces that embedded 1-3 timestamps in the pre-specified timestamp option in response to ICMP B|BBBB probes, we inferred 29,930 (38.7%) of these to represent the in-bound interface on the router on at least one pt2pt link. However, the majority of UDP G|BBBB probes across these pt2pt links obtain zero timestamps and would be classified by [14] as off-path. In our data, between 77.1% and 90.0% of interfaces visited embedded zero timestamps, depending on the VP. Techniques relying on pre-specified timestamps to infer off-path addresses are unreliable.

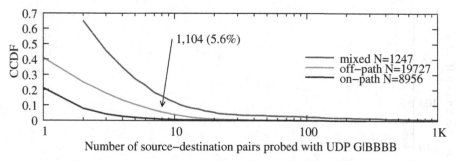

Fig. 4. CCDF of the number of source-destination pairs an interface was observed in a traceroute path, grouped by classifications made with UDP G|BBBB probes and the technique from [14]. 1,104 (5.6%) of interfaces always inferred to be off-path using the technique from [14] that we infer to represent the in-bound interface of the router were traversed in at least eight source-destination pairs in our data.

Because hop B might be observed in multiple traceroutes to destinations G_1, G_2, G_N, and therefore be counted N times, particularly for interfaces close to our VP [11], we next examine the variability of classifications made using pre-specified timestamps. Table 2 reports the number of interfaces that behave consistently regardless of the destination probed; 70.9% – 74.5% do not insert a timestamp when the in-bound interface is visited regardless of the destination probed. This result partly explains Marchetta et al.'s surprising result that most classified addresses in traceroute paths are off-path: it seems routers that insert 1-3 timestamps when probes are addressed to them with ICMP B|BBBB probes often do not insert timestamps when they forward UDP G|BBBB probes.

We next investigate the possibility that the prevalence of off-path inferences are due to load-balancing routers. As with Marchetta et al. [14], the UDP probes for the traceroute towards G contain no IP options, while the UDP probes G|BBBB to infer on- and off- path interfaces do. Routers that per-flow load-balance IPv4 packets using bytes 20-23 (where the transport header would be located if the IP header contained no options) may forward probes based on the first four bytes of a pre-specified timestamp option rather than on the first four bytes of the UDP header (source and destination ports). However, this explanation is unlikely to explain the prevalence of off-path inferences for two reasons. First, per-destination load-balancers are the most common form of load balancer, i.e. they do not consider bytes 20-23 when forwarding a packet. Augustin et al. reported that 70% of source-destination pairs traversed such a load balancer in their data, while 39% traversed a per-flow load balancer [3]. Second, figure 4 presents a CCDF of the number of source-destination pairs an interface was observed in a traceroute, grouped by the classifications made using the technique from [14]. 5.6% of interfaces were consistently inferred to be off-path despite being traversed by at least eight source-destination pairs with UDP G|BBBB probes. We are at least 99% confident the hop prior to B did not per-flow load balance these probes on a path avoiding B. Figure 5 shows a scatter-plot of interfaces that we inferred to be received on the in-bound interface on a pt2pt

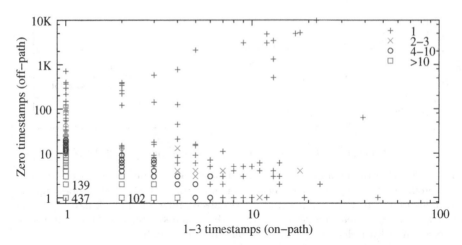

Fig. 5. Scatter plot of in-bound interfaces inferred to be on-path toward some destinations and off-path toward others (i.e. have mixed timestamp behavior). The symbol shape reflects the frequency of the on-path:off-path ratio in our data. Most interfaces are inferred to be on-path for just one source-destination pair using the technique from [14] despite being the in-bound interface of a pt2pt link.

link, but which were inferred to be on-path for some source-destination pairs and off-path for others using the technique from [14]; that technique infers the majority of interfaces to be on-path for a few destinations, and off-path for most. We attempted to traverse some interfaces with hundreds of UDP G|BBBB probes; the technique from [14] inferred these interfaces to be on-path only a few times.

4   Conclusion and Future Work

Traceroute has an important role in overcoming the visibility issue of AS topology data because we have no other way of uncovering some peerings. However, researchers must first overcome traceroute artifacts such as third-party addresses which cause us to deduce false AS links and paths. Using traceroutes from eight Ark monitors to 80K randomly chosen destinations and a method derived from first principles, we showed (counter to the result in [14]) that the majority of IP addresses in traceroute paths are the in-bound interface on a pt2pt link, and that current techniques using pre-specified timestamps to infer third-party addresses are not reliable. We also release our code used to collect these measurements so others can reproduce our work. In future work, we plan to use these eight Ark VPs with public BGP data available to investigate incongruities between BGP and traceroute paths where the incongruity is inferred on a pt2pt link. Deriving a technique that accurately infers AS links from traceroute paths remains an important and currently unsolved problem.

Acknowledgments. The work was supported by U.S. NSF grant CNS-0958547, DHS S&T Cyber Security Division (DHS S&T/CSD) BAA 11-02 and SPAWAR

Systems Center Pacific via N66001-12-C-0130, and by Defence Research and Development Canada (DRDC) pursuant to an Agreement between the U.S. and Canadian governments for Cooperation in Science and Technology for Critical Infrastructure Protection and Border Security. This material represents the position of the author and not of NSF, DHS, or DRDC.

References

1. IP address hitlist, PREDICT ID USC-LANDER/internet_address_hitlist_it52w (January 2, 2013), http://www.isi.edu/ant/lander
2. Ager, B., Chatzis, N., Feldmann, A., Sarrar, N., Uhlig, S., Willinger, W.: Anatomy of a large European IXP. In: SIGCOMM 2012 (2012)
3. Augustin, B., Friedman, T., Teixeira, R.: Measuring load-balanced paths in the Internet. In: IMC 2007 (2007)
4. Augustin, B., Krishnamurthy, B., Willinger, W.: IXPs: Mapped? In: IMC 2009 (2009)
5. Bender, A., Sherwood, R., Spring, N.: Fixing Ally's growing pains with velocity modeling. In: IMC 2008 (2008)
6. Giotsas, V., Zhou, S., Luckie, M., Claffy, K.: Inferring multilateral peering. In: CoNEXT 2013 (2013)
7. Govindan, R., Tangmunarunkit, H.: Heuristics for Internet map discovery. In: IN-FOCOM 2000 (2000)
8. Heidemann, J., Pradkin, Y., Govindan, R., Papadopoulos, C., Bartlett, G., Bannister, J.: Census and survey of the visible Internet. In: IMC 2008 (2008)
9. Hyun, Y., Broido, A., Claffy, K.: On third-party addresses in traceroute paths. In: PAM 2003 (2003)
10. Keys, K., Hyun, Y., Luckie, M., Claffy, K.: Internet-scale IPv4 alias resolution with MIDAR. IEEE/ACM Transactions on Networking 21(2) (April 2013)
11. Lakhina, A., Byers, J.W., Crovella, M., Xie, P.: Sampling biases in IP topology measurements. In: INFOCOM 2003 (2003)
12. Luckie, M.: Scamper: a scalable and extensible packet prober for active measurement of the Internet. In: IMC 2010 (2010)
13. Luckie, M., Dhamdhere, A., Claffy, K., Murrell, D.: Measured impact of crooked traceroute. CCR 14(1) (January 2011)
14. Marchetta, P., de Donato, W., Pescapé, A.: Detecting third-party addresses in traceroute traces with IP timestamp option. In: Roughan, M., Chang, R. (eds.) PAM 2013. LNCS, vol. 7799, pp. 21–30. Springer, Heidelberg (2013)
15. Oliveira, R., Pei, D., Willinger, W., Zhang, B., Zhang, L.: In search of the elusive ground truth: the Internet's AS-level connectivity structure. In: SIGMETRICS 2008 (2008)
16. Oliveira, R., Zhang, B., Zhang, L.: Observing the Evolution of Internet AS Topology. In: SIGCOMM 2007 (2007)
17. Postel, J.: Internet protocol (September 1981)
18. Sherry, J., Katz-Bassett, E., Pimenova, M., Madhyastha, H.V., Anderson, T., Krishnamurthy, A.: Resolving IP aliases with prespecified timestamps. In: IMC 2010 (2010)
19. Spring, N., Mahajan, R., Wetherall, D.: Measuring ISP topologies with Rocketfuel. In: SIGCOMM 2002, Pittsburgh, PA, USA (2002)
20. Zhang, Y., Oliveira, R., Zhang, H., Zhang, L.: Quantifying the pitfalls of traceroute in AS connectivity inference. In: Krishnamurthy, A., Plattner, B. (eds.) PAM 2010. LNCS, vol. 6032, pp. 91–100. Springer, Heidelberg (2010)

Ingress Point Spreading: A New Primitive for Adaptive Active Network Mapping

Guillermo Baltra, Robert Beverly, and Geoffrey G. Xie

Naval Postgraduate School, Monterey, CA
{gbaltra,rbeverly,xie}@nps.edu

Abstract. Among outstanding challenges to Internet-wide topology mapping using active probes is balancing efficiency, e.g. induced load and time, with coverage. Toward maximizing probe utility, we introduce Ingress Point Spreading (IPS). IPS utilizes ingress diversity discovered in prior rounds of probing to rank-order available vantage points such that future probes traverse all known paths into a target network. We implement and deploy IPS to probe ~49k random prefixes drawn from the global BGP table using a distributed collection of vantage points. As compared to existing mapping systems, we discover 12% more unique vertices and 12% more edges using ~50% fewer probes, in half the time.

1 Introduction

Accurate and complete maps of the Internet topology are important to both security and networking research. As a piece of critical infrastructure, understanding network structure, interconnectivity and vulnerabilities is a first step toward protecting the Internet and making it more robust. Further, topology data is essential to network research that creates new protocols, performs modeling, designs clean-slate architectures, or examines Internet evolution and economics.

However, obtaining Internet topologies remains a challenging task [4]. The sheer size of the network implies that the accuracy of collected topologies can depend on the number, location, and probing rate of available vantage points (VPs) [16]. Topological inferences of paths, aliases, and structure can be brittle or lead to false conclusions [19]. Compounding the measurement difficulty, the Internet is non-stationary and dynamic. While mapping systems such as Archipelago (Ark) [10], Rocketfuel [17], and iPlane [13] have achieved Internet scale and produced important research insights [20][5], recent research, e.g. [2][18][7], shows that their performance, particularly in terms of probing efficiency as measured by the return of topological data per probing packet, can benefit significantly from an *adaptive* approach where the source and destination of each probe packet are judiciously chosen based on knowledge gained from prior probes and an understanding of network provisioning.

In this paper, we propose a new adaptive interface-level network mapping technique which we term "Ingress Point Spreading" (IPS). Underlying IPS is the observation that a target autonomous system (AS) is typically multi-homed and multi-connected. According to two 2010 studies [12,6], the number of these peering links, and thus the number of distinct ingress router interfaces for external traffic to enter the AS, are on the rise. We henceforth call these interfaces

M. Faloutsos and A. Kuzmanovic (Eds.): PAM 2014, LNCS 8362, pp. 56–66, 2014.

the *ingress points* of the target network. Intuitively, two probes would likely reveal more of a target network's topological structure if the probes were to enter the network via distinct ingress points. IPS aims to increase probing efficiency by first inferring the number of ingress points for a target network and then, for each new probe, selecting the VP with the highest likelihood to traverse an ingress point that has not yet been covered.

To evaluate the performance of IPS, we implement and deploy an Internet mapping system that integrates IPS with another recently proposed adaptive mapping primitive (subnet centric probing [2]). The system uses one day's worth of prior probing results to infer potential ingress points at different notional network boundaries for each target prefix. Rather than being agnostic to network structure, our system is designed to discover: i) the degree of subnetting within edge networks through an iterative interrogation process; and ii) sources of path diversity into networks by finding and exploiting the target's ingress points. This paper therefore makes the following three primary contributions:

1. Design and implementation of an Internet mapping system that integrates IPS with a complementary adaptive primitive originally proposed in [2].
2. Real-world deployment of the new mapping system. Specifically, we probed a sample set of 49,000 random destination prefixes in December, 2013.
3. Compared to data collected by a popular, currently deployed mapping system in the same time period for the same set of prefixes, our system finds more interfaces and edges, using only half of the total number of probes. This result is in contrast to prior efforts that demonstrate probing savings, but at the expense of lower topological recall.

2   Methodology

At the heart of our methodology is discovering network ingresses and predicting the ingress through which traffic from an available VP will enter a target network. Our intuition is straightforward: by ensuring that our probing uses all available ingresses, we more completely explore the target network, as well as exercise diverse paths to reach the target. As an additional benefit, a focus on ingress diversity matches an explicit higher-level goal of understanding topological connectivity, mapping disjoint paths, and characterizing ways in which portions of the network can become disconnected.

This section first describes probing properties that motivate a focus on ingress points, then details modifications to existing algorithms to support an ingress-centric approach. We then provide our algorithm to rank-order VPs on a per-destination network basis in order to maximize each probe's topological coverage.

2.1   Vantage Point Importance

It is well-known that the VPs used in active probing strongly influence the inferred topology [16]. A natural question is why we focus on the *order* of VPs employed when probing a particular destination network. If all VPs are used,

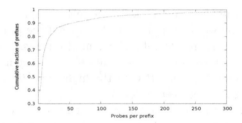

Fig. 1. Distribution of probes required per prefix probed by SCP. Because more than half of the prefixes are probed fewer than 10 times, VPs selection is important.

then the order in which they are used assumes only small importance. Instead, we consider two situations that commonly arise in topology probing: i) the set of VPs is large; or ii) the system must balance coverage and efficiency. For example, we may wish to use a subset of the VPs that result in the most topological coverage while exploring the destination network – thereby saving needless probing.

To characterize VP importance, we examine the popular CAIDA Ark system [10]. Ark divides the entire routed address space into logical /24 subnetworks, and in each "cycle," probes a random address within each /24 using a random VP. Ark assimilates the union of 21 of probing to obtain a high resolution map. For N cycles and M VPs, the expected number of unique VPs that explore a given /24 prefix (Y) in Ark is given by:

$$E[Y] = M - \frac{(M-1)^N}{M^{N-1}} \tag{1}$$

Examining one team of CAIDA probing from June, 2013, we see that $M = 18$ VPs were used. Thus, on average, each /24 in the union of $N = 21$ cycles is explored by: $E[Y] = 12.6$ VPs, and not all VPs are utilized even though $N > M$.

As a second example, the Subnet Centric Probing (SCP) algorithm of [2], which we also employ in our complete system, uses a variable number of probes per prefix in order to balance efficiency and coverage. To better understand the implications of SCP on VP selection, we used SCP with 60 Ark VPs to probe 1500 prefixes selected at random from the global Routeviews BGP view [14]. Figure 1 shows the number of probes per prefix versus the cumulative fraction of prefixes when using SCP. We observe that over half of the prefixes are probed fewer than 10 times, while $\approx 90\%$ of the prefixes see 50 or fewer probes.

This exploratory analysis of CAIDA's data and SCP support two observations. First, even when the number of probes is larger than the number of VPs, using randomly selected VPs is sub-optimal. Second, for systems such as SCP that attempt to maximize efficiency, the number of VPs used is frequently less than the total available. Thus, *the order in which VPs are employed matters*.

2.2   Recursive Subnet Inference

Intelligent selection of VPs, described in detail in the next subsection, is only a partial topology mapping solution. Just as important is the selection of destinations to probe. To this end, we take inspiration from the SCP algorithm proposed in [2]. However, our practical experience in implementing SCP directly revealed two impediments. First, per-flow load-balancing, as commonly found in the Internet, perturbs SCP's stopping criterion by artificially influencing the path edit distance. Second, SCP's dependence on edit distance requires pair-wise comparisons between probes that originate at the same VP – and thus prevents the full utilization of multiple VPs.

Instead, we implement the Recursive Subnet Inference (RSI) technique which takes inspiration from SCP. The input to RSI is a network prefix, i.e. network and subnet mask. Rather than simply splitting the prefix into its constituent /24 subnetworks, as is done with e.g. Ark, RSI attempts to discover the internal subnetting structure of the given prefix. Abstractly, RSI performs a binary search over the address space represented by an input prefix, pruning those branches of the tree that do not reveal new topology information.

To interrogate a prefix, RSI uses the same Least Common Prefix (LCP) principle as defined in [2]. Given an input prefix and mask p/m, LCP splits the prefix into two halves and probes a center address of each from a different VP. More formally, $LCP(p/m) = (d_1, d_2)$ where the two destination addresses are:

$$d_1 = p + 2^{32-m-2} + 1 \tag{2}$$
$$d_2 = p + 3\left(2^{32-m-2}\right) + 1 \tag{3}$$

Note that LCP readily adapts to 128bit IPv6 prefixes in the future. We term the initial two probes to the two halves of the input prefix the "parent probes." For each input prefix, RSI maintains the set of discovered interfaces within the destination AS. By only considering those interfaces within the destination AS, RSI is agnostic to which VP issues the probes, thereby accommodating IPS.

Let I denote the set of all unique router interfaces discovered that belong to the AS of the target prefix. Let P_i denote the set of router interfaces within the target's AS discovered by the i'th probe. Then, RSI splits an input prefix into two halves and recursively operates on those two smaller prefixes (which leads to additional probing using different VPs) if the following condition holds:

$$|P_i \setminus I| \geq \tau \tag{4}$$

where we set $\tau = 1$ such that probing terminates for a prefix only if no new interfaces are discovered. The interface set is then updated: $I = I \bigcup P_i$.

2.3   Ingress Point Spreading

Given our analysis of the importance of VPs (§2.1), and a probing strategy that may use fewer probes than VPs (§2.2), we turn to implementing a primitive that extracts the most benefit from each probe via intelligent VP selection.

At a high-level, we assume M VPs that will explore X destinations within a prefix (p/m), where it is frequently the case that $X < M$. The problem is to select the VP for each of the X destinations to be probed. Practically, we view RSI as requiring a pool of VPs to serve as the origin of RSI's probes, where we rank-order the VPs to provide maximum per-probe topological coverage.

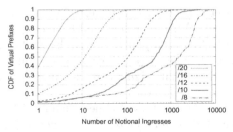

Fig. 2. Distribution of ingresses into prefixes of different logical size, as discovered during a prior round of probing. By expanding the size of the notional prefix, all VPs can be rank-ordered by their path diversity.

The Ingress Point Spreading (IPS) algorithm computes a per-destination network rank-ordered list of VPs based on *prior rounds* of probing. IPS seeks to utilize all of the ingress points discovered in prior rounds of probing such that future probing can induce probe traffic to flow through each of these known ingresses, thereby exploring more of the destination network's topology. By utilizing specific VPs, IPS spreads probes across ingresses. By spreading the probes across ingresses, RSI explores diverse paths, thereby preventing its early termination (as per the stopping criterion in eq. 4).

IPS employs an abstraction we term the "notional prefix ingress." A notional prefix is simply an expansion to a larger prefix aggregate containing the target prefix, while a notional prefix ingress is the first router interface hop that leads to a next hop whose IP is within the notional prefix.

IPS maintains a mapping of VPs to ingresses, i.e. which VP resulted in which ingress being traversed while probing the prefix. The notional prefix is important as there may be too few ingresses discovered from prior probing into the destination network. To obtain as much path diversity as possible, we perform an expansion to utilize ingresses into notional prefixes that represent a larger IP address aggregate containing the target prefix. Note that the notional prefix has no implied relationship to real-world BGP route aggregation; it is simply a means for IPS to expand its ingress search space for a given target network.

To provide intuition over the available notional ingresses as a function of the size of the notional prefix, we analyzed an entire cycle of probing data from CAIDA's Ark spanning June 2-4, 2013 in Figure 2. While using a /20 results in 99.4% of the notional /20 prefixes having 10 or fewer ingresses, expansion to a /16 provides more than 10 ingresses for more than half of the notional prefixes. Taken further, more than 60% of the notional /8's have 1,000 or more notional ingresses. Thus, by using our expansion technique combined with notional ingresses, IPS can adapt to best utilize any number or location of available VPs.

To illustrate, consider probing the prefix 205.155.0.0/16. Figure 3(a) is a simplified example showing traces from prior rounds of probing from six VPs (numbered 1-6) to various destinations (the red colored nodes). The /16 prefix to be probed in the current round is shaded in red and encompasses three previous destinations and two ingresses into the /8 that lead to known paths into the /16 prefix. The VPs 1 and 2 are selected as the first two VPs in the rank order list

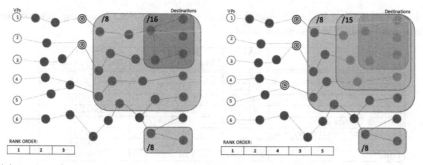

(a) Target /16 prefix with two ingresses (b) Expansion to find notional ingresses

Fig. 3. Ingress Point Spreading (IPS): Example where six VP are rank-ordered relative to the destination prefix on the basis of the notional ingresses the VPs traversed in prior probing

depicted at the bottom of Figure 3, as these two VPs resulted in traversing the diverse ingresses in the prior round. Since VPs 2 and 3 share the same ingress router into the /8 prefix, the latter is included at the end of the list.

However, we wish to obtain a total order over all of the VPs (typically, many more than six). IPS then expands its ingress search space to include 205.154.0.0/15 as shown in Figure 3(b) (green shaded box). In this example, the expansion results in one additional destination and one more ingress. VP 4 then becomes the third in the rank-order as it traversed the diverse ingress into the notional prefix in the prior round. Following the same reasoning used for VP 3, VP 5 is included at the end of the list.

IPS continues to expand its search space, i.e. 205.152.0.0/14, 205.152. 0.0/13, ..., 205.0.0.0/8, where the larger aggregates are notional prefixes containing 205.155.0.0/16, until all VPs are ordered. At each step, more notional ingress points may be identified which are used to rank order additional VPs to be used with RSI. RSI sends at least as many parent traces as there were notional ingresses to the original input prefix, but may send more.

3   Results

This section details our initial findings from deploying the combined RSI and IPS primitives described in §2. As a baseline, we implement the current Ark strategy[1] of subdividing the routed address space into /24's and select a random VP from which to probe a random address within the /24. Herein, we refer to the Ark method and resulting topology data synonymously as "Ark."

As part of the pre-probing process, we provide IPS with one day's worth of probing results as published by CAIDA [1]. We use CAIDA data as input to IPS to demonstrate that IPS can utilize not only prior rounds of our own probing, but also external sources of data (which, from a probing load perspective, are

---

[1] Direct comparison with published Ark data is not possible as we do not use "teams."

Table 1. Comparing RSI+IPS and Ark performance metrics. The same 49k random prefixes were probed in December, 2013.

Metric	Ark	RSI+IPS (Aug. 2013 trained)	RSI+IPS (Dec. 2013 trained)
Prefixes Probed	48,905	48,905	48,905
Vertices	464,544	521,513	520,903
Edges	906,680	1,024,295	1,034,101
Probes	4,041,289	2,056,562	2,052,842
Vertices (inside dest)	121,137	135,209	134,575
Vertices (intersection w/ ark)		309,997	309,971
Ingresses	31,138	38,532	39,020
Time	26h 55m	13h 38m	14h 47m

a sunk cost). To gain some initial understanding of IPS's sensitivity to training data and age, we perform two experiments, one where IPS is trained using data from Aug 28, 2013, and the second with Dec 18, 2013 training data. However, the probing itself was all performed between Dec 20-22, 2013.

From Routeviews [14], we randomly select 50,000 prefixes without regard to prefix size or origin AS. Of these original prefixes, we find 48,905 that were probed by both our IPS and Ark method. The natural changes in availability of VPs and routing require us to eliminate the 1,095 prefixes in order to fairly compare the two techniques. We probe these 48,905 prefixes using CAIDA's "topology-on-demand" service [9], where we have implemented RSI+IPS using 59 globally distributed VPs.

Table 1 summarizes our aggregate results. Two findings bear highlighting: not only is our combined RSI and IPS system significantly more efficient (using $\approx 50\%$ of the number of probes as compared to Ark and taking approximately half the time), we discover *more* topological information.

Examining the intersection of vertices, we observe that 309,997 vertices are common to both RSI+IPS (August) and Ark. RSI+IPS discovers 211,516 vertices not in Ark, while Ark discovers 154,547 vertices that RSI+IPS does not.

Figure 4(a) shows the distribution of the per-prefix difference of discovered vertex counts between our system versus Ark. Surprisingly, we find that our system performs worse than Ark for approximately 66% of the prefixes. Rather, RSI+IPS is significantly superior to Ark for a small number of prefixes, thereby contributing to the overall superior topological coverage. In contrast, Figure 4(b) shows that Ark and our system perform comparably in terms of edge discovery for approximately 80% of the prefixes, while we are superior for 10%. Again, the tail of the distribution is long – there are a small number of prefixes where we discover significantly more topological information. For future work, we will explore ways of refining the RSI stopping criterion as expressed in Eq. 4 to increase the percentage of networks for which our system has a better coverage. The fact that RSI+IPS performs better on some prefixes while Ark does better on others explains why a high number of interfaces and edges are uniquely discovered by each method.

To understand the performance variations, we examine the distribution of the number of notional ingresses discovered for each prefix. Figure 5 shows two interesting phenomena. First, neither Ark nor our system discovers any ingresses for approximately 70% of the prefixes, as ICMP blocking and other forms of packet filtering may be prevalent, particularly for enterprise networks. However, among those destination where probing within the target network is feasible, IPS finds significantly more ingresses than Ark. Based on the prefix's origin AS, we find that the top three prefixes for which IPS performs the best against Ark (as measured by additional vertices) are national ISP networks with hundreds of peering links while the bottom three prefixes belong to enterprise networks that have a small number of peering links. Furthermore, for those prefixes with at least one notional ingress, the relative performance of IPS has a medium correlation (with a Pearson correlation efficient of ~0.35) with the number of ingresses discovered. The correlation is more significant (~0.45) if we consider only the set of ~2000 prefixes with at least five discovered ingresses. Both of these findings confirm that IPS does a good job of leveraging available ingresses to increase probing efficiency. Of particular interest is that the size of the network prefix (in terms of IP address space) has a correlation of ~0.52 to the performance difference, implying that our system performs better on smaller networks, while it often prematurely stops probing large prefixes. Adding a random component to RSI, or a lower probing threshold proportional to the network size may alleviate the performance differential of these prefixes. The results also suggest that the performance of IPS may be enhanced with a more effective network ingresses inference. We defer these to future work.

4   Related Work

Ever since the advent of network mapping research, emphasis has been placed on eliminating unnecessary probes to increase probing efficiency. Earlier notable efforts on this front include the development of the Rocketfuel [17], Doubletree [7] and DIMES [15] systems. These systems avoid traversing the same hops more than once by carefully choosing the starting point and the time to live (TTL) of each new traceroute packet used for probing. Follow-on studies [8,2,18] generalize and extend such techniques into a class of adaptive probing primitives, termed "set cover," characterized by a common requirement for determining a minimum number of probes to cover a set of previously discovered interfaces.

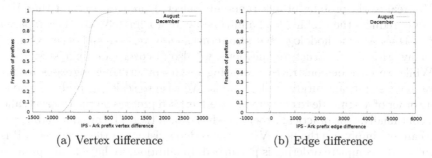

(a) Vertex difference   (b) Edge difference

Fig. 4. CDF of per-prefix coverage difference $((RSI + IPS) - Ark)$

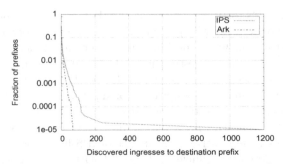

Fig. 5. CDF of per-prefix number of notional ingresses discovered

Recent efforts (e.g., [2,16,3,11]) in developing adaptive mapping approaches center around leveraging information beyond the hops traversed before. The additional information considered includes knowledge of common subnetting practice, BGP route data, network latency characteristics, and potential path diversity from different VPs. The work that is most related to this paper is the vantage point spreading (VPS) primitive proposed in [2]. IPS shares with VPS a similar intuition for increasing path diversity into target networks. The key difference is that IPS uses a more refined criterion of path diversity to drive the selection of VPs, and as such, is able to explicitly maximize the likelihood that a new probe will enter a destination network through a new ingress point. While IPS requires prior probing data in order to infer possible ingress points into each destination network, this data is naturally accumulated by production mapping systems as part of their functionality.

5   Conclusion

Significant prior work has considered the problem of balancing efficiency and coverage in active probing-based topology collection. We contribute to this body of work by explicitly taking into consideration target network ingresses, and the diversity of available vantage points (VPs) toward those ingresses, by developing the Ingress Point Spreading (IPS) algorithm. IPS rank-orders VPs for a given target prefix on the basis of ingresses discovered from prior rounds of probing. Thus, unlike prior approaches, IPS is not memoryless.

Via real-world probing of 49k randomly selected prefixes, we find that IPS not only reduces the probing load and time by approximately 50% as compared to CAIDA's Ark methodology, but also returns *more* vertices and edges. Crucial to many critical infrastructure questions, we also discover more ingresses.

While we have demonstrated promising results by utilizing ingresses to our advantage, significant future work remains. We wish to scale our probing by one more order of magnitude to encompass all advertised prefixes on the Internet, and run continually. Our practical experience has shown that VPs are unreliable, yet IPS cannot simply use the next VP in the ordered list when the preferred VP is down, as the complete ordering is perturbed. In addition, we have found prefixes with significant topology that goes undiscovered by RSI due to the particular deterministic selection of destinations causing premature termination. We must accommodate all of these issues in future work.

Our hope is that this work contributes to the continual progress being made on topology mapping systems. Moving forward, we additionally plan to integrate IPS with recent advances in topology set coverage and change detection.

Acknowledgments. We thank Young Hyun, kc claffy, Justin Rohrer, Arthur Berger, our shepherd Bruce Maggs, and the anonymous reviewers for invaluable feedback and support. This work supported in part by the Department of Homeland Security (DHS) Cyber Security Division under contract N66001-2250-58231. Views and conclusions are those of the authors and should not be interpreted as representing the official policies, either expressed or implied, of the U.S. government or DHS.

References

1. The CAIDA UCSD IPv4 Routed/24 Topology Dataset (2013),
   `http://www.caida.org/data/active/ipv4_routed_24_topology_dataset.xml`
2. Beverly, R., Berger, A., Xie, G.G.: Primitives for active Internet topology mapping: Toward high-frequency characterization. In: Proceedings of the 10th ACM SIGCOMM Conference on Internet Measurement, pp. 165–171 (2010)
3. Chen, M., Xu, M., Xu, K.: A delay-guiding source selection method in network topology discovery. In: IEEE International Conference on Communications (2011)
4. Claffy, K., Hyun, Y., Keys, K., Fomenkov, M.: Internet mapping: From art to science. In: IEEE Cybersecurity Applications and Technologies Conference (March 2009)
5. Dainotti, A., Squarcella, C., Aben, E., Claffy, K., Chiesa, M., Russo, M., Pescap, A.: Analysis of Country-wide Internet Outages Caused by Censorship. In: Internet Measurement Conference (IMC), pp. 1–18 (November 2011)
6. Dhamdhere, A., Dovrolis, C.: The Internet is flat: Modeling the transition from a transit hierarchy to a peering mesh. In: Proceedings of ACM CoNEXT (2010)
7. Donnet, B., Raoult, P., Friedman, T., Crovella, M.: Efficient algorithms for large-scale topology discovery 33(1), 327–338 (2005)
8. Gonen, M., Shavitt, Y.: An O(log_n)-approximation for the set cover problem with set ownership. Inf. Process. Lett. 109(3) (2009)
9. Hyun, Y.: On-demand IPv4 and IPv6 topology measurements (2012)
10. Hyun, Y., Claffy, K.: Archipelago measurement infrastructure (2013),
    `http://www.caida.org/projects/ark/`
11. Kardes, H., Gunes, M., Oz, T.: Cheleby: A subnet-level Internet topology mapping system. In: COMSNETS, pp. 1–10. IEEE (2012)
12. Labovitz, C., Iekel-Johnson, S., McPherson, D., Oberheide, J., Jahanian, F.: Internet inter-domain traffic. In: Proceedings of ACM SIGCOMM (2010)
13. Madhyastha, H.V., Isdal, T., Piatek, M., Dixon, C., Anderson, T., Krishnamurthy, A., Venkataramani, A.: iPlane: An information plane for distributed services. In: Proceedings of NSDI, pp. 367–380 (2006)
14. Meyer, D.: University of Oregon RouteViews (2013), `http://www.routeviews.org`
15. Shavitt, Y., Shir, E.: DIMES: Let the Internet measure itself. SIGCOMM Computer Communication Review 35(5), 71–74 (2005)

16. Shavitt, Y., Weinsberg, U.: Quantifying the importance of vantage points distribution in Internet topology measurements. In: IEEE INFOCOM (March 2009)
17. Spring, N., Mahajan, R., Wetherall, D.: Measuring ISP topologies with Rocketfuel. ACM SIGCOMM Computer Communication Review 32(4), 133–145 (2002)
18. Bourgeau, T., Friedman, T.: Efficient IP-level network topology capture. In: Roughan, M., Chang, R. (eds.) PAM 2013. LNCS, vol. 7799, pp. 11–20. Springer, Heidelberg (2013)
19. Willinger, W., Alderson, D., Doyle, J.C.: Mathematics and the Internet: A source of enormous confusion and great potential. Notices of the AMS 56(5) (2009)
20. Wu, J., Zhang, Y., Mao, Z.M., Shin, K.G.: Internet routing resilience to failures: analysis and implications. In: Proceedings of ACM CoNEXT (2007)

On Searching for Patterns
in Traceroute Responses

Nevil Brownlee

The University of Auckland, New Zealand
nevil@auckland.ac.nz

Abstract. We study active traceroute measurements from more than 1,000 vantage points towards a few targets over 24 hours or more. Our aim is to detect patterns in the data that correspond to significant operational events. Because traceroute data is complex and noisy, little work in this area has been published to date. First we develop a measure for the differences between successive traceroute measurements, then we use this measure to cluster changes across all vantage points and assess the meaning and descriptive power of these clusters. Large-scale operational events stand out clearly in our 3D visualisations; our clustering technique could be developed further to make such events visible to the operator community in near-real time.

1 Introduction

In April 2012 the author spent some time at RIPE NCC in Amsterdam, working with traceroute data from RIPE's Atlas project. Atlas is "a global network of probes that measure Internet connectivity and reachability" [7]. By mid-2013 it had about 3600 tiny Linux probes deployed world-wide providing Atlas 'vantage points;' about 1500 of them made half-hourly traceroute measurements, three UDP probes per step, to a set of fixed destinations. The resulting data provides a view of the global Internet. This paper reports on efforts to find and display patterns observable in the traceroute responses.

Of particular interest were patterns caused by routing changes that affected significant parts of the Internet, for example because a high-capacity router or backbone link had failed. To detect such patterns we needed to find sets of probes that saw traceroute changes that occurred at about the same time, and that involved similar sets of IP addresses. A simple strategy to achieve that was to use hierarchical agglomerative clustering to group probes that saw similar changes, and to develop simple visualisations that allowed us to see patterns in the probes' traceroutes.

Traceroute can produce unexpected results in many different ways, so traceroute data is inherently noisy. Any technique for clustering relies on computed 'distances' between pairs of objects. We realised early on that we would have to 'clean up' our data before using it to compute distances; section 4 presents our data-cleaning methods. Our objects are Atlas probes, each of which provides a set of half-hourly traceroutes. We needed to compute distances between probes

M. Faloutsos and A. Kuzmanovic (Eds.): PAM 2014, LNCS 8362, pp. 67–76, 2014.

Table 1. Dataset summary information. The last three columns show average values for the 14 destinations.

name	start date	hours	active probes	varying probe %	traces
tdi	22 Feb	48	1340	99.25	121736
may1	1 May	24	1591	94.72	70475
may7	1 May	24	1533	97.46	70812

based on their traceroutes. Our algorithms for measures of distance between probes are presented in subsections 4.1 and 4.2. Section 5 presents results of our analyses. Section 6 summarises our contributions and future plans.

2   Related Work

Many researchers have investigated global Internet routing behaviour by collecting and analysing BGP data. For example, Lad et al. [3] used BGP data from RouteViews[1] and RIPE RIS[2] to create a topology graph that "weighs a link by the number of routes using that link." Their tool, Link-Rank, visualises aggregate route changes within the AS-level topology; they demonstrate how that can be used to detect various kinds of routing problems.

In 2012 King et al. [2] presented several different methods of visualising Internet outages, and pointed out that using "coordinated views" can help in understanding those outages. For packets sent from "malware-infected PCs" they used Mercator projections for the number of hosts and packets using symbols plotted in geolocated positions showing where the packets originated. To visualise the address blocks for those packets they used Wessels' IPv4 heat-map tool[3], colouring pixels on a Hilbert curve for each /24 subnet to show the number of source IPv4 addresses in each /24 subnet. They displayed both of those visualisations in successive frames of a movie, with each frame covering a 320-second interval.

In [6], Quan et al assumed that events occurring at the same time suggest a common root cause. They developed a "simple clustering algorithm that helps identify spatial clusters of network events based on correlations in event timing," and used it to make a 2D visualisation of such events – essentially a simple plot of address block vs time, with coloured dots showing when events occurred.

3   Datasets

In this project our data sources are Atlas probes. Each probe provides a time series of IPv4 traceroutes (Traces), one for each half-hour (TimeBin). A Trace is a sequence of Hops, each with two components: the responding host's IP address(es), the RTTs for responses from those addresses, and an error indication.

---

[1] http://www.routeviews.org/

[2] https://www.ripe.net/data-tools/stats/ris/routing-information-service

[3] http://maps.measurement-factory.com/software/

Table 2. Statistics for *may1* dataset

ID	destination	inst	hops	% multi-responder			% A traces	% A probes	% * traces	% * probes
				hops	traces	probes				
5016	j.root-servers.net	70	585381	9.12	34.01	39.26	1.00	1.25	0.95	5.27
5001	k.root-servers.net	17	608995	5.65	22.26	26.12	7.57	8.62	1.93	6.12
5004	f.root-servers.net	49	633507	9.12	31.61	36.25	0.18	0.26	0.03	0.66
5008	labs.ripe.net	1	639826	6.55	27.96	32.08	0.25	0.33	0.08	0.66
5005	i.root-servers.net	43	663644	9.77	29.35	37.83	0.13	0.20	0.02	0.66
5002	tt01.ripe.net	1	685521	12.32	50.84	63.03	0.13	0.20	0.03	1.12
5006	m.root-servers.net	6	800726	22.26	81.69	85.92	14.69	32.50	12.58	28.09
5017	ronin.atlas	1	812731	21.75	92.47	96.78	0.13	0.26	0.02	0.66
5011	c.root-servers.net	8	848329	27.10	92.63	95.60	0.19	0.33	0.07	0.72
5009	a.root-servers.net	8	961161	14.31	79.13	89.01	15.17	83.62	14.06	83.68
5010	b.root-servers.net	1	979508	17.68	76.34	83.75	0.13	0.20	0.09	0.86
5012	d.root-servers.net	1	985951	17.02	57.32	61.29	0.19	0.33	0.20	4.28
5015	h.root-servers.net	2	1073730	21.50	77.36	83.41	0.14	0.26	0.12	3.16
5020	carson	1	1137892	16.70	55.29	59.83	0.47	0.53	0.18	1.58

We analysed datasets from early 2012, as set out in Table 1. Each dataset has Traces for all of its online probes to 14 fixed destinations (see Table 2). Dataset *tdi* covers two days that include the Telstra-Dodo incident[10], which occurred at 1340-1425 (AEDST) – i.e. 0240-1525 UTC – on 23 Feb 12, leaving "millions of customers without Internet connectivity." Thus, *tdi* covers a 48-hour period around a large known Internet routing incident. *may1* and *may7* cover two single days selected arbitrarily. The number of probes on-line increased from 1340 in February to about 1560 in May 2012, showing that more probes were deployed over that interval.

Table 2 shows summary statistics for the 14 fixed destinations in dataset *may1*; our other two datasets have similar variations among the destinations. Most of Table 2's destinations are root servers, the number of anycast instances each has is shown in the 'inst' column. The other destinations are individual servers. The total number of hops seen in each trace is shown on the 'hops' column; j.root has the smallest, most likely because it has the most instances, allowing shorter paths from probes to reach it. The same is true for f, k and i roots. On the other hand, labs.ripe.net also saw a fairly low number of hops, we surmise that is because the Atlas project has the highest concentration of its probes in Europe.

On average, between 95% and 99% of the online probes in each dataset saw some changes in their Traces to the 14 destinations. Within the *may1* dataset, the number of probes that saw varying Traces was between 26% and 98%. These high percentages demonstrate the variability of Internet routing.

Table 2's '% A' columns show the percentage of traces and probes that contained an A error response. m.root and a.root have unusually high A percentages; we surmise that they are connected to ISPs that block traceroutes close to the end of many Traces. Table 2's '% *' columns show precentages for Hops that received no responses, and thus no IP address information.

4 Methodology

Traces can misbehave in many different ways. Inspecting our data showed one common behaviour: incomplete Traces (those that did not reach their destination) often continue for many unanswered (* RTTs, with no IP addresses) or administratively blocked ('A' error code) Hops. For such Traces, we find the first 'A' Hop, delete any following Hops, then we delete any unanswered Hops before the 'A' Hop. 'Cleaning up' Traces in this way deletes Hops that do not provide any address information, thereby preventing them from producing misleadingly high Trace edit distance values.

4.1 Measuring Changes between Successive Traces: *Edit Distances*

For each probe we needed to measure how often, and by how much, its source-to-destination path changed. We chose to do that using Levenshtein Edit Distance [4], *ed*, i.e. the number of inserts, deletes or swaps needed to construct a Trace from the one in its preceding TimeBin, using Hop IP addresses as symbols. That approach yields a vector of *ed* values for each probe, with high values indicating Timebins when large path changes occured.

We compute *ed* for each pair of *Traces* using a linear programming implementation similar to the one described in [1]; that requires a method of computing the difference between any two *Hops* in the Traces. If both Hops have only single responding hosts – i.e. IP addresses – the Hop difference is either 0 if the two IP addresses are the same, or 1. However, up to 27% of the Hops we observed for a single destination had multiple responders, indicating that their Traces include load-balanced sections. Considering Table 2 again, we see that load-balanced Hops appear in up to 93% of the Traces, and as many as 96% of the probes saw at least one load-balanced path segment.

For load-balanced paths, we decided to use values between 0 and 1 to indicate how different the sets of addresses in pairs of hops were. We assume that router interfaces within an ISP PoP are most likely to have addresses within a /24 address block. That allows us to use an *approximate match* where each of two Hop IP addresses have the same leading 24 bits. Figure 1 shows the match length cumulative distributions for each destination. About 30% of these matches differ at bit 0, i.e. they are completely different, but more than 90% differ by bit 25, indicating path changes that used a different PoP. For pairs of Hops where one or both Hops have multiple IPv4 addresses, we compute the Hop difference as $hd = u/(u + m)$, where m is the number of approximately matched addresses, and u the number of unmatched addresses.

When our datasets were collected the Atlas probes could only perform 'classic' traceroutes; our approximate matching algorithm works well to reduce the noise level in our edit distance calculations. Our project was only concerned with observing patterns of changes in our Traces. For us, classic traceroute gives an effective view of all the paths in the Traces for every TimeBin.

At this point, we made 3D plots of *ed* over time (x axis), with the probes in probe ID order on our y axis. We refer to these as *cornfield* plots – the edit

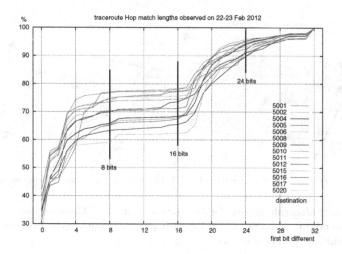

Fig. 1. *tdi* dataset: Hop match lengths cumulative distributions for 14 fixed destinations, for all matches with *at least one multi-responding Hop*. More than 90% of these matches differ by bit 25, indicating path changes that used a different PoP.

distances are upright (z axis) like corn stalks, and patterns caused by route changes stand out like crop circles in a cornfield. These plots clearly showed lines of high *ed* values at times when paths to a (single) destination changed for many probes at the same time, as shown in Fig. 2(a).

To gain insight into which probes had changing paths, we needed to group together the probes with similar changes. We chose to do that using single-link clustering (*slink*) [8], a simple form of hierarchical agglomerative clustering, and implemented it by following its very clear description in [5]. Clustering algorithms need to know a *distance* between any two of the objects being clustered. Our objects to be clustered are probes, for each probe we have a vector of edit distances; we compute *cs*, the cosine similarity [9] of two such vectors, then use $1 - cs$ as the *distance* between them. Since we are trying to detect significant changes, we exclude the probes that showed no change at all.

We used *slink* to compute a dendrogram for the probes; that dendrogram lists the probes in an order that gathers the 'least-different' probes close together. Since our datasets include 1340 to 1533 probes, it is difficult to see clear probe clusters in a tree-style visualisation of a destination's dendrogram. Instead, we modified our cornfield plots to show the probes in dendrogram order on the y axis, as shown in Fig. 2(b).

Our first attempts to interpret our cornfield plots were inconclusive, mostly because our edit distance (*ed*) values are rather noisy. In particular, they are dependent on the number of Hops in any probe's Traces. To minimise that effect we compute the standard deviation of each probe's *ed* values, then colour the *ed* stalks so that we can distinguish those with unusually high *ed* values (plotted in red).

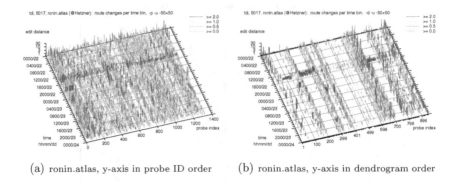

(a) ronin.atlas, y-axis in probe ID order   (b) ronin.atlas, y-axis in dendrogram order

Fig. 2. Dataset *tdi* cornfield plots for destination ronin.atlas. Colour shows edit distance in 'probe standard deviation' units for each probe. Using dendrogram order brings similarly-behaving probes together.

Displaying the probes in dendrogram order makes the behaviour of similar probes much more obvious. Figure 2(a) plots the probes in ID order. There were three times (1430-1530 on 22 Feb 13 UTC) when many probes saw changes, but those probes are spread out across the y axis. Figure 2(b) shows probes in dendrogram order; the same probes show changes at the same times, but we can see that there are several obvious probe clusters. Probes that saw few changes appear as almost empty lines along the x axis, i.e. over time, while probes that saw frequent changes have many high *ed* values. Overall, because similar probes are grouped together, we can see their behaviour over time more clearly.

4.2   Trace Uncommon Distances

Although edit distance is sensitive to changes that occur at the same time for different probes, it is insensitive to changes of IP addresses. In order to distinguish probes for which different addresses changed at the same time, we needed another measure based on changes in path addresses.

Figure 3 shows the Hop addresses for probe IDs 1324 and 2602 for Traces to i-root in our *may1* dataset. The integers at the start of each Trace show the number of times that path was used. For both these probes, the most common path had no multi-address Hops, four Traces (occurring within the same TimeBins) had one multi-address Hop, and the third used a path to a different i-root instance. The lines starting with *uncommon* show the probe's *uncommon* IP addresses, i.e. those that did not appear in every Trace.

To compute the *uncommon distance, ucd*, between two Traces, we count the number of uncommon address blocks that appear in both Traces, *ubt*, and in the Trace with most uncommon blocks, *mub*. Then $ucd = 1 - (ubt/mub)$. Pairs of traces that saw similar sets of uncommon blocks will have smaller *ucd* values.

```
probe 1324, dest=192.36.148.17, i-root:
43  89.37.15.5/20 37.128.239.42/32 80.97.248.13/32 145.236.18.91/32 95.158.131.242/22 85.29.25.10/32
                                                    193.140.13.2/32 192.36.148.17/32  s
 4  89.37.15.5/20 37.128.239.42/32 80.97.248.13/32 145.236.18.91/32 95.158.131.242/22 82.222.10.157/18
                                                    85.29.8.165/19   193.140.13.2/32 192.36.148.17/32  s
 1  89.37.15.5/20 37.128.239.5/32 62.40.125.137/20 109.105.97.5/32  194.146.105.187/32 192.36.148.17/32  s

   uncommon: 80.97.248.13/32,145.236.18.91/32,95.158.131.242/22,85.29.25.10/32,193.140.13.2/32,
             82.222.10.157/18,62.40.125.137/20,109.105.97.5/32,194.146.105.187/32

probe 2602, dest=192.36.148.17, i-root:
42  77.70.97.1/32 89.190.204.244/32 193.169.198.199/32 95.158.131.242/22  85.29.25.10/32 193.140.13.2/32  f
 4  77.70.97.1/32 89.190.204.244/32 193.169.198.199/32 95.158.131.242/22 82.222.10.157/18
                                                        85.29.8.165/19   193.140.13.2/32  f
 1  77.70.97.1/32 89.190.198.146/19                     80.81.192.229/25 192.36.148.17/32  s

   uncommon: 193.169.198.199/32,95.158.131.242/22,85.29.25.10/32,193.140.13.2/32,82.222.10.157/18,
             80.81.192.229/25,192.36.148.17/32
```

Fig. 3. Examples of paths showing addresses for Hops that succeeded and failed. The *uncommon* lines show blocks that did not appear in all paths.

4.3 Clustering Distance between Probe Pairs

On testing our *uncommon distance* algorithms, we found that the distances it yields are not sufficient for single-link clustering to work well. Instead we use both algorithms together, with equal weight. The resulting dendrograms separate out clusters of probes that saw path changes at the same time, and those clusters are made up of sub-clusters of probes that saw the same uncommon addresses at those times.

5 Observations

We made sheets of cornfield plots for all 14 destinations for each of our datasets. Unfortunately we did not find any patterns in our *tdi* data that could have been caused by the Telstra-Dodo incident; we believe that is because on 23 February 2012 there were only 40 Atlas probes were deployed in all of Australia.

In Figure 4 we show four examples of cornfield plots, all for our *may1* dataset. To understand events in them, we analysed their 'uncommon Hops' log files, mapping IP addresses to network providers by using whois at the Regional Internet Registry (RIR) websites.

Figure 4(a) shows edit distances for Traces to m-root (RIPE NCC), an anycast nameserver with six instances. Probes numbered 365-550 on this plot have high *ed* values at 1230, followed by *ed* values below 0.5 standard deviations for the rest of the day. All the Traces to probes 365-550 reached m-root via SFINX, the French Internet Exchange, hence they were destined for the Paris instance of m-root. The event at 1230 was caused by a routing change; the first 26 Traces went via Cogent, the remaining 22 went via Tiscali. Since the *ed*'s after 1230 were much lower than before, it is clear that during that time the route via Tiscali was more stable than before.

Again, probes numbered 271-362 have high *ed* values at 2230. Their Traces were mostly carried by Level3; at 2230 a different route, still within Level3 but two hops shorter, appeared, producing the observed high *ed* values.

74   N. Brownlee

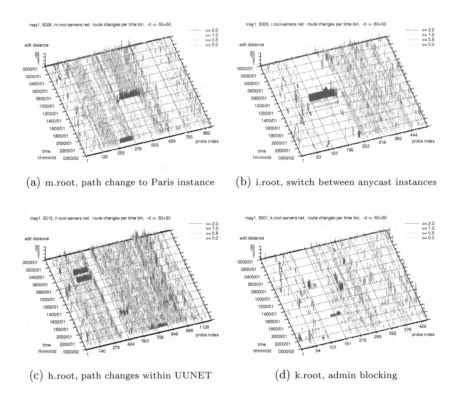

(a) m.root, path change to Paris instance

(b) i.root, switch between anycast instances

(c) h.root, path changes within UUNET

(d) k.root, admin blocking

Fig. 4. Cornfield plots for four destinations. -d = probes in dendrogram order probes, -u = ed in std dev units, 50+50 = equal weight for *ed* and *uncommon* distances.

Traces to i-root (Netnod), an anycast nameserver with 43 instances, are shown in Figure 4(b). Probes numbered 120-212 on this plot have high *ed* values at 1130 and 1200. Most of their traces reached the i-root instance in Ankara via Novatel (Bulgaria) and ULAK, the Turkish national academic network, but a few reached its Stockholm instance via NORDUnet and Netnod, or its Frankfurt instance via various European providers. Also, many of these traces stopped one hop short of their destination instance; perhaps this could indicate short-term overloads at the destination instances.

Figure 4(c) shows edit distances for Traces to h-root (U.S. Army Research Lab), which has two instances. Probes numbered 190-300 on this plot have high *ed's*. No Traces from the Atlas probes reached h-root, their last hop was always to DoD NIC in the DREN network. Perhaps DREN simply discards DNS requests to h-root from most of the Internet? Further, all the Traces for probes 190-300 pass through UUNET; the high *ed* values we see were caused by routing changes within that network.

Traces to k-root (RIPE NCC), an anycast nameserver with 17 instances, are shown in Figure 4(d). Probes numbered 139-180 on this plot have high *ed* values at 1800. All their traces reach the London instance of k-root via PacketExchange

Abovenet. From 1800 through the rest of 1 May, Traces were administratively blocked.

6   Conclusions and Future Work

We have shown that simple clustering algorithms are sufficient to reveal patterns in traceroute data caused by path changes that are seen by different probes – presumably because of routing changes, or link or router failures – at the same times. To implement single-link clustering we have used two simple distance measures: *edit distance*, using Levenshtein distance between pairs of Traces, and *uncommon distance*, using sets of IP address blocks that do not appear in all the Traces for a pair of probes.

We handle Trace hops that include load-balanced paths, i.e. those that return RTTs for several different IP addresses, by using an approximate match algorithm. For each address pair we compute the number of their leading bits that match, and assume that the addresses match if their first 24 bits are the same, i.e. that ISPs use at most /24 subnets for router interfaces in their PoPs. Our cornfield plots reveal changes for quite small sets of probes, indicating that noise from approximate-matching errors is not sufficient to impair our clustering process.

We find that a total clustering distance using 50% edit distance + 50% uncommon distance works well for clustering our Atlas probe data, enabling us not only to observe changes in the Traces (visualised as 'cornfield plots,') but also to discover which addresses were involved in those changes.

In developing our algorithms we were not concerned with computing speed. All our programming is done in Ruby, producing code that is simple to understand. Nonetheless, running them on a Lenovo T61 laptop, for each destination in a day's dataset, we find that the elapsed time for processing Trace data took at most 15.7 minutes, with 69% of that time spent computing the edit distances. For all 14 destinations, one day's data takes about 3.5 hours.

In the three datasets we have analysed, events occur over one to three Time-Bins, i.e. they appear to last no longer that 1.5 hours. They are of two kinds: short-term changes followed by a return to the 'normal' state, and longer-term changes in global routing. Long-term changes can be distinguished in our cornfield plots, for example where routing stability improves the edit distances decrease. We find that our cornfield plots are an effective way to visualise Trace changes, since one can see a whole dataset in a single 2D projection of the 3D cornfield.   We propose several topics for future work:

- We will investigate other probe distance measures and clustering algorithms.
- So far we have recognised path change clusters by observing them as visual patterns in our cornfield plots. We need to automate that process.
- In section 5 we comment on which address blocks were involved in clusters of probes with paths that changed. Again, that process could be automated.

With these two processes automated, it would be possible to run this analysis in near-real time, for example to produce a report every few hours, or perhaps cornfield plots that were updated every half-hour. Such reports could make service providers aware of large-scale path changes before large numbers of end users are affected by them.

Acknowledgment. Thank-you to my colleagues at RIPE NCC for their help and encouragement through the early stages of this project, especially Emile Aben, Robert Kisteleki and Daniel Karrenberg. Thanks to Bradley Huffaker at CAIDA, for our helpful discussions of visualisation and clustering. Last, thanks to the PAM referees for their very helpful comments.

Atlas data is available from RIPE NCC, the Ruby programs we developed for this project can be obtained by emailing a request to this paper's author.

References

1. Allison, L.: Dynamic programming algorithm (dpa) for edit-distance, http://www.csse.monash.edu.au/~lloyd/tildeAlgDS/Dynamic/Edit/
2. King, A., Huffaker, B., Dainotti, A., Claffy, K.: A coordinated view of the temporal evolution of large-scale internet events. In: First IMC Workshop on Internet Visualization, WIV 2012 (2012), http://ant.isi.edu/wiv2012/program.html
3. Lad, M., Massey, D., Zhang, L.: Visualizing internet routing changes. IEEE Transactions on Visualization and Computer Graphics 12(6) (November 2006)
4. Levenshtein, V.I.: Binary Codes Capable of Correcting Deletions, Insertions and Reversals. Soviet Physics Doklady 10, 707 (1966)
5. Matteucci, M.: Hierarchical clustering algorithms, http://home.dei.polimi.it/matteucc/Clustering/tutorial_html/hierarchical.html
6. Quan, L., Heidemann, J., Pradkin, Y.: Visualizing sparse internet events: network outages and route changes. In: First IMC Workshop on Internet Visualization, WIV 2012 (2012), http://ant.isi.edu/wiv2012/program.html
7. RIPE Network Coordination Centre. Ripe atlas, https://atlas.ripe.net/
8. Sibson, R.: Slink: An optimally efficient algorithm for the single-link cluster method. The Computer Journal 16(1), 30–34 (1973)
9. Singhal, A.: Modern information retrieval: a brief overview. IEEE Data Engineering Bulletin 24, 35–43 (2001)
10. Taylor, J.: How did dodo break the internet? (February 24, 2012), http://www.zdnet.com/how-did-dodo-break-the-internet-1339332390/

Volume-Based Transit Pricing:
Is 95 the Right Percentile?

Vamseedhar Reddyvari Raja[1], Amogh Dhamdhere[2], Alessandra Scicchitano[3],
Srinivas Shakkottai[1], kc claffy[2], and Simon Leinen[3]

[1] Texas A&M University, College Station, TX 77843, USA
[2] CAIDA/UCSD, San Diego, CA 92093, USA
[3] SWITCH, Switzerland
vamseedhar.reddyvaru@neo.tamu.edu

Abstract. The 95th percentile billing mechanism has been an industry *de facto* standard for transit providers for well over a decade. While the simplicity of the scheme makes it attractive as a billing mechanism, dramatic evolution in traffic patterns, associated interconnection practices and industry structure over the last two decades motivates an obvious question: is it still appropriate? In this paper, we evaluate the 95th percentile pricing mechanism from the perspective of transit providers, using a decade of traffic statistics from SWITCH (a large research/academic network), and more recent traffic statistics from 3 Internet Exchange Points (IXPs). We find that over time, heavy-inbound and heavy-hitter networks are able to achieve a lower 95th-to-average ratio than heavy-inbound and moderate-hitter networks, possibly due to their ability to better manage their traffic profile. The 95th percentile traffic volume also does not necessarily reflect the cost burden to the provider, motivating our exploration of an alternative metric that better captures the costs imposed on a network. We define the *provision ratio* for a customer, which captures its contribution to the provider's peak load.

1   Introduction

The industry standard for transit billing is the 95th *percentile billing* method [1, 2] wherein a transit provider measures the utilization of a customer link in 5-minute bins over the duration of a month, and then computes the 95th Percentile of these utilization values as the billing volume. The 95th Percentile method has several attractive properties. First, this method is simple to implement, and uses data (e.g., SNMP) that the provider typically already collects. Second, it approximates the load that a customer causes the provider, while "forgiving" a few bursts (the top 5% of samples are ignored). While this transit billing method has remained fairly standard for over a decade, traffic patterns have evolved dramatically, from the dominance of client-server traffic in the early days of the Internet, to the rise and fall in popularity of peer-to-peer applications, to the rise of streaming video. Given that the traffic profile of a transit customer depends on the popularity of underlying applications, it is not clear that a transit billing scheme that may have been rational a decade ago is still appropriate.

In this work, we revisit the 95th Percentile billing scheme from the perspective of a provider, to investigate whether this scheme approximately achieves its intended objective of providing an easy-to-compute approximation of a customer's traffic load

M. Faloutsos and A. Kuzmanovic (Eds.): PAM 2014, LNCS 8362, pp. 77–87, 2014.

to the provider. We first use 10 years of historical data from SWITCH, a Swiss research/academic network, and more recent data from 3 Internet Exchange Points (IXPs) to investigate how the 95th Percentile of a customer's traffic relates to: (1) its total traffic volume, (2) its nature as a predominantly inbound/outbound customer, and (3) its behavior as a heavy vs. moderate hitter. Second, we study the *fairness* of the 95th percentile scheme, and define a new metric called the *provision ratio* to investigate the relationship between the 95th Percentile of customer and the contribution of that customer to the provider's traffic load.

Analysis of these data sets reveals evidence that over the years the customers with a predominantly outbound traffic profile are able to maintain a lower 95th-to-average ratio than predominantly inbound customers, meaning that they have a lower billing volume for the same amount of traffic sent. Furthermore, the 95th-percentile pricing mechanism is *unfair*, because for many customers the 95th Percentile may not reflect their cost burden to the provider, as there is little overlap between the customer's peak and the overall (provider) peak traffic. Our results motivate the need to look for alternatives to the 95th Percentile billing method that can better approximate a customer's cost burden to the provider without adding too much additional measurement or computational overhead.

2   Datasets

SWITCH Dataset: Our first dataset comes from SWITCH, a Swiss Research/Academic network which provides Internet connectivity to major universities and organizations in Switzerland. Currently, SWITCH connects about 50 research and education sites, acting as a transit provider for traffic that originates or is destined to those networks. SWITCH also provides connectivity to the public Internet via commercial providers, and hosts content caches of two large content providers. For traffic billing, SWITCH measures the utilization of each border router interface in both inbound and outbound directions in 5-minute intervals. To present a longitudinal analysis, we use historical datasets from SWITCH from January 2003 to December 2012.

IXP Dataset: The second dataset consists of traffic statistics published by 3 Internet Exchange Points (IXPs) – Budapest Internet Exchange (BIX), Slovak Internet Exchange (SIX), and Interlan Internet Exchange (ILAN). These IXPs publish MRTG graphs with 5-minute utilization (inbound and outbound) for each network connected to the public peering fabric of the IXP. We collected these graphs every day for the month of August 2013 and used Optical Character Recognition tools [3] to parse them. BIX had 62 networks connected to its public peering fabric, while SIX and ILAN had 48 and 55 networks, respectively. Networks connect to IXPs to create (settlement-free) peering connections with other participating networks, and so the traffic statistics we see at an IXP are for a connected network's peering traffic[1]. Castro et al. [3] showed that transit traffic and peering traffic have similar diurnal patterns and peak-to-valley ratios; in fact, the transit traffic for a network can be well-approximated as a multiplicative factor of the peering traffic. In our analysis we consider the IXP as proxy for a transit provider, and the networks connected to it as its customers.

---

[1] While not explicitly disallowed, transit sale over the shared IXP fabric is rare [4].

3   Longitudinal Study of 95th Percentile Billing

We first describe two common methods of computing the 95th Percentile traffic volume, and how the two methods can treat customers differently. We then classify networks based on two criteria: (i) major direction of traffic (inbound, outbound, and balanced); and (ii) volume of traffic (heavy-hitter and moderate-hitter), and present a longitudinal view of the traffic properties of these network types.

3.1   Calculation of 95th Percentile

Although 95th Percentile billing is the industry standard, there are two common implementations and several possible variations. The first method measures the inbound and outbound traffic in every 5 minutes over the month, calculates the 95th percentile for each direction, and uses the maximum of these two values. Most transit provider references to computing the 95th Percentile use this method, e.g., [5, 6], so we use it in our subsequent analysis. The second method records the maximum of inbound and outbound traffic in each five minute interval, and calculates the 95th Percentile value from the resulting data set. This second method seems to be less common although we found a few transit providers that bill using this method [7, 8]. The second method will yield a value greater than or equal to the first method, and the results will differ significantly for customers with balanced traffic profiles, but with inbound peaks occurring at different times from outbound peaks. We computed the 95th Percentile for each network in the SWITCH dataset over 10 years. We found that the median ratio of the 95th Percentile value for each network, computed using these two methods is close to 1, but the widest difference induces a 20% higher transit bill using the second method.

3.2   Classification of Networks

Direction of Traffic: We divide networks into three categories based on the dominant direction of traffic. For each network, we measure the traffic that terminates within that network (inbound) and traffic that originates from that network (outbound). If the inbound traffic of the network is more than twice the outbound traffic we classify it as *heavy-inbound*, and if the outbound traffic is more than twice the inbound traffic we classify the network as *heavy-outbound*. Networks that do not satisfy either condition are classified as *balanced*. Typically, content providers are heavy-outbound, while eyeball providers are heavy-inbound.

Volume of Traffic: We next classify networks based on the volume of traffic they generate/consume over a month into *heavy-hitter and moderate-hitter* networks. To define the two classes we evaluated the traffic contribution by the top 20% of networks in each month of the SWITCH and IXP datasets. The top 20% of networks consistently contributed between 80 and 90% of total traffic in the SWITCH dataset, and 75% of total traffic in the IXP dataset. Based on this observation, we classify the top 20% of networks in each month as *heavy-hitter networks* and the rest as *moderate-hitter networks*.

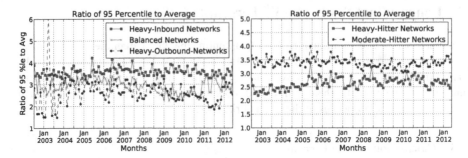

Fig. 1. Mean 95th Percentile to average ratio for different network types in the SWITCH dataset. Heavy-inbound networks have a larger 95th Percentile to average ratio than heavy-outbound networks. Also, moderate-hitter networks have a larger ratio than heavy-hitter networks.

3.3 95th Percentile to Average Ratio

For each customer network, we first evaluate the 95th Percentile to average traffic ratio; the average reflects the total volume of traffic, whereas the 95th Percentile value gives an idea of the peak, and is also the traffic volume for which the customer is billed. If the two significantly differ, it suggests that the customer is paying primarily for its bursti-ness. Figure 1 shows the mean of the 95th Percentile to average traffic ratio over time for networks in the SWITCH dataset classified by traffic direction and traffic volume.

First, we observe that the 95th Percentile to average ratio has been fairly stable over the years for each type of network, despite the dramatic changes in overall inter-domain traffic patterns that have occurred during the same time. In the last 4 years, the mean ratio for heavy-outbound networks is between 2 and 3, while the mean for heavy-inbound networks is between 3.25 and 4. For balanced networks, the ratio is less than 3.25. Hence, heavy-inbound networks in general have higher 95th Percentile traffic compared to heavy-outbound or balanced networks for the same average traffic. Consequently, heavy-inbound networks have a higher billing volume than heavy-outbound networks for the same amount of total traffic sent. We observe that the mean ratio is between 2.25 and 3 for heavy-hitter networks, especially in the last 4 years. However, the mean ratio always exceeds 3 for moderate-hitter networks in those 4 years.

Table 1 shows the mean 95th Percentile to average ratio for different classes of net-works in the IXP dataset. We observe that the mean ratio is higher for heavy-inbound networks than for heavy-outbound networks, consistent with our analysis of the SWITCH dataset. With the exception of BIX, the mean 95th Percentile to average ra-tio for networks at the other two IXPs is larger for moderate-hitter networks than for heavy-hitter networks, meaning that moderate-hitter networks have a burstier traffic profile than heavy-hitter networks.

3.4   Skewness of the Traffic Distribution

The above analysis shows that heavy-inbound and moderate-hitter networks have a higher 95th-to-average ratio as compared to other networks, meaning that their traf-

Table 1. Mean 95th Percentile to average ratio for IXPs, using different network classifications. Heavy-inbound and moderate-hitter networks (except at BIX) generally have higher ratios.

IXP	Heavy-inbound	Balanced	Heavy-outbound	Heavy-hitter	Moderate-hitter
SIX	2.6	-	1.7	1.4	1.9
BIX	2.82	2.3	2.1	2.59	1.94
ILAN	2.62	1.9	2.21	1.7	2.386

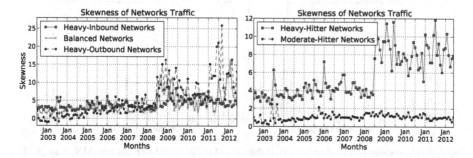

Fig. 2. Mean skewness for different network types in the SWITCH dataset. Heavy-outbound networks have a higher skewness, especially in the last 4 years. Heavy-hitter networks have larger skewness than moderate-hitter networks.

fic profile is likely to be burstier. Figure 2 illustrates the difference by plotting the mean skewness of the traffic distribution for each network type.

Skewness reveals how much the traffic distribution leans to one side of the mean; for a random variable X: Skewness $= E\left[(X - \mu)^3\right] / \left(E\left[(X - \mu)^2\right]\right)^{3/2}$, where μ is the mean. If a probability distribution function is unimodal, then higher positive skew implies few values higher than the mean, i.e., the 95th Percentile value would be closer to the average. The empirical probability mass function for the traffic of each network is unimodal for our data sets. Heavy-outbound networks have high positive skew (the mean is between 5 and 25), especially in the last 4 years[2], compared to heavy-inbound networks or balanced networks, whose mean skewness is between 0 and 12 and 5 and 15, respectively. Similarly, heavy-hitter networks have higher positive skew than moderate-hitter networks. Table 2 shows the mean skew of traffic for networks at each IXP, classified according to dominant traffic direction and traffic volume. As in the SWITCH dataset, heavy-outbound and heavy-hitter networks generally have a larger skewness than heavy-inbound and moderate-hitter networks.

In summary, the 95th-to-average ratio has been stable for various classes of networks in our dataset over the last decade, indicating that a high-percentile billing scheme is still useful. Certain networks (particularly heavy-outbound and heavy-hitter networks) are able to achieve a lower 95th Percentile to average ratio (perhaps using intelligent means of traffic shaping), and hence a lower billing volume for the same total amount

---

[2] The level shifts around 2009 coincide with SWITCH connecting to AMS-IX, acquiring hundreds of new peers, though the set of customers over which we compute statistics is unchanged.

Table 2. Mean skewness for networks in the IXP dataset. Heavy-hitter networks and heavy-outbound networks generally have higher skewness.

IXP	Heavy-inbound	Balanced	Heavy-outbound	Heavy-hitter	Moderate-hitter
SIX	-0.56	-	0.04	0.3	-0.88
BIX	-1.6	-0.4	-0.19	-0.88	0.317
ILAN	-0.122	0.07	0.29	0.253	-0.11

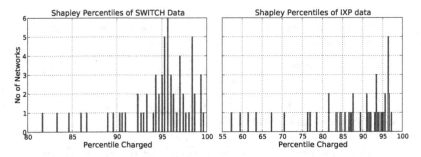

Fig. 3. Shapley value percentiles: SWITCH dataset (Mar 2012) and IXP dataset (SIX, Aug 2013)

of transit traffic. Traffic smoothing may allow networks to achieve a lower transit bill, but this says little about the contribution of those networks to the provider's peak traffic. The 95th Percentile of a network does not account for *when* the peaks occur, and so it is unclear whether it is fair to charge each customer using the same percentile.

4   Fairness of 95th Percentile Billing

Motivated by the preceding discussion, we now focus on the fairness of the 95th Percentile billing mechanism. We consider a billing mechanism fair if the amount of resources used by a network is reflected in the amount it is charged. An appealing idea in this context is the Shapley value, which assigns costs to the members in a cooperative game [9]. It possesses many attractive properties – it is *efficient*, i.e., the sum of costs assigned to each member is the total cost to the system, and it is *symmetric*, i.e., two members that have the same contribution will be assigned the same cost.

4.1   Shapley Value Percentile Billing

Stanojevic et al. [10] presented a model of the ISP cost allocation problem as a cooperative game. The cost function of a group is the 95th Percentile of the total traffic obtained by adding the traffic of all members in that group. This cost estimate is consistent with the idea that the transit provider must provision for peak traffic, and is itself billed by its provider based on this value. The Shapley value (ϕ_i) of network i is then uniquely defined by $\phi_i = \frac{1}{N!} \sum_{\pi \in \Pi} (\mathcal{V}(S(\pi, i) - \mathcal{V}(S(\pi, i) \backslash i))$ where $\mathcal{V}$ is the cost function, Π is the set of all possible permutations of players $\mathcal{N}$ and $S(\pi, i)$ is the set of all players in ordering π before i and including i.

Once we determine the Shapley value of each network, we need to map it to a billing percentile. Let the volume corresponding to the 95th Percentile value of the total traffic be $\mathcal{V}$. Then (by efficiency) the Shapley values of the customer networks will satisfy $\mathcal{V} = \sum_i \phi_i$. Let the volume corresponding to the 95th Percentile of network i be x_i. Then the total volume billed by the transit provider under the 95th Percentile billing scheme is $\sum_i x_i$, which we define as $\mathcal{X}$. Trivially, $\mathcal{X} \geq \mathcal{V}$. For an apples-to-apples comparison between the two billing schemes, we define the normalized Shapley value of network i as $s_i = \phi_i \mathcal{X}/\mathcal{V}$, so that the total billing volume in both cases is $\mathcal{X}$. Then each network can be charged based on a percentile that yields the traffic volume closest its normalized Shapley value, which is the "Shapley value percentile" of that network.

Computation of the Shapley value is quite complex—with N users, it has complexity order of $\mathcal{O}(N!)$. Even for a moderate size ISP, which has around 50 users, the complexity is of the order of 10^{64}. Stanojevic et al. [10] used a Monte Carlo approximation, which achieves a good trade-off between accuracy and complexity. We used this approximation to find the Shapley value percentile for the SWITCH dataset (month of March 2012) and the SIX IXP (August 2013). The results are shown in Figure 3. Clearly, the Shapley value percentiles are widely different from the 95th Percentile .

In addition to computational complexity, the Shapley value percentile can be any-where between 0 and 100. This approach lacks the ability of restricting the charging percentiles to a fixed range. The handicaps of directly using the Shapley value motivate a need for a simple proxy that captures its essence. A key observation is that a traffic profile has greater Shapley value when it is concentrated during the peak periods when demand is highest. Thus, Shapley value percentile billing would charge users with high peak traffic higher than users with off peak traffic.

4.2 Overlap Rank

Building on the intuition developed in the last section that it is fair to charge more to networks with traffic during peak periods than off-peak periods, we will show how the current 95th Percentile billing mechanism can lead to unfairness as it does not consider peak and off-peak periods. We define the peak periods of a transit provider as those in which the total traffic carried by the transit provider exceeds the 95th Percentile of the provider's total traffic. We similarly define the peak slots for customer networks. Based on the number of peak slots of networks that overlap with peak slots of the total traffic, we rank the networks from highest to lowest and call it the *overlap rank*. Thus, a network with rank 0 has the maximum number of peak slots that occur during the same time intervals as the peak slots of the transit provider. We also rank networks based on their 95th Percentile and call it the 95th Percentile rank.

Figure 4 plots overlap rank vs. percentile rank (normalized to 100) for the IXP dataset (first 3 plots) and one month (January 2012) from the SWITCH dataset (far right). If networks with high 95th Percentile rank also had high overlap rank, most points would appear on the diagonal, and imply that 95th Percentile billing is charging the contrib-utors who necessitate the provisioning of large transit links. Figure 4 tells a different story. The points below the diagonal, especially those in the red shaded area (16% of networks for SWITCH) have a high 95th Percentile rank but a low overlap rank, which means that their peaks are mostly in the peak period, but their billing volume is

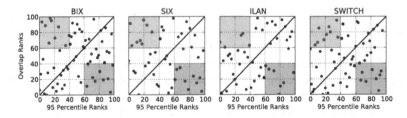

Fig. 4. Overlap rank vs 95th Percentile rank for IXP dataset (Aug 2013) and one month of SWITCH dataset (Jan 2012). A large fraction of networks lie far from the diagonal, meaning they have a large billing volume but little overlap with the provider's peaks, or vice versa.

relatively lower. Analogously, the points above the diagonal line, especially in the gray region (15% of networks for SWITCH) correspond to low 95th Percentile rank and high overlap rank. Their contribution to the peak period is low but they have a relatively high billing volume. Similar observations can also be made from the IXP graphs in Figure 4.

4.3 Provision Ratio

The overlap rank considers only the cardinality of overlap slots, without accounting for diverse traffic volumes. A good proxy for the Shapley value should capture the volume during peak slots, appropriately normalized with the amount of traffic generated by the network. We define the **provision ratio** (PR) of a network as the ratio of the average traffic during the peak slots of total traffic to the 95th Percentile of that network's traffic.

$$\text{PR of network } i = \frac{\text{Total traffic of network } i \text{ during peak slots / \# of peak slots}}{95^{th} \text{ Percentile of network } i\text{'s traffic}}.$$

The PR is essentially the ratio of traffic contributed by the network during the peak time slots (or average capacity provided to that network during these peaks) to the peak traffic of that network (excluding the top 5% of bursts); It can be viewed as the fraction of a network's peak traffic that occurs during the provider's peak periods. We propose that the PR can be an important component of a billing mechanism, because it captures the contribution of a network's traffic to the provider's peak. The PR is also robust to the exact thresholds used to compute it – we found that in our datasets, the provision ratio is robust to the exact threshold for defining a peak slot, e.g., if we change the 95th Percentile to 85th percentile, the provision ratio does not change significantly.

The provision ratio is not equal to the Shapley value percentile in an absolute sense, but in a relative sense it appears to have the right characteristics. To quantify the similarity between the two, we find the percentage of orders preserved between all possible pairs of networks in both datasets. A transit provider with N customers will have $^N C_2$ customer pairs. For each pair, order is preserved if the network that is charged a higher Shapley percentile also has a higher provision ratio. We find that for the SWITCH dataset, the provision ratio preserves between 76% and 82% of orders in the SWITCH dataset (each month of 2012) and 89%, 75%, and 82% for the SIX, BIX, and ILAN IXPs, respectively (August 2013). The strong similarity of orders indicates that provision ratio is indeed order preserving.

4.4　Towards a New Billing Mechanism

One could argue that the 95th Percentile billing scheme is an approximation, aiming for simplicity and predictability over fairness. At the other extreme is Shapley value pricing, which charges each user differently based on their actual contribution to the provider's costs. An open challenge is how to achieve both objectives – fairness and low computational complexity. We are currently exploring the use of the provision ratio in a scheme that determines the optimal percentile to charge a given customer. The objective of this scheme would be to vary the billing percentile per customer, and to use the provision ratio as a measure of the contribution of a customer to the provider's peak traffic. This pricing scheme would automatically assign lower billing percentiles (i.e., give discounts) to customers whose peak traffic does not contribute significantly to the provider's peak, and higher percentiles to customers that contribute most to the provider's peak. An important criterion for such a scheme is that the provider should be able to communicate information about its peak and off-peak periods to customers, without having to make its traffic profile available publicly. For this purpose, the provider could design a tool that accepts a customer's traffic profile and analyzes it in relation to its own traffic to determine the percentile at which it would charge the customer. Such a scheme would retain the attractive properties of burstable billing (because it is still based on a billing percentile), while better accounting for a network's contribution to total provider costs. Our initial investigation indicates that this problem can be formulated as a convex optimization, and hence solved efficiently.

5　Related Work

While network service pricing has been studied extensively, relatively little work has focused on specific mechanisms in the transit business, i.e., volume based pricing based on the 95th Percentile rule. As early as 1999, Brownlee et al. [11] experimented with an alternative to the 95th Percentile pricing mechanism, the "third quartile day", which they showed was a better estimate of the bandwidth requirements for customers of New Zealand's Kawaihiko network. Norton discussed 95th Percentile pricing in his white papers, particularly the possibility of ISPs gaming the scheme to get free transit [12], and the impact of streaming video on the statistics of customer traffic [13]. Dmitropoulos et al. [2] studied the 95th Percentile billing method using traffic traces, and investigated how the 95th Percentile computed for a given network depends on factors such as the averaging window size and the effect of flow aggregation. In the context of broadband users, Stanojevic et al. [10] used the Shapley value approach to quantify the contribution of each broadband user to the total costs of the access provider. Valancius et al. [14] proposed that transit providers implement tiered pricing using just a few tiers based on the volume of traffic and the cost of carrying it to maximize their profits. However, their approach was targeted at properly structuring pricing tiers, i.e., the price per unit of traffic that the provider charges to a customer. The focus of our work is on the underlying traffic percentile at which a provider charges its customers.

6   Conclusions

In this paper, our goal was to empirically examine the effectivenvess of the 95th percentile pricing scheme, using a decade of historical traffic data from a transit provider network and more recent data from three European IXPs. Our analysis shows that over the years, certain networks have lower 95th-to-average ratio than others – for the datasets we studied, networks with predominantly inbound traffic have higher 95th-to-average ratios, and would incur a higher billing volume than those with predominantly outbound traffic (for the same amount of total traffic), and similarly for moderate hitters vs. heavy hitters. Furthermore, we find that the 95th percentile pricing scheme can be unfair, as the 95th Percentile traffic of a network is often unrelated to the amount of time that network's peak traffic overlaps that of its provider, nor does it accurately represent the contribution of that network to the provider's peak traffic. We define a new metric, the Provision Ratio (PR) for a network, which is easy to compute and is able to capture the contribution of a customer traffic to the provider's peak.

Acknowledgements. We thank our shepherd, Sergey Gorinsky, and the anonymous reviewers for their constructive comments. This material is based upon work supported in part by NSF grants CNS-1149458, CNS-1017064 and a Cisco URP grant. Any opinions, findings, and conclusions or recommendations expressed in this material are those of the authors and do not necessarily reflect the views of NSF or Cisco.

References

[1] Odlyzko, A.: Internet pricing and the history of communications. Computer Networks 36 (2001)
[2] Dimitropoulos, X., Hurley, P., Kind, A., Stoecklin, M.P.: On the 95-percentile billing method. In: Moon, S.B., Teixeira, R., Uhlig, S. (eds.) PAM 2009. LNCS, vol. 5448, pp. 207–216. Springer, Heidelberg (2009)
[3] Castro, I., Stanojevic, R., Gorinsky, S.: Using Tuangou to reduce IP transit costs. IEEE/ACM Transactions on Networking (2013)
[4] Norton, W.B.: Transit Traffic at Internet Exchange Points? Drpeering.net blog: http://drpeering.net/AskDrPeering/blog
[5] G4 Communications: 95th Percentile Usage Billing Policy, http://www.g4communications.com/docs/G4_95th_Percentile_Usage.pdf
[6] Axis Internet: 95th Percentile, http://www.axint.net/95th
[7] AboveNet: Monitoring 95-percentile, http://john.de-graaff.net/wiki/doku.php/links/95-percentile
[8] Cline Communications: 95th Percentile billing, http://clinecommunications.net/?ID=33
[9] Roth, A.E.: The Shapley Value: Essays in Honor of Lloyd S. Shapley (1988)
[10] Stanojevic, R., Laoutaris, N., Rodriguez, P.: On Economic Heavy Hitters: Shapley Value Analysis of 95th-percentile Pricing. In: Proceedings of IMC (2010)

[11] Brownlee, N., Fulton, R.: Kawaihiko and the Third-Quartile Day. IEEE Communications 38(8) (2000)

[12] Norton, W.B.: Transit Tactic - Gaming the 95th Percentile. Drpeering.net white paper: http://drpeering.net/

[13] Norton, W.B.: Video Internet: The Next Wave of Massive Disruption to the U.S. Peering Ecosystem. Drpeering.net white paper: http://drpeering.net/

[14] Valancius, V., Lumezanu, C., Feamster, N., Johari, R., Vazirani, V.V.: How many tiers?: pricing in the Internet transit market. In: Proceedings of ACM SIGCOMM (2011)

Dissecting Round Trip Time on the Slow Path with a Single Packet

Pietro Marchetta[1], Alessio Botta[1], Ethan Katz-Bassett[2], and Antonio Pescapé[1]

[1] University of Napoli Federico II, Napoli, Italy
[2] University of Southern California, Los Angeles, USA

Abstract. Researchers and operators often measure *Round Trip Time* when monitoring, troubleshooting, or otherwise assessing network paths. However, because it combines all hops traversed along both the forward and reverse path, it can be difficult to interpret or to attribute delay to particular path segments.

In this work, we present an approach using a single packet to dissect the RTT in chunks mapped to specific portions of the path. Using the IP Prespecified Timestamp option directed at intermediate routers, it provides RTT estimations along portions of the slow path. Using multiple vantage points (116 PlanetLab nodes), we show that the proposed approach can be applied on more than 77% of the considered paths. Finally, we present preliminary results for two use cases (home network contribution to the RTT and per-Autonomous System RTT contribution) to demonstrate its potential in practical scenarios.

1 Introduction and Motivation

A common metric used to estimate the delay over a network path is the Round Trip Time (RTT) [1], defined as the length of time it takes to send a data packet toward a destination and receive its response. Monitoring RTT provides useful information about the network status when managing testbeds and operational networks [28]. However, an RTT sample comprises all the delays experienced by the data packet and its response along the forward and reverse path respectively, and it also includes the time the destination takes to inspect the incoming packet and generate the proper response. As a consequence, it can be difficult to interpret RTT values or tease apart the contributing factors.

From this point of view, dissecting the RTT into chunks related to specific portions of the network path may be helpful, making it possible to evaluate the relative impact of each subpath on the total experienced RTT. This approach is particularly useful in several scenarios. In a home network, one could isolate the impact of the home network on the RTT experienced toward a destination of interest, such as a website or network service. A large corporatation with multiple providers may want to evaluate the impact of its access networks when considering performance optimization and traffic engineering. Service providers may be interested in assessing if the ISP of a particular user has a great impact on the RTT, thus potentially representing the main cause of poor performance perceived by the user.

M. Faloutsos and A. Kuzmanovic (Eds.): PAM 2014, LNCS 8362, pp. 88–97, 2014.

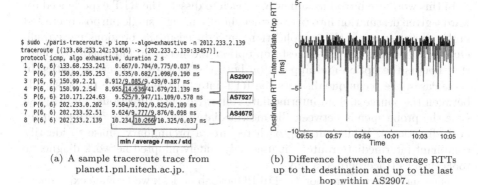

(a) A sample traceroute trace from planet1.pnl.nitech.ac.jp.

(b) Difference between the average RTTs up to the destination and up to the last hop within AS2907.

Fig. 1. Inaccuracy of traditional approaches for dissecting RTT

Unfortunately, accurately dissecting RTT is not a trivial task, especially through active measurements. One possibility is to rely on the RTTs reported by traceroute, i.e. the time it takes to send the TTL-limited probe and receive the ICMP Time Exceeded reply. However, it is not uncommon to observe RTT of intermediate hops higher than the RTT of the destination, as reported in the sample trace of Fig. 1(a)[1]. Another possibility is to use the ping command to monitor both the RTT to an intermediate hop and to the destination. For example, let us assume that our goal is to evaluate the impact of the provider, AS2907 (SINET-AS), on the RTT experienced toward the destination. We monitored the RTTs up to the last hop within AS2907 (150.99.2.54) and the destination by issuing pairs of ICMP Echo Request packet probes closely in time with the ping command. We launched one probe pair every 200 ms for 10 minutes and computed the average RTT obtained in one second bins. Finally, we computed the difference between the average RTT to the destination and to the intermediate hop. Fig. 1(b) presents the results. For about half of the bins, the intermediate hop had an average RTT higher than the RTT of the destination, making it hard to understand how the intermediate hop contributes to overall latency. Preliminary analysis suggests the this problem holds even for sophisticated ping variants that control RTT variance [21].

The inaccuracy of the two methods described above is determined by specific factors: (i) due to path asymmetry [12], the intermediate hop may not be part of the reverse path from the destination, thus its RTT is not part of the RTT of the destination; (ii) the two RTT samples are obtained by employing two distinct packet probes that potentially experience different network conditions or paths;[2] (iii) the two solicited devices may require a different amount of time to inspect the probe and generate the response [11]; finally (iv) when using ping, the forward path up to the intermediate hop may not represent a subpath of the forward path toward the destination, since fowarding is destination-based.

---

[1] This forward path is stable and unique, according to paris-traceroute [2].

[2] For example, due to load balancers located along the reverse paths [2].

In this work, we introduce a new approach to dissect the RTT experienced toward a given destination into two distinct chunks, using a single purposely crafted probe packet to avoid the complications introduced in the previous paragraph. Our approach uses the IP Timestamp option and needs an intermediate router that honors the option and appears on both the forward and reverse paths. In these cases, the technique dissects the RTT into (a) the time the probe spends between the source and an intermediate router (in both directions) and (b) the time the probe spends between the intermediate router and the destination (in both directions). While our approach requires a preliminary phase to identify compliant intermediate routers, it uses only widely adopted network diagnostic tools such as traceroute and ping.

Using multiple vantage points (116 PlanetLab nodes), we provide experimental results about the degree of applicability of our approach as well as case studies demonstrating its utility in practical scenarios.

2   Dissecting Round Trip Time

In this section, after a brief recap of the IP Prespecified Timestamp option, we describe the approach we propose to dissect the RTT in chunks.

Background. Although IP options headers [22] are not universally supported on the Internet [5, 9], researchers have used them as the basis for a number of recent measurement techniques [8, 14, 16, 17, 19, 20, 25, 26]. In this work, we use the IP Prespecified Timestamp option [22] (hereafter TS option) to dissect the RTT. This option lets the sender specify up to four IP addresses in the header of the packet, to request timestamps from the corresponding routers. We adopt the notation proposed by Sherry *at al.* [25]: X |ABCD refers to an ICMP Echo Request packet where X is the targeted destination and ABCD is the ordered list of prespecified IPs from which a timestamp is requested. Note that the position of each prespecified address in the ordered list ABCD is essential since it implies that B cannot insert its own timestamp before A, C before B, and so on. Typically, when the packets are not filtered along the path [9], the incoming option is replicated by the destination inside the ICMP Echo Reply. The TS option has been used to infer aliases [19, 25], to infer routers statistics such as traffic shape and CPU load [8], to identify third-party addresses and hidden routers in traceroute trace [17, 20], to reconstruct reverse paths [14], to infer link latency [24], and to identify symmetric link traversal [15].

Dissecting RTT. Our approach makes it possible to dissect the RTT toward a destination that (i) provides at least one timestamp when probed with D |DDDD and (ii) is not an extra-stamper [25], i.e. it does not provide more than one timestamp when probed with D |DXXX where X is an IP address surely not involved on the traversed path. On these paths, we can dissect the RTT into chunks by exploiting a *compliant* router located along the path (see Fig. 2): a compliant node *W* (i) is part of both the forward and reverse path under investigation; (ii) honors the TS option and provides standard timestamps [22],

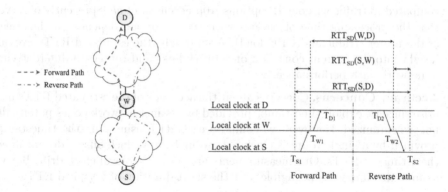

Fig. 2. Baseline scenario (S: source - W: compliant node - D: destination)

Fig. 3. Timestamps collected with D|WDDW and related RTT chunks

i.e milliseconds since midnight UT; (iii) provides timestamps both on the forward and reverse path. Hereafter we adopt the following notation: $RTT_{S,D}(X, Y)$ is the time taken by probes sent from the source S to the destination D to travel from X to Y on the forward path and from Y to X on the reverse path. This is a portion of the RTT of the entire path, i.e. $RTT_{S,D}(S, D)$.

Let W be a compliant node between the source S and the destination D. Besides $RTT_{S,D}(S, D)$, our approach estimates $RTT_{S,D}(S, W)$ and $RTT_{S,D}(W, D)$ by using the same single-packet probe. To this end, we send a D |WDDW probe from S to D. Once S receives the reply, six timestamps are available: (a) the sending and receiving time at the source (T_{S1} and T_{S2}); (b) the timestamp provided by W along the forward (T_{W1}) and reverse path (T_{W2}); (c) the two timestamps provided by the targeted destination D (T_{D1} and T_{D2}). These timestamps allow us to easily compute the RTT chunks (see Fig. 3 as reference): $RTT_{S,D}(S, D)$ as T_{S2}-T_{S1}, $RTT_{S,D}(W, D)$ as T_{W2}-T_{W1} and $RTT_{S,D}(S, W)$ as $RTT_{S,D}(S, D)$-$RTT_{S,D}(W, D)$.[3] When the destination provides only one timestamp when probed with D |DDDD, we send probe packets formatted like D |WDWW, rather than D |WDDW, to dissect the RTT.

To identify the compliant nodes and to monitor the path, we use widely adopted network diagnostic tools such as traceroute and ping: the ping option `-T tsprespec` sends ICMP Echo Request packets with a customized TS option.

The Slow Path. Packets can traverse a router either through the *fast* (hardware) or the *slow* (route processor/software) path. The IP option on our probes causes routers to inspect them and process them on the slow path. Previous work showed that IP options traffic experiences higher RTT, jitter, and packet loss,

---

[3] Note how it would be possible to estimate also several one way delays: from S to D (T_{D1}-T_{S1}), D to S (T_{S2}-T_{D2}), S to W (T_{W1}-T_{S1}), W to D (T_{D1}-T_{W1}), D to W (T_{W2}-T_{D2}) and W to S (T_{S2}-T_{W2}). However, unlike the RTT considered in this paper, one way delays are potentially biased if clocks at the various nodes are not properly synchronized, a common case in the Internet.

compared to traffic without IP options [10]. Ferguson *et al.* [8] recently observed that the processing time of packets with the TS option depends on the status of the router (traffic and CPU load). Accordingly, the estimated RTTs provide insight into the current condition of network links and routers, a different view of network path performance.

Accuracy Concerns. Concerns about the accuracy of the estimated RTTs may arise since we exploit timestamps provided by distinct network nodes potentially not synchronized. However, we compute each RTT using only the timestamps provided by a single router's clock. Accordingly, any clock offsets do not affect the estimated RTTs. Our measurements are subject to local clock drift, but we assume this impact is negligible over the short duration of a typical RTT.

3 Evaluation

In this section we first describe the results of an experimental campaign aiming at evaluating the applicability of the proposed approach. Then, we describe two use cases to show the utility of the proposed approach.

Degree of Applicability. We conducted a study to evaluate how many nodes per path will allow our approach to dissect the RTT (i.e. are compliant). To identify compliant nodes on a path between a source S and a destination D, we first need to discover all the nodes along the path. To this end, we collect an ICMP traceroute from S toward D. Let us suppose that the destination D provides two timestamps when probed with D |DDDD. For each discovered address Y, we send two packet probes D |YDDY and D |DYYY: if D |YDDY collects four timestamps, then Y is a compliant node. Indeed, four timestamps imply that Y inserted the first timestamp along the forward path (otherwise, D would not have been able to insert its own timestamp), and Y inserted its second timestamp along the reverse path (because the destination D inserted its timestamp before).[4] Non-compliant nodes (i) simply ignore the TS option (D |YDDY and D |DYYY collect none and one timestamp, respectively) or (ii) provide a timestamp only on the forward path (D |YDDY and D |DYYY collect between two and three timestamps and one timestamp respectively) or (iii) provide a timestamp only on the reverse path (D |YDDY and D |DYYY collect one and more than one timestamp, respectively). We refer to the latter two cases as *forward* and *backward stampers*. Forward stampers are nodes that do not appear on the reverse path while backward stampers are more challenging to explain: these nodes are discovered along the forward path but insert a timestamp only when traversed on the reverse path. Load balancing and off-path addresses [13,17,18] may explain this behavior.[5] When the destination provides only one timestamp,

---

[4] Previous work exploited a similar approach to assess symmetric link traversal [15,16].

[5] Standard-compliant routers set as source address of Time Exceeded replies the address associated to the outgoing interface causing Traceroute to report addresses associated to interfaces not actually traversed by the traffic sent to the Traceroute destination [13,17,18].

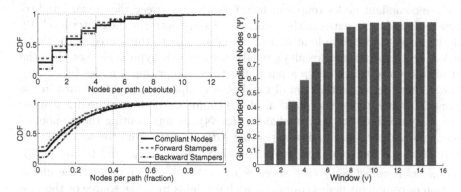

Fig. 4. Compliant nodes per path   **Fig. 5.** Compliant nodes relative position

we make use of D |YDYY probes instead of D |YDDY. In this case, a node is
compliant when D |YDYY collects at least three timestamps.

To generate a hitlist of suitable destinations, we extracted the addresses that
provided at least one timestamp when probed with D |DDDD in a large-scale ex-
perimental campaign from our previous work [5]. Of 1.7M IP addresses probed,
36% replied providing timestamps. From these addresses, we randomly selected
one representative IP for each AS [4]. The final hitlist comprises 3,133 distinct
ASes, including all Tier-1 ISP networks[6] and 35 out of 50 top-10 ASes for each
region, according to the APNIC weekly routing table report. We then performed
another experimental campaign using 116 PlanetLab nodes [3] as vantage points
(VPs). Each VP made the following steps for each destination of the hitlist:
first, it sent two probes, D |DDDD and D |DXXX, to check if the destination is
still responsive and is not an extra-stampers (see Sec. 2). Second, it performed
a traceroute toward the destination. Third, for each address Y discovered along
the path, it sent a D |YDDY (or D |YDYY depending on the number of times-
tamps provided by the destination) and D |DYYY. After removing about 90 K
paths toward extra-stamping destinations and 50 K paths toward addresses unresponsive for a subset of vantage points due to in-transit filtering, our final
dataset comprises 223,548 distinct paths.

Fig. 4 reports the compliant nodes observed per path. Ideally, we would like
all intermediate routers to be compliant, in order to split the RTT into all the
available chunks. On the other hand, just a single compliant node (W) allows
us to split the RTT into $RTT_{S,D}(S, W)$ and $RTT_{S,D}(W, D)$, thus providing
much more information on the network status than a classic RTT estimation.
We found that about 77.4% of the paths contain at least one compliant node
and 27.3% contain more than four compliant nodes. On average, we observed 2.5
compliant nodes, 2.1 forward stampers, and 2.7 backward stampers per path.
This result means that, on average, about 17% of the nodes in each scanned
path are compliant.

---

[6] http://en.wikipedia.org/wiki/Tier_1_network#List_of_tier_1_networks. August 1, 2013.

Since compliant nodes represent meeting points between the forward and reverse path and most paths in the Internet are asymmetric at the router level [12, 23], we expect most compliant nodes to appear close to the source or the destination. Our experimental results partially confirm this hypothesis. Let Ω be the set of traceroute traces and p a particular trace comprising n nodes $(a_1, .. , a_i, .. , a_n)$. Also, let C be the overall number of compliant nodes contained in the dataset. To investigate the position of the compliant nodes, we used a *window* ν to compute the *bounded compliant nodes* $\Phi(p, \nu)$ representing the number of compliant nodes on the path p appearing within ν hops from the source *or* the destination, i.e the compliant nodes contained in $(a_1, .. a_\nu)$ and $(a_{n-\nu}, .. a_n)$. The *global bounded compliant nodes* $\Psi(\nu) = \frac{\sum_{p \in \Omega} \Phi(p,\nu)}{C}$ represent the global fraction of compliant nodes contained within ν hops from the source or the destination when considering all the paths. Fig. 5 depicts how the global bounded compliant nodes varies with ν. If the hypothesis is true, then the global bounded compliant nodes should quickly tend to one. The figure shows evident though not sharp growth: about 72% of all the compliant nodes occur within 5 hops from the source or the destination, with about 15% appearing just one hop after the source or before the destination. These results confirm that the majority of the compliant nodes are located near the two end points of the paths, while there is also a significant percentage of compliant nodes in the middle of the paths.

Applications. We now report preliminary potential use cases of the proposed approach.

Per-Autonomous System RTT contribution. Our approach can isolate the RTT contribution of entire ASes. Consider again the trace in Fig. 1(a). Our goal is to isolate the RTT contribution of the provider network, AS2907. To this end, we monitored the path by using both the ping command and our approach (the last hop within AS2907, 150.99.2.54, is a compliant node). As anticipated in Sec. 1, when using ping to estimate the RTT up to the last hop within AS2907 and up to the destination with packet probes sent closely in time, we observed inconsistent results, as reported in Fig. 1(b). Often, the average RTT up to the intermediate hop is higher than the RTT up to the destination (see the negative difference values in Fig. 1(b)). Our approach, instead, always provides coherent results. As shown in Fig. 6(a), the estimated contribution of the AS2907 is always a fraction of the whole RTT. Results obtained with ping do not provide any meaningful information about the impact of the AS2907 on the end-to-end performance. As shown in Fig. 6(b), according to ping, the AS2907 RTT contribution represents on average 106% of the whole RTT, an unreasonable result. On the other hand, thanks to our approach, we can conclude that the AS2907 RTT contribution on the slow path is on average 76.8% of the whole RTT. The packet probes spent more than two-third of the time within the provider network.

Our approach also isolates the RTT contribution of a target AS network when the first hop within this AS is a compliant node. In the dataset collected to evaluate the applicability, the last hop within the provider AS (the first hop within the targeted AS) is a compliant node in $44,846$ $(22,236)$ paths, about 20% (9.95%) of the paths.

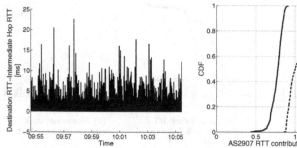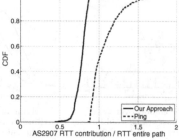

(a) Difference between the average RTTs up to the destination and up to the last hop within AS2907.

(b) AS2907 RTT contribution as fraction of the entire RTT.

Fig. 6. Isolating the RTT contribution of AS2907 over the path of Fig.1(a)

Home network contribution to the RTT. The impact of home networks on Internet performance has recently attracted an increasing interest from the research community [6,27]. However, classic diagnostic tools or simply probing the home gateway are not always able to reliably state if the home network is the cause of the performance degradation [7].

When the home gateway behaves as a compliant node, our approach allows us to evaluate the RTT toward any destination, as well as the contribution of the home network, by using a single packet probe. [7] As a case study, we monitored the RTT toward a top-ranked Italian journal website (repubblica.it). The monitored home network is connected to the Internet via an ADSL connection provided by Telecom Italia. The laptop in charge of monitoring is connected via Wi-Fi to a NETGEAR DGN2200v3, a common commercial modem-router compliant with our approach. To monitor the RTT, we used D |WDDW packet probes where W is the private address of the modem-router: We approximate the home network contribution as $RTT_{S,D}(S, W)$.

Fig. 7(a) shows the trend over time of the RTT chunks. In the beginning, the home network is unloaded. However, from 9:14 to 9:23, another Wi-Fi connected host started downloading and uploading large files through the Internet. During the overloaded period, the RTT grows in median by 356% (from 69.8 ms to 249 ms) but the home network played just a marginal role (see Fig. 7(b)). On average, packets spent 4.7% and 2.6% of the entire RTT within the home network during the unloaded and overloaded period, respectively. At the same time, we observed spurious latency spikes inside the home network probably caused by the packet-by-packet impact of contention-induced transmission delays over the wireless link (these spikes disappear on the wired connection). In the worst cases, the spikes represent more than 60% of the total RTT experienced in both

---

[7] In these experiments, the precise border of the home network clearly depends on when and how the home router handles the IP option. For instance, if the home router inserts its own timestamp before putting the probe on an overloaded buffer (an instance of home network bufferbloat), such buffering delay is not included in the home network contribution.

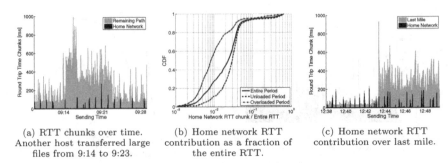

(a) RTT chunks over time. Another host transferred large files from 9:14 to 9:23.

(b) Home network RTT contribution as a fraction of the entire RTT.

(c) Home network RTT contribution over last mile.

Fig. 7. Home network RTT contribution toward repubblica.it monitored through a wireless link and an ADSL connection.

the unloaded and overloaded period. These results suggest that the stable performance degradation observed during the overloaded period is not caused by the home network but by congestion of the last mile.[8] Indeed, by replicating the experiment while monitoring the RTT on the last mile and isolating the home network contribution, we observed that downloading and uploading large files through the Internet does not affect the intra-home network delay while it determines a dramatic growth of the delay on the last mile (see Fig. 7(c)).

4   Conclusion

We presented an approach using a single packet to accurately dissect the RTT on the slow path in chunks mapped to specific portions of the end-to-end path. We observed how using other techniques based on ping and traceroute to this end may provide misleading results. Our approach uses the IP Timestamp option and a compliant router along the path. A large-scale measurement study we performed from 116 vantage points comprising 223K traced paths showed that 2.5 router per path on average are compliant. As preliminary evidence of the use of our approach, we presented two case studies, showing how it allows us to isolate the RTT contribution of the home network and of an entire AS.

Acknowledgements. This work is partially funded by the MIUR projects: PLATINO (PON01_01007), SMART HEALTH (PON04a2_C), and S^2−MOVE (PON04a3_00058).

References

1. Almes, G., Kalidindi, S., Zekauskas, M.: A round-trip delay metric for IPPM. Technical report, RFC 2681 (September 1999)
2. Augustin, B., et al.: Avoiding traceroute anomalies with Paris traceroute. In: ACM SIGCOMM IMC, pp. 153–158. ACM (2006)
3. Bavier, A., et al.: Operating system support for planetary-scale network services. In: NSDI (2004)
4. Cymru, T.: (2012), http://www.team-cymru.org/Services/ip-to-asn.html

---

[8] The physical connection between a customer's home and the DSLAM or the CMTS.

5. de Donato, W., Marchetta, P., Pescapé, A.: A hands-on look at active probing using the IP prespecified timestamp option. In: Taft, N., Ricciato, F. (eds.) PAM 2012. LNCS, vol. 7192, pp. 189–199. Springer, Heidelberg (2012)
6. DiCioccio, L., Teixeira, R., May, M., Kreibich, C.: Probe and pray: Using UPnP for home network measurements. In: Taft, N., Ricciato, F. (eds.) PAM 2012. LNCS, vol. 7192, pp. 96–105. Springer, Heidelberg (2012)
7. DiCioccio, L., Teixeira, R., Rosenberg, C.: Impact of home networks on end-to-end performance: controlled experiments. In: ACM HomeNets (2010)
8. Ferguson, A., Fonseca, R.: Inferring router statistics with IP timestamps. In: ACM CoNEXT Student Workshop (2010)
9. Fonseca, R., Porter, G., Katz, R., Shenker, S., Stoica, I.: IP options are not an option, Univ. of California, Berkeley (2005)
10. Fransson, P., Jonsson, A.: End-to-end measurements on performance penalties of IPv4 options. In: IEEE GLOBECOM (2004)
11. Govindan, R., Paxson, V.: Estimating router ICMP generation delays. In: PAM (2002)
12. He, Y., Faloutsos, M., Krishnamurthy, S.: Quantifying routing asymmetry in the Internet at the AS level. In: IEEE GLOBECOM (2004)
13. Hyun, Y., Broido, A., et al.: On third-party addresses in traceroute paths. In: "Passive and Active Measurement" Workshop 2003 (2003)
14. Katz-Bassett, E., et al.: Reverse traceroute. In: NSDI (2010)
15. Madhyastha, H.V.: An information plane for Internet applications. UW dissertation (2008)
16. Madhyastha, H.V., Katz-Bassett, E., Anderson, T., Krishnamurthy, A., Venkataramani, A.: iPlane Nano: Path prediction for peer-to-peer applications. In: NSDI (2009)
17. Marchetta, P., de Donato, W., Pescapé, A.: Detecting third-party addresses in traceroute traces with IP timestamp option. In: Roughan, M., Chang, R. (eds.) PAM 2013. LNCS, vol. 7799, pp. 21–30. Springer, Heidelberg (2013)
18. Marchetta, P., Persico, V., Katz-Bassett, E., Pescapé, A.: Don't trust traceroute (completely). In: ACM CoNEXT Student Workshop (2013)
19. Marchetta, P., Persico, V., Pescapé, A.: Pythia: yet another active probing technique for alias resolution. In: ACM CoNEXT, pp. 229–234 (2013)
20. Marchetta, P., Pescapè, A.: Drago: Detecting, quantifying and locating hidden routers in traceroute IP paths. In: IEEE Global Internet Symposium (2013)
21. Pelsser, C., Cittadini, L., Vissicchio, S., Bush, R.: From Paris to Tokyo: On the suitability of ping to measure latency. In: IMC 2013, pp. 427–432. ACM (2013)
22. Postel, J.: Internet protocol: DARPA Internet program protocol specification. RFC 791 (1981)
23. Schwartz, Y., Shavitt, Y., Weinsberg, U.: On the diversity, stability and symmetry of end-to-end Internet routes. In: IEEE INFOCOM Workshops (2010)
24. Sherry, J.: Applications of the IP timestamp option to Internet measurement. Undergraduate Honor Thesis (2010)
25. Sherry, J., Katz-Bassett, E., Pimenova, M., Madhyastha, H., Anderson, T., Krishnamurthy, A.: Resolving IP aliases with prespecified timestamps. In: ACM SIGCOMM IMC (2010)
26. Sherwood, R., Spring, N.: Touring the Internet in a TCP sidecar. In: ACM SIGCOMM IMC, pp. 339–344. ACM (2006)
27. Sundaresan, S., de Donato, W., Feamster, N., Teixeira, R., Crawford, S., Pescapè, A.: Broadband Internet performance: A view from the gateway. SIGCOMM 2011 41(4), 134 (2011)
28. Zeng, H., Kazemian, P., Varghese, G., McKeown, N.: A survey on network troubleshooting. Technical report, TR12-HPNG-061012, Stanford University (2012)

Is Our Ground-Truth for Traffic Classification Reliable?[*]

Valentín Carela-Español[1], Tomasz Bujlow[2], and Pere Barlet-Ros[1]

[1] UPC BarcelonaTech, Spain
{vcarela,pbarlet}@ac.upc.edu
[2] Aalborg University, Denmark
tbu@es.aau.dk

Abstract. The validation of the different proposals in the traffic classification literature is a controversial issue. Usually, these works base their results on a ground-truth built from private datasets and labeled by techniques of unknown reliability. This makes the validation and comparison with other solutions an extremely difficult task. This paper aims to be a first step towards addressing the validation and trustworthiness problem of network traffic classifiers. We perform a comparison between 6 well-known DPI-based techniques, which are frequently used in the literature for ground-truth generation. In order to evaluate these tools we have carefully built a labeled dataset of more than 500 000 flows, which contains traffic from popular applications. Our results present *PACE*, a commercial tool, as the most reliable solution for ground-truth generation. However, among the open-source tools available, *NDPI* and especially *Libprotoident*, also achieve very high precision, while other, more frequently used tools (e.g., *L7-filter*) are not reliable enough and should not be used for ground-truth generation in their current form.

1 Introduction and Related Work

During the last decade, traffic classification has considerably increased its relevance, becoming a key aspect for many network related tasks. The explosion of new applications and techniques to avoid detection (e.g., encryption, protocol obfuscation) have substantially increased the difficulty of traffic classification. The research community have thrown itself into this problem by proposing many different solutions. However, this problem is still far from being solved [1].

Most traffic classification solutions proposed in the literature report very high accuracy. However, these solutions mostly base their results on a private ground-truth (i.e., dataset), usually labeled by techniques of unknown reliability (e.g., ports-based or DPI-based techniques [2–5]). That makes it very difficult to compare and validate the different proposals. The use of private datasets is derived

[*] This research was funded by the Spanish Ministry of Economy and Competitiveness under contract TEC2011-27474 (NOMADS project), by the Comissionat per a Universitats i Recerca del DIUE de la Generalitat de Catalunya (ref. 2009SGR-1140) and by the European Regional Development Fund (ERDF).

M. Faloutsos and A. Kuzmanovic (Eds.): PAM 2014, LNCS 8362, pp. 98–108, 2014.

Table 1. DPI-based techniques evaluated

Name	Version	Applications
PACE	1.41 (June 2012)	1000
OpenDPI	1.3.0 (June 2011)	100
NDPI	rev. 6391 (March 2013)	170
L7-filter	2009.05.28 (May 2009)	110
Libprotoident	2.0.6 (Nov 2012)	250
NBAR	15.2(4)M2 (Nov 2012)	85

from the lack of publicly available datasets with payload. Mainly because of privacy issues, researchers and practitioners are not allowed to share their datasets with the research community. To the best of our knowledge, just one work has tackled this problem. Gringoli et al. in [6] published anonymized traces without payload, but accurately labeled using GT. This dataset is very interesting to evaluate Machine Learning-based classifiers, but the lack of payload makes it unsuitable for DPI-based evaluation.

Another crucial problem is the reliability of the techniques used to set the ground-truth. Most papers show that researchers usually obtain their ground-truth through port-based or DPI-based techniques [2–5]. The poor reliability of port-based techniques is already well known, given the use of dynamic ports or well-known ports of other applications [7, 8]. Although the reliability of DPI-based techniques is still unknown, according to conventional wisdom they are, in principle, one of the most accurate techniques.

Some previous works evaluated the accuracy of DPI-based techniques [3, 5, 9, 10]. These studies rely on a ground-truth generated by another DPI-based tool [5], port-based technique [3] or a methodology of unknown reliability [9,10], making their comparison very difficult. Recently, a concomitant study to ours [10] compared the performance of four DPI-based techniques (i.e., *L7-filter*, *Tstat*, *NDPI* and *Libprotoident*). This parallel study confirms some of the findings of our work presenting *NDPI* and *Libprotoident* as the most accurate open-source DPI-based techniques. In [11] the reliability of *L7-filter* and a port-based technique was compared using a dataset obtained by GT [6] showing that both techniques present severe problems to accurately classify the traffic.

This paper presents two main contributions. First, we publish a reliable labeled dataset with full packet payloads [12]. The dataset has been artificially built in order to allow us its publication. However, we have manually simulated different behaviours to make it as representative as possible. We used VBS [13] to guarantee the reliability of the labeling process. This tool can label the flows with the name of the process that created them. This allowed us to carefully create a reliable ground-truth that can be used as a reference benchmark for the research community. Second, using this dataset, we evaluated the performance and compared the results of 6 well-known DPI-based techniques, presented in Table 1, which are widely used for the ground-truth generation in the traffic classification literature.

These contributions pretend to be a first step towards the impartial validation of network traffic classifiers. They also provide to the research community some insights about the reliability of different DPI-based techniques commonly used in the literature for ground-truth generation.

2   Methodology

The Testbed. Our testbed is based on VMWare virtual machines (VM). We installed three VM for our data generating stations and we equipped them with Windows 7 (W7), Windows XP (XP), and Ubuntu 12.04 (LX). Additionally, we installed a server VM for data storage. To collect and accurately label the flows, we adapted Volunteer-Based System (VBS) developed at Aalborg University [13]. The task of VBS is to collect information about Internet traffic flows (i.e., start time of the flow, number of packets contained by the flow, local and remote IP addresses, local and remote ports, transport layer protocol) together with detailed information about each packet (i.e., direction, size, TCP flags, and relative timestamp to the previous packet in the flow). For each flow, the system also collects the process name associated with that flow. The process name is obtained from the system sockets. This way, we can ensure the application associated to a particular traffic. Additionally, the system collects some information about the HTTP content type (e.g., *text/html*, *video/x-flv*). The captured information is transmitted to the VBS server, which stores the data in a MySQL database. The design of VBS was initially described in [13]. On every data generating VM, we installed a modified version of VBS. The source code of the modified version was published in [14] under a *GPL license*. The modified version of the VBS client captures full Ethernet frames for each packet, extracts HTTP *URL* and *Referer* fields. We added a module called *pcapBuilder*, which is responsible for dumping the packets from the database to PCAP files. At the same time, INFO files are generated to provide detailed information about each flow, which allows us to assign each packet from the PCAP file to an individual flow. We also added a module called *logAnalyzer*, which is responsible for analyzing the logs generated by the different DPI tools, and assigning the results of the classification to the flows stored in the database.

Selection of the Data. The process of building a representative dataset, which characterizes a typical user behavior, is a challenging task, crucial on testing and comparing different traffic classifiers. Therefore, to ensure the proper diversity and amount of the included data, we decided to combine the data on a multidimensional level. Based on w3schools statistics, we selected Windows 7 (55.3 % of all users), Windows XP (19.9 %), and Linux (4.8 %) - state for January 2013. Apple computers (9.3 % of overall traffic) and mobile devices (2.2 %) were left as future work. The selected applications are shown below.

- Web browsers: based on w3schools statistics: Chrome and Firefox (W7, XP, LX), Internet Explorer (W7, XP).
- BitTorrent clients: based on CNET ranking: uTorrent and Bittorrent (W7, XP), Frostwire and Vuze (W7, XP, LX)

- eDonkey clients: based on CNET ranking: eMule (W7, XP), aMule (LX)
- FTP clients: based on CNET ranking: FileZilla (W7, XP, LX), SmartFTP Client (W7, XP), CuteFTP (W7, XP), WinSCP (W7, XP)
- Remote Desktop servers: built-in (W7, XP), xrdp (LX)
- SSH servers: sshd (LX)
- Background traffic: DNS and NTP (W7, XP, LX), NETBIOS (W7, XP)

The list of visited websites was based on the top 500 websites according to Alexa statistics. We chose several of them taking into account their rank and the nature of the website (e.g., search engines, social medias, national portals, video websites) to assure the variety of produced traffic. These websites include: Google, Facebook, YouTube, Yahoo!, Wikipedia, Java, and Justin.tv. For most websites we performed several random clicks to linked external websites, which should better characterize the real behavior of the real users and include also other websites not included in the top 500 ranking. This also concerns search engines, from which we manually generated random clicks to the destination web sites. Each of the chosen websites was processed by each browser. In case it was required to log into the website, we created fake accounts. In order to make the dataset as representative as possible we have simulated different human behaviors when using these websites. For instance, on Facebook, we log in, interact with friends (e.g., chat, send messages, write in their walls), upload pictures, create events or play games. On YouTube, we watched the 10 most popular videos, which we randomly paused, resumed, and rewound backward and forward. Also, we randomly made some comments and clicked *Like* or *Not like* buttons. The detailed description of actions performed with the services is listed in our technical report [15]. We tested the P2P (BitTorrent and eDonkey) clients by downloading files of different sizes and then leaving the files to be seeded for some time, in order to obtain enough of traffic in both directions. We tried to test every FTP client using both the active transfer mode (PORT) and passive transfer mode (PASV), if the client supports such mode.

Extracting the Data for Processing. Each DPI tool can have different requirements and features, so the extracting tool must handle all these issues. The PCAP files provided to PACE, OpenDPI, L7-filter, NDPI, and Libprotoident are accompanied by INFO files, which contain the information about the start and end of each flow, together with the flow identifier. Because of that, the software, which uses the DPI libraries, can create and terminate the flows appropriately, as well as to provide the classification results together with the flow identifier. Preparing the data for NBAR classification is more complicated. There are no separate INFO files describing the flows, since the classification is made directly on the router. We needed to extract the packets in a way that allows the router to process and correctly group them into flows. We achieved that by changing both the source and destination MAC addresses during the extraction process. The destination MAC address of every packet must match up with the MAC address of the interface of the router, because the router cannot process any packet which is not directed to its interface on the MAC layer. The source MAC address was set up to contain the

Table 2. Application classes in the dataset

Application	No. of flows	No. of Megabytes
Edonkey	176581	2823.88
BitTorrent	62845	2621.37
FTP	876	3089.06
DNS	6600	1.74
NTP	27786	4.03
RDP	132907	13218.47
NETBIOS	9445	5.17
SSH	26219	91.80
Browser HTTP	46669	5757.32
Browser RTMP	427	3026.57
Unclassified	771667	5907.15

identifier of the flow to which it belongs, so the flows were recognized by the router according to our demands. To the best of our knowledge, this is the first work to present a scientific performance evaluation of NBAR.

The Classification Process. We designed a tool, called *dpi_ benchmark*, which can read the PCAP files and provide the packets one-by-one to *PACE*, *OpenDPI*, *L7-filter*, *NDPI* and *Libprotoident*. All the flows are started and terminated based on the information from the INFO files. After the last packet of the flow is sent to the classifier, the tool obtains the classification label associated with that flow. The labels are written to the log files together with the flow identifier, which makes us later able to relate the classification results to the original flows in the database. A brief description of the DPI-tools used in this study is presented in Table 1. Although some of the evaluated tools have multiple configuration parameters, we have used in our evaluation the default configuration for most of them. A detailed description of the evaluated DPI-tools and their configurations can be found in [15].

Classification by *NBAR* required us to set up a full working environment. We used GNS3 - a graphical framework, which uses Dynamips to emulate our Cisco hardware. We emulated the 7200 platform, since only for this platform supported by GNS3 was available the newest version of Cisco IOS (version 15), which contains Flexible NetFlow. The router was configured by us to use Flexible NetFlow with *NBAR* on the created interface. Flexible NetFlow was set up to create the flows taking into account the same parameters as are used to create the flow by VBS. On the computer, we used *tcpreplay* to replay the PCAP files to the router with the maximal speed, which did not cause packet loss. At the same time, we used *nfacctd*, which is a part of PMACCT tools, to capture the Flexible NetFlow records sent by the router to the computer. The records, which contain the flow identifier (encoded as source MAC address) and the name of the application recognized by *NBAR*, were saved into text log files. This process is broadly elaborated in our technical report [15].

The Dataset. Our dataset contains 1 262 022 flows captured during 66 days, between February 25, 2013 and May 1, 2013, which account for 35.69 GB of pure packet data. The application name tag was present for 520 993 flows (41.28 % of all the flows), which account for 32.33 GB (90.59 %) of the data volume. Additionally, 14 445 flows (1.14 % of all the flows), accounting for 0.28 GB (0.78 %) of data volume, could be identified based on the HTTP *content-type* field extracted from the packets. Therefore, we were able to successfully establish the ground truth for 535 438 flows (42.43 % of all the flows), accounting for 32.61 GB (91.37 %) of data volume. The remaining flows are unlabeled due to their short lifetime (below ~1 s), which made VBS incapable to reliably establish the corresponding sockets. Only these successfully classified flows will be taken into account during the evaluation of the classifiers. However, all the flows are included in the publicly available traces. This ensures data integrity and the proper work of the classifiers, which may rely on coexistence of different flows. We isolated several application classes based on the information stored in the database (e.g., application labels, HTTP *content-type* field). The classes together with the number of flows and the data volume are shown in Table 2. We have published this labeled dataset with full packet payloads in [12]. Therefore, it can be used by the research community as a reference benchmark for the validation and comparison of network traffic classifiers.

3 Performance Comparison

This section provides a detailed insight into the classification results of different types of traffic by each of the classifiers. All these results are summarized in Table 3, where the ratio of correctly classified flows (i.e., precision or true positives), incorrectly classified flows (i.e., errors or false positives) and unclassified flows (i.e., unknowns) are respectively presented. The complete confusion matrix can be found in our technical report [15].

Regarding the classification of P2P traffic, *Edonkey* is the first application studied. Only *PACE*, and especially *Libprotoident*, can properly classify it (precision over 94 %). *NDPI* and *OpenDPI* (that use the same pattern), as well as *NBAR*, can classify almost no *Edonkey* traffic (precision below 1 %). *L7-filter* classifies 1/3 of the flows, but it also produces many false positives by classifying more than 13 % of the flows as *Skype*, *NTP*, and *finger*. The wrongly classified flows in *NDPI* were labeled as *Skype*, *RTP* and *RTCP*, and in *NBAR* as *Skype*. The classification of *BitTorrent* traffic, the second P2P application studied, is not completely achieved by any of the classifiers. *PACE* and *Libprotoident* achieve again the highest precision (over 77 %). The rest of the classifiers present severe problems to identify this type of traffic. When misclassified, the *BitTorrent* traffic is usually classified as *Skype*.

The performance of most DPI tools with more traditional applications is significantly higher. FTP traffic is usually correctly classified. Only *L7-filter* and *NBAR* present problems to label it. The false positives produced by *L7-filter* are because the traffic is classified as *SOCKS*. Table 3 also shows that all the classifiers can properly classify *DNS* traffic. Similar results are obtained for *NTP*, which almost all the classifiers can correctly classify it. However, *NBAR* completely miss the classification of this traffic. *SSH* was evaluated in its *Linux* version. Table 3 shows that *NBAR* almost classified all the flows while the rest of classifiers labeled more than 95 % of them.

Similar performance is also obtained with *RDP*, usually employed by VoIP applications, as shown in Table 3. Again, *L7-filter* and *NBAR* can not classify this application at all. The false positives for *L7-filter*, *Libprotoident*, and *NBAR* are mainly due to *Skype*, *RTMP*, and *H323*, respectively.

Unlike previous applications, the results for *NETBIOS* are quite different. Surprisingly, *NBAR* and *NDPI* are the only classifiers that correctly label *NET-BIOS* traffic. *PACE* can classify 2/3 of this traffic and *OpenDPI* only 1/4. On the other hand, the patterns from *L7-filter* and *Libprotoident* do not properly detect this traffic. The wrongly classified flows in *Libprotoident* are labeled as *RTP* and *Skype*, and in *L7-filter* as *Edonkey*, *NTP*, and *RTP*.

We also evaluated *RTMP* traffic, a common protocol used by browsers and plugins for playing *FLASH* content. It is important to note that only *Libpro-toident* has a specific pattern for *RTMP*. Because of that, we have also counted as correct the *RTMP* traffic classified as *FLASH* although that classification is not as precise as the one obtained by *Libprotoident*. *L7-filter* and *NBAR* can not classify this type of traffic. The rest of the classifiers achieve a similar precision, around 80 %. The surprising amount of false positives by *NDPI* is because some traffic is classified as *H323*. *L7-filter* errors are due to wrongly classified traffic as *Skype* and *TSP*.

Table 3 also presents the results regarding the *HTTP* protocol. All of them but *L7-filter* can properly classify most of the *HTTP* traffic. *L7-filter* labels all the traffic as *finger* or *Skype*. *NDPI* classifies some *HTTP* traffic as *iMessage_Facetime*. The amount of errors from PACE is surprising, as this tool is usually characterized by very low false positive ratio. All the wrong classifications are labeled as *Meebo* traffic. The older *Meebo* pattern available in *OpenDPI* and the newer from *NDPI* seems not to have this problem.

Most incorrect classifications for all the tools are due to patterns that easily match random traffic. This problem especially affects L7-filter and, in particular, with the patterns used to match *Skype*, *finger* and *ntp* traffic. The deactivation of those patterns would considerably decrease the false positive ratio but it would disable the classification of those applications. In [4], the authors use a tailor-made configuration and post-processing of the L7-filter output in order to minimize this overmatching problem.

3.1 Sub-classification of HTTP Traffic

Our dataset also allows the study of *HTTP* traffic at different granularity (e.g., identify different services running over *HTTP*). However, only *NDPI* can subclassify some applications at this granularity (e.g., *Youtube*, *Facebook*). Newer versions of *PACE* also provide this feature but we had no access to it for this study. Table 4 presents the results for four applications running over *HTTP* identified by *NDPI*. Unlike the rest of tools that basically classify this traffic as *HTTP*, *NDPI* can correctly give the specific label with precision higher than 97 %. Furthermore, the classification errors are caused by traffic that *NDPI* classifies as *HTTP* without providing the lower level label.

Table 3. DPI evaluation

Application	Classifier	% correct	% wrong	% uncl.	Application	Classifier	% correct	% wrong	% uncl.
Edonkey	PACE	94.80	0.02	5.18	SSH	PACE	95.57	0.00	4.43
	OpenDPI	0.45	0.00	99.55		OpenDPI	95.59	0.00	4.41
	L7-filter	34.21	13.70	52.09		L7-filter	95.71	0.00	4.29
	NDPI	0.45	6.72	92.83		NDPI	95.59	0.00	4.41
	Libprotoident	98.39	0.00	1.60		Libprotoident	95.71	0.00	4.30
	NBAR	0.38	10.81	88.81		NBAR	99.24	0.05	0.70
BitTorrent	PACE	81.44	0.01	18.54	RDP	PACE	99.04	0.02	0.94
	OpenDPI	27.23	0.00	72.77		OpenDPI	99.07	0.02	0.91
	L7-filter	42.17	8.78	49.05		L7-filter	0.00	91.21	8.79
	NDPI	56.00	0.43	43.58		NDPI	99.05	0.08	0.87
	Libprotoident	77.24	0.06	22.71		Libprotoident	98.83	0.16	1.01
	NBAR	27.44	1.49	71.07		NBAR	0.00	0.66	99.34
FTP	PACE	95.92	0.00	4.08	NETBIOS	PACE	66.66	0.08	33.26
	OpenDPI	96.15	0.00	3.85		OpenDPI	24.63	0.00	75.37
	L7-filter	6.11	93.31	0.57		L7-filter	0.00	8.45	91.55
	NDPI	95.69	0.45	3.85		NDPI	100.00	0.00	0.00
	Libprotoident	95.58	0.00	4.42		Libprotoident	0.00	5.03	94.97
	NBAR	40.59	0.00	59.41		NBAR	100.00	0.00	0.00
DNS	PACE	99.97	0.00	0.03	RTMP	PACE	80.56	0.00	19.44
	OpenDPI	99.97	0.00	0.03		OpenDPI	82.44	0.00	17.56
	L7-filter	98.95	0.13	0.92		L7-filter	0.00	24.12	75.88
	NDPI	99.88	0.09	0.03		NDPI	78.92	8.90	12.18
	Libprotoident	99.97	0.00	0.04		Libprotoident	77.28	0.47	22.25
	NBAR	99.97	0.02	0.02		NBAR	0.23	0.23	99.53
NTP	PACE	100.00	0.00	0.00	HTTP	PACE	96.16	1.85	1.99
	OpenDPI	100.00	0.00	0.00		OpenDPI	98.01	0.00	1.99
	L7-filter	99.83	0.15	0.02		L7-filter	4.31	95.67	0.02
	NDPI	100.00	0.00	0.00		NDPI	99.18	0.76	0.06
	Libprotoident	100.00	0.00	0.00		Libprotoident	98.66	0.00	1.34
	NBAR	0.40	0.00	99.60		NBAR	99.58	0.00	0.42

Table 4. HTTP sub-classification by *NDPI*

Application	% correct	% wrong	% unclassified
Google	97.28	2.72	0.00
Facebook	100.00	0.00	0.00
Youtube	98.65	0.45	0.90
Twitter	99.75	0.00	0.25

Another sub-classification that can be studied with our dataset is the *FLASH* traffic over *HTTP*. However, the classification of this application is different for each tool making its comparison very difficult. *PACE*, *OpenDPI* and *NDPI* have a specific pattern for this application. At the same time, these tools (as well as *L7-filter*) have specific patterns for video traffic, which may or may not run over *HTTP*. In addition, *NDPI* has specific labels for *Google*, *Youtube* and *Facebook* that can also carry *FLASH* traffic. *Libprotoident* and *NBAR* do not provide any pattern to classify *FLASH* traffic over *HTTP*. Table 5 shows that *NDPI* can correctly classify 99.48 % of this traffic, 25.48 % of which is classified as *Google*, *Youtube* or *Facebook*. *PACE* and *OpenDPI* can properly classify around 86 % of the traffic. The errors produced in the classification are almost always related to traffic classified as *HTTP* with the exception of *L7-filter* that classifies 86.49 % of the traffic as *finger*.

Table 5. FLASH evaluation

Classifier	% correct	% wrong	% unclassified
PACE	86.27	13.18	0.55
OpenDPI	86.34	13.15	0.51
L7-filter	0.07	99.67	0.26
NDPI	99.48	0.26	0.26
Libprotoident	0.00	98.07	1.93
NBAR	0.00	100.00	0.00

4   Discussion

This section extracts the outcomes from the results obtained during the performance comparison. Also, we discuss the limitations of our study. Table 6 presents the summary of the results from Section 3. The *Precision* (i.e., first column) is computed similarly to Section 3, but we take into account all the applications together (i.e., 100 * # correctly classified flows / # total flows). However, this metric is dependent on the distribution of the dataset. Because of that, we also compute a second metric, the *Average Precision*. This statistic is independent from the distribution and is calculated as follow:

$$Avg.\ Precision = \frac{\sum_{i=1}^{N} \frac{correctly\ classified\ i\ flows}{total\ i\ flows}}{N} \tag{1}$$

where N is the number of applications studied (i.e., $N = 10$).

As it can be seen in Table 6, *PACE* is the best classifier. Even while we were not using the last version of the software, PACE was able to properly classify 94 % of our dataset. Surprisingly for us, *Libprotoident* achieves similar results, although this tool only inspect the first four bytes of payload for each direction. On the other hand, *L7-filter* and *NBAR* perform poorly in classifying the traffic from our dataset. The more fair metric, *Avg. Precision*, presents similar results. *PACE* is still the best classifier, however, it has increased the difference by several points to the second best classifier, *Libprotoident*. Unlike before, *NDPI* is almost as precise as *Libprotoident* with this metric. *L7-filter* and *NBAR* are still the tools that present the worst performance.

Table 6. Summary

Classifier	% Precision	% Avg. Precision
PACE	94.22	91.01
OpenDPI	52.67	72.35
L7-filter	30.26	38.13
NDPI	57.91	82.48
Libprotoident	93.86	84.16
NBAR	21.79	46.72

Nonetheless, the previous conclusions are obviously tied to our dataset. Although we have tried our best to emulate the real behavior of the users, many applications, behaviors and configurations are not represented on it. Because of that, it has some limitations. In our study we have evaluated 10 well-known applications, however adding more applications as *Skype* or *Spotify* is part of our ongoing future work. The results obtained from the different classifiers are directly related to those applications. Thus, the introduction of different applications could arise different outcomes. The traffic generated for building the dataset, although has been manually and realistically created, is artificial. The backbone traffic would carry different behaviors of the applications that are not fully represented in our dataset (e.g., P2P clients running on port 80). Therefore, the performance of the tools studied could not be directly extrapolated from the current results, but it gives an idea of their precision in the evaluated set of applications. At the same time, the artificially created traffic allowed us to publish the dataset with full packet payloads.

5   Conclusions

This paper presents the first step towards validating the reliability of the accuracy of the network traffic classifiers. We have compared the performance of six tools (i.e., *PACE, OpenDPI, L7-filter, NDPI, Libprotoident*, and *NBAR*), which are usually used for the traffic classification. The results obtained in Section 3 and further discussed in Section 4 show that *PACE* is, on our dataset, the most reliable solution for traffic classification. Among the open-source tools, *NDPI* and especially *Libprotoident* present the best results. On the other hand, *NBAR* and *L7-filter* present several inaccuracies that make them not recommendable as a ground-truth generator.

In order to make the study trustworthy, we have created a dataset using VBS [13]. This tool associates the name of the process to each flow making its labeling totally reliable. The dataset of more than 500 K flows contains traffic from popular applications like *HTTP, Edonkey, BitTorrent, FTP, DNS, NTP, RDP, NETBIOS, SSH*, and *RDP*. The total amount of data properly labeled is 32.61 GB. Furthermore, and more important, we release to the research community this dataset with full payload, so it can be used as a common reference for the comparison and validation of network traffic classifiers.

As the future work, we plan to extend this work by adding new applications to the dataset (e.g., Skype, Games) and especially focus on HTTP-based applications. We also plan to introduce new tools to the study (e.g., NBAR2).

References

1. Dainotti, A., et al.: Issues and future directions in traffic classification. IEEE Network 26(1), 35–40 (2012)
2. Valenti, S., Rossi, D., Dainotti, A., Pescapè, A., Finamore, A., Mellia, M.: Reviewing Traffic Classification. In: Biersack, E., Callegari, C., Matijasevic, M. (eds.) Data Traffic Monitoring and Analysis. LNCS, vol. 7754, pp. 123–147. Springer, Heidelberg (2013)
3. Fukuda, K.: Difficulties of identifying application type in backbone traffic. In: Int. Conf. on Network and Service Management (CNSM), pp. 358–361. IEEE (2010)
4. Carela-Español, V., et al.: Analysis of the impact of sampling on NetFlow traffic classification. Computer Networks 55, 1083–1099 (2011)
5. Alcock, S., et al.: Libprotoident: Traffic Classification Using Lightweight Packet Inspection. Technical report, University of Waikato (2012)
6. Gringoli, F., et al.: Gt: picking up the truth from the ground for internet traffic. ACM SIGCOMM Computer Communication Review 39(5), 12–18 (2009)
7. Dainotti, A., et al.: Identification of traffic flows hiding behind TCP port 80. In: IEEE Int. Conf. on Communications (ICC), pp. 1–6 (2010)

8. Karagiannis, T., et al.: Transport layer identification of P2P traffic. In: 4th ACM Internet Measurement Conf. (IMC), pp. 121–134 (2004)
9. Shen, C., et al.: On detection accuracy of L7-filter and OpenDPI. In: 3rd Int. Conf. on Networking and Distributed Computing (ICNDC), pp. 119–123. IEEE (2012)
10. Alcock, S., Nelson, R.: Measuring the Accuracy of Open-Source Payload-Based Traffic Classifiers Using Popular Internet Applications. In: IEEE Workshop on Network Measurements (2013)
11. Dusi, M., et al.: Quantifying the accuracy of the ground truth associated with Internet traffic traces. Computer Networks 55(5), 1158–1167 (2011)
12. [Online]: Traffic classification at the Universitat Politècnica de Catalunya, UPC BarcelonaTech (2013),
    http://monitoring.ccaba.upc.edu/traffic_classification
13. Bujlow, T., et al.: Volunteer-Based System for classification of traffic in computer networks. In: 19th Telecommunications Forum TELFOR, pp. 210–213. IEEE (2011)
14. [Online]: Volunteer-Based System for Research on the Internet (2012),
    http://vbsi.sourceforge.net/
15. Bujlow, T., et al.: Comparison of Deep Packet Inspection (DPI) Tools for Traffic Classification. Technical report, UPC BarcelonaTech (2013)

Detecting Intentional Packet Drops
on the Internet via TCP/IP Side Channels

Roya Ensafi, Jeffrey Knockel, Geoffrey Alexander, and Jedidiah R. Crandall

Department of Computer Science, University of New Mexico, USA
{royaen,jeffk,alexandg,crandall}@cs.unm.edu

Abstract. We describe a method for remotely detecting intentional packet drops on the Internet *via* side channel inferences. That is, given two arbitrary IP addresses on the Internet that meet some simple requirements, our proposed technique can discover packet drops (*e.g.*, due to censorship) between the two remote machines, as well as infer in which direction the packet drops are occurring. The only major requirements for our approach are a client with a global IP Identifier (IPID) and a target server with an open port. We require no special access to the client or server. Our method is robust to noise because we apply intervention analysis based on an autoregressive-moving-average (ARMA) model. In a measurement study using our method featuring clients from multiple continents, we observed that, of all measured client connections to Tor directory servers that were censored, 98% of those were from China, and only 0.63% of measured client connections from China to Tor directory servers were not censored. This is congruent with current understandings about global Internet censorship, leading us to conclude that our method is effective.

1   Introduction

Tools for discovering intentional packet drops are important for a variety of applications, such as discovering the blocking of Tor by ISPs or nation states [1]. However, existing tools have a severe limitation: they can only measure when packets are dropped in between the measurement machine and an arbitrary remote host. The research question we address in this paper is: can we detect drops between two hosts without controlling either of them and without sharing the path between them? Effectively, by using idle scans our method can turn approximately 1% of the total IP address space into conscripted measurement machines that can be used as vantage points to measure IP-address-based censorship, without actually gaining access to those machines.

Antirez [2] proposed the first type of idle scan, which we call an IPID idle port scan. In this type of idle scan an "attacker" (which we will refer to as the *measurement machine* in our work) aims to determine if a specific port is open or closed on a "victim" machine (which we will refer to as the *server*) without using the attacker's own return IP address. The attacker finds a "zombie" (*client* in this paper) that has a global IP identifier (IPID) and is completely idle. In this

M. Faloutsos and A. Kuzmanovic (Eds.): PAM 2014, LNCS 8362, pp. 109–118, 2014.

paper, we say that a machine has a global IPID when it sends TCP RST packets with a globally incrementing IPID that is shared by all destination hosts. This is in contrast to machines that use randomized IPIDs or IPIDs that increment per-host. The attacker repeatedly sends TCP SYN packets to the victim using the return IP address of the zombie, while simultaneously eliciting RST packets from the zombie by sending the zombie SYN/ACKs with the attacker's own return IP address. If the victim port that SYN packets are being sent to is open, the attacker will observe many skips in the IPIDs from the zombie. Nmap [3] has built-in support for the IPID idle scan, but often fails for Internet hosts because of noise in the IPID that is due to the zombie sending packets to other hosts. Our method described in this paper is resistant to noise, and can discover packet drops in either direction (and determine which direction). Nmap cannot detect the case of packets being dropped from client to server based on destination IP address, which our results demonstrate is a very important case.

Two other types of idle scans were presented by Ensafi *et al.* [4], including one that exploits the state of the SYN backlog as a side channel. Our method is based on a new idle scan technique that can be viewed as a hybrid of the IPID idle scan and Ensafi *et al.*'s SYN backlog idle scan. Whereas Ensafi *et al.*'s SYN backlog idle scan required filling the SYN backlog and therefore causing denial-of-service, our technique uses a low packet rate that does not fill the SYN backlog and is non-intrusive. The basic insight that makes this possible is that information about the server's SYN backlog state is entangled with information about the client's IPID field. Thus, we can perform both types of idle scans (IPID and SYN backlog) to detect drops in both directions, and our technique overcomes the limitations of both by exploiting the entanglement of information in the IPID and treating it as a linear intervention problem to handle noise characteristic of the real Internet.

This research has several major contributions:

- A non-intrusive method for detecting intentional packet drops between two IP addresses on the Internet where neither is a measurement machine.
- An Internet measurement study that shows the efficacy of the method.
- A model of IPID noise based on an autoregressive-moving-average (ARMA) model that is robust to autocorrelated noise.

Source code and data are available upon request, and a web demonstration version of the hybrid idle scan is at `http://spookyscan.cs.unm.edu`. The types of measurements we describe in this paper raise ethical concerns because the measurements can cause the appearance of connection attempts between arbitrary clients and servers. In China there is no evidence of the owners of Internet hosts being persecuted for attempts to connect to the Tor network, thus our measurements in this paper are safe. However, we caution against performing similar measurements in other countries or contexts without first evaluating the risks and ethical issues. More discussion of ethical issues, additional details about the ARMA model, and other information not included here due to space limitations are available in the extended version of this paper [5].

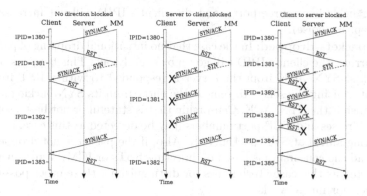

Fig. 1. Three different cases that our method can detect. MM is the measurement machine.

The rest of the paper is structured as follows: After describing the implementation of our method in Section 2, we present our experimental methodology for the measurement study in Section 3 and the ARMA model in Section 4. Results from the measurement study are in Section 5, followed by a discussion of related work in Section 6 and then the conclusion.

2   Implementation

In order to determine the direction in which packets are being blocked, our method is based on information flow through both the IPID of the client and the SYN backlog state of the server, as shown in Figure 1. Our implementation queries the IPID of the client (by sending SYN/ACKs from the measurement machine and receiving RST responses) to create a time series to compare a base case to a period of time when the server is sending SYN/ACKs to the client (because of our forged SYNs). We assume that the client has global IPIDs and the server has an open port.

Global IPIDs were explained in Section 1. The SYN backlog is a buffer that stores information about half-open connections where a SYN has been received and a SYN/ACK sent but no ACK reply to the SYN/ACK has been received. Half-open connections remain in the SYN backlog until the connection is completed with an ACK, aborted by a RST or ICMP error, or the half-open connection times out (typically between 30 and 180 seconds). The SYN/ACK is retransmitted some fixed number of times that varies by operating system and version, typically three to six SYN/ACKs in total. This SYN backlog behavior on the server, when combined with the global IPID behavior of the client, enables us to distinguish three different cases (plus an error case):

– **Server-to-client-dropped:** In this case SYN/ACKs are dropped in transit from the server to the client based on the return IP address (and possibly other fields like source port), and the client's IPID will not increase at all (except for noise).

- **No-packets-dropped:** In the case that no intentional dropping of packets is occurring, the client's IPID will go up by exactly one. This happens because the first SYN/ACK from the server is responded to with a RST from the client, causing the server to remove the entry from its SYN backlog and not retransmit the SYN/ACK. Censorship that is stateful or not based solely on IP addresses and TCP port numbers may be detected as this case, including filtering aimed at SYN packets only. Also, if the packet is not dropped, but instead the censorship is based on injecting RSTs or ICMP errors, it will be detected as this case. Techniques for distinguishing these other possibilities are left for future work.

- **Client-to-server-dropped:** In this case RST responses from the client to the server are dropped in transit because of their destination IP address (which is the server). When this happens the server will continue to retransmit SYN/ACKs and the client's IPID will go up by the total number of transmitted SYN/ACKs including retransmissions (typically three to six). This may indicate the simplest method for blacklisting an IP address: null routing.

- **Error:** In this case networking errors occur during the experiment, the IPID is found to not be global throughout the experiment, a model is fit to the data but does not match any of the three non-error cases above, the data is too noisy and intervention analysis fails because we are not able to fit a model to the data, and/or other errors.

Noise due to packet loss and delay or the client's communications with other machines may be autocorrelated. The autocorrelation comes from the fact that the sources of noise, which include traffic from a client that is not idle, packet loss, packet reordering, and packet delay, are not memoryless processes and often happen in spurts. The accepted method for performing linear intervention analysis on time series data with autocorrelated noise is ARMA modeling, which we describe in Section 4.

3   Experimental Setup

All measurement machines were Linux machines connected to a research network with no packet filtering. Specifically, this network has no stateful firewall or egress filtering for return IP addresses.

One measurement machine was dedicated to developing a pool of both client and server IP addresses that have the right properties for use in measurements. Clients were chosen by horizontally scanning China and other countries for machines with global IPIDs, then continually checking them for a 24-hour period to cull out IP addresses that frequently changed global IPID behavior (*e.g.*, because of DHCP), went down, or were too noisy. A machine is considered to have a global IPID if its IPID as we measure it by sending SYN/ACKs from alternating source IP addresses and receiving RSTs never incrementing outside the ranges $[-40, 0)$ or $(0, 1000]$ per second when probed from two different IP addresses. This range allows for non-idle clients, packet loss, and packet reordering. It is possible to build the time series in different ways where negative IPID differences are never observed, but in this study our time series was the differences in the client's IPIDs in the order in which they arrived at the measurement machine. Our range of $[-40, 0)$ or $(0, 1000]$ is based on our observations of noise typical of the real Internet. The IPID going up by 0 is a degenerate case and means the IPID is not global.

Servers were chosen from three groups: Tor directory authorities, Tor bridges, and web servers. The ten Tor directory authorities were obtained from the Tor source code and the same ten IPs were tested for every day of data. Three Tor bridges were collected daily both through email and the web. Every day seven web servers were chosen randomly from the top 1000 websites on the Alexa Top 1,000,000 list [6]. All web server IPs were checked to make sure that they stood up for at least 24 hours before being selected for measurement. Furthermore, we checked that the client and server were both up and behaving as assumed between every experiment (*i.e.*, every five minutes).

A round of experiments was a 24-hour process in which measurements were carried out on the two measurement machines. Each 24-hour period had 22 hours of experiments and 2 hours of down time for data synchronization. For each measurement period on each of the two machines performing direct measurements, ten server machines and ten client machines from the above process were chosen for geographic diversity: 5 from China, 2 from countries in Asia that were not China, 1 from Europe, and 2 from North America. IP addresses were never reused except for the Tor directory authorities, so that every 24-hour period was testing a set of 20 new clients, 10 new servers, and the 10 directory authorities.

For each of the twenty clients and twenty servers geographical information provided by MaxMind was saved. MaxMind claims an accuracy of 99.8% for identifying the country an IP address is in [7]. For each of the twenty server machines, a series of SYN packets was used to test and save its SYN/ACK retransmission behavior for the analysis in Section 4.

Every hour, each of our two main measurement machines created ten threads. Each thread corresponded to one client machine. Each thread tested each of the ten server IP addresses sequentially using our idle scan based on the client's IPID. No forged SYNs were sent to the server during the first 100 seconds of a test, and forged SYNs with the return IP address of the client were sent to the server at a rate of 5 per second for the second 100-second period. Then forged RST packets were sent to the server to clear the SYN backlog and prevent interference between sequential experiments. A timeout period of sixty seconds was observed before the next test in the sequence was started, to allow all other state to be cleared. Each experiment lasted for less than five minutes, so that ten could be completed in an hour. Every client and server was involved in only one experiment at a time. Each client/server pair was tested once per hour throughout the 24-hour period, for replication and also to minimize the effects of diurnal patterns. Source and destination ports for all packets were carefully chosen and matched to minimize assumptions about what destination ports the client responds on.

4   Analysis

In this section we give an overview of our intervention analysis based on ARMA modeling. More details are available in the extended version of the paper [5].

We model each time series $y_1, \ldots, y_n$ as a *linear regression with ARMA errors*, a combination of an autoregressive-moving-average (ARMA) model with external linear regressors. An ARMA(p, q) model combines an AR model of order p and an MA model of order q. We use a linear regression with ARMA errors to model our time series data. This specifies that every element in a time series can be written as a constant plus the linear combination of regressors $x_1, \ldots, x_r$ with an ARMA-modeled error term, e_t:

$$y_t = c + \sum_{i=1}^{r} \beta_i x_{it} + e_t, \qquad e_t = z_t + \sum_{i=1}^{p} \phi_i e_{t-i} + \sum_{i=1}^{q} \theta_i z_{t-i}$$

where z_t is a white noise series and ϕ_i, θ_i, and β_i are ARMA model parameters to be fitted. We use the regressors x_i for *intervention analysis*, i.e., for analyzing our experimental effect on the time series at a specific time.

For each experiment, we pick regressors according to which times the server (re)transmits SYN/ACK's in response to SYN's. For a server that (re)transmits r SYN/ACK's in response to each SYN, we have r regressors. We call time t_1 the time of the first transmission in response to the first of our forged SYN's, and we call t_{i+1} the time the server would send the ith retransmission in response to that SYN. Then we define regressor x_i as the indicator variable

$$x_{ij} = \begin{cases} 1 & \text{if } t_i \leq j \text{ and either } j < t_{i+1} \text{ or } i = r \\ 0 & \text{otherwise} \end{cases}$$

In other words, x_1 is zeros until the time the server transmits the first SYN/ACK then ones until the server begins retransmitting SYN/ACK's. The remaining x_i are zeros until the time the server would begin retransmitting its ith SYN/ACK then ones until if/when the $(i+1)$th SYN/ACK's would begin being retransmitted. This definition allows us to model any of the possible level shifts in any case of packet drop as a linear combination of all x_i. See Figure 2 for an illustration.

For intervention analysis, we use hypothesis testing over a value β_r, which represents the difference in IPID differences between when we do or do not send forged SYN packets to the server. Then we determine the case by a series of one-sided hypothesis tests performed with significance $\alpha = 0.01$ according to the following breakdown, where k_1 and k_2' are thresholds between cases:

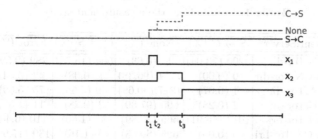

Fig. 2. For a server that retransmits $r - 1$ SYN/ACK's, each case can be expressed as the linear combination of regressors $x_1, \ldots, x_r$; shown is when $r = 3$ with SYN/ACK transmissions responding to the first forged SYN occurring at t_1, t_2, and t_3

- **Server-to-client-dropped** if we reject the null hypothesis that $\beta_r \geq k_1$.
- **No-packets-dropped** if we reject the null hypotheses that $\beta_r \leq k_1$ and that $\beta_r \geq k_2'$.
- **Client-to-server-dropped** if we reject the null hypothesis that $\beta_r \leq k_2'$.
- **Error** if none of the above cases can be determined.

For details about the linear regression step, removal of outliers, and how we choose the thresholds, see the extended version of the paper [5].

5   Results

Table 1 shows results from 5 days of data collection, where $S \to C$ is **Server-to-client-dropped**, *None* is **No-packets-dropped**, $C \to S$ is **Client-to-server-dropped**, and *Error* is **Error**. *CN* is China, *Asia-CN* is other Asian countries, *EU* is Europe, and *NA* is North America. For server types, *Tor-dir* is a Tor directory authority, *Tor-bri* is a Tor bridge, and *Web* is a web server.

Our expectation would be to observe **Server-to-client-dropped** for clients in China and Tor servers because of Winter and Lindskog's observation that the SYN/ACKs are statelessly dropped by the "Great Firewall of China" (GFW) based on source IP address and port [8]. We would expect to see **No-packets-dropped** for most web servers from clients in China, unless they host popular websites that happen to be censored in China. Similarly, in the expected case we should observe **No-packets-dropped** for clients outside of China, regardless of server type. We expect a few exceptions, because censorship happens outside of China and because the GFW is not always 100% effective. In particular, Tor bridges are not blocked until the GFW operators learn about them, and some routes might not have filtering in place. Our results are congruent with all of these expectations.

In 5.9% of the client/server pairs we tested, multiple cases were observed in the same day. In some cases it appears that noise caused the wrong case to be detected, but other cases may be attributable to routes changing throughout the day [9]. That the data is largely congruent with our expectations demonstrates

Table 1. Results from the measurement study

Client,Server	$S \rightarrow C$ (%)	None (%)	$C \rightarrow S$ (%)	Error (%)
CN,Tor-dir	2200 (73.04)	19 (0.63)	504 (16.73)	289 (9.59)
Asia-CN,Tor-dir	0 (0.00)	1171 (96.38)	1 (0.08)	43 (3.54)
NA,Tor-dir	1 (0.07)	1217 (90.69)	49 (3.65)	75 (5.59)
EU,Tor-dir	2 (0.28)	695 (97.89)	2 (0.28)	11 (1.55)
CN,Tor-bri	1012 (58.91)	565 (32.89)	31 (1.80)	110 (6.40)
Asia-CN,Tor-bri	0 (0.00)	626 (80.88)	9 (1.16)	139 (17.96)
NA,Tor-bri	0 (0.00)	657 (78.21)	30 (3.57)	153 (18.21)
EU,Tor-bri	0 (0.00)	313 (78.25)	9 (2.25)	78 (19.50)
CN,Web	28 (2.15)	995 (76.30)	36 (2.76)	245 (18.79)
Asia-CN,Web	1 (0.17)	569 (97.43)	1 (0.17)	13 (2.23)
NA,Web	0 (0.00)	606 (93.37)	0 (0.00)	43 (6.63)
EU,Web	0 (0.00)	305 (90.24)	0 (0.00)	33 (9.76)
All Web	29 (1.01)	2475 (86.09)	37 (1.29)	334 (11.62)
All Tor-bri	1012 (27.12)	2161 (57.90)	79 (2.12)	480 (12.86)
All Tor-dir	2203 (35.09)	3102 (49.40)	556 (8.85)	418 (6.66)

the efficacy of the approach, and some of the data points that lie outside our expectations have patterns that suggest that a real effect is being measured, rather than an error. For example, of the 28 data points where web servers were blocked from the server to the client in China, 20 of those data points are the same client/server pair.

38% of the data we collected does not appear in Table 1 because it did not pass liveness tests. Every 5-minute data point has three associated liveness tests. If a server sends fewer than 2.5 SYN/ACKs in response to SYNs from the measurement machine, a client responds to less than $\frac{3}{5}$ of our SYN/ACKs, or a measurement machine sending thread becomes unresponsive, that 5-minute data point is discarded.

Two out of the ten Tor directory authorities never retransmitted enough SYN/ACKs to be included in our data. Of the remaining eight, two more account for 98.8% of the data points showing blocking from client to server. These same two directory authorities also account for 72.7% of the **Error** cases for directory authorities tested from clients in China, and the case of packets being dropped from server to client (the expected case for China and the case of the majority of our results) was never observed for these two directory authorities.

When Winter and Lindskog [8] measured Tor reachability from a virtual private server in China, there were eight directory authorities at that time. One of the eight was completely accessible, and the other seven were completely blocked in the IP layer by destination IP (*i.e.*, **Client-to-server**). In our results, six out of ten are at least blocked **Server-to-client** and two out of ten are only blocked **Client-to-server** (two had all results discarded). Winter and Lindskog also observed that Tor relays were accessible 1.6% of the time, and we observed that directory authorities were accessible 0.63% of the time. Our results have geographic diversity and their results can serve as a ground truth because they tested from within China. In both studies the same special treatment of directory authorities compared to relays or bridges was observed, as well as a small percentage of cases where filtering that should have occurred did not.

To evaluate the assumption that clients with a global IPID are easy to find in a range of IP addresses that we desire to measure from, take China as an example. On average, 10% of the IP addresses in China responded to our probes so that we could observe their IPID, and of those 13% were global. So, roughly 1% of the IP address space of China can be used as clients for measurements with our method, enabling experiments with excellent geographic and topological diversity.

6 Related Work

Related work directly related to idle scans [2,3,4] was discussed in Section 1. Other advanced methods for inferring remote information about networks have been proposed. Qian *et al.* [10] demonstrate that firewall behavior with respect to sequence numbers can be used to infer sequence numbers and perform off-path TCP/IP connection hijacking. Chen *et al.* [11] use the IPID field to perform advanced inferences about the amount of internal traffic generated by a server, the number of servers in a load-balanced setting, and one-way delays. Morbitzer [12] explores idle scans in IPv6.

iPlane [13] sends packets from PlanetLab nodes to carefully chosen hosts, and then compounds loss on specific routes to estimate the packet loss between arbitrary endpoints without access to those endpoints. This does not detect IP-address-specific packet drops. Our technique, in contrast, can be used to detect intentional drops of packets based on IP address and requires no commonalities between the measurement machine's routes to the server or client and the routes between the server and client. Queen [14] utilizes recursive DNS queries to measure the packet loss between a pair of DNS servers, and extrapolates from this to estimate the packet loss rate between arbitrary hosts.

7 Conclusion

We have presented a method for detecting intentional packet drops (*e.g.*, due to censorship) between two almost arbitrary hosts on the Internet, assuming the client has a globally incrementing IPID and the server has an open port. Our method can determine which direction packets are being dropped in, and is resistant to noise due to our use of an ARMA model for intervention analysis. Our measurement results are congruent with current understandings about global Internet censorship, demonstrating the efficacy of the method.

Acknowledgments. We would like to thank the anonymous PAM 2014 reviewers and our shepherd, Jelena Mirkovic, as well as Terran Lane, Patrick Bridges,

Michalis Faloutsos, Stefan Savage, and Vern Paxson for helpful feedback on this work. This material is based upon work supported by the National Science Foundation under Grant Nos. #0844880, #1017602, #0905177, and #1314297.

References

1. arma: Research problem: Five ways to test bridge reachability. Tor Blog (December 1, 2011), https://blog.torproject.org/blog/research-problem-five-ways-test-bridge-reachability
2. Antirez: new tcp scan method. Posted to the bugtraq mailing list (December 18, 1998)
3. Lyon, G.: Nmap Network Scanning: The Official Nmap Project Guide to Network Discovery and Security Scanning. Insecure.Org LLC, Sunnyvale, CA, USA (2009)
4. Ensafi, R., Park, J.C., Kapur, D., Crandall, J.R.: Idle port scanning and non-interference analysis of network protocol stacks using model checking. In: Proceedings of the 19th USENIX Security Symposium, USENIX Security 2010. USENIX Association (2010)
5. Ensafi, R., Knockel, J., Alexander, G., Crandall, J.R.: Detecting intentional packet drops on the Internet via TCP/IP side channels: Extended version CoRR abs/1312.5739 (2013), http://arxiv.org/abs/1312.5739
6. Alexa: Alexa top 1,000,000 sites, http://www.alexa.com/topsites
7. MaxMind: How accurate are your GeoIP databases? http://www.maxmind.com/en/faq#accurate
8. Winter, P., Lindskog, S.: How the Great Firewall of China is Blocking Tor. In: Free and Open Communications on the Internet. USENIX Association (2012)
9. Paxson, V.: End-to-end internet packet dynamics. SIGCOMM Comput. Commun. Rev. 27(4), 139–152 (1997)
10. Qian, Z., Mao, Z.M.: Off-path TCP sequence number inference attack - how firewall middleboxes reduce security. In: Proceedings of the 2012 IEEE Symposium on Security and Privacy, SP 2012, pp. 347–361. IEEE Computer Society, Washington, DC (2012)
11. Chen, W., Huang, Y., Ribeiro, B.F., Suh, K., Zhang, H., de Souza e Silva, E., Kurose, J., Towsley, D.: Exploiting the IPID field to infer network path and end-system characteristics. In: Dovrolis, C. (ed.) PAM 2005. LNCS, vol. 3431, pp. 108–120. Springer, Heidelberg (2005)
12. Morbitzer, M.: TCP Idle Scans in IPv6. Master's thesis, Radboud University Nijmegen, The Netherlands (2013)
13. Madhyastha, H.V., Isdal, T., Piatek, M., Dixon, C., Anderson, T., Krishnamurthy, A., Venkataramani, A.: iPlane: an information plane for distributed services. In: Proceedings of the 7th Symposium on Operating Systems Design and Implementation, OSDI 2006, pp. 367–380. USENIX Association, Berkeley (2006)
14. Wang, Y.A., Huang, C., Li, J., Ross, K.W.: Queen: Estimating packet loss rate between arbitrary internet hosts. In: Moon, S.B., Teixeira, R., Uhlig, S. (eds.) PAM 2009. LNCS, vol. 5448, pp. 57–66. Springer, Heidelberg (2009)

The Need for End-to-End Evaluation
of Cloud Availability

Zi Hu[1,2], Liang Zhu[1,2], Calvin Ardi[1,2], Ethan Katz-Bassett[1],
Harsha V. Madhyastha[3], John Heidemann[1,2], and Minlan Yu[1]

[1] USC/CS Dept.
[2] USC/ISI
[3] U. of California, Riverside

Abstract. People's computing lives are moving into the cloud, making
understanding cloud availability increasingly critical. Prior studies of Internet outages have used ICMP-based pings and traceroutes. While these
studies can detect network availability, we show that they can be inaccurate at estimating *cloud* availability. Without care, ICMP probes can
underestimate availability because ICMP is not as robust as application-
level measurements such as HTTP. They can *overestimate* availability
if they measure reachability of the cloud's edge, missing failures in the
cloud's back-end. We develop methodologies sensitive to five "nines" of
reliability, and then we compare ICMP and end-to-end measurements
for both cloud VM and storage services. We show case studies where one
fails and the other succeeds, and our results highlight the importance
of application-level retries to reach high precision. When possible, we
recommend end-to-end measurement with application-level protocols to
evaluate the availability of cloud services.

1 Introduction

Cloud computing is a distributed computing paradigm that allows users to easily
access and configure remote computing resources in a scalable manner. As the
cloud grows in importance, it will host more applications and services from the
small (such as new and developing web applications) to the large (Amazon,
Netflix, etc.).

As we depend on them more and more, services that run in the cloud need to
be highly available. Despite this need and news reports highlighting major cloud
outages [17], there have been few *systematic*, third party studies of how reliable
the cloud actually is. While recent systems might use one [25] or multiple [2]
cloud providers to improve reliability, there is a poor understanding of reliable
methods to externally and empirically measure cloud reliability.

Many general network availability and measurement studies use ICMP-based
methodologies [14,15,12,23,10], sometimes focusing on routing problems [15] or
outages in edge networks [12,23]. Studies likely use ICMP because more routers
respond to it than to other types of probes [18,19] and because ICMP probes are
less likely to elicit complaints [24,18]. However, distrust of ICMP in the network

M. Faloutsos and A. Kuzmanovic (Eds.): PAM 2014, LNCS 8362, pp. 119–130, 2014.

Table 1. Datasets used in this paper

start	duration (days)	target service (provider)		sources (VPs)	method tries/interval
2013-03-11	+33	VM	(Amazon)	23	3× / 10 min.
2013-03-11	+33	storage	(Amazon, Google, Microsoft)	23	3× / 10 min.
2013-06-18	+17	VM	(Amazon)	54	9× / 11 min.
2013-06-18	+75	storage	(Amazon, Google, Microsoft)	54	9× / 11 min.

operator community [1] calls into question the accuracy and reliability of using only ICMP to measuring availability. While effective for network measurements, ICMP is not perfect, and care must be taken to consider filtering, rate limiting, and depreferential service.

The contribution of this paper is to develop and compare mechanisms to measure cloud reliability. We show that ICMP-based measurements are inaccurate at measuring cloud availability and that *end-to-end measurements* are *necessary* to establish cloud availability.

We first compare ICMP and HTTP to measure cloud reliability at the network and application levels, and then apply them to several cloud VM and storage services. We evaluate the effect of retries and show that ICMP has a higher loss rate than random packet loss alone predicts (Section 3). While ICMP and HTTP nearly always agree, they sometimes disagree. ICMP occasionally experiences a period of loss from some vantage points and thus will *overestimate* cloud outages—a weakness of the methodology. Less frequently, we see that HTTP probing shows outages that last for extended periods from some vantage points; ICMP would *underestimate* these outages because of its failure to reach the provided service. We conclude that, although application-level methods such as HTTP probing incur the cost of provisioning and accessing cloud resources, they are necessary to accurately assess cloud reliability.

2   Methodology

We use two methods to study availability: ICMP probes at the network level, and end-to-end probes with HTTP at the application level. We target both cloud VMs and storage services of three providers. Our work results in four datasets (Table 1), all available on request.

2.1   Outage Causes

We measure outages in *cloud services* by taking observations from many *vantage points* (VPs). Section 2.4 details our VP selection and infrastructure. To understand what these measurements tell us, we must consider potential sources of failure that can occur from the VP to the cloud. These problems may occur near the VP, in the network, near the cloud provider, at the cloud front-end, or inside the cloud infrastructure.

We see several possible failures: (1) DNS lookup failures; (2) routing problems, either near the VP, in the network, or at the provider; (3) random packet loss in the network; (4) rate limiting, either near the VP, in the network, or at the provider; and (5) service outages inside the cloud infrastructure.

While all of these problems can interfere with use of the cloud, some, such as packet loss, are commonplace and the end user is responsible to recover from them. Others affect some measurements differently. Our goal is to understand how the choice of measurement methodologies emphasizes different failures.

2.2 Outage Detection at the Network and Application Level

We measure cloud status every 10 or 11 minutes (see Table 1), sending ICMP and HTTP probes with retries. We record the results from many vantage points. We consider the overall response to be positive if the initial probe or any of the retries succeeds.

For network-level tests, we send an ICMP echo request, considering only positive replies as successful, and lack of a reply or any error code as negative. For end-to-end testing, we retrieve a short file over HTTP with `curl`. A positive response is a HTTP status code of 200 OK; any other HTTP status code is a negative response. We record curl error codes to distinguish some failure cases.

In both cases, if the initial request fails, we try two and eight additional times for the datasets that begin on 2013-03-11 and 2013-06-18, respectively. We then record the result as I or $\bar{\text{I}}$ for ICMP success or failure, and H or $\bar{\text{H}}$ for HTTP. In the 2013-03-11 datasets, we do not do ICMP retries unless HTTP probes fail, in which case we then perform ICMP retries in conjunction with HTTP retries.

To diagnose problems, we observe the probe at the service itself (when possible), and we record ICMP and TCP traceroutes between the VP and service.

Since routing outages near the vantage point will skew our observations, we calibrate our measurements by probing two *control sites* at USC/ISI and University of Washington. We probe these sites with the same method as probing the cloud. We discard cloud measurements when either of these control sites is unavailable.

2.3 Targets: Cloud Storage and VMs

We probe two cloud targets: virtual machines (VMs) and online storage.

Virtual Machines: We test VMs at Amazon only. Google's VM service is not yet public, and Microsoft VMs filter inbound and outbound ICMP traffic.

For Amazon VMs, we instantiate a `micro` VM on Amazon's Elastic Compute Cloud (EC2) running Ubuntu 12.04 in all eight regions (May 2013). We install `lighttpd` HTTP daemon and serve static, 1 kB files. We modify the firewall on each VM to allow all traffic. Each VM is given a public IP address. We probe this IP address directly. We expect both ICMP and HTTP probes to reach our VM at the kernel and application-level.

Storage: We test storage on three providers: Amazon Simple Storage Service (S3), Microsoft Azure, and Google Cloud Storage. Each provider exports an

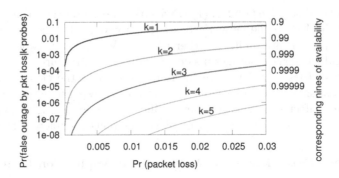

Fig. 1. Probability of false positive caused by random packet loss

HTTP-based storage abstraction. We store 1 kB files on all available regions in each provider.

For ICMP probes to storage, we ping the hostname in the URL of the stored object. We expect that this probe contacts only the front-end for the service. HTTP probes retrieve data from the storage back-end. Providers do not, in general, provide details about their back-end storage architecture, and we expect data to be replicated in each datacenter and often across datacenters. HTTP, however, is an end-to-end test for storage.

2.4 Sources: Vantage Points

We probe each of our targets from *vantage points* in PlanetLab [5], using 23 starting 2013-03-11 and 54 starting 2013-06-18. We limit the number of VPs to reduce cloud costs, and select them from universities around the world. We expect PlanetLab nodes to be well connected, allowing us to focus on cloud availability. We follow best practices in taking measurements from PlanetLab [24].

3 Evaluating the Need for Retries

A range of possible root causes can explain an outage (Section 2.1). To understand what measurement says about the cloud, we must first rule out mundane causes like packet loss.

While packet loss is rare, cloud outages are much rarer, so random packet loss will dominate careless observations. We next show that ICMP requires at least 5 retries, and even HTTP benefits from application-level retries in addition to kernel-level TCP retransmissions.

3.1 A Simple Analytic Model

Packet loss in the network can be correlated (burst losses due to congestion, filtering) and random (queue overflow over medium timescales). We limit distortion from congestive loss by spacing probes 2 s apart, avoiding most short-term

Pr(first try fails)		
Target	ICMP	HTTP
Amazon/VM	.00585	.00232
Amazon/storage	.00574	.00435
Google/storage	.00631	.00217

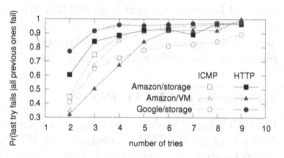

Fig. 2. Comparing loss and reties for each target and method. Left: table of probability *first* try fails. Right: conditional probability kth retry fails, given failure of prior tries. Dataset: VMs (2013-06-18+17), storage (2013-06-18+75).

outages [22,9]. Our probe rate (a few packets per second) is low enough to avoid rate limiting, although, in Section 4.1, we see some cases where *all* packets are dropped.

Having ruled out most sources of correlated loss, we next evaluate random loss. We first establish an analytic model of packet loss, assuming a fixed loss rate that affects packets independently. We then compare that to our experimental observations.

The curved lines in Figure 1 evaluate the probability of falsely inferring an outage caused by random packet loss, as a function of packet loss rate (the x-axis). We assume k tries for each probe and declare the service down when all tries fail. For packet loss p, we model loss of the request or response:

$$\Pr\left(\text{outage} \mid k \text{ probes}\right) = (p + (1 - p)p)^k \qquad (1)$$

Without retries ($k = 1$), the false outage rate approximates the loss rate. Since wide area packet loss can be around 1%, *measurement without retries will show false outages and skew estimates of cloud reliability.* Fortunately, if we assume packet loss is independent, then a few retries drive the false outage rate well below typical cloud outage rates. For example, with three tries and 1% packet loss, probe loss will be around 10^{-5}, or five nines of availability. If we assume network loss rates peak at a few percent, 4–6 tries may be appropriate. Our data starting 2013-06-18 uses 9 retries to rule out random loss.

3.2   ICMP Measurements

We next compare our model against experimental results for ICMP. The dotted lines in Figure 2 show the probability the kth try fails if all previous $k - 1$ tries failed. We evaluate this by considering the first k tries from each observation.

With ICMP, we see that retries help. An initial loss is followed by a second loss only 35-45% of the time, so 55–65% of the time the second try succeeds, suggesting that the first try was random loss. This effect diminishes with more retries, generally plateauing around 5 or 6 retries. When we compare long-term observed loss rates to short-term ICMP retries, we see that losses are generally *more* correlated than predicted by our analytic model. That is, it usually takes more retries to recover from an initial loss than are predicted, but, with enough retries, we often recover from an initial loss.

3.3 Retries and HTTP Probes

For HTTP-based probing, we retry at the application level, but the kernel also does retries for the TCP connection. Our HTTP client (curl) has a 10 s application timeout. The OS (Linux-2.6.32) does 3 SYN transmissions in this time, providing 2 network-level retries "for free" for each application retry.

We see this benefit in the Figure 2's left table, where single-try HTTP losses rates are much lower than ICMP. Kernel-level retries help even with application retries, as seen in Figure 2's right graph where the basic HTTP failure rate for Amazon/storage and Google/storage is half that of ICMP. However, even HTTP benefits from multiple application-level retries before the conditional benefit of additional tries plateaus. We recommend 6 application-level tries even for HTTP probes.

Application-level probes show even higher levels of conditional failure than network-level, with 50% of second HTTP attempts failing on average, presumably because of the additional kernel-level retries. However, this result means that 50% of second attempts *succeed*—application-level failures are sometimes transient. We thus recommend retries even for end-to-end tests.

4 Comparing Network and Application-Level Probing

We next compare network- and application-level probes to judge cloud availability. We use our control sites to rule out problems near vantage points, and we use sufficient retries to avoid effects of random packet loss and transient network issue in the middle, leaving outages at or near the cloud as the primary problem. Cloud services are made up of Internet-facing front-ends with sophisticated back-end clusters. In some cases, ICMP may be handled by the front-ends, while HTTP's end-to-end tests reach into the back-end. Our goal is to compare this difference. While the protocols almost always agree, there are many small disagreements. We next show several causes of disagreement through representative examples.

4.1 Comparing ICMP and HTTP Probing

We first compare ICMP and HTTP probing, showing representative examples of several causes of disagreement. These results show the need for end-to-end measurement with application-level protocols.

Method Agreement: Figure 3 shows the percent of disagreement between ICMP and HTTP over 17 days. Both approaches give the same result in the vast majority of measurement rounds. They disagree in at most 3% of rounds

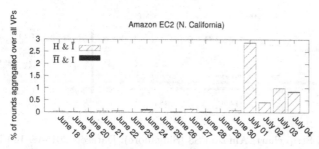

Fig. 3. Quantifying disagreements between HTTP and ICMP probes. This includes either HTTP success and ICMP failure (red striped bar) or HTTP failure and ICMP success (blue bar). Dataset: 2013-06-18+17.

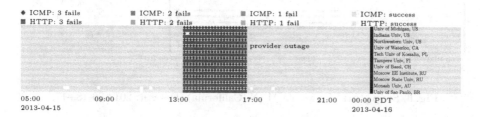

Fig. 4. Strip chart: Amazon VM (Singapore). Dataset: 2013-03-11+33.

in a given day, and, on most days, they disagree in 0.5% or less of the rounds. The high agreement is because the monitored service is almost always up, and both methods detect it as such. On three days (June 23, 25, 29), we see complete agreement (no outages). We also see that both methods report outages on some days (for example, June 18 and 24).

To illustrate the details of an outage, Figure 4 shows a *strip chart* for a provider-confirmed outage at one Amazon EC2 site [3]; ICMP and HTTP report the outage consistently. In this chart, each column of data shows one round of measurements (with 24-hour boundaries as vertical black lines), and each pair of rows shows ICMP and HTTP observations from one VP (the blue top is ICMP, and the lower red is HTTP). Light colors represent successful probes, medium colors represent failures of some tries (but eventual success). Dark blue diamonds show ICMP-determined outages (all ICMP tries fail); dark red squares show an HTTP outage (all HTTP tries fail). White areas show cases where one of the control nodes failed to respond to either ICMP or HTTP, or where we are unable to upload data to our collection site.

As a second example, Figure 5 shows a case where both ICMP and HTTP report intermittent failures from one VP. We see intermittent problems from Koszalin University of Technology in Poland to Amazon S3's Singapore site. In fact, we observe intermittent failures between that source and destination pair for the entire duration of our measurement. This case shows that sometimes network problems between the VP and cloud (such as routing problems) persist for some time. Both ICMP and HTTP report outages for this VP.

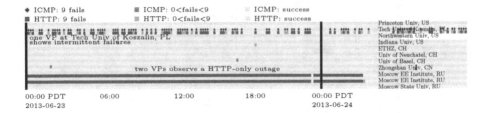

Fig. 5. Strip chart: Amazon S3 (Singapore). Dataset: 2013-06-18+75.

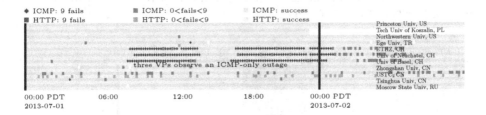

Fig. 6. Strip chart: Amazon VM (N. California). Dataset: 2013-06-18+17.

Method Disagreement: However, HTTP and ICMP probes can also show disagreement. We see disagreement in 0.01% to 3% of observations, as shown by the stacked bars in Figure 3. The source of the disagreement is usually ICMP failures with HTTP success (the bottom, red striped bars), but sometimes ICMP succeeds and HTTP fails (the much smaller blue bars on top).

As a first example where ICMP fails but HTTP succeeds, Figure 6 shows a case where three Swiss universities could not reach Amazon/VM in California. We see with `tcpdump` that filtering happens on the return path. Since the three VPs reporting this ICMP-only outage are at different sites in the same country, we hypothesize that reverse path changes–possibly to a path that filtered ICMP–caused the outage. In this case, despite ICMP reporting multiple outages, we can still fetch the data in the cloud, meaning that ICMP over-counts outages.

We also see the reverse case, where HTTP fails but ICMP succeeds, overestimating cloud availability. Figures 5 and 7 show two VPs in Russia observing an HTTP-only outage to both Amazon S3 and EC2 in Singapore. We observe route changes before and after the outage, and we confirm our probes (here TCP SYNs) reach the VM and replies are sent but do not reach the VP. We cannot confirm the root cause for this outage, although we guess there may be problems in a load-balancer at the cloud's edge.

4.2 Differences between Probing VMs and Storage

In addition to comparing network and application probing, we also probe different targets: virtual machines and storage. The *target* affects what the probing

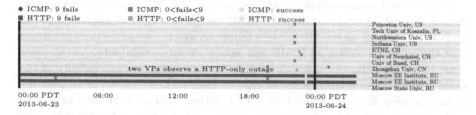

Fig. 7. Strip chart: Amazon VM (Singapore). Dataset: 2013-06-18+17.

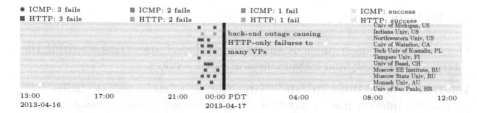

Fig. 8. Strip chart: Amazon S3 (Japan). Dataset: 2013-03-11+33.

mechanism sees. We next show that *end-to-end measurements are essential to observe outages in cloud storage* and other systems with complex back-ends.

Figure 8 shows an outage for Amazon S3 in Tokyo on April 16. Only HTTP measurements detect this outage; ICMP reports that all is well. This outage is confirmed by Amazon outage report [3].

To understand this discrepancy, we must consider what exactly ICMP and HTTP measure when observing a storage system. For storage systems, a user accesses a front-end system with a URL, but data retrieval exercises the back-end storage system. ICMP measures only to this front-end, while HTTP provides an end-to-end test, verifying that the storage system is functioning (at least for one stored object). We can therefore infer this outage was *inside* Amazon's storage system and not in the network from the VP to the datacenter. We conclude that *ICMP will overestimate the availability of cloud storage*, supporting our recommendation for *end-to-end outage testing for higher-level cloud services*.

To understand the root cause of these storage outages, we next use errors reported by our storage retrieval tool (curl). We look at the error returned from each failed attempt of storage retrieval from the 2013-06-18+75 storage dataset. We see that most of these (87%) are due to DNS lookup failure, with the second largest cause (10%) due to TCP connection setup failure. In contrast, for VMs (dataset: 2013-06-18+17), almost all failures (99%) are caused by TCP connection setup failures. All of the storage systems use DNS to map a request into the storage back-end systems. These DNS failures can represent either random loss of the request in the network, or failure of the storage system's DNS mechanism to identify a storage server. Since applications that use cloud storage will follow a similar process as curl which is used in our measurements, these types of outages reflect intermittent problems that should be reported.

Based on our measurement results, we show that ICMP probes can be inaccurate at estimating cloud availability. ICMP is not as robust as application-level measurements such as HTTP. ICMP's failure to solicit a response does not mean that the service is down, so ICMP can *underestimate* availability. At the same time, ICMP can also *overestimate* availability as it measures reachability of the cloud's edge, missing failures in the cloud's back-end. We therefore suggest using application-level probes such as HTTP rather than network-level probes to evaluate cloud reliability; the examples in this section present the motivation for a longer-term study.

5 Related Work

Our work builds upon previous efforts in two broad areas: characterizing the Internet's availability and measurement of cloud services.

Internet Availability: To date, a large number of measurement studies have probed the Internet from a distributed set of vantage points in order to characterize the Internet's availability. While some studies rely on passive measurements of Internet traffic to detect the onset of outages (for example, [27,4]), such monitoring is possible only by instrumenting a popular service. Therefore, most measurement studies of the Internet's availability have instead relied on continuous probing of a large number of end-hosts. These studies have focused on identifying outages [14,23], network failures [6,28], characterizing the typical duration of outages [14,10,15], and pinpointing their root causes [8,13]. Some studies have paid particular attention to measurement methodology of paths [7] and of the edge [23]. However, all of these studies have in common a reliance on ICMP-based probes. While ICMP may be necessary for Internet-wide studies, our results show that application-level measurements should be used when possible, and they are essential to understanding availability of cloud services, where ICMP-based probing can both over- and under-predict outages.

Measurements of Cloud Services: Some recent work has begun on measure and characterize the performance offered by cloud services. CloudCmp measures the compute, storage, and network performance offered by various cloud services with the goal of enabling application providers to choose from these services [16]. Others have performed measurements of cloud services in order to determine when it is beneficial for applications to be hosted in the cloud [11,21]. To the best of our knowledge, we are the first to investigate the methodology of active monitoring of the availability of cloud services. Motoyama et al. pursue a complementary approach of inferring outages from indirect information in Twitter posts [20]; further investigation is necessary to correlate outages in web services to outages of the underlying cloud services on which they are deployed.

6 Conclusion

This paper compared network and application level measurements sensitive of cloud service availability. We compare ICMP and HTTP over two types of services (VMs and storage) and three providers. We find that ICMP can both over- and under-report outages, suggesting that it is important to use end-to-end measures (such as HTTP) to best characterize cloud service availability. Our study raises concerns about the use of ICMP for monitoring availability and suggests that earlier results should be revisited. We are using these approaches as part of a long-term study of cloud availability. Part of our ongoing work is to understand cloud availability in order to deploy highly-available systems at low cost across various cloud providers, just as existing work uses multiple providers to provide low latency at low cost [26].

References

1. Outages mailing list. Mailing List, http://www.outages.org
2. Abu-Libdeh, H., Princehouse, L., Weatherspoon, H.: RACS: A case for cloud storage diversity. In: SoCC (2010)
3. Amazon. AWS Service Health Dashboard, http://status.aws.amazon.com/
4. Choffnes, D.R., Bustamante, F.E., Ge, Z.: Crowdsourcing service-level network event monitoring. In: SIGCOMM (2010)
5. Chun, B., Culler, D., Roscoe, T., Bavier, A., Peterson, L., Wawrzoniak, M., Bowman, M.: PlanetLab: An overlay testbed for broad-coverage services. In: SIGCOMM CCR (2003)
6. Cunha, I., Teixeira, R., Feamster, N., Diot, C.: Measurement methods for fast and accurate blackhole identification with binary tomography. In: IMC (2009)
7. Cunha, I., Teixeira, R., Veitch, D., Diot, C.: Predicting and tracking internet path changes. In: SIGCOMM (2011)
8. Dhamdhere, A., Teixeira, R., Dovrolis, C., Diot, C.: Netdiagnoser: troubleshooting network unreachabilities using end-to-end probes and routing data. In: CoNEXT (2007)
9. Flach, T., Dukkipati, N., Terzis, A., Raghavan, B., Cardwell, N., Cheng, Y., Jain, A., Hao, S., Katz-Bassett, E., Govindan, R.: Reducing web latency: the virtue of gentle aggression. In: SIGCOMM (2013)
10. Gummadi, K.P., Madhyastha, H.V., Gribble, S.D., Levy, H.M., Wetherall, D.: Improving the reliability of Internet paths with one-hop source routing. In: OSDI (2004)
11. Hajjat, M., Sun, X., Sung, Y.-W.E., Maltz, D., Rao, S., Sripanidkulchai, K., Tawarmalani, M.: Cloudward bound: planning for beneficial migration of enterprise applications to the cloud. In: SIGCOMM (2010)
12. Heidemann, J., Pradkin, Y., Govindan, R., Papadopoulos, C., Bartlett, G., Bannister, J.: Census and survey of the visible Internet. In: IMC (2008)
13. Javed, U., Cunha, I., Choffnes, D.R., Katz-Bassett, E., Krishnamurthy, A., Anderson, T.: PoiRoot: Investigating the root cause of interdomain path changes. In: SIGCOMM (2013)
14. Katz-Bassett, E., Madhyastha, H.V., John, J.P., Krishnamurthy, A., Wetherall, D., Anderson, T.: Studying black holes in the Internet with Hubble. In: NSDI (2008)

15. Katz-Bassett, E., Scott, C., Choffnes, D.R., Cunha, I., Valancius, V., Feamster, N., Madhyastha, H.V., Anderson, T., Krishnamurthy, A.: LIFEGUARD: Practical repair of persistent route failures. In: SIGCOMM (2012)
16. Li, A., Yang, X., Kandula, S., Zhang, M.: Cloudcmp: comparing public cloud providers. In: IMC (2010)
17. Lohr, S.: Amazon's trouble raises cloud computing doubts (April 2011), http://www.nytimes.com/2011/04/23/technology/23cloud.html
18. Luckie, M., Hyun, Y., Huffaker, B.: Traceroute probe method and forward IP path inference. In: IMC (2008)
19. Madhyastha, H.V., Isdal, T., Piatek, M., Dixon, C., Anderson, T., Krishnamurthy, A., Venkataramani, A.: iPlane: An information plane for distributed services. In: OSDI (2006)
20. Motoyama, M., Meeder, B., Levchenko, K., Voelker, G.M., Savage, S.: Measuring online service availability using Twitter. In: WOSN (2010)
21. Palankar, M.R., Iamnitchi, A., Ripeanu, M., Garfinkel, S.: Amazon S3 for science grids: a viable solution? In: DADC (2008)
22. Paxson, V.: End-to-end internet packet dynamics. In: SIGCOMM (1997)
23. Quan, L., Heidemann, J., Pradkin, Y.: Trinocular: understanding internet reliability through adaptive probing. In: SIGCOMM (2013)
24. Spring, N., Peterson, L., Bavier, A., Pai, V.: Using PlanetLab for network research: Myths, realities, and best practices. SIGOPS Oper. Syst. Rev. (2006)
25. Wood, T., Cecchet, E., Ramakrishnan, K.K., Shenoy, P., van der Merwe, J., Venkataramani, A.: Disaster recovery as a cloud service: economic benefits & deployment challenges. In: HotCloud (2010)
26. Wu, Z., Butkiewicz, M., Perkins, D., Katz-Bassett, E., Madhyastha, H.V.: Spanstore: Cost-effective geo-replicated storage spanning multiple cloud services. In: SOSP 2013 (2013)
27. Zhang, M., Zhang, C., Pai, V., Peterson, L., Wang, R.: PlanetSeer: Internet path failure monitoring and characterization in wide-area services. In: OSDI (2004)
28. Zhang, Z., Zhang, Y., Hu, Y.C., Mao, Z.M., Bush, R.: iSPY: Detecting IP prefix hijacking on my own. In: SIGCOMM (2008)

Exposing Inconsistent Web Search Results with Bobble

Xinyu Xing[1], Wei Meng[1], Dan Doozan[1], Nick Feamster[1],
Wenke Lee[1], and Alex C. Snoeren[2]

[1] Georgia Institute of Technology
[2] University of California, San Diego
{xxing8,wei,ddoozan3,feamster,wenke}@gatech.edu,
snoeren@cs.ucsd.edu

Abstract. Given their critical role as gateways to Web content, the search results a Web search engine provides to its users have an out-sized impact on the way each user views the Web. Previous studies have shown that popular Web search engines like Google employ sophisticated personalization engines that can occasionally provide dramatically inconsistent views of the Web to different users. Unfortunately, even if users are aware of this potential, it is not straightforward for them to determine the extent to which a particular set of search results differs from those returned to other users, nor the factors that contribute to this personalization.

We present the design and implementation of Bobble, a Web browser extension that contemporaneously executes a user's Google search query from a variety of different world-wide vantage points under a range of different conditions, alerting the user to the extent of inconsistency present in the set of search results returned to them by Google. Using more than 75,000 real search queries issued by over 170 users during a nine-month period, we explore the frequency and nature of inconsistencies that arise in Google search queries. In contrast to previously published results, we find that 98% of all Google search results display some inconsistency, with a user's geographic location being the dominant factor influencing the nature of the inconsistency.

1 Introduction

Web search engines have emerged as the *de facto* gateway to the Internet, with the major players like Google and Bing locked in a heated battle to attract users from around the world. Personalization is a key tool for adding value to search results: Each search engine tailors search results not only to the query term, but also based on the profile of the user [1, 3]. Web search personalization aims to return the search results that are most relevant to each user, based upon the user's past search history, clicks, geographic location, device type, and other features that may help identify the user's preferences and predispositions [3]. Ideally, personalization identifies results that closely match the user's preferences and intent, improving user satisfaction and ultimately increasing revenue for the search engine.

In practice, Web search personalization may also hide certain results from users, when personalized results preempt search results that would have otherwise been included [7]. Because search personalization algorithms are effectively a "black box",

M. Faloutsos and A. Kuzmanovic (Eds.): PAM 2014, LNCS 8362, pp. 131–140, 2014.

users have little to no information about the information that personalization algorithms might prevent them from seeing. Moreover, personalization frequently occurs without the user's involvement—or even explicit agreement—so users may not even be aware that their search results have been tailored according to their profile and preferences. The goal of our work is to expose and characterize inconsistencies that result from personalization. In particular, we seek to quantify the extent to which search personalization algorithms return results that are inconsistent with those that would be returned to other users, and expose any differences to the user—in real time.

We present Bobble, a Chrome Web browser extension that allows users to see how the search results that Google returns to them differ from the results that are returned to other users. Bobble captures a user's search query and reissues it from a subset of over 300 world-wide vantage points, including both dedicated PlanetLab measurement nodes and the hosts of other consenting Bobble users. In contrast to research tools that have been developed to measure search personalization offline [5], we intend users to use Bobble while they browse the Web, providing them critical insight into how their online experience is being potentially distorted by personalization.

To understand the nature of the inconsistencies uncovered by Bobble, we study more than 75,000 real search queries issued by hundreds of Bobble users over nine months. We quantify the extent to which personalization affects search results and determine how users' Google search results vary based on factors ranging from their geographic locations to their past search histories. Our study study focuses exclusively on Google search, one of the more widely used search engines, but we expect that similar phenomena exist for other popular search engines. We find that 98% of Google Web searches return at least one set of inconsistent search results—typically from a vantage point in a different geographic region than the user, even though Bobble performs these searches without exposing any information that links to the searchers' Google profiles.

In sum, our study provides the first large-scale glimpse into the nature of inconsistent results that arise from search personalization and opens many avenues for future research. We quantify on how geography and search history may influence search results, but others have noted that many other factors (*e.g.*, device type, time of day) may also affect the results that a user sees for a given search term [5]. Bobble has been deployed and publicly available for 21 months; users and researchers can extend it to measure how other factors might induce inconsistencies in search results.

2   Related Work

Researchers have previously studied means to personalize Web search results. Dou *et al.* performed a large-scale evaluation and analysis of five personalized search algorithms using a twelve-day MSN query log [2]. They find that profile-based personalization algorithms are sometimes unstable. Teevan *et al.* conduct a user study to investigate the value of personalized Web search [11]. In contrast, we are less interested in the distinction between different personalization methods, and focus instead on the effects of a single search personalization algorithm. We aim to quantify the effects of different personalization factors on search inconsistency.

In a contemporaneous study, Hannak *et al.* measure the personalization of Google search. The bulk of their effort focuses on understanding the features leading to personalization, but they also conduct a limited study of real-world personalization by hiring 200 US-based workers to search a fixed set of 120 search terms using their own Google accounts [5]. They find that any given slot in the first page of search results has less than a 12% chance of being personalized. Directly comparing their result to ours is challenging, because we do not consider reordering. We instead focus on the set of results returned, not their order. Moreover, our study considers a larger set of real queries from a global set of locations, conducted over a longer time period. We find that almost all results are subject to some form of personalization. We do, however, replicate their method in Section 6 and find that personalization is more than twice as likely than their work suggests.

Personalization is not limited to Web search. Previous research has built distributed systems to understand the effect of information factors in a number of online services. For example, Mikians *et al.* develop a distributed system to demonstrate the existence of price discrimination on e-commerce sites and discover the effects of information factors on price discrimination [6]. They find the factors that contribute to price discrimination include the customer's geographic location, personal information, and origin URL. Guha *et al.* explore several approaches to determine how advertising networks adjust the advertisements that they display based on users' personal information [4].

3 Bobble

To identify inconsistencies in Google search results that result from personalization based upon geography or personal history, we design, implement and deploy Bobble, a distributed system that monitors and displays inconsistent search results that Google returns for user search queries in real time.

3.1 Design and Implementation

Bobble has three components: a Chrome browser extension, hundreds of Chrome browser agents, and a centralized data collection server. Our Chrome browser extension[1] runs on a Google user's Chrome browser, and passively collects the Google user's searching activities including the Google user's search terms and corresponding search results. Chrome browser agents—running both inside users' Chrome browser extensions and in Chrome browser emulators that we install on PlanetLab nodes across the Internet—perform Google searches without signing in to a Google account or revealing a trackable browser cookie to Google. The central Bobble server coordinates the agents and archives users' search activities, their IP addresses, and the search results from the Chrome browser agents.

Bobble follows four steps to reveal inconsistencies in search results. When a user issues a Google search query (Step 1), Bobble browser extension delivers the search terms to the central Bobble server (Step 2), where they are placed in a global work queue. To protect user privacy, all subjects' Google identities are hashed by a one-way SHA-1 hash function. Asynchronously, Chrome browser agents periodically poll

---

[1] The Bobble Chrome browser extension is available from the Google Chrome store and our project website http://bobble.gtisc.gatech.edu/.

Table 1. The number of terms that generate inconsistent sets of search results when searching 1,000 distinct terms from Chrome browsers / agent on different OSes

	with same browser	with Chrome agent	p-value
Windows	11 / 1,000	16 / 1,000	0.1725
Linux	23 / 1,000	21 / 1,000	0.7517
Mac	15 / 1,000	15 / 1,000	1.0

the Bobble server for pending search terms (Step 3) and reissue them locally as search queries to Google without signing into a Google account or revealing Google a trackable browser cookie (Step 4). Each agent pushes the results it receives from Google to the Bobble server.

To establish a baseline for comparing inconsistencies in search results, we would ideally like to also reissue the user's query locally from a separate browser session that is not signed into Google and does not pass session cookies to Google. We call these anonymous queries "organic", as they are as free as possible from user-specific influences (in contrast to queries that are issued when a user is logged in or passing browser cookies to Google). Unfortunately, collecting true organic results is challenging due to the technical and usability obstacles surrounding logging the user out in order to issue such a query from an extension running within the same Web browser. Instead, Bobble collects organic search results by issuing a duplicate query from a nearby Chrome browser agent. (Section 3.2 presents a detailed discussion of the effects of using a nearby agent to stand-in for the user's browser.)

3.2 Validation

To evaluate whether Bobble accurately reports results that regular users would actually receive, we first validate that Bobble's Chrome browser agent correctly emulates major version releases of Chrome browsers—specifically, that the results returned to a Bobble agent reflect those that would be returned to an actual query issued by a user in her Web browser. Second, we measure the effects of collecting organic search results indirectly by issuing queries from nearby agents as opposed to inside the user's browser.

Do Bobble Agents Emulate Browser Behavior? We begin by ensuring that the Google search results collected using the Chrome browser agent do not differ statistically from the results obtained when the query is issued from the Google home page viewed with the Chrome browser itself. We randomly select 1,000 unique search terms from the daily top-20 Google trending search terms between August 2011 and December 2011 and search each of these terms three times from machines running Linux, Windows, and Mac operating systems. On each machine, we run a Chrome browser agent and two Google Chrome browsers with the same release version. We use the Selenium Chrome driver [9] to automate the two Chrome browsers and one browser agent to perform the same Google search simultaneously.

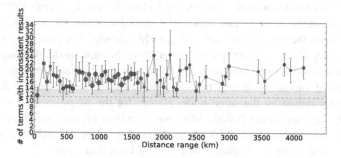

Fig. 1. The count variations of inconsistent sets of search results vs. the distance variations between a pair of PlanetLab nodes

One might expect that simultaneously issued queries from identical Web browsers would return identical sets of results, since the queries do not involve any search history and are issued from the same location at essentially the same time. While this expectation generally rings true, it is not always the case. Table 1 shows the number of terms that generate inconsistent search results when comparing the first set of results returned to a Web browser to those returned to both the second instance of the browser and the Bobble agent; neither are non-zero. To test if the proportion of inconsistent results generated by our browser agent is statistically different from that of the browser, we conduct a two-sample proportion test. Table 1 shows that the proportion tests for the three operating systems are not statistically significant at the 0.05 level (*i.e.*, all p-values are greater than .05). In other words, we observe no significant difference observed in the proportion of inconsistent results generated by the Bobble browser agents and a real Chrome browser. We thus conclude that Bobble agents are reasonably accurate substitutes for real users executing search queries from within browser.

Are PlanetLab queries similar to real users? Bobble does not collect organic search results from within a user's own browser since this would require issuing duplicate queries from the user's browser and forcibly signing out the user and clearing the user's cookies. Instead, Bobble issues queries from an agent running on the closest PlanetLab node to obtain an approximation of what the Google user's organic search results would be. To identify how well this approximation holds with distance, we conduct the following experiment from 308 PlanetLab [8] nodes on which Bobble was deployed.

Using the same 1,000 search terms as before, Bobble browser agents search every term twice, back-to-back. Across the 308 nodes, 8–13 out of 1,000 terms generate inconsistent Google results with a 95% statistical confidence level[2]. This inconsistency may be due to caching, a sudden DNS change, updates to Google's indicies with their data center, or a myriad other possibilities. Regardless, we view this as a "noise floor" against which to judge inconsistency.

We now consider the number of terms that generate inconsistent search results when searches are performed on different PlanetLab nodes in the same country at varying

---

[2] When constructing confidence intervals, we consider searches from distinct browser agents to be independent trials from the same underlying distribution.

geographic distances from each other. Figure 1 plots the average number of terms that result in inconsistent search results with a 95% confidence interval as a function of the distance between the two agents (according to Maxmind). The pink band represents the inconsistency observed from queries issued from the same node. Although there is no clear relationship between distance and consistency, only results returned to nodes within 50 km of another node bear the same statistical level of resemblance as back-to-back queries issued by the same node. Hence, for the purposes of our study, we only consider queries where Bobble was able to collect organic search results from a PlanetLab node located within 50 km of the issuing agent. We selected the 50-km threshold because of the geographic distribution of PlanetLab nodes.

4   Data

On January 17, 2012, we released Bobble on both our project website and the Google Chrome store. As of October 25, 2012, we had collected 100,451 search queries. For each query, we record the corresponding Google search results returned to both the browser on which a Google user installs our Bobble Chrome extension and the Chrome browser agents that reissued the query. We obtain organic search results browser agents running on PlanetLab nodes no further than 50 kilometers from the user issuing the query. Using this criterion, we obtained organic search results for 76,307 of the search queries (75.96%).

To use 76,307 search queries for our analysis, we divided our data set into two categories: search queries issued by Google users while signed in to their Google accounts (signed-in Google users) and search queries issued by Google users while signed out (*i.e..*, anonymous Google users). There are 66,138 search queries (86.67%) issued by 174 distinct signed-in users, and 10,169 search queries (13.33%) issued by anonymous Google users.

5   Location-Based Inconsistency

We now analyze how geographic location affects search inconsistency. Search inconsistency contributed by geographic locations is a joint consequence of both location-based personalization and data diversity across different data centers. We analyze how geographic location contributes to search inconsistency that appears in different Google searches (Section 5.1) and validate that the inconsistencies we observe are in fact due to personalization, as opposed to inconsistencies across data centers (Section 5.2).

For each search query, we group the sets of search results from PlanetLab nodes into sets, each of which contains a unique result set. We compare the number of search results on the first page, as well as the rank, title and URL of each Google result. We use a nearby PlanetLab node's search results to represent the set of organic search results for a Google user in that region. If there is more than one unique search result set for a user's search query, we consider the results to be inconsistent, and we also deem geographic location to be a contributing factor to this inconsistency.

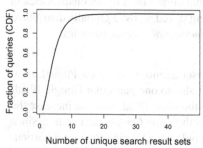

Fig. 2. CDF plot: the distribution of the number of search queries

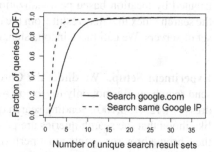

Fig. 3. The distribution of the number of search queries when sending queries to *google.com* and a Google IP address, respectively

5.1 Results

We find that 74,594 out of the 76,307 search queries (97.76%) generate at least one inconsistent set of organic search results due to geographic location. Figure 2 shows the fraction of search queries that generate different numbers of inconsistent sets of search results. This result indicates that organic search results of most Google search queries are tailored on the basis of the location where these searches are performed, even though Google users neither sign into their accounts nor uncover their browser cookies to Google personalized search services. In the following section, we further design a careful examination to explore whether the observed search inconsistency results from location-based personalization rather than data diversity across different Google data centers.

To quantify the effect of geographic location on search inconsistency, we classified the inconsistent search results in three ways:

- At least one search result appears in the top-three search results of other PlanetLab nodes but not at all in a Google user's organic search result set. We find that 23,394 out of 76,307 search queries (30.66%) give rise to this situation.
- At least one search results appears in the top-10 (but not top-3) search results of other PlanetLab nodes, but does not appear in a Google user's organic search result set; 65,939 out of 76,307 search queries (86.41%) fit this situation.
- At least one search result appears in the Google user's organic search result set but does not appear in search results of other PlanetLab nodes; 1,434 search queries out of 76,307 search queries (1.88%) fit this situation.

Considering the fact that the top-10 Google search results receive about 90% of clicks and the top-3 Google search results usually receive the most attention [10], the inconsistency that arises due to location likely has significant implications for a user's experience.

5.2 Distributed Index Inconsistencies

To validate the observed search inconsistency is in fact derived from location-based personalization rather than data diversity across different data centers, we conduct an experiment. In particular, we modify Bobble to attempt to isolate the inconsistency contributed by location-based personalization from that contributed by inconsistencies in the search index that may result from the index being stored across a globally distributed set of servers. We call these inconsistencies *distributed index inconsistencies*.

Experiment Setup. We direct the Chrome browser agents running on PlanetLab to send search queries not only to google.com but also to one particular Google IP address (74.125.130.100). Sending search queries to the same IP address can increase the likelihood that the search queries are processed by the same Google data center. Since the Chrome browser agents must perform any Google search twice (one on a particular data center and the other on a data center geographically nearby), which increases the risk of our Chrome browser agents being profiled as a search bot and challenged by Google CAPTCHA system, we limit our experiment to a subset of submitted daily search queries.

Quantifying Distributed Index Inconsistencies. We collect 23,362 search queries from 149 Google users. We then compare the numbers of unique search result sets for each collected search query when it is searched on google.com and the particular Google IP address. For all of the collected search queries, we observed that every search query sent to google.com nearly always generates a larger number of unique search result sets than it is sent to the particular Google IP address. Figure 3 shows that searching on google.com produces more inconsistent result sets than searching on the particular Google IP address does. This discrepancy likely results from the fact that directing a search to a particular Google IP address significantly reduces the influence of data diversity upon search inconsistency.

Another interesting observation from Figure 3 is that approximately 98% of search queries have at least one set of inconsistent search results, even though the influence of data diversity upon search inconsistency is nearly removed. Note Appendix indicates that the inconsistency within a single data center is minimal. We therefore believe that (1) these observed search inconsistency results from location-based personalization when the search terms are searched on the particular Google IP address, (2) location-based personalization contributes significantly to search inconsistency.

6   Profile-Based Inconsistency

We also explore how a user's profile (*i.e.*, search history) contributes to search inconsistencies. In particular, we treat the search queries (and corresponding results) independently based on the way that a user issues a search query. Table 2 summarizes our results. For the case of queries corresponding to signed-in users, 42,454 of 66,138 search queries (64.19%) generate results that are inconsistent with respect to the organic search results. For the anonymous users, 5,976 out of 10,169 search queries (58.77%) yield inconsistent search results.

In contrast to Hannak *et al.*'s prior study [5], we find that the profile-based personalization results in significant inconsistencies. Here, we replicate Hannak *et al.*'s

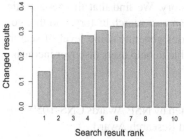

Fig. 4. % of search results changed at each rank

Table 2. How location and user profile contribute to search inconsistency. Location has more effect on inconsistency than search history does.

Signed-in data set		Signed-out data set	
Location	Profile	Location	Profile
97.64%	64.19 %	97.80%	58.77%

experimental method. Figure 4 shows the percentage of search results changed at each rank in our data set. The average is 28.6%, compared to 11.7% as reported by Hannak *et al.* (see Figure 5 in previous work [5]). One possible reason for this discrepancy is the difference in the measurement method. Previous work recruited differnt Google users to search the same set of keywords, where the keywords were chosen such that they were deemed to not be related to user profiles. In contrast, we perform our study in a more natural setting because it measures the influence of the profile-based personalization using each user's own search queries. Because a user's past queries are typically relevant to personalization that may occur in the future, we observe that profile-based personalization has more influence on Google users' search results.

In addition to inconsistencies in the search result sets, we also discovered the following inconsistencies:

- For signed-in users, 22,405 out of 66,138 search queries (33.88%) have at least one search result that shows in the profile-based personalized search result set but not in the organic search result set.
- For anonymous users, 3,148 out of 10,169 search queries (30.96%) have at least one search result that shows in the profile-based personalized search result set but not in the organic search result set.
- For signed-in users, 7,352 out of 66,138 search queries (11.12%) have at least one search result that shows in the top 3 of the organic search result set but not in the profiled-based personalized search result set.
- For anonymous users, 1,484 out of 10,169 search queries (14.59%) have at least one search result that shows in the top 3 of organic search result but not in the profiled-based personalized search result set.

Table 2 also shows that the Google search inconsistencies resulting from signed-in users' profiles are stronger than those resulting from signed-out users' profiles. Finally, we also observe location-based factors introduce more inconsistencies than profile-based factors do.

7 Conclusion

We have designed, implemented, and deployed Bobble, a distributed system that tracks and monitors the inconsistency of search results for user search queries. Using Bobble, we collect user search terms and results and measure the search inconsistency that arise from both geographic location and search history. We find that the geographic location contributes more to search inconsistency than user search history, and that geographic location causes about 98% of search queries generate some level of search inconsistency. We have made Bobble publicly available to help users discover inconsistent results resulting from their own queries.

Acknowledgments. This work was partially supported by NSF Awards CNS-1059350, CNS-1162088, CNS-1255274 and a Google Focused Research Award.

References

1. More personalization on bing with adaptive search, `http://www.youtube.com/watch?v=CgrzhyHCnfw`
2. Dou, Z., Song, R., Wen, J.-R.: A large-scale evaluation and analysis of personalized search strategies. In: Proceedings of the 16th International Conference on World Wide Web. ACM (2007)
3. Making search more relevant, `http://www.google.com/goodtoknow/data-on-google/more-relevant/`
4. Guha, S., Cheng, B., Francis, P.: Challenges in measuring online advertising systems. In: Proceedings of the 10th ACM SIGCOMM Conference on Internet Measurement. ACM (2010)
5. Hannak, A., Sapieżyński, P., Kakhki, A.M., Krishnamurthy, B., Lazer, D., Mislove, A., Wilson, C.: Measuring Personalization of Web Search. In: Proceedings of the Twenty-Second International World Wide Web Conference (WWW 2013), Rio de Janeiro, Brazil (May 2013)
6. Mikians, J., Gyarmati, L., Erramilli, V., Laoutaris, N.: Detecting price and search discrimination on the internet. In: Proceedings of the 11th ACM Workshop on Hot Topics in Networks. ACM (2012)
7. Pariser, E.: The Filter Bubble: What the Internet is Hiding from You. Penguin Press (2011)
8. Planetlab: An open platform for developing, deploying, and accessing planetary-scale services, `http://planet-lab.org/`
9. Selenium - web browser automation, `http://seleniumhq.org/`
10. What is a #1 google ranking worth? `http://training.seobook.com/google-ranking-value`
11. Teevan, J., Dumais, S.T., Horvitz, E.: Beyond the commons: Investigating the value of personalizing web search. In: Proceedings of the Workshop on New Technologies for Personalized Information Access (2005)

Appendix: Inconsistency within a Single Data Center

As a sanity check, we search the same set of 1,000 keywords in Section 3.2 by sending the corresponding queries twice in succession, but this time explicitly to the same Google IP address. We repeat the validation process sixteen times. Approximately 8 out of 1,000 (0.8%) keywords generate inconsistent search results on average, presumably because the Google indices stored on different servers in the same data center are different. We conclude that inconsistency within a single data center is minimal.

Modern Application Layer Transmission Patterns from a Transport Perspective*

Matt Sargent[1], Ethan Blanton[3], and Mark Allman[2]

[1] Case Western Reserve University, Cleveland, OH, USA
[2] International Computer Science Institute, Berkeley, CA, USA
[3] Independent Scientist, South Bend, IN, USA

Abstract. We aim to broadly study the ways that modern applications use the underlying protocols and networks. Such an understanding is necessary when designing and optimizing lower-layer protocols. Traditionally—as prior work shows—applications have been well represented as bulk transfers, often preceded by application-layer handshaking. Recent suggestions posit that application evolution has eclipsed this simple model, and a typical pattern is now a series of transactions over a single transport layer connection. In this initial study we examine application transmission patterns via packet traces from two networks to better understand the ways that modern applications use TCP.

1 Introduction

In this study we seek to broadly understand the ways that modern applications use the underlying protocols and networks. In particular, we are interested in the transmission patterns of applications as viewed at the transport layer. While previous studies have documented these issues to some degree, we are motivated by the following two points.

- We aim to ensure that our mental models of application-imposed behavior are up-to-date. For instance, [14] suggests that while application behavior varies, when simulating Internet traffic a reasonable rule of thumb is to use connection sizes described by the log-normal distribution. In other words, a TCP connection is established, a given number of bytes sent, and then the connection is torn down. This behavior approximates traditional applications like HTTP/1.0 and FTP. However, some in the community have stated their belief that applications' use of TCP has evolved to a more transaction-oriented nature wherein an application re-uses connections for a number of small transactions (e.g., as part of a web application) [5].
- Second, good network engineering crucially depends on an empirical understanding of the system. For instance, intrusion detection systems must understand the difference between an abandoned connection and a quiescent application. Another example is understanding the importance of the so-called "last window" problems in TCP (e.g., [6]). The amount of justifiable additional complexity in TCP to deal with such problems depends on whether there is one "last window" in a connection (e.g., the bulk transfer case) or there are numerous "last windows" (e.g., at the end of every transaction in a connection with many transactions).

---

* Work supported in part by NSF grants CNS-0831535 and CNS-1213157.

M. Faloutsos and A. Kuzmanovic (Eds.): PAM 2014, LNCS 8362, pp. 141–150, 2014.

Table 1. Data overview

	CCZ	ICSI
Time	2/11–3/12	9/12–3/13
Length (hrs)	98	1,176
Total Conns.	6.5M	56.9M
Conns. w/o Data	2.6M	27.9M
Port Filtered	-	1.4M
Remaining	3.9M	27.6M

Table 2. Prevalence of N periods at various positions

Location	CCZ	ICSI
No N	31%	51.2%
Internal-only	14.4%	18.3%
Trailing-only	32.3%	20.7%
Internal & Trailing	22.3%	9.8%

As an initial check on these two points we examine packet traces from the Lawrence Berkeley National Laboratory (LBNL) and the International Computer Science Institute (ICSI). For each connection we compute the maximum duration between data segments. Bulk transfers would tend to show sub-second gaps, while multiple distinct transactions would likely show a larger maximum gap driven by application behavior. We find that in both datasets, the *proportion* of connections with maximum gaps of more than one second and the *duration* of the gaps increases over time. In the LBNL dataset roughly 55% of the connections have a maximum silent period of at most 275 msec in both 2003 and 2013. The distributions then diverge with 4% more connections containing a gap of at least 1 second in 2013 than in 2003 and 12% more connections having a gap of at least 10 seconds. Similarly, in the ICSI data, the distribution of the maximum gap per connection is similar for 2007 and 2013 data up to 1 second—covering about two-thirds of the connections. However, 13% more connections have a maximum gap of at least 10 seconds in 2013 than in 2007. While this analysis is simple and anecdotal it suggests an in-depth exploration of modern application behavior is warranted.

We use packet-level traces from two vantage points—a small research laboratory and a small residential network—as the basis of an initial study into application patterns from TCP's perspective. We contribute both an application agnostic methodology and an initial understanding of modern TCP-based applications.

2   Related Work

There are two general classes of related work. First, there is a vast and long-standing vein of work that characterizes and models specific application protocols. These studies span much time and many protocols, from the largely outdated (e.g., [12]) to a rich understanding of early web traffic (e.g., [3,4]) to modern applications (e.g., [17]). A second class of previous work attempts to identify applications based on the behavior they exhibit on the network (e.g., [8,9]). We do neither of these things, preferring to understand the traffic patterns applications impose on the transport protocol.

3 Data

We analyze the two sets of packet traces summarized in Table 1.[1] The first dataset is gathered from the border of a residential fiber-to-the-home network, the Case Connection Zone (CCZ) [1]. The CCZ connects roughly 90 residences (200-300 users) with bi-directional 1 Gbps fiber. While the connection is abnormal for US residential users, we find in previous work that actual use of the bandwidth is modest—topping out at roughly 10 Mbps in the typical case—and the application mix is in line with previous studies of residential network users [15]. Our second dataset is gathered from the border of the International Computer Science Institute, and covers roughly 100 users. In both cases we gather data between the 11th–17th of each month. We capture all packets from our ICSI vantage point. Our measurement capabilities within the CCZ network are more modest and we collect a one-hour trace from a random time for each day. As we develop in more detail in [15], the CCZ measurement apparatus does not often drop packets during the collection process, with no detectable measurement-based loss in the majority of the traces and the loss rate reaching 0.013% in the worst case. The tracing apparatus at ICSI experiences more measurement-based loss than the CCZ monitor, with an average loss rate of roughly 2.1%. We account for measurement-based loss in our analysis by either not considering missing packets or inferring their existence (by noting progression of TCP's sequence space for missing packets), as appropriate.

We prune the datasets before use for two reasons. First, we do not consider connections that do not have at least one byte of data flowing form the monitored network to the remote network. This rule largely removes scanning and backscatter. Further, in the ICSI dataset we noticed two large traffic anomalies that turned out to be part of an independent experiment: (i) a large crawl of the *whois* databases and (ii) a large backhauling of data to Amazon's EC2. These activities are sufficiently voluminous to affect our results. Therefore, since this traffic is also abnormal, we filter it from further analysis. Table 1 shows the number of connections we remove from further analysis.

4 Dividing Connections

Our general strategy for analyzing application behavior is to take stock of the amount and temporal location of silence in TCP connections. Under this model, traditional bulk data transmission would show few instances where a connection was not actively transmitting data in one or both directions except at the beginning and end of a connection. Of course, our approach is not fool-proof. For instance, streaming may look like bulk transfer in that there are few silent periods, but may be pushing only as fast as required for the given media and not as hard as a bulk transfer. While this is also an important aspect of application behavior to understand, we leave it for future work.

Given our data, we do not have details of the precise application operations. Additionally, our lack of application payload precludes a study based on application protocol semantics.[2] We approximate application behavior with the following process:

---

[1] Note, the LBNL data we present in § 1 is anecdotal in that each trace covers only a single hour. We believe it is useful for motivating the problem, it is not sufficient for deeper analysis and therefore not used in the remainder of the paper.

[2] Additionally, encrypted traffic is not amenable to such analysis.

ON/OFF Periods: As a first cut we divide connections into ON and OFF periods with respect to the transmission behavior of the local host (the host close to our monitor) in the connection. Each connection begins in an OFF period and transitions to an ON period when we observe the local host sending a data segment. Transitioning from an ON period to an OFF period happens when two conditions are met: (i) all outstanding data sent by the local host is acknowledged (ACKed)[3], and (ii) either the local host sends an ACK containing no data or at least 5 msec passes without the local host sending another data segment. Note that once we are in an ON period we are able to deal with loss from the local host by advancing the TCP sequence number based on local packets being sent after the loss or by noticing a gap in the sequence space once rule (i) is met and all of the outstanding data has been ACKed. Lost packets during an ON period will not change the length of the ON period that we detect. Rule (ii) ensures that the local TCP does not have application data waiting to be sent. A bare ACK indicates directly that the TCP buffer is empty. The 5 msec rule is otherwise necessary to account for TCP's slow start behavior [7,2]. Consider a local host that sends a single segment; when that segment is ACKed, criteria (i) is met. However, in slow start, we expect the local host to use the ACK to open the congestion window and transmit additional data. Therefore, data coming within a short amount of time should be considered part of TCP's dynamics and not part of the application's dynamics. We studied the length of the OFF periods without criteria (ii) to find a reasonable threshold, and thresholds of 1–10 msec show similar results. The 5 msec threshold is a somewhat arbitrary choice within that range.

Refinement: Two-Way Traffic: The ON/OFF analysis only accounts for traffic in one direction (from the local to the remote). This approach does not reveal the applications' full complexities, but reconstructing the TCP state of hosts distant from a monitor is known to be difficult [13]. Therefore, we use the following heuristics to glean enough information about returning data to conduct our analysis without reconstructing the entire state of the remote host. We couple the ON/OFF classification above with information about the data flow from the remote host to the local host to refine our classification into four types: Local-only periods are ON periods where we do not observe data sent by the remote host, Remote-only periods are OFF periods where we observe data sent by the remote host, Both periods are ON periods where we also find data sent by the remote host, and None periods are OFF periods where we find no data sent from the remote host. N periods are a first approximation of the silent periods we describe at the beginning of this section. We find that R periods hide silence at times. Consider the case where a single data segment is sent from the remote just after the start of an OFF period and then the connection goes silent for a long period of time. In this case, we classify the entire period as R, when most of the period is in fact silent. We remedy this by terminating an R period—at the point of the last data segment arrival—if twice the minimum observed RTT for the connection elapses without another data segment from the remote host. Twice the minimum RTT provides some robustness to network and TCP behaviors while ensuring that the model transitions in a timely fashion. An N period is inserted for the remaining duration of the shortened R period. R periods that do not trigger this rule may still contain some silence, but the duration of this error is

---

[3] Note, this criteria naturally keep original transmissions and their retransmissions in the same period.

bounded by twice the minimum RTT. Together, these heuristics provide a conservative estimate of the silent periods. Any N period in the analysis is a true silent period, but there may be short application silences hidden in L, R, or B periods.

As a next step, we build a map for each connection that consists of a string corresponding to the order of the various periods in the connection. For instance, a map of NLR indicates an initial OFF period, then a period of local data transmission and the connection ending with a period of data transmission from only the remote host. We find over 155 k and 579 k unique maps within our CCZ and ICSI datasets, respectively. This shows the that applications display significant variety in their behavior. Over millions of connections, we find an average of 25 and 50 connections share each map in the CCZ and ICSI datasets, respectively. Further, we find that there are 12 "popular" maps, or maps that make up at least 1% of the connections, in the CCZ dataset and 10 popular maps in the ICSI dataset. Three maps—NBN, NLR and $NLRN$—are popular in both datasets. Popular maps account for a total of 63% of the connections in both datasets. These results underscore the vast heterogeneity in application behavior observed.

Next, we analyze where N periods fall within connections. Since many connections start with an N period following the three-way handshake due to TCP dynamics, we ignore initial N periods for this analysis. Table 2 shows the prevalence of N periods in various locations within the connection. First, we find that about one half to two thirds of the connections in both datasets contain periods where the application is silent. We believe this illustrates that the majority of the connections are not simple bulk transfers. Further, we find that of the connections with silent periods a plurality have only "trailing" silent periods (e.g., persistent HTTP keeping a connection open in case further requests are forthcoming, but ultimately closing with no such requests). Finally, we find that between a quarter and a third of the connections have an internal silent period, indicating an application pause. We present in-depth analysis in the next two sections.

5 Trailing Silent Periods

We first study trailing silent periods, or connections that transfer data and then go silent before terminating. Persistent HTTP follows this model, as connections speculatively persist after the "final" response in case the browser subsequently needs more objects. This mechanism aids performance by allowing subsequent transactions to avoid the overhead of starting a new connection [11]. As we note above, 54.6% and 30.5% of connections from CCZ and ICSI, respectively, end with a silent period. Note that these connections may not violate the bulk transfer model of TCP behavior, as they may behave as bulk transfers that simply do not close immediately when activity completes.

The left plot in Figure 1 shows the distribution of the duration of trailing silent periods. Trailing silence of less than 1 second happens in about 30% and 20% of the connections for CCZ and ICSI, respectively. These likely represent applications finishing processing tasks before closing the connection. On the other hand, we find that just under half of the trailing silent periods last longer than 10 seconds in both datasets. This likely indicates the application speculatively leaving a connection open in case further work materializes—which never happens in these cases. These trailing silent periods can be lengthy, with nearly 20–25% of the periods extending beyond 2 minutes. Further, 10% of the trailing silent periods exceed 4 minutes in each dataset.

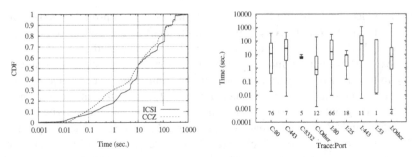

Fig. 1. Duration of trailing N periods

We next study the behavior of specific applications [4] with respect to trailing silent periods. The right plot in Figure 1 shows the characteristics of each port that contributes at least 1% of the connections with trailing silent periods. The labels on the x-axis indicate the dataset—"C" for CCZ, "I" for ICSI—and port number for the applications, with "other" being a combination of all ports not shown independently. The number just above the x-axis shows the percentage of connections with trailing silent periods that the given port is responsible for in the given dataset. For each port, the box shows the quartiles of the distribution of the duration of the trailing silent periods and the whiskers show the 1st and 99th percentiles.

The figure shows that at least three-quarters of the connections with trailing silent periods across datasets are likely web traffic (ports 80 and 443) and web traffic generally shows the longest trailing silent periods. Additionally, we find three times as much "other" traffic in the CCZ data as in the ICSI data. This is natural in that CCZ traffic contains more peer-to-peer traffic that is widely distributed across the port range and therefore confounds such simple port-based classification (see [15] for details). We find that CCZ traffic using port 8332[5] has short and highly uniform trailing silent periods. The "other" traffic generally has the largest spread of trailing silent periods, as one might expect, given that it is an amalgamation of different applications. The ICSI dataset includes many SMTP connections with trailing silent periods; while half of these are at least 10 seconds, the 99th percentile is only 19 seconds, which suggests that a fairly tight timeout is in play. Finally, we find that TCP-based DNS traffic in the ICSI dataset is responsible for roughly 1% of the trailing silent periods. Two ICSI hosts are responsible for most of this DNS traffic, and the general pattern of their connections is consistent with a single, short DNS lookup followed by a 2 minute timeout—which is consistent with the behavior specified in RFC 1035 [10].

6   Internal Silent Periods

Our next analysis is of silent periods that happen between periods of activity within connections. These periods indicate an application imposing a non-bulk transfer structure

---

[4] Our traces include only packet headers and therefore we rely on port numbers to identify applications—as crude as that can sometimes be.

[5] As discussed in [15], we have not been able to fully disambiguate this traffic between Bitcoin and an experimental security camera application known to be in use within the CCZ.

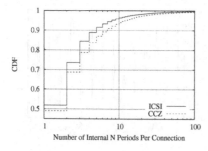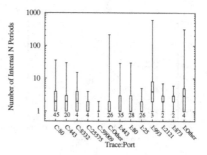

Fig. 2. Number of internal N periods per connection

on their activity. There could still be periods in which the application—and therefore TCP—tries to move data as fast as possible in bulk transfer fashion, but these silent periods indicate that is not the applications' exclusive goal.

Silent Periods Per Connection: Recall from Table 2 that 36.7% and 28.1% of the connections in the CCZ and ICSI datasets, respectively, contain at least one internal silent period. From this we understand that a non-trivial fraction of the connections are not solely concerned with bulk transfer. The left plot in Figure 2 shows the distribution of the number of internal silent periods per connection in our two datasets. We find general agreement between the datasets with roughly half the connections having only one internal silent period, and over 90% of the connections having no more than ten internal silent periods. Therefore, while we find that internal silent periods are not rare, we also find that they are in general not numerous on a per-connection basis.

The right plot in Figure 2 breaks down the number of silent periods per connection by port for ports that contribute at least 1% of the connections with internal silent periods. Again, the overall fraction of connections is given just above the x-axis, the bars represent quartiles and the whiskers show the 1st and 99th percentiles. We find that over 60% of the connections with internal silent periods in both datasets are web traffic (ports 80 and 443). Further, most of the popular ports have a median of one internal silent period per connection and the 75th percentile is under 10 periods across ports. This is consistent with the overall distribution given in the left figure and shows that popular ports do not drastically depart from the overall distribution. We do find that IMAP connections at ICSI (port 993) show a large 99th percentile—604 silent periods. This is expected for email clients that leave connections open for pushed email.

Silent Period Duration: We next assess the duration of internal silent periods, as we show in Figure 3. This plot shows that most such periods are short—with at least 30% lasting at most 100 msec and two thirds lasting at most 1 second. These durations are consistent with the "active off" periods previously identified in web traffic [4]. However, more than 10% of the internal silent periods across connections last at least 10 seconds. These periods likely represent applications that run out of networking tasks.

The duration of internal silent periods is not as uniform across applications as their number, as shown in Figure 3. For example, SMTP (port 25) is largely rapid exchanges, with 75% of silent periods lasting less than about 100 msec and no silent period lasting more than a few seconds. On the other hand, web traffic (ports 80 and 443) show

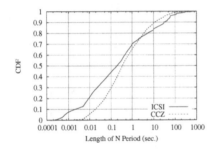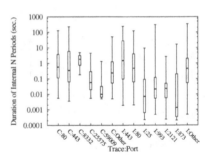

Fig. 3. Duration of internal N periods

significantly longer internal silent periods in both the ICSI and CCZ traces. Interestingly, we note that port 443 has longer internal silent periods than port 80 in both datasets—but more exaggerated in the ICSI dataset. We speculate that this may be due to more aggressive caching of HTTPS connections to avoid the higher setup cost of SSL/TLS.

We now turn from focusing on individual internal silent periods to the amount of aggregate silence we find across an entire connection. We calculate the total fraction of each connection with least one internal silent period that is spent in silence. We find that two thirds of the connections are fairly uniformly distributed between nearly no silence and roughly 90% silence across the connection. However, in the other one-third of the connections across datasets over 90% of the connection is silent—with roughly 20% of the connections in both datasets showing near total silence. The distribution of the number of silent periods for connections that are at least 90% silent shows that these connections have more silent periods than the overall distribution (which is shown in Figure 2)—indicating that a single silent period is not driving the overall behavior.

The Last Window Problem: TCP's loss recovery depends on the acknowledgment of packets received. The information in returning ACKs is used to drive retransmission decisions, by assuming that multiple incoming ACKs that do not acknowledge outstanding data indicate that the data was lost. However, ACKs are sent only when data is received, and there is no data after the last window to generate new ACKs. Hence, it is comparatively more difficult for TCP to determine that the final packets of a window have been lost; in many algorithms, this situation is detected only by a relatively long retransmission timeout (RTO). TCP also uses ACKs to trigger the transmission of new data. However, after a period of silence there are no incoming ACKs, and thus this "ACK clock" cannot be used to immediately pace out new data. This can lead to either a large burst of segments [7,16] or the need to wait a full RTT for ACKs for the new data to return [16]. In other words, events that happen in a routine and timely fashion most of the time can be problematic at the "end" of a connection. A silent period within a connection can manifest the same behaviors.

Various proposals exist to deal with TCP's "last window" (e.g., [6]). However, understanding the frequency of this phenomenon is crucial to determining how much complexity should be added to TCP to deal with the issue. Our approach to assess this is to treat the window before a silent period as a "last window" as long as the silent

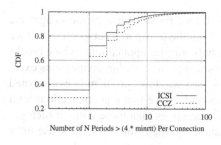

Fig. 4. # of N periods > RTO

Table 3. Length and diversity of connection maps

Class	Med.	Mean	StdDev	# Cnns
CCZ Active	2	2.80	1.13	139k
CCZ Simple	3	3.45	1.34	2.5M
CCZ Complex	8	20.0	199	1.4M
ICSI Active	2	2.66	5.15	4.3M
ICSI Simple	4	4.79	3.88	19.8M
ICSI Complex	8	27.2	714	7.8M

period is relatively long, which we define as roughly the length of an RTO. We use this approximation because of the recommendation that TCP collapse its congestion window after an RTO worth of idle time [2]. Since the specifics of the RTO vary across implementations we use $4 \times minRTT$ as an approximation.

We find that 65–71% of the connections have internal silent periods that last at least $4 \times minRTT$—which represents at least a doubling of last windows (i.e., one internal and one actual last window). Figure 4 shows the distribution of the number of silent periods that exceed $4 \times minRTT$ per connection. We find that 32% and 24% of the connections that have internal silent periods for CCZ and ICSI, respectively, have 2–10 silent periods of at least $4 \times minRTT$. These results show that a non-trivial number of connections would benefit from techniques that mitigate last window issues.

7 Application Complexity

We next assess the diversity of patterns of activity within connections. For this analysis, we classify connections into three types: (i) "active" connections consist only of L, R, and B periods, with no N period, (ii) "simple" connections may have initial and/or trailing N periods, but all other periods must be L, R, or B (note that active connections are a subset of simple connections) and (iii) "complex" connections which may have any combination of periods. Table 3 shows a summary of our analysis. The data suggests that active and simple connections are much more likely to consist of a small number of exchanges followed by termination, whereas complex connections—those with at least one internal N period—display a large diversity of internal structure, involving a comparatively larger number of exchanges and period transitions.

The tendency of simple connections to be classic bulk transfers is strong. Out of the CCZ simple connections, 90% of the maps (2.2M connections) consist of no more than two periods containing data—with 60% being LR, with or without initial and trailing N periods—suggesting a simple request-response bulk transfer. The ICSI data is somewhat more diverse, with the corresponding maps accounting for 47% of the simple connections. Further, 40% of the connections are either LR or RL with or without initial and trailing N periods. This suggests that the simple connections in the ICSI dataset are somewhat more complicated than in the CCZ dataset, but the overall diversity remains markedly lower than for complex connections.

8   Conclusions

This paper makes several initial contributions: (i) we provide an application agnostic methodology for studying application patterns from the transport's perspective, (ii) we confirm that TCP is non-trivially used for non-bulk transfer applications, which breaks our often-employed mental model, (iii) while silent periods within connections exist, they are mostly short, (iv) we find that TCP's "last window" problem is exacerbated by the transactional nature of some connections and (v) we find that connections with internal silent periods have more complicated interactions than those without such periods. We stress that this is an initial investigation and the results in some sense offer more questions than answers—which we are grappling with as future work.

References

1. Case Connection Zone, http://caseconnectionzone.org/
2. Allman, M., Paxson, V., Blanton, E.: TCP Congestion Control, RFC 5681 (September 2009)
3. Arlitt, M., Williamson, C.: Web Server Workload Characterization: The Search for Invariants (Extended Version). IEEE/ACM Transactions on Networking 5(5) (October 1997)
4. Barford, P., Crovella, M.: Generating Representative Web Workloads for Network and Server Performance Evaluation. In: ACM SIGMETRICS (July 1998)
5. Cheng, Y.: Re: [tcpm] Adopting draft-fairhurst-tcpm-newcwv. IETF TCPM Mailing List (December 2012)
6. Dukkipati, N., Cardwell, N., Cheng, Y., Mathis, M.: TCP Loss Probe (TLP): An Algorithm for Fast Recovery of Tail Losses. Internet-Draft draft-dukkipati-tcpm-tcp-loss-probe-00.txt, Work in progress (July 2012)
7. Jacobson, V.: Congestion Avoidance and Control. In: ACM SIGCOMM (1988)
8. Karagiannis, T., Papagiannaki, K., Faloutsos, M.: BLINC: Multilevel Traffic Classification in the Dark. In: ACM SIGCOMM (2005)
9. Kim, H., Claffy, K., Fomenkov, M., Barman, D., Faloutsos, M., Lee, K.: Internet Traffic Classification Demystified: Myths, Caveats, and the Best Practices. In: ACM SIGCOMM CoNEXT (December 2008)
10. Mockapetris, P.: Domain Names - Implementation and Specification. RFC 1035 (November 1987)
11. Nielsen, H., Gettys, J., Baird-Smith, A., Prud'hommeaux, E., Lie, H., Lilley, C.: Network Performance Effects of HTTP/1.1, CSS1, and PNG. In: ACM SIGCOMM (September 1997)
12. Paxson, V.: Empirically-Derived Analytic Models of Wide-Area TCP Connections. IEEE/ACM Transactions on Networking 2(4) (August 1994)
13. Paxson, V.: Automated Packet Trace Analysis of TCP Implementations. In: ACM SIGCOMM (September 1997)
14. Paxson, V., Floyd, S.: Difficulties in Simulating the Internet. IEEE/ACM Transactions on Networking 9(4), 392–403 (2001)
15. Sargent, M., Stack, B., Dooner, T., Allman, M.: A First Look at 1 Gbps Fiber-To-The-Home Traffic. Technical Report 12-009, International Computer Science Institute (August 2012)
16. Visweswaraiah, V., Heidemann, J.: Improving restart of idle TCP connections. Technical Report 97-661, University of Southern California (November 1997)
17. Xu, Y., Yu, C., Li, J., Liu, Y.: Video Telephony for End-consumers: Measurement Study of Google+, iChat, and Skype. In: ACM Internet Measurement Conference (October 2012)

Third-Party Identity Management Usage on the Web

Anna Vapen[1], Niklas Carlsson[1], Anirban Mahanti[2], and Nahid Shahmehri[1]

[1] Linköping University, Linköping, Sweden
[2] NICTA, Sydney, NSW, Australia

Abstract. Many websites utilize third-party identity management services to simplify access to their services. Given the privacy and security implications for end users, an important question is how websites select their third-party identity providers and how this impacts the characteristics of the emerging identity management landscape seen by the users. In this paper we first present a novel Selenium-based data collection methodology that identifies and captures the identity management relationships between sites and the intrinsic characteristics of the websites that form these relationships. Second, we present the first large-scale characterization of the third-party identity management landscape and the relationships that makes up this emerging landscape. As a reference point, we compare and contrast our observations with the somewhat more understood third-party content provider landscape. Interesting findings include a much higher skew towards websites selecting popular identity provider sites than is observed among content providers, with sites being more likely to form identity management relationships that have similar cultural, geographic, and general site focus. These findings are both positive and negative. For example, the high skew in usage places greater responsibility on fewer organizations that are responsible for the increased information leakage cost associated with highly aggregated personal information, but also reduces the user's control of the access to this information.

1 Introduction

With an increasing demand for personalized services, many websites ask their users to create personal user accounts and authenticate themselves before service. To simplify account creation and increase personalization opportunities, many sites use third-party identity management services. These services allow a user's digital identity and some personal information to be shared across multiple distinct sites; however, they also come with their own reliability, privacy, and security concerns [9,13].

Third-party identity management providers typically offer simplified authentication, using a *single-sign-on* (SSO) [13] service. In a typical authentication scenario, the browser of a user wanting to use such identity service interacts with two additional parties: a *relying party* (RP) and an *identity provider* (IDP).

M. Faloutsos and A. Kuzmanovic (Eds.): PAM 2014, LNCS 8362, pp. 151–162, 2014.
© Springer International Publishing Switzerland 2014

Fig. 1. Huffington Post login example   **Fig. 2.** Methodology overview

An RP such as Yahoo can offer that users use their account with a third-party IDP such as Facebook or Google, to login to Yahoo and access its services. In this case, the selected IDP, say Facebook, would provide the authentication service and the user would only need to remember their digital identity with Facebook to access Yahoo. More formally, we say that two sites have an RP-IDP relationship, if the user log in to one of the sites (the RP) using the other site (the IDP). Figure 1 illustrates a more complex scenario. The Huffington Post site allows local login as well as authentication at multiple trusted third-party IDPs, including both Facebook and Google. Notice that Huffington Post uses Yahoo as IDP, illustrating that Yahoo can act as both IDP and RP. While the figure only shows a snippet of this complex situation, clearly, the relationships between these sites are nested.

In this paper we consider any third-party login collaborations in which an RP is using one or more external IDPs in the login process. In addition to SSO service, third-party identity providers are increasingly also used to share and modify information across sites. Following this trend, in addition to authentication protocols, such as OpenID[1] (e.g., used in part by Google), our study shows that these services are increasingly implemented using authorization protocols, such as OAuth[2] (e.g., used by Facebook). Authorization protocols have the added functionality that they, on behalf of the user, can allow one site (or service) to perform actions on a different site.

In this paper, we present (i) a novel Selenium-based data collection methodology that allows us to accurately identify and validate RP-IDP relationships that are not easily captured by pattern-matching crawlers (Section 2), and (ii) a large-scale characterization of the identified RP-IDP relationships[3], studying how websites select their IDPs (Section 3). Our methodology and analysis capture the impact on IDP selection of things such as relative site popularity, cultural/geographic biases, and the intrinsic website characteristics. To put distribution and selection characteristics in perspective, we compare our results against what is observed for third-party content delivery relationships. To the

---

[1] OpenID (official website), http://openid.net/, May 2013.

[2] OAuth (official website), http://oauth.net/, May 2013.

[3] Datasets are available at
   http://www.ida.liu.se/divisions/adit/data/pam14.html.

best of our knowledge, at the time of writing, there are no other large-scale studies of the third-party identity management landscape and its structure.

In general, we find that IDP usage is highly skewed, with a small set of IDPs accounting for most of the world-wide usage. These IDPs are typically globally popular sites (such as Facebook, Twitter, and Google) that have a large user base. The tendency to select popular services as IDPs has resulted in a pronounced rich-gets-richer effect. For example, 90% of the RP-relationships are to an IDP among the top-100 most popular sites according to Alexa, and 50% of the observed RP-IDP relationships have a site-rank ratio of at least 10^3 (ratio between the RP and IDP ranks). In contrast, the third-party content provider relationships are relatively evenly distributed among Alexa ranks, with 50% of the observed content provider relationships having a site-rank ratio of at least four, suggesting a relatively weaker bias towards more popular sites. We also find that IDP selection is more biased towards the same cultural/geographic region than what is observed for third-party content provider selection, and websites appear to have a slight preference for selecting IDPs that provide similar service as the website.

2   Methodology

2.1   Data Collection

At the core of the third-party identity management landscape are the relationships between relaying parties (RPs) and identity providers (IDPs). To identify relationships for a wide range of sites, we employed a novel two-step approach. In the first step, we use a logarithmic sampling technique to pick a sample set of sites with varying popularities. In the second step, we use a Selenium-based crawling tool that allows us to accurately identify and validate RP-IDP relationships that are not easily captured by pattern-matching crawlers. Figure 2 summarizes our methodology.

Popularity-Based Logarithmic Sampling: The size of the Web precludes identification of all RP-IDP relationships. Instead, we collect a "sample" set of sites and study these for potential IDP usage. For our sampling we retrieved the Alexa[4] list on April 17, 2012 of the top 1 million most popular websites worldwide. Based on Web popularity following power-law distributions [5], we then placed 80,000 points uniformly on a logarithmic range $[1, 10^6]$ (ensuring that the number of points in segment $[10^x, 10^{x+1}]$ is independent of x) and sampled the sites with a popularity rank closest to each point. After removal of duplicates we had a sample set with 35,620 sites.

Relationship Identification: To identify RP-IDP relationships of each sampled site, we built a novel Selenium-based[5] crawling tool. Our crawler is built as a cloud-based proxy, and acts like a human user, which may click on many

---

[4] Alexa (official website), http://www.alexa.com, April 2012.

[5] Selenium. http://seleniumhq.org/, March 2012.

different available GUI elements, react to pop-ups, and take a range of other GUI-driven actions. In comparison with pattern-matching tools, we have found that our Selenium-based tool does a very good job identifying relationships associated with more complex Web 2.0 websites. It captures relationships that are non-trivial and not easily identified even using manual methods. This is important as many websites today use clickable images which may not match the actual IDPs, and/or hide the IDPs within their design.

Our crawler is multi-threaded, explores each site down to a depth two from the starting page, and uses regular-expression-based pattern matching on all elements (including not only links but also clickable images, pop-ups, and similar) to find elements related to authentication. The tool initially prioritizes clicking on object elements that match pre-defined patterns and therefore are potential authentication related elements. When all matched elements on a page are clicked, the tool continues clicking all other clickable elements until a specified per-site timeout value of 25 minutes is reached.

2.2 Statistics and Complementary Datasets

For both the sampled sites and the identified IDPs, we used the Selenium-based crawler and complementing scripts to collect statistics and information about each site. The crawl included the download of $1.4 \cdot 10^8$ objects (totaling 1.6 TB), the identification and analysis of $2.5 \cdot 10^7$ links. Out of the 35,620 sampled websites, 1,865 websites were classified as RPs. We also observed 50 IDPs and 3,329 unique RP-IDP relations. Finally, complementing scripts were used to obtain additional ownership, cultural, and geographic information regarding all observed (sampled and non-sampled) sites. These complementary datasets are primarily supportive and are discussed when used.

2.3 Validation

To ensure a fairly clean dataset, our Selenium-based data collection tool is designed to carefully identify true RP-IDP relationships and avoid false positives. The accuracy of our tool was validated using semi-manual relationship identification and classification. To obtain as exhaustive and accurate a list of RP-IDP relationships as possible we first built yet another crawling tool that identified candidate relationships much more loosely (and hence resulted in many false positives!) that we could later manually verify/reject by examining the identified objects that suggested such a linkage. We also carefully explored all sites on the top-200 list manually for relationships. By combining these two approaches we built a list of relationships involving the top-200 sites.

Out of a total of 69 RPs, 32 IDPs, and 186 relationships, the tool identified 23, 12, and 36, respectively. While the tool clearly does not find all relationships, it is very successful in avoiding false positives. The single false positive for IDPs (`vkontakte.ru`), is due to a name change from `vkontakte.ru` to `vk.com`. The three potentially false RPs (`wordpress.com`, `uol.com.br`, and `onet.pl`) are all blog hosts, portals and website hosts. Their users create sub-sites which may

Table 1. Top-10 list of global IDPs. ([a] Facebook is a well-known OAuth-only provider, but has in the past been an RP in OpenID. [b] Google and Yahoo also occasionally uses OAuth. [c] The OpenID field allows general login with any OpenID IDP, although some restrictions may occur.)

IDP rank	Alexa rank	IDP/federation	Protocol	Number of RPs
1	2	facebook.com	OAuth[a]	1293
2	10	twitter.com	OAuth	378
3	9	qq.com	OAuth	278
4	1	google.com	OpenID[b]	250
5	4	yahoo.com	OpenID[b]	141
6	16	sina.com.cn	OAuth	127
7	-	openID	OpenID[c]	87
8	4173	vkontakte.ru	OAuth	73
9	25	weibo.com	OAuth	64
10	12	linkedin.com	OAuth	63

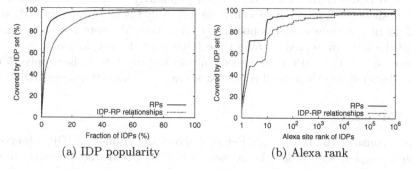

(a) IDP popularity   (b) Alexa rank

Fig. 3. RPs that are served by the most popular IDPs

allow third-party authentication. The third site `onet.pl`, also shares content with Facebook. Finally, out of the 13 false relationships, roughly half are due to sub-domain matches and name changes (as discussed above), and the rest are due to misclassified content provider relationships.

While omitted, it should be noted that our conclusions have been tested and validated using multiple crawlers. The use of our semi-manual dataset further strengthens our belief in the generality of our results. We have not found any major biases in the set of relationships included.

3 Characterization Results

3.1 The Big Players

Table 1 summarizes the top-10 globally most popular IDPs in our dataset, the number of (sampled) RPs that these IDPs help, and the primary protocol used

for third-party authentication. For reference, we also provide the Alexa ranks of
the services.

We note that some of the most popular sites on the Web also are the most used
IDPs. The low Alexa rank for vkontakte.ru is largely due to a domain name
change (to vk.com with an Alexa rank of 41), as many RPs use the old domain
name. Interestingly, the general OpenID field that allows the user to input any
OpenID provider is only used by 87 of the sampled sites and no specialized
IDP makes the list. In fact, we observe that OAuth is the dominating protocol.
Among the top-10 IDPs in Table 1, eight IDPs use OAuth as their primary
protocol and nine use OAuth for some of their relationships.

These results suggest that many sites choose to use popular sites as their
IDPs. The users are more likely to already have accounts with these sites, and in
many cases these sites may already have access to large amounts of personal information that could help the RP improve their personalization and service. This
observation may also provide some insight as to why identity management federations such as OpenID and third-party services that specialize only in identity
management have struggled to take off [11].

We next take a closer look at the relative popularity of the IDPs. Figures 3(a)
and 3(b) show the fraction of RPs that are served by the most popular IDPs and
the IDPs of a certain global popularity, respectively. We note that more than
75% of the RPs are served by 5% of the IDPs, and the majority of these 75%
are made up by the IDPs with Alexa ranks in the top 100. In fact, only 15 of
the 44 IDPs outside the top-10 Alexa list serve more than 10 sampled IDPs.

3.2   IDP Usage

We next consider the IDP usage. Figure 4 shows the number of IDPs observed
for each sampled site. While the average is highest for the most popular sites,
we note that there are some less popular sites that use a large number of IDPs.
Among the nine sampled websites with more than ten IDPs, six of the sites are
news sites and all nine use a login widget from gigya.com, providing the sites
with a selection of IDPs.

Figure 5 breaks down the IDP usage for each popularity segment, based on
which IDPs the sites in each segment are using. We can see that the RPs with the
most popular sites on average use the most IDPs, and that the top-ranked IDPs
are the most popular IDP choices for sites belonging to all popularity segments.
For all segments, the IDPs that rank in the top-10 contribute for more than 75%
of the IDP usage.

3.3   Comparison with Content Services

To put popularity skew and biases in perspective, in the following we compare
our observations with those observed in the more traditional content delivery
context. First, we consider the site-rank of the biggest *service providers* and
service users. In the context of identity management, these entities correspond to
the third-party IDPs and the RPs, respectively. In the context of content delivery,

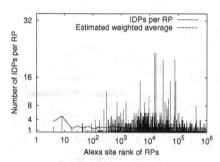
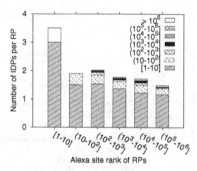

Fig. 4. Number of IDPs per sampled RP   **Fig. 5.** Breakdown of the average number of IDPs selected per RP and popularity segment

these entities correspond to the third-party content providers that deliver the content and the site that the content is delivered on behalf of, respectively. This comparison provides a natural reference point, as both IDPs and third-party content providers serve clients on behalf of the origin site.

Figure 6(a) shows the service provider breakdown; i.e., the fraction of user sites (RPs, for example) that are served by each third-party service provider (IDP, for example) of varying global Alexa rank. Figure 6(b) shows the service user breakdown; i.e., the fraction of third-party relationships that these sites are responsible for. We note that the content provider usage is distributed much more evenly across popularities than the IDP usage, which is heavily skewed towards the most popular sites.

In general, we find that IDPs often provide service for less popular RPs, whereas in the context of content delivery, it is much more common that the third-party content is served by less popular sites. While these less popular sites in some cases are backed up by a big company, the differences are striking. Figure 7 shows the relative difference in site rank between providers (e.g., IDPs) and service user sites (e.g., RPs) for the two types of relationships. These results show that the identity management landscape is significantly more skewed towards the big players than the content delivery ecosystem. For example, while 50% of the observed content provider relationships have a site-rank ratio of at least 4 (suggesting only a light bias towards more popular sites), the corresponding RP-IDP site-rank ratio is at least 10^3 (between the RP and IDP ranks).

3.4 Service-Based Analysis

To gain a better understanding of the sites that are more likely to act as an RP or IDP, we manually classified the top-200 sites, as well as each of the identified IDPs, based on the primary service they provide. For this analysis, we manually labeled each site into one of nine service classes. While alternative classifications are possible, the classes used here were inspired by those used by Gill et al. [5]. Table 2 lists the service classes and the statistics for each class.

These results show that the use of IDPs is greatest among sites that share information/news/data. This is consistent with significant use of OAuth. How-

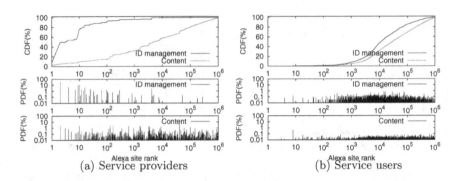

(a) Service providers

(b) Service users

Fig. 6. Comparison with content delivery

Table 2. Manual site classification results for top-200 list

Type	Sites		Relationships			
	Total	RPs	Total	Per page	Per RP	Breakdown
Social/portal	84	23 (27%)	55	0.65	2.39	47 social, 4 tech, 3 commerce, 1 info
Tech	24	8 (33%)	40	1.67	5.00	26 social, 12 tech, 1 commerce, 1 info
Commerce	20	5 (25%)	6	0.30	1.20	3 social, 2 commerce
News	17	11 (65%)	28	1.65	2.55	28 social
Video	18	8 (44%)	24	1.33	3.00	22 social, 1 commerce, 1 info
Info	14	7 (50%)	11	0.79	1.57	10 social, 1 commerce
Filesharing	12	7 (58%)	22	1.83	3.14	22 social
Ads	6	0 (0%)	0	0	0	-
CDN	5	0 (0%)	0	0	0	-

ever, it is also interesting to see that sites of some other service classes (e.g., tech and video sites) often use more IDPs per RP, in the case that they decide to act as an RP. We conjecture that the high number of IDPs per RP for tech sites reflects that these sites are early adopters of these technologies. This conjecture is supported by the fact that these sites to a much larger extent than other sites give their users the option of using specialized IDPs, which provide identity management as their only service.

We find that both tech and commerce sites have a relative preference for picking IDPs from within their own category. For example, the tech sites are responsible for 12/40 (30%) of the tech IDP relationships observed from the top-200 sites, and 2/5 (40%) of the IDPs used by RPs classified as commerce sites are to IDPs that are commerce sites. These sites may have to rely more on domain knowledge to maintain credibility within their communities than other type of sites. News and file sharing sites, on the other hand, only use IDPs classified as social (e.g., Facebook and Twitter). This usage may be motivated by a desire to form "personal" relationships and connect with more users.

Table 3. Percent (%) unique third-party relationships that are to a local IDP or content provider (CP) in the same geographic region as the sampled site, using each of our three location mappings

	Method (local (%))					
	Whois		Servers		Audience	
Region	IDPs	CPs	IDPs	CPs	IDPs	CPs
North America	97.0	91.7	95.8	88.8	95.8	82.2
Europe	0.4	21.2	0.9	21.5	0.9	22.0
Asia	61.3	25.7	71.8	45.5	53.6	41.3
Others	0.0	9.1	0.0	10.6	1.3	9.7

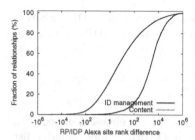

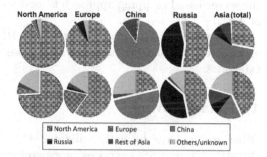

Fig. 7. Difference in site-rank ratio between service user/provider. (Alexa rank of user divided by rank of provider.)

Fig. 8. Geographic distribution of third-party relationships. Top row: Identity management. Bottom row: Content delivery.

3.5   Cultural and Geographic Analysis

We next try to glean some insight as to whether there may be some preference for selecting IDPs with similar geographic or cultural focus. Due to factors such as global user populations, it is difficult to uniquely assign each site to a single geographic region. We make no claims regarding the absolute number of sites that pick a "local" IDP. Instead, our observations are discussed relative to what is observed for third-party content delivery relationships.

While the general conclusions of our results appear to hold true for a wide range of mapping approaches, in this section we present results using three diverse methods: (i) a whois services based on where sites are registered, (ii) an online geo-location service located in the US to map the location of the servers, and (iii) statistics provided by Alexa estimating the region in which the site's primary user audience is located.

Table 3 shows the percentage of local relationships, for each of the three mapping approaches. We use one row for sample sites mapped to different parts of the world, and list how large a percentage of the third-party providers are considered local. The region "others", which includes South America, Africa and Oceania, is only responsible for 2-3.5% of the relationships. In the above results we exclude the unmapped relationships.

While the correct geographic location of a service/site in non-trivial and the exact percentage of sites classified as "local" clearly depends on the method used, our results allow two major observations. First, we note that there is a tendency for selecting local IDPs in all geographic regions with major IDPs, with the exception of Europe and Other, which primarily use major American IDPs. Second, and more importantly, the fraction of "local" IDPs is larger than the fraction of "local" content providers for all regions except for Europe and Other. It should be noted that the IDP usage in Europe and Other overall is much smaller than in the other regions. This stronger locality preference (with the exception of European sites) is further illustrated in Figure 8, which shows the geographic breakdown for sites mapped to the regions with the most usage. Here, the server-based mapping approach is used and we include a further breakdown of Asia.

A closer look at the data reveals that info RPs only choose local IDPs, whereas social, tech, file sharing, and news RPs use more non-local IDPs than other categories.

4   Related Work

Other works have formally validated OAuth [3, 8], Facebook Connect [7], OpenID [12], and SSO services in general [1]. For OAuth, a long laundry list of problems and threats has been identified, including phishing, eavesdropping, and various problems related to tokens [6]. It has also been shown that SSO services are vulnerable to cross-site scripting attacks [1] and that OpenID is vulnerable to cross-site request forgery attacks [12]. However, perhaps the biggest weakness in SSO is the implementation of the protocols themselves [3, 10]. For example, Wang et al. [13] presents an experimental study of the security of some of the most popular SSO services.

It should also be noted that identity management solutions can greatly affect user behavior. For example, as users get used to authenticating with unknown third-parties and following the path of least resistance, they may not take security precautions or read privacy agreements, making them increasingly susceptible to phishing attacks [4]. This last uncertainty has prompted many users to be cautious and afraid of using (unknown) third-party services, and may be another reason why we observe that many sites select popular IDPs. This shift away from specialized OpenID solutions may also hamper the development and/or adoption of large-scale identity federations with stronger authentication methods [2].

Complementing prior work, we provide a large-scale characterization in which we analyze relationships and third-party selection in the identity management landscape.

5   Discussion and Conclusions

This paper studies how websites are using third-party identity providers. We present a novel data collection methodology, which combines a Selenium-based crawler and a log-based sampling technique, and use the collected datasets to characterize global IDP usage. To provide a reference point for discussion, we compare our observations with the selection of third-party content providers. Our methodology and analysis captures how factors such as relative site popularities, cultural/geographic biases, and the intrinsic characteristics of the websites influence the relationships between RPs and IDPs.

Our study shows that a small number of IDPs dominate the IDP space. These IDPs are typically popular web services with a large international user base, and already have access to large amounts of sensitive user data. As these companies are under public scrutiny, they will hopefully take greater care to securely store and handle sensitive user information. However, the many RPs using a few IDPs can also result in a large attack surface. The fact that OAuth is dominating OpenID also raises some privacy concerns, as it typically involves sharing of more user data.

A rich-gets-richer phenomena appears to be at play with the tendency of RPs selecting highly popular services as IDPs. Instead of picking specialized IDPs, which provide authentication as their primary service, RPs are choosing IDPs with higher popularity ranking than themselves. Today, many specialized IDPs, such as Clickpass, Vidoop, and MyopenID are therefore disappearing, being acquired, and/or going out of business.

Our characterization and dataset is the first large-scale measurement-based study of the identity management landscape and its structure, and is expected to provide an important stepping stone towards better understanding third-party identity management and their impact on Web users. Future work includes a large-scale security and privacy evaluation of alternative identity management solutions that take into account the observed relationship tendencies observed in the current identity management landscape.

References

1. Armando, A., Carbone, R., Compagna, L., Cuellar, J., Pellegrino, G., Sorniotti, A.: From multiple credentials to browser-based single sign-on: Are we more secure? In: Camenisch, J., Fischer-Hübner, S., Murayama, Y., Portmann, A., Rieder, C. (eds.) SEC 2011. IFIP AICT, vol. 354, pp. 68–79. Springer, Heidelberg (2011)
2. Bonneau, J., Herley, C., van Oorschot, P.C., Stajano, F.: The quest to replace passwords: A framework for comparative evaluation of web authentication schemes. In: Proc. IEEE Symposium on S&P (May 2012)
3. Chari, S., Jutla, C., Roy, A.: Universally composable security analysis of oauth v2.0. Technical report, Cryptology ePrint Archive, Report 2011/526 (2011)
4. Dhamija, R., Dusseault, L.: The seven flaws of identity management: Usability and security challenges. IEEE Security & Privacy 6(2), 24–29 (2008)
5. Gill, P., Arlitt, M., Carlsson, N., Mahanti, A., Williamson, C.: Characterizing organizational use of web-based services: Methodology, challenges, observations, and insights. ACM Transactions on the Web (TWEB) 5(4), 19:1–19:23 (2011)
6. Lodderstedt, T., McGloin, M., Hunt, P.: Oauth 2.0 threat model and security considerations. Internet-Draft, IETF (October 2011)

7. Miculan, M., Urban, C.: Formal analysis of facebook connect single sign-on authentication protocol. In: Proc. SOFSEM (January 2011)
8. Pai, S., Sharma, Y., Kumar, S., Pai, R.M., Singh, S.: Formal verification of oauth 2.0 using alloy framework. In: Proc. CSNT (June 2011)
9. Pfitzmann, B., Waidner, M.: Analysis of liberty single-sign-on with enabled clients. IEEE Internet Computing 7(6), 38–44 (2003)
10. Sun, S.-T., Beznosov, K.: The devil is in the (implementation) details: an empirical analysis of oauth sso systems. In: Proc. ACM CCS (October 2012)
11. Sun, S.-T., Boshmaf, Y., Hawkey, K., Beznosov, K.: A billion keys, but few locks: The crisis of web single sign-on. In: Proc. NSPW (September 2010)
12. Sun, S.-T., Hawkey, K., Beznosov, K.: Systematically breaking and fixing openid security: Formal analysis, semi-automated empirical evaluation, and practical countermeasures. Computers & Security 31(4), 465–483 (2012)
13. Wang, R., Chen, S., Wang, X.: Signing me onto your accounts through facebook and google: a traffic-guided security study of commercially deployed single-sign-on web services. In: Proc. IEEE Symposium on S&P (May 2012)

Understanding the Reachability
of IPv6 Limited Visibility Prefixes

Andra Lutu[1,2], Marcelo Bagnulo[2], Cristel Pelsser[3], and Olaf Maennel[4]

[1] Institute IMDEA Networks, Spain
[2] University Carlos III of Madrid, Spain
[3] IIJ Innovation Institute, Japan
[4] Loughborough University, UK

Abstract. The main functionality of the Internet is to provide global connectivity for every node attached to it. In light of the IPv4 address space depletion, large networks are in the process of deploying IPv6. In this paper we perform an extensive analysis of how BGP route propagation affects global reachability of the active IPv6 address space in the context of this unique transition of the Internet infrastructure. We propose and validate a methodology for testing the reachability of an IPv6 address block active in the routing system. Leveraging the global visibility status of the IPv6 prefixes evaluated with the BGP Visibility Scanner, we then use this methodology to verify if the visibility status of the prefix impacts its reachability at the interdomain level. We perform active measurements using the RIPE Atlas platform. We test destinations with different BGP visibility degrees (i.e., limited visibility - LV, high visibility - HV and dark prefixes). We show that the IPv6 LV prefixes (v6LVPs) are generally reachable, mostly due to a less-specific *HV* covering prefix (v6HVP). However, this is not the case of the dark address space, which, by not having a covering v6HVP is largely unreachable.

1 Introduction

The fundamental task envisioned for the Internet is to provide reachability for every node attached to the network. The Border Gateway Protocol (BGP) is currently responsible for the exchange of network reachability information and the selection of paths according to specified routing policies. By tweaking the BGP configurations, the network operators are able to express their interdomain routing preferences, designed to accommodate myriad economic and technical goals. However, these routing policies can at time affect the global visibility of a certain prefix, both willingly or unknowingly/accidentally [13]. Given the complex interactions between policies in the Internet, the origin AS by itself cannot ensure that only by configuring a routing policy it can also achieve the anticipated results [7]. Consequently, policies may affect the propagation of routes, making some paths unavailable at a global level, and sometimes preventing a prefix to be learned altogether. Moreover, the definition of routing policies is a complicated process, involving a number of subtle tuning operations prone to errors.

Over the last few years, much has been said about global connectivity (or the lack of it) in the IPv6 Internet due to the routing policies of a few Autonomous Systems(ASes) (e.g., [2]). In this paper, we aim to establish if IPv6 prefix visibility at the interdomain

M. Faloutsos and A. Kuzmanovic (Eds.): PAM 2014, LNCS 8362, pp. 163–172, 2014.
© Springer International Publishing Switzerland 2014

level has an impact on the reachability of the address space advertised in the Internet. Using the interdomain route propagation process reflected in the global routing tables as an expression of routing policy interaction, we introduce the concept of **Limited-Visibility Prefix (LVP)**. We define *LVPs* as stable long-lived Internet routes that are advertised by at least two different ASes, but visible in *less than* 95% of all the global routing tables analyzed. Though some legitimate routing policies of an AS limit the visibility of its prefixes in the Internet, the latter can also stem from human operator errors or unpredicted interplay with the external netting of otherwise correctly defined routing policies. Contrariwise, we define the **High-Visibility Prefixes (HVPs)** as the set of prefixes that are propagated in *at least* 95% of all the available global routing feeds. We also identify the **Dark Prefixes (DPs)** [9], which represent the subset of *LVPs* that are not covered by any *HV* less-specific prefix. These prefixes represent address space that, in the absence of a default route, may not be globally reachable. We use the BGP Visibility Scanner [11] to evaluate the visibility status of the IPv6 prefixes announced in the global routing system. The tool uses the routing data retrieved from the RIPE RIS and RouteViews projects to performs a differential analysis to retrieve *LVPs* on a daily basis, which are then made available on-line.

We further focus on measuring the reachability of the prefixes in all of the three above-mentioned sets of prefixes, i.e. HVP, LVP and DP. We propose a methodology for testing the reachability of an IPv6 *prefix*, which relies on the use of traceroute probes to test the destination prefix. We calibrate the proposed measurement methodology by testing a large set of so-called *anchor* prefixes, which we know a priori to contain at least one reachable address. We compile a set of approximatively 70,000 such prefixes, which we test from a major Japanese ISP using different traceroute approaches. We then apply the proposed methodology from multiple vantage points in the Internet, including 100 RIPE Atlas active probes. We thus show that the IPv6 LVPs (v6LVPs) are generally reachable, mostly due to the less-specific *HV* covering prefixes. However, this is not the case of the dark address space, which is largely unreachable.

2   The BGP Visibility Scanner for IPv6

In this section we describe the BGP Visibility Scanner - a tool we propose for identifying *LVPs* at the interdomain level. We have publicly released an initial version of the BGP Visibility Scanner[1] in November 2012, allowing any network operator to check if the AS originates LVPs. The earlier version of this tool is documented in [11]. Since it became operational, the tool has been well received by the operational community and it still attracts a large amount of attention and feedback. The methodology used for the BGP Visibility Scanner is structured in three steps: First, we retrieve the raw BGP routing data at two different times every day. Second, we clean the raw data in order to obtain the Global Routing Tables (GRTs), by applying two different cleansing filters. Third, we verify in two sub-steps the visibility of each prefix within the sample of identified GRTs using the Visibility Scanner Algorithm. We now further expand on the steps we take in order to retrieve, parse, clean and process the raw BGP routing data to distinguish the set of *LVPs* and *DPs*.

---

[1] The BGP Visibility Scanner is publicly available at **visibility.it.uc3m.es**

2.1 Retrieving and Refining the Raw Routing Data

We work with publicly available routing data, retrieved from the RouteViews and RIPE RIS projects. These two repositories periodically receive BGP routing table *snapshots*, i.e. one time instance of a routing table, from over 400 active BGP peers for both IPv4 and IPv6. In this first step of the methodology, we retrieve the publicly available routing data. We choose to do so at two different times during the day, i.e., at 8h00 and 16h00. We process these two different snapshots per day in order to be certain that we only work with routes that are stable expression of routing policies at the interdomain level.

In the second step of our methodology, we parse the raw data in order to identify what we define to be *global routing tables (GRTs)*. Only by comparing the GRTs from the BGP peers, we can further identify the sets of *HV* and *LV* prefixes. For the purpose of this paper, we loosely define the GRT as the entire routing table provided by a *Default Free Zone (DFZ)*[2] network to its customers requesting a full routing feed. The routing table maintained in one of the so-called DFZ routers is commonly known as the *global routing table*. Realistically speaking though, due to the current operational status of the Internet routing, such a GRT of the BGP routing is an idealized concept. However, Internet Service Providers (ISPs) do maintain their own version of the *global routing table*, which is propagated to customer networks upon request. This is not a formal definition, but it properly captures the main idea of the kind of data we require.

In order to identify the feeds which constitute a GRT, the primary characteristic of the routing feeds on which we focus is the actual size of the routing table snapshot. Based on the BGP Analysis Report [1], we consider that *a complete routing feed from a monitor should have no less than **10,000** IPv6 routing entries*. Consequently, we check over 200 routing feeds collected from the two repositories, and keep approximatively 110 BGP feeds that comply with the imposed lower-limit of prefix number.

Additionally, we perform a couple of "sanitary" checks on the data contained in the identified GRTs, in order to further discard the information that is of no interest for our study. Hence, we apply the *bogon filter* on all the GRTs. Bogon prefixes are a class of routes that should never appear in the Internet. Bogons are defined as *Martians*, representing reserved and local address space or *Fullbogons*, which include the IP space that has been allocated to a Regional Internet Registry (RIR), but has not been assigned by that RIR to an actual Internet Service Provider (ISP) or other end-user. We use the periodically updated filters from The Bogon Reference [4] in order to make sure that we eliminate any possible bogon route included in the GRTs.

2.2 The Visibility Scanner Algorithm: The Labeling Mechanism

We now apply the **Visibility Scanner Algorithm** for identifying prefixes with *stable* limited visibility in the Internet. It is important to filter out the cases of limited visibility caused by other factors unrelated to routing policies, e.g. BGP convergence or internal routes advertised only to the collector. In order to discard any internal paths leaking towards the collectors, we remove all the routes learned from only one monitor which

---

[2] Conceptually, the so-called *Default Free Zone (DFZ)* represents the set of BGP-speaking routers that do not need a default route to forward packets towards any destination in the Internet.

is also the route originating AS. Next, in order to further avoid that the converging prefixes emerge as false positive limited visibility prefixes in our results, we analyze two samples taken 8-hours apart of routing data. We evaluate the *visibility degree* at every sampling moment and assign *visibility labels* based on our results. We define the *visibility degree* as the number of GRTs which contain (i.e., "see") a certain prefix, and the *visibility label* as the visibility status of each prefix, i.e. *LV* for Limited Visibility and *HV* for High Visibility. We then compare the per-prefix visibility of each prefix, as observed at each sampling time and apply the prefix visibility prevalence sieve.

The Labeling Mechanism: Based on the visibility degree of the prefixes at each of the two sampling moments (i.e. 08h00 and 16h00), we assign a *visibility labels* at each sampling moment to all the prefixes discovered. *We define Limited Visibility prefixes as prefixes present in less than* 95% *of the active monitors at a sampling time*. Otherwise, the prefixes are defined as High Visibility prefixes. Ideally, a *HV* prefix should be contained in absolutely all the routing tables contained in the sample. The choice of the 95% allows for a 5% error in the sampling, including possible glitches that may appear in the data. Moreover, according to our threshold sensitivity analysis, we find that the set of *LVPs* is not particularly sensitive to the values of the prevalence sieve threshold.

Visibility Label Prevalence Sieve: When deriving the final per-day visibility label, we account for the dynamics of a prefix in time. The high visibility of a prefix in at least one monitor sample hints the fact that the route could reach all the observed ASes. Should this change during the analyzed time, it might be a cause of, for example, topology changes or failures. Therefore, we consider that *the HV label always prevails*, i.e. if a prefix is tagged as *HV* in one of the samples, it is tagged as *HV* in the final set.

Otherwise, when no *HV* label is tagged, we analyze the cases of *LV* prefixes emerging in our results. If a prefix appears only at one sampling time and it is tagged as *LVP*, this might be a sign that the prefix is in the process of being withdrawn or, contrariwise, in the process of converging after just being injected. These particular routes cannot be qualified within our study, thus we filter out any prefix with only one label in a day and that label being *LV*. The only case where a prefix has limited visibility and mark it accordingly, is when the two labels assigned at each sampling time are both *LVP*.

Identifying Dark Prefixes: Once we have identified the two main sets of prefixes, i.e. the *LVPs* and the *HVPs*, we can now identify the set of Dark Prefixes. For each of the prefix in the LVP category, we build the covering trie of less specific HV prefixes, from which we ultimately retrieve its root prefix (i.e. the smallest covering HV prefix). In the eventuality of not identifying any such globally visible less-specific prefix, we mark the LV prefix as *Dark* and continue our analysis.

3   The IPv6 Limited Visibility Prefixes

We collect more than *500* routing feeds on a daily basis, for each of the two different sampling moments, i.e., 8h00 and 16h00. After the *cleansing process*, we distinguish, in average, *110 GRTs* injected to the public repositories by unique ASes. We then compare the content of the 110 GRTs in order to identify the LVPs. In rough numbers, the daily overall total number of prefixes identified is approximatively *16,500 prefixes*. Out of these, on average *150 prefixes* are singled out as leaked internal routes and, consequently, discarded from our analysis. Furthermore, we remove the converging routes

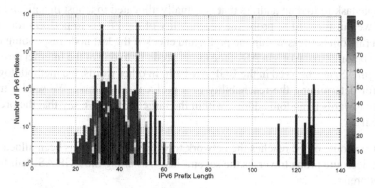

Fig. 1. Distribution of IPv6 prefixes on prefix length. The bars are color-coded to show the visibility degree of the prefixes: from dark blue for LV, going to dark red for HV.

that may otherwise emerge as limited visibility in the visibility scanner. This incurs the elimination of about *10* additional prefixes in average. For the remaining prefixes we continue our visibility analysis and assign LV/HV visibility tags.

Finally, we identify an average of *3,500 IPv6 prefixes* that are tagged *LVP* and approximatively *12,500* prefixes marked *HVP*. Therefore, 20% of all the IPv6 prefixes identified from the analyzed routing tables are LVPs. This is consistent with the result for the IPv4 LVPs, where out of all the prefixes learned, 20% have limited visibility [11]. When checking how the two sets of prefixes overlap, we find that there are more than *500* LV prefixes without a covering HVP, which we mark *DP*. This represents approximately 14% of the whole set of v6LVPs and 3.75% of the v6HVP set. When comparing with the situation in IPv4, where in average only 3% of the LVPs (and 0.6% of the HVPs) are marked as *dark*, we conclude that we have almost 5 times more IPv6 dark address space. This is relevant because these prefixes may have limited reachability. We have observed more than 13% of all IPv6 active ASes inject LVPs, while less than 5% of all IPv6 active ASes originate DPs. In IPv4, we see that 9% of all ASes originate LVPs, while only 2% are also injecting DPs. This result further hints the early stages of development of the IPv6 architecture, previously established in [6].

For the rest of the analysis we perform in the paper, we use the LVP dataset derived on the 8th of August, 2013. The dataset consists of 12,621 v6HVPs and 3,444 v6LVPs, out of which 473 are v6DPs. Figure 1 depicts the distribution of IPv6 prefixes per prefix length, color-coded to match the visibility degree of the prefixes in question. All the prefixes with a length longer than /48 are labeled as v6LVPs by the BGP Visibility Scanner i.e. /48's do not propagate globally in the IPv6 routing system. This is consistent with the status in IPv4, where every prefix more-specific than /24 is labeled LVP.

4   Traceroute Probing for Reachability

In this section, we try to verify if the limited visibility of such prefixes have an actual impact in the reachability of the addresses in them.

We propose a methodology for determining if a prefix is reachable from a given vantage point in the Internet. The challenge for doing this with IPv6 prefixes is that it is not a simple task to find an address that is actually allocated to a host in a given prefix. The idea we put forward to probe the reachability of a prefix is to perform traceroute towards a random address within the prefix and check if the last node responding to the traceroute belongs to the origin AS of the target prefix or to one of the Internet providers of the origin AS, as observed in the BGP AS-Path. In other words, the methodology we propose for determining the reachability of a prefix is as follows. We send a traceroute probe towards a random address within the target prefix. We say that the prefix is reachable if :

1. The traceroute probe reaches the network to which the prefix has been allocated.
2. The traceroute probe traverses the second-last[3] AS along the BGP AS-Path for the target prefix.

We consider this latter hypothesis because there may be cases where, even if the probe does reach its destination, it might happen that the origin AS of the source IP for the last ICMP message received is actually the transit provider of the target AS. This happens because it is a common operational practice that ASes use addresses from their providers for their transit links. As a result, the router within the destination network that issues the last message of the traceroute process will do so using an source address from its ISP's address space. We do acknowledge that this may also be due to reachability problems in the last hop, which our methodology is unable to distinguish.

4.1 Traceroute Probing Approach

We begin by discussing the different traceroute probing methods and how we select the most suited approach. Traceroute is one of the most widely used network measurement tools, useful both to network operators and researchers. The original traceroute tool [8] sends UDP probes and it will be our *default* measurement approach. We further refer to this test as *default UDP traceroute probing*. The major weakness of the default UDP traceroute is that, in the current operational routing system, firewalls are likely to filter the probes sent to these unlikely ports, thus impacting the quality of the measurements. In order to avoid this problem, several other approaches are available. We use a modified UDP traceroute method which, instead of using high-numbered unlikely ports, sends packets on port 53. We further refer to this probing method as "UDP traceroute". A second approach we use is the so-called *ICMP traceroute*, which uses *ICMP echo request* instead of UDP probes. The last approach we use is *TCP traceroute*, which employs TCP SYN probes to port 80. The advantage of this approach is that the probes cannot be easily distinguished from normal requests to web servers, so they are less likely to be discarded along the path.

We establish which of the above-mentioned traceroute approaches is the most efficient by testing the status of a large set of control IPv6 addresses with all the listed probing methods. We use a set of 70.000 IPv6 addresses which are known to be reachable. This is made up of addresses from many sources, including DNS entries, Alexa's

---

[3] Usually, in the BGP AS-Path the last hop represent the origin AS of the prefix, while the first hop represents the AS whose routing table we analyze. Following this order, the second-last hop (2LH) in the AS-Path corresponds to the transit provider of the origin AS.

top sites, and several other sources. We check the reachability status of these 70,000 IPv6 addresses from a machine inside a major Japanese ISP's network. We do so by using all the above-mentioned traceroute probing approaches. Our results show that the most efficient probing method is *ICMP traceroute*, which successfully reached 99% of all the 70,000 probable IP addresses. Consequently, the traceroute probing method we further employ in our study is the ***ICMP traceroute***. This results is consistent with the observations of Luckie et al. in [10].

4.2   Validating the Measurement Methodology

We validate our methodology by testing a set of reachable IPv6 prefixes, which are known to contain at least one reachable address. The way we do this is by tacking a reverse engineering approach. For each of the previously identified 70,000 reachable IPv6 addresses, we map the covering prefix installed in the BGP routing tables. We use public routing data information to determine the most-specific prefixes covering each of these reachable addresses. The set of prefixes determined represents address space known to contain at least one address which is successful to ICMP traceroute probing. These prefixes form the target set of prefixes which we use for validation.

We start by sending ICMP traceroute probes from a machine within the major Japanese ISP towards a **randomly selected IPv6 address** within each of the prefixes determined above. According to the proposed methodology, we consider that the traceroute probe reached its destination when the traceroute probe traverses either the origin AS of the destination address, either the second-last AS appearing in the BGP AS-Path towards the target prefix. In order to identify the 2LH towards a prefix, we analyze the AS-Path information in the BGP routing table of the AS from which we are generating the traceroute messages, i.e., the major Japanese ISP.

After parsing the results of our traceroute tests, we learn that the ICMP traceroute probes successfully reached more than 96% of these *a-priori* reachable prefixes. Consequently, the methodology we propose is able to identify with 96% accuracy the reachability status of an IPv6 prefixes. For the other 4% of prefixes, our methodology is unable to determine reachability. This may be due to several reasons, including ICMP filtering or routers silently discarding packets.

5   Reachability Measurements and Results

5.1   Local Reachability Measurements

In order to establish the reachability for prefixes with the three different classes of interdomain visibility, we perform ICMP traceroute probing from a machine inside a major Japanese ISP's network. Regarding the target address space to be tested, we first re-define the set of LVPs and DPs *locally*, by analyzing only the routing table snapshot of the Japanese ISP. We are thus able to identify a total of 13,195 IPv6 prefixes present in the routing table, which we further label as High-Visibility Prefixes. These prefixes may not be globally High-Visibility, since there may be other routing tables not "seeing" some of these prefixes. We label all the rest of prefixes learned from the rest of the routing tables collected from the public repositories as Limited Visibility, which reach a total number of 2,359 prefixes. In order to check if any of the Limited Visibility prefixes are in fact Dark Prefixes from the point of view of the ISP, we check which v6LVPs have a less-specific v6HVP in the ISP's routing table to offer global reachability. We are thus able to single out a total number of 511 Dark Prefixes.

From the results of the measurements we learn that, in the case of the locally-defined v6HVPs, 92% of the target high-visibility prefixes are reachable from the ISP's network. This is consistent with the precision of our methodology, so we cannot make claims about reachability problems in the HVP set. In the case of the locally-defined v6LVPs which have a covering high-visibility IPv6 prefix (i.e., they are not dark), we observe that 94% of the prefixes are reachable from the Japanese ISP's network. Likewise, this is consistent with the precision of our tool so we cannot make any claims about reachability problems in the LVP set. We next evaluate the reachability status for the DPs and we learn that more than 95% of these prefixes traceroute ended in a network or destination unreachable error messages. Consequently, less than 5% of the dark address space is reachable from the Japanese ISP. We can then claim that within the precision of our methodology, DPs do present reachability problems.

5.2   RIPE Atlas Measurements and Results

Previously, we have seen that the non-dark LVPs defined for the Japanese ISP do not exhibit reachability issues, due to the covering HVPs. However, this was not the case for the local dark address space, which has less than 5% reachability. In this section, we use the RIPE Atlas platform [3] to run **larger-scale measurements for characterizing the reachability of the global dark address space**.

We zoom out from the previous localized analysis of reachability, and test the reachability of the DPs from 100 different probes active in the RIPE Atlas platform. We run the measurements both towards the globally defined set of IPv6 dark prefixes, i.e. the 473 v6DPs derived from analyzing 110 BGP routing tables, and also towards the set of IPv4 dark prefixes, i.e., 3,200 v4DPs derived from analyzing 154 global BGP routing tables. We send ICMP traceroute probes towards a random target address within each of the v6 and v4 DPs.. We proceed to verifying the reachability results in accordance with the methodology specified in Section 4. Point 2) of the proposed methodology requires to verify if the traceroute probe traverses the provider of the origin AS for the target prefix. As opposed to the case of the major Japanese ISP for which we have the BGP routing table to analyze, we now do not have access to the BGP routing tables corresponding to the 100 Atlas probes used. In order to overcome this issue, we build a set of *probable* second-last hops which may be traversed towards all the possible destination ASes. We do so by analyzing all the available routing tables from all the ASes active in RIPE RIS and/or Routeviews, and monitoring the ASes appearing as 2LHs towards every active destination AS. Thus, we state that the target prefix is reachable if *the traceroute probe traverses **any** of the probable second-last ASes to the origin AS of the target prefix.*

After processing all the traceroute results from each of the 100 probes towards a Dark Prefix, we conclude that the average reachability degree for a v6DP is of 46.5%, whereas for v4DPs this decreases to only 17.4%. To further understand this result, we

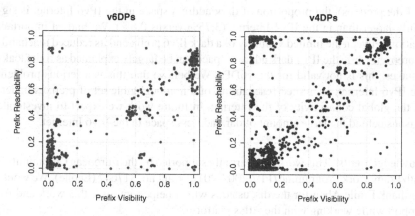

Fig. 2. Scatterplot of reachability probability against the DP's visibility, for v6DPs and for v4DPs

verify how the DP reachability correlates with the visibility degree of a DP. We show in Figure 2 the scatterplots both for IPv6 and IPv4 DPs' reachability against their visibility within the corresponding sample of ASes analyzed. We observe that for the v6DPs, depicted in the left-side plot, there is a stronger correlation between reachability and visibility than for the v4DPs. This happens because, for the v4DPs, we see a high number of prefixes with very limited visibility, but which are highly reachable from the sample of 100 probes chosen. We observe that in the v4 plot from Figure 2 there are approximatively 8% of IPv4 prefixes with visibilities smaller than 0.2 and reachability larger than 0.2. As previously noted in [5], this may be due to default routing in IPv4. In [12], the authors explain many of the real-life operational reasons for which this type if v4DPs emerge in the Internet. For example, we observe in the lower-left corner of the IPv4 plot in Figure 2 a very large number of v4DP (approximatively 72% of all the v4DPs) with a reduced visibility degree and a corresponding low reachability degree. These v4DPs may be route leaks which, as we learn from [12], often occur in the Internet. Consequently, the lack of reachability observed for v4DPs is largely explained by the fact that these prefixes are unintended to be visible in the Internet to begin with. At the same time, even if the v6DPs do not follow the known symptoms of route leaks or anomalies previously learned from the IPv4 cases, they do struggle with important lack of reachability. This further supports the hypothesis that, while in IPv4 the DPs are in majority results of mistakes or slips in the network configuration, for IPv6 we understand this as a side-effect of the early stages of development of the network.

6   Conclusions

In this paper, we perform an extensive analysis of how BGP route propagation affects global reachability of the active IPv6 address space, in the context of IPv6 penetration growing in the Internet.We proposed a methodology to measure the reachability status of the active LVP IPv6 prefixes, which represent address space that is not present in all the global routing tables of the operational networks. We find that, while the fraction of limited visibility address space is similar in the IPv4 and the IPv6 Internet (about

20% of the prefixes), the proportion of dark address space in the IPv6 Internet is significantly larger than in the IPv4 Internet (3.75% versus 0.6%). We find an important correlation between the limited visibility of a dark IPv6 prefix and its reduced reachability. Moreover, while the IPv4 dark address space can be largely explained as route leaks or mistakes, this is not valid for the v6DPs. We believe that this is a serious problem for the IPv6 Internet, as limited reachability of a non-negligible set of prefixes undermines the global connectivity of the Internet. In future work we expect to investigate the reasons behind the large amount of dark address space in the IPv6 Internet.

Acknowledgements. This work was partially supported by the European Community's Seventh Framework Programme (FP7/2007-2013) grant no. 317647 (Leone). We would like to thank Emile Aben for the discussions which helped improve this work and for his support while working with the Atlas platform.

References

1. BGP Routing Table Analysis Report, http://bgp.potaroo.net/
2. IPv6 internet broken - NANOG mailing list, http://mailman.nanog.org/pipermail/nanog/2009-October/013997.html
3. Ripe Atlas, https://atlas.ripe.net/
4. The Bogon Reference, http://www.cymru.com/BGP/bogons.html
5. Bush, R., Maennel, O., Roughan, M., Uhlig, S.: Internet optometry: Assessing the broken glasses in internet reachability. In: Proceedings of the 9th ACM SIGCOMM Conference on Internet Measurement Conference, IMC 2009 (2009)
6. Dhamdhere, A., Luckie, M., Huffaker, B., Claffy, K., Elmokashfi, A., Aben, E.: Measuring the deployment of ipv6: topology, routing and performance. In: Proceedings of the 2012 ACM Conference on Internet Measurement Conference, IMC 2012 (2012)
7. Griffin, T., Huston, G.: BGP Wedgies, RFC 4264 (2005)
8. Jacobson, V.: Traceroute, ftp://ftp.ee.lbl.gov/traceroute.tar.gz
9. Labovitz, C., Ahuja, A., Bailey, M.: Shining Light on Dark Address Space. Tech. Rep. TR-2001-01, Arbor Netwoks, Ann Arbor, Michigan, USA (November 2001)
10. Luckie, M., Hyun, Y., Huffaker, B.: Traceroute probe method and forward ip path inference. In: Proceedings of the 8th ACM SIGCOMM Conference on Internet Measurement (2008)
11. Lutu, A., Bagnulo, M., Maennel, O.: The BGP Visibility Scanner. In: IEEE Global Internet Symposium, GI 2013 (April 2013)
12. Lutu, A., Bagnulo, M., Cid-Sueiro, J., Maennel, O.: Separating wheat from chaff: Winnowing unintended prefixes using machine learning. In: Proceedings of 33rd IEEE International Conference on Computer Communications, IEEE INFOCOM 2014 (to appear, 2014)
13. Zhang, K., Yen, A., Zhao, X., Massey, D., Wu, S.F., Zhang, L.: On detection of anomalous routing dynamics in BGP. In: Mitrou, N.M., Kontovasilis, K., Rouskas, G.N., Iliadis, I., Merakos, L. (eds.) NETWORKING 2004. LNCS, vol. 3042, pp. 259–270. Springer, Heidelberg (2004)

Violation of Interdomain Routing Assumptions

Riad Mazloum[1], Marc-Olivier Buob[1], Jordan Augé[1], Bruno Baynat[1],
Dario Rossi[2], and Timur Friedman[1,*]

[1] UPMC Sorbonne Universités
[2] Telecom ParisTech

Abstract. We challenge a set of assumptions that are frequently used to model interdomain routing in the Internet by confronting them with routing decisions that are actually taken by ASes, as revealed through publicly available BGP feeds. Our results quantify for the first time the extent to which such assumptions are too simple to model real-world Internet routing policies. This should introduce a note of caution into future work that makes these assumptions and should prompt attempts to find more accurate models.

1 Introduction

Figure 1a illustrates a case of what is called *multi-exit routing* in the Internet. From BGPmon's [1] publicly-available feed of the BGP interdomain route updates of numerous routers, we know that the autonomous system (AS) in the middle of the figure, AS6762, has two different routes by which to reach the address prefix 103.11.245.0/24, the advertisement for which is originated by AS5845, on the figure's far right. One route, on top, goes via AS10026 and AS45932, while the other, on the bottom, goes via AS1299. Which of these routes will AS6762 advertise to the ASes that neighbor it on the left, AS262589 and AS26615?

The AS in the middle is Telecom Italia's Sparkle, the world's 9th most important AS as reported by CAIDA's AS Rank service [2]. The top route goes via Pacnet, which is a customer of Sparkle according to CAIDA's AS Relationships database [3]. The bottom route is via TeliaNet, which the database tells us is Sparkle's peer. The standard assumption is that an AS will always route through a paying customer rather than a peer, from which it receives no revenue. And indeed Sparkle advertises the route via its paying customer Pacnet to the top-left neighbor, INTERNEXA. However, the BGP feeds also tell us that Sparkle advertises a different route, the one via its peer TeliaNet, to the bottom-left neighbor, Tim Cellular. It appears that the assumption does not hold.

What is wrong? Could there be an error in the AS Relationships database that we are relying upon? Suppose, for instance, that TeliaNet was in fact a

---

* Collaboration through the LINCS laboratory. Full institutional affiliation of UPMC Sorbonne Universités authors: Sorbonne Universités, UPMC Univ Paris 06, UMR 7606, LIP6, F-75005, Paris, France.

M. Faloutsos and A. Kuzmanovic (Eds.): PAM 2014, LNCS 8362, pp. 173–182, 2014.

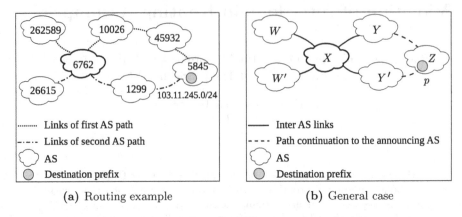

<table>
<tr><td>········ Links of first AS path</td><td>——— Inter AS links</td></tr>
<tr><td>–·–· Links of second AS path</td><td>- - - - Path continuation to the announcing AS</td></tr>
<tr><td>⬭ AS</td><td>⬭ AS</td></tr>
<tr><td>◉ Destination prefix</td><td>◉ Destination prefix</td></tr>
</table>

(a) Routing example   (b) General case

Fig. 1. Multi-exit routing example and general case

paying customer of Sparkle, rather than its peer. Then, Sparkle's routing through both Pacnet and TeliaNet would be perfectly coherent with the assumption that Sparkle will prefer to route through its customers.

However, this scenario would violate another common assumption: that an AS with two customers will route through the one that offers a shorter sequence of AS hops to the destination prefix. Since the route via TeliaNet is just two hops, it should be chosen instead of the route via Pacnet, which takes three hops, but this is not the case. If Sparkle were to override this choice, which BGP practices allow, it would be to select Pacnet in place of TeliaNet, and not advertise routes via both of them, as it does.

The scientific community already knows that network operators do not always implement interdomain routing policies in ways that are consistent with the simplifying assumptions that are made for modeling purposes. However, *the degree to which reality defies the assumptions has not previously been quantified.* This paper looks at 4 million routes that we collected from IPv4 BGP feeds, and in particular at 204 thousand instances of multi-exit routing that those feeds reveal. In 33% of the multi-exit cases, the assumption about routing preferentially to customers over peers and to peers over providers is not coherent with the relationships that are described by CAIDA. In fully 57% of the cases, the path length assumption does not hold.

This paper proceeds in Sect. 2 by providing some background for readers who are not familiar with the details of BGP. In this context, we formalize four commonly-held assumptions, and cite examples in the literature where they are made. (The assumptions described above are composites of these four assumptions.) Sect. 3 describes our methodology for confronting the assumptions with the data. Results appear in Sect. 4. The paper wraps up with related work (Sect. 5) and a conclusion pointing to future work (Sect. 6).

Our contributions are to formalize commonly-held assumptions about interdomain routing and AS relationships and propose two methods to identify violations of the models. Also, we provide the first quantification of such violations to be based upon publicly-available data.

2 Interdomain Routing and Our Set of Assumptions

2.1 BGP Background

BGP is the interdomain routing protocol that allows an AS to learn how to route to destinations in other ASes. A BGP route describes the *AS Path*, or sequence of ASes, to be traversed on the way to a *prefix*, which is a set of contiguous IP addresses. The *BGP next hop* is the egress point to use at the IP level in order to follow the route. Routes are exchanged between routers in the same AS through *iBGP* sessions, and between routers in different ASes via *eBGP*.

In the general case, a BGP router learns several routes toward a given destination. It is free to accept just some of them and to modify these. The router then elects one route (the *best route*) by following the *selection steps* of the *BGP decision process* [4], typically modeled as in Table 1. At each step, routes dominated by at least one other route are discarded. When, after one of these steps, there remains just one element in the set, this element is the best route.

Table 1. Selection steps of the BGP decision process

1. Highest local preference	5. eBGP over iBGP
2. Shortest AS Path length	6. Lowest IGP cost
3. Lowest origin type	7. Tie break rules
4. Lowest multi-exit discriminator	

The router is free to modify a best route before forwarding it to its neighboring routers and it is free to select which of those routers will receive the route.

One modifiable parameter that affects the choice of best routes is the *local preference*. If a router receives two routes ϱ and ϱ' toward the same destination with a higher value of `local_pref` assigned to ϱ, then ϱ is preferred to ϱ'.

2.2 AS Relationships

ASes use BGP to implement their contractual commercial agreements, which are typically modeled by three types of economic relationship.

- *Customer-to-provider (c2p)*: a customer pays a provider for transit service to the rest of the Internet for its traffic and its customers' traffic.
- *Peering (peer)*: a pair of ASes transit traffic between them or their customers to destinations belonging to them or their customers, free of charge.
- *Sibling-to-sibling (s2s)*: a pair of ASes transit traffic for each other and for their respective clients to every destination in the Internet, free of charge.

Gao [5] proposed a way to infer AS relationships based upon observed BGP routes, opening the way to much subsequent work.

2.3   A Set of Interdomain Routing Assumptions

This section describes four common assumptions about interdomain routing, citing selected papers that make each assumption.

(A1) iBGP valid

The assumption is that any BGP route has the potential to be propagated within an AS to all routers of that AS. In other words, route propagation is *only* governed by routing decisions taken by the different routers in the AS and there are no parts of the AS to which a route cannot be forwarded.

This assumption seems justified since an AS should guarantee this property in order to assure that all of its routers are selecting the best routes [6–10].

(A2) Policy through eBGP only

Routing policy is only applied by routers through their participation in interdomain (i.e., eBGP) sessions. This assumption implies that the `local_pref` value is not modified by routers through their iBGP sessions. If a router were to modify the `local_pref` value for some or all of the routes in an iBGP session, this could affect the choices of all routers in the AS to which this route is forwarded.[1]

This assumption is made to simplify the model of route propagation in an AS [6,8–10].

(A3) Customer over peer, peer over provider

The assumption that an AS always prefers to send traffic through a customer over a peer and through a peer over a provider so as to maximize the presumed economic benefits. Sending traffic through a customer means that the customer will pay for it, while sending though a provider means that one has to pay the provider. [6,8,10].

An AS will implement this hierarchy by assigning a higher `local_pref` value to routes learned from a customer than to routes learned from a provider.

(A4) Only one relationship type

In the literature, each AS interconnection is typically modeled as a single economic relationship [5,8–16]. This assumption rules out, for instance, an AS being the peer of another AS in one part of the world, while being that AS's customer in another location. This is a convenient assumption to make because the main source of data consists of AS paths conveyed on BGP routes. These paths provide only AS-level information, and do not reveal, for instance, in cases where there are several possible egress points through which traffic can pass from one AS to another, which ones are used.

3   Methodology

If we had detailed knowledge of the routing decisions made by BGP routers, it would be possible to challenge, and possibly invalidate, the individual assumptions described in the previous section. Unfortunately, this information is

---

[1] There is a way to influence a routing decision before the local preference step, which is to use a vendor-specific *weight* attribute. It allows a router to prefer routes based upon which router it received them from. For the purposes of (A2), modifying weights through iBGP sessions has the same violation impact as modifying local preferences.

unavailable to us. However, the publicly-available BGP feeds do allow us to challenge combinations of assumptions.

The novelty of our approach lies in the way that we use observed instances of multi-exit routing as a means to identify assumption violations. An instance, which we call a *multi-exit*, arises when an AS uses multiple next-hop ASes to reach a given destination prefix. Briefly, we process the feeds to identify multi-exits (Sect. 3.1), and then we examine each one for incoherencies in either the AS path length, the AS relationships, or both (Sect. 3.2). Each incoherency reveals a case in which one or more common assumptions have been violated.

3.1   Observing Multi-exits

Not all multi-exits can be observed through BGP feeds, but we can see them when an AS advertises two or more routes to a common destination prefix to its neighboring ASes. Fig. 1b illustrates the general case: an AS X announces to its neighbors W and W' different routes to a destination prefix p, each route having a different next-hop AS, Y or Y'.

We observe multi-exits as follows. A BGP snapshot at a given instant t is the set of all of the BGP routes being used by the vantage points at that time. The AS Path of a route is a sequence of AS numbers $(AS_1, \ldots, AS_i, \ldots, AS_k)$. For each AS AS_i of the AS Path and for each destination prefix p related to this path, we extract the next-hop AS AS_{i+1} used by AS_i to reach the destination p. In this way we build the set of *BGP triplets*, $\mathcal{T}_{\mathrm{BGP}} = \{(AS_i, AS_{i+1}, p)\}$. Looking at these triplets, a multi-exit is observed whenever we detect two (or more) triplets of the form (AS_i, AS_{i+1}, p) and (AS_i, AS'_{i+1}, p).

3.2   Observing Incoherencies in Multi-exits

We now present simple criteria for detecting, in a multi-exit, two types of incoherency with a set of common assumptions. Each incoherency reveals an instance in which one or more assumptions have been violated. Note that while observed incoherencies allow us to reveal assumption violations, the inverse is not necessarily the case. If an assumption is violated by an AS for which there is no multi-exit in our database, our techniques will not reveal this violation. Furthermore, it is possible, even in a multi-exit, for a violation to not manifest itself as an observable incoherency. Hence, our results provide a lower bound on the number of actual violations present at the time of the BGP snapshot.

Incoherent AS Path Lengths. We observe incoherent AS Path lengths as follows. Assume that X, in Fig. 1b, through a router R (not shown), announces to its neighbor W a route ϱ that it has received from Y, and simultaneously, through another router R' (not shown), announces to its neighbor W' a route ϱ' that it has received from Y'. If any of the first four steps of the BGP decision process (see Table 1) had been decisive, assumptions (A1) and (A2) require that R and R' will have selected the same route. Since each has selected a different route, the decision process will have passed steps 1 and 2, meaning that routes ϱ and ϱ' had the same `local_pref` values and identical AS Path lengths.

Our first criterion is thus to check the AS path length of routes identified in a multi-exit. If an AS announces two routes ϱ and ϱ' toward the same destination, and the AS Path lengths of ϱ and ϱ' differ, we deduce that either (A1) or (A2), or both, have been violated. Since our observations do not allow us to distinguish violations of (A1) from violations of (A2), we state merely that a path length incoherency reveals a violation of the *composite assumption* (A1 $\oplus$ A2).

Incoherent AS Relationships. We observe incoherent AS relationships as follows. According to (A3), an AS assigns higher values of `local_pref` to its customers than to its peers, which in turn receive higher values than do the providers. Also, according to (A4), there is only one relationship between two ASes, which means that there is one value of `local_pref` per neighboring AS and that this value further corresponds to the type of the relationship. Further, according to (A1), if an AS X is observed to do multi-exit routing through two different ASes Y and Y' then routes learned from those ASes have the same value of `local_pref`. Finally, according to (A2), Y and Y' *must* have identical types of relationship with X (e.g., they are both customers of X).

As a consequence, our second criterion is to examine the relationships between an AS and its next-hop ASes in a multi-exit. This requires the availability of an AS relationship database. We consider *c2p* and *peer* relationships, leaving out the special case of *s2s* without affecting our conclusions. If the relationships differ, then we can infer that at least one of the assumptions in the composite set (A1 $\oplus$ A2 $\oplus$ A3 $\oplus$ A4) is violated.

4   Results

4.1   Data Sources

Our study is based on two types of data: BGP updates and AS relationships. We parsed IPv4 BGP updates from BGPmon, which gathers data provided by RouteViews[2] and peers to some other BGP routers [1].

We ran our analysis on snapshots taken in August 2012, then January, March, and August 2013. Results presented here are based on a snapshot taken on 24 March 2013 at 10:00:00 GMT. Table 2 lists some snapshot statistics and results. The other snapshots were similar.[3]

To increase the likelihood that each route that has been introduced has indeed had a chance to propagate to all of the vantage points, we apply a route stability filter. We consider a route stable if it is the last one received by a BGP router concerning a prefix and it has been received at least 24 hours ago without being withdrawn. The filter causes us to slightly undercount multi-exits, and its effect on the overall results is negligible.

---

[2] http://www.routeviews.org/

[3] All of our data is publicly available at http://top-hat.info/routing-assumptions/.

We also remove from AS paths any ASNs reported by CAIDA [3] to belong to Internet exchange points (IXPs). In principle, these do not play a role in the routing policy of the ASes they interconnect.

Table 2. Snapshot statistics and results

routes		3,948,447
stable routes		3,493,673
prefixes		459,532
vantage points		35 routers in 32 ASes
triplets		13,852,998
unique triplets		8,257,351
transit ASes	6,762	100%
transit ASes having multi-exits	1,441	21%
MEs (multi-exits)	204,423	100%
MEs with incoherence	129,590	63%
MEs with incoherent path length only	62,051	30%
MEs with incoherent relationships only	12,229	6%
MEs with both incoherencies	55,310	27%

There is limited publicly available ground truth for AS relationships. From the projects that aim to infer them, we chose CAIDA's relationship dataset [3] since it is the only one we know to have a fully public methodology. For the 34.6% of their inferences that they were able to validate against either public or privately-obtained ground truth, they report accuracy of 99.6% for c2p relationships and 98.7% for peer relationships [17].

4.2 Quantifying Multi-exits

We observed 204,423 multi-exits, each having usually 2, but in some cases as many as 5, next-hop ASes. These constitute 2.7% of the (AS, destination prefix) pairs in our database (the remainder having just one next-hop AS), so by this metric multi-exits might seem to be rare. However, of the 6,762 transit ASes in our dataset, we observed 21% to be performing multi-exit routing. We found multi-exits in the ASes ranked 1 through 38 in CAIDA's AS ranking [2], including in all of the dozen or so ASes that are generally considered to be tier 1. So, multi-exit observations reveal information about ASes that play a central role in Internet routing.

4.3 Quantifying Incoherences

Fully 63% of the multi-exits in our dataset show incoherencies. AS Path length incoherencies, implying a violation of composite assumption (A1 ⊕ A2), showed up in 57% of multi-exits. AS relationship incoherencies, implying a violation of (A1 ⊕ A2 ⊕ A3 ⊕ A4), appeared in 33% of the multi-exits. There is overlap, with 27% of multi-exits revealing both kinds of incoherency.

4.4   Possible Causes for Violations

We speculate on reasons for these assumptions to be violated.

Traffic Engineering. From our conversations with people familiar with large operators, we believe that the assumptions don't fully capture contemporary traffic engineering practices. An AS might prefer, for example, to send some traffic through a peer rather than a customer, or through a provider rather than a peer, intentionally violating (A3). This could happen when the customer has insufficient bandwidth. It could also arise when a router in a large AS is geographically closer to a peer than to a customer, and the revenue that would be generated by routing via the customer is outweighed by the cost of carrying the traffic internally to the egress point for that customer.

Complex or Hybrid AS Relationships. Previous work [15,17] has highlighted the existence of complex or hybrid relationships, in which, for example, one large AS might be another's peer on one continent and its customer elsewhere. Such relationships violate (A4), and to be implemented (A2) must be violated. The CAIDA AS relationship database [17] is built using an understanding of this sort of relationship, but it provides as output only one relationship per AS pair.

Misconfigurations. A router misconfiguration might cause any one of the assumptions to be violated. For example, an incorrect value of `local_pref` could result in an AS inadvertently favoring a provider over a customer, violating (A3).

Erroneous AS Relationships. An alternative is that assumptions are not violated as often as our results indicate, but rather that CAIDA's database is not indicating the correct AS relationships, despite its high accuracy in cases where it has been validated. However, it would need to be incorrect in a large portion of cases in order to change our overall conclusions.

5   Related Work

As we have described in previous sections, many papers in the literature [5–17] have employed various assumptions about interdomain routing. Some of these papers, as well as others, have looked at violations of these assumptions.

Feamster et al. [18] give some examples of violations of (A1) that can appear. Gill et al. [19] queried 100 network operators for their private data, finding that 77% of ASes do not modify the value of local preference, i.e., they are coherent with (A2). The same survey reports that 87% of the concerned ASes are also coherent with (A3). Mühlbauer et al. [9] compared the routes that actually propagate to vantage points with the routes that ought to propagate, revealing violations of (A3). Giotsas et al. [20] show that relationships between pairs of ASes for IPv4 routes differ in 13% of the cases from those for IPv6 routes. Roughan et al. [21] summarize lessons about modeling ASes based on an extensive study of common assumptions. They observe, notably, that modeling an AS interconnection by a single connection is insufficient. Mühlbauer et al. [8] similarly show the weaknesses in modeling an AS as an atomic entity.

Our work goes further by providing a method for detecting violations of commonly employed assumptions using publicly available data. We supply the first quantification of the extent of observable violations.

Our finding that violations can be observed in a large portion of transit ASes, including all of the biggest ones, does not mean, however, that previous work that made simplifying assumptions should be considered invalid. Most work on AS relationship inference [5, 11–17] makes only assumption (A4). As we have noted, our method does not allow us to specify precisely which of a set of assumptions have been violated, and so we cannot say how often (A4) in particular does not hold. Furthermore, if (A4) is indeed violated, it might not be to a degree that would change previous results.

Our results might pose more serious questions for other work. Javed et al. [10] use the four assumptions to reduce the set of ASes that may be the root cause for an routing event in the network. If the assumptions are violated, the final set might not contain the root cause AS. Buob et al. [6] aim to solve a problem in which the assumptions are respected.

6   Conclusion and Future Work

This paper formalized four assumptions about interdomain routing in the Internet that are commonly used in the literature. We employed a data-driven method to challenge these assumptions, making novel use of so-called "multi-exit" scenarios to reveal incoherencies between sets of these assumptions and actual interdomain routing decisions. We observe multi-exits in 21% of transit ASes in a BGP snapshot from March 2013, and find that that in 63% of these multi-exits at least one assumption is violated. Other snapshots showed similar results. Given this, we believe that future work should use these assumptions with caution.

We expect that our technique of using multi-exits to reveal characteristics of interdomain routing behavior can be further developed. Studying how they change over time could, for instance, tell us more about how ASes perform traffic engineering. We also believe that much more can be revealed by combining the BGP data with IP level measurements, which is part of our future work.

Acknowledgments. We thank Martin Levy of Hurricane Electric for taking the time to impress upon us the weaknesses in assumptions (A2) and (A3). We also thank the anonymous reviewers and Matthew Luckie for their feedback. The research leading to these results has received funding from the European Union's Seventh Framework Programme (FP7/2007-2013) under grant agreements no. 287581 – OpenLab, and no. 318627 – mPlane.

References

1. Yan, H., Oliveira, R., Burnett, K., Matthews, D., Zhang, L., Massey, D.: BGPmon: A real-time, scalable, extensible monitoring system. In: Proc. CATCH (2009)
2. CAIDA: The CAIDA AS Ranking service, http://as-rank.caida.org/
3. CAIDA: The CAIDA AS Relationships dataset, http://www.caida.org/data/active/as-relationships/
4. Rekhter, Y., Li, T.: A border gateway protocol 4 (BGP-4). RFC 1771, Internet Engineering Task Force (March 1995)
5. Gao, L.: On inferring autonomous system relationships in the Internet. IEEE/ACM Trans. Netw. 9(6), 733–745 (2001)
6. Buob, M.O., Meulle, M., Uhlig, S.: Checking for optimal egress points in iBGP routing. In: Proc. DRCN (2007)
7. Teixeira, R., Shaikh, A., Griffin, T., Voelker, G.M.: Network sensitivity to hot-potato disruptions. In: Proc. SIGCOMM (2004)
8. Mühlbauer, W., Feldmann, A., Maennel, O., Roughan, M., Uhlig, S.: Building an AS-topology model that captures route diversity. In: Proc. SIGCOMM (2006)
9. Mühlbauer, W., Uhlig, S., Fu, B., Meulle, M., Maennel, O.: In search for an appropriate granularity to model routing policies. In: Proc. SIGCOMM (2007)
10. Javed, U., Cunha, I., Choffnes, D., Katz-Bassett, E., Anderson, T., Krishnamurthy, A.: PoiRoot: Investigating the root cause of interdomain path changes. In: Proc. SIGCOMM (2013)
11. Subramanian, L., Agarwal, S., Rexford, J., Katz, R.: Characterizing the Internet hierarchy from multiple vantage points. In: Proc. Infocom (2002)
12. Di Battista, G., Patrignani, M., Pizzonia, M.: Computing the types of the relationships between autonomous systems. In: Proc. Infocom (2003)
13. Xia, J., Gao, L.: On the evaluation of AS relationship inferences. In: Proc. Globecom (2004)
14. Dimitropoulos, X., Krioukov, D., Huffaker, B., Claffy, K., Riley, G.: Inferring AS relationships: Dead end or lively beginning? In: Nikoletseas, S.E. (ed.) WEA 2005. LNCS, vol. 3503, pp. 113–125. Springer, Heidelberg (2005)
15. Dimitropoulos, X., Krioukov, D., Fomenkov, M., Huffaker, B., Hyun, Y., Claffy, K., Riley, G.: AS relationships: inference and validation. ACM SIGCOMM CCR 37(1), 29–40 (2007)
16. Shavitt, Y., Shir, E., Weinsberg, U.: Near-deterministic inference of AS relationships. In: Proc. ConTEL (2009)
17. Luckie, M., Huffaker, B., Dhamdhere, A., Giotsas, V., Claffy, K.: AS relationships, customer cones, and validation. In: Proc. IMC (2013)
18. Feamster, N., Balakrishnan, H.: Detecting BGP configuration faults with static analysis. In: Proc. NSDI (2005)
19. Gill, P., Schapira, M., Goldberg, S.: A survey of interdomain routing policies. ACM SIGCOMM CCR (to appear, 2014)
20. Giotsas, V., Zhou, S.: Detecting and assessing the hybrid IPv4/IPv6 As relationships. In: Proc. SIGCOMM (2011)
21. Roughan, M., Willinger, W., Maennel, O., Perouli, D., Bush, R.: 10 lessons from 10 years of measuring and modeling the Internet's Autonomous Systems. IEEE JSAC 29(9), 1810–1821 (2011)

Here Be Web Proxies*

Nicholas Weaver[1], Christian Kreibich[2], Martin Dam[3], and Vern Paxson[4]

[1] ICSI / UC San Diego
[2] ICSI / Lastline
[3] Aalborg University
[4] ICSI / UC Berkeley

Abstract. HTTP proxies serve numerous roles, from performance enhancement to access control to network censorship, but often operate *stealthily* without explicitly indicating their presence to the communicating endpoints. In this paper we present an analysis of the evidence of proxying manifest in executions of the ICSI Netalyzr spanning 646,000 distinct IP addresses ("clients"). To identify proxies we employ a range of detectors at the transport and application layer, and report in detail on the extent to which they allow us to fingerprint and map proxies to their likely intended uses. We also analyze 17,000 clients that include a novel proxy location technique based on traceroutes of the responses to TCP connection establishment requests, which provides additional clues regarding the purpose of the identified web proxies. Overall, we see 14% of Netalyzr-analyzed clients with results that suggest the presence of web proxies.

1 Introduction

The World Wide Web continues to take center stage in people's use of the Internet. Indeed, for many users the web remains synonymous with the Internet itself. The plain-text nature of the web's workhorse protocol, HTTP, makes it particularly tempting to interpose on its flows using proxy servers, and HTTP remains one of the few protocols with explicit support for proxying. As a consequence, HTTP proxies have become widespread and different stakeholders employ them for a wide array of reasons. To the Internet's users, however, the actual prevalence and nature of web proxies remains a *terra incognita*. The typically transparent nature of web proxies means that users may remain unaware of their existence unless the proxy significantly malfunctions or induces significant changes to the connection payload.

In this work we present the results of extensive measurements probing for the presence of web proxies by conducting HTTP connections from end-user browsers to custom web servers under our control. We do so using Netalyzr [11], which contains a large and growing suite of proxy detection techniques. In 646,000 distinct addresses ("clients") analyzed by Netalyzr, 14% of clients show evidence of HTTP proxying through one or more tests, suggesting that a significant fraction of all end-user HTTP traffic passes through web proxies either on the host or in the network.

* This work is supported by the National Science Foundation under grants CNS-0831535, CNS-1213157, and CNS-1223717, and the Department of Homeland Security (DHS) Science and Technology Directorate, Cyber Security Division (DHS S&T/CSD) Broad Agency Announcement 11-02, and SPAWAR Systems Center Pacific via contract number N66001-12-C-0128, with additional support from Amazon, Google and Comcast.

M. Faloutsos and A. Kuzmanovic (Eds.): PAM 2014, LNCS 8362, pp. 183–192, 2014.
© Springer International Publishing Switzerland 2014

We make two contributions. First, compared to the results we presented in the original 2010 Netalyzr paper [11], we now substantially broaden both the dataset (roughly seven times more sessions) and the depth of the analysis: we categorize the actual modifications, fingerprint proxy implementations, and, when feasible, deduce the purpose of the proxies' presence. Second, we introduce additional testing methods, including a proxy location technique based on traceroutes of the SYN-ACK packets responding to TCP connection requests. Given the improved measurement apparatus, we find nearly twice the fraction of HTTP-proxied sessions compared to our 2010 results.

We start by discussing the basic modes of operation in real-world proxies and presenting related work (Section 2). Next, we summarize Netalyzr's current proxy-detection test suite (Section 3), followed by a detailed presentation of our proxy fingerprinting and classification methodology (Section 4). We then present our findings (Section 5), including both identified proxies as well as a set of proxies whose purpose remains elusive, and a look at the most heavily proxied countries around the world. We conclude with a reflection on our findings (Section 6).

2   Background and Related Work

Web proxies examine and potentially alter some or all of a user's HTTP request and response traffic, sometimes even when the user has not explicitly configured the browser to route traffic through a particular proxy. In this work we consider both proxies co-located with the user's computer (such as security products) as well as in-path network elements.

Web proxies can employ two main strategies for modifying payload: TCP termination, and packet rewriting. A proxy employing TCP termination actively responds to the browser's TCP connection request, establishing a full transport connection with the browser, and creating a new, separate TCP connection with the target server. Once established, the proxy relays the content streams from both endpoints, potentially altering them at will. While we might expect the proxy to use its own IP address for the connection to the server, some proxies reuse the client's IP address. Doing so increases implementation complexity, but also provides transparency, and avoids any server-perceived centralization of behavior deemed abusive because it emanates in high volume from a single IP address.[1]

Packet-rewriting proxies, by contrast, modify traffic as it flows through them, potentially also injecting additional traffic, such as in the case of HTTP 404 error rewriting we observe in some NATs in Section 5. Packet-rewriting proxies work best for tasks that require only minor changes that can fit into a single packet, such as replacing a response entity with a redirection script.

A substantial body of work covers Internet censorship detection [1,16,14], focusing on the general problem of triggering and understanding censorship mechanisms implemented using proxies or packet-injection tools.

---

[1] For example, BlueCoat's knowledge base (https://kb.bluecoat.com/index?page=content&id=KB3119&actp=RSS) specifically suggests enabling the "reflect-client-ip" configuration item (namely, use the client's IP address rather than the proxy's IP) in transparent mode, when Google detects a possible abuse situation. Operators can install such a proxy wherever symmetric routing ensures return traffic will transit it.

Two academic studies have focused on specific proxy effects. The "Tripwires" work of Reis et al. [13] detected systems that modified HTTP content by performing an XML-RPC fetch and checking to see whether the returned content matched the expected content of the page itself. Huang et al. [10] used web ads in both Flash and Java to detect proxies based on flaws that make incorrect associations between hostnames and content to cache (per CERT VU 435052, as discussed below).

Finally, Auger proposed cache-detection using timing [2], where the origin server returns content after first observing an artificial delay. Objects that load quicker than the delay indicate the browser must be receiving the content from a caching proxy.

3 Detecting Web Proxies

In principle we can detect the presence of a proxy any time it permutes a connection's properties. We base our basic detection approach on employing an HTTP client and server under our control to exchange precisely known HTTP messages and then look for deviations from the expected. We implemented this approach using the ICSI Net-alyzr, our popular user-driven, web-based connectivity analysis service that runs in a Java applet in the browser. See the original paper [11] for architectural and operational details, as well as general biases in our dataset, which remain largely unchanged. Ne-talyzr includes a range of tests that detect proxy implementation technologies, implementation artifacts and proxy limitations. Each user-initiated test session runs through a full suite of tests, of which we now describe in detail those relevant to HTTP proxy analysis. Since we have enhanced Netalyzr's test suite over time, we include for each of the test a description of the approximate number of distinct clients that observed the given results for the particular test.

Non-responsive Server Test (116,500 of clients tested): We expect TCP-terminating proxies, unless specifically customized, to respond with a SYN-ACK to a client's connection request before attempting to contact the client's intended origin server. We can test for this behavior by connecting to a server that we know will not accept the connection request [18]. For Netalyzr, we employ a server interface that sends a RST packet in response to all incoming requests, regardless of port. If the Netalyzr client's attempt to connect to this server on port 80 initially succeeds, this indicates the presence of a TCP-terminating proxy.

Proxy Traceroute (17,000 clients): The previous test indicates the presence of a TCP-terminating proxy but does not illuminate its location. We added to Netalyzr a new test to pinpoint the proxy's location, as follows. For any port on which the previous test flagged the presence of a proxy, the Netalyzr client attempts a TCP connection to our *traceroute server*. Upon receipt of an incoming SYN (likely sent by an in-path proxy), this server conducts a traceroute from server toward client using SYN-ACK packets. This traceroute terminates upon receiving the TCP handshake's pure ACK, rather than an ICMP "TTL exceeded" response. We do not perform a similar test outbound from the client, because while the client can technically invoke commands such as traceroute directly, the issues of platform dependence, increased intrusiveness of the client, and the potential lack of required user privileges for a TCP-based traceroute make this approach problematic.

HTTP 404 Fetches (448,000 clients): While investigating DNS "error traffic monetization" [17], we discovered a proxy vendor whose product modifies HTTP 404 error responses. To detect this behavior, Netalyzr attempts to fetch three custom 404 "page not found" error pages. One returns just a blank 404 page, one returns a copy of Apache's default 404 page, and one returns Netalyzr's custom 404 page. We then watch for any alterations to the content.

Previously Documented Tests. In addition to the new tests described above, we used several existing Netalyzr tests in our analysis of web proxies.

Customized HTTP Fetch (633,000 clients): RFC 2616 [6] specifies that systems should treat HTTP header names as case-insensitive, and, with a few exceptions, free of ordering requirements. Netalyzr leverages these properties by implementing its own HTTP engine and fetching a custom page from the server, using mixed-cased request and response headers in a known order. Any changes indicate a proxy. This test also aids in the identification of the proxy's purpose. Some proxies declare their presence and/or function in a header, while others may modify the HTML document or transfer encoding in a manner which reflects the proxy's function, or serve as a base for further investigation (Section 4).

Non-HTTP Fetch (646,000 clients): In addition to a fetch using standard HTTP, Netalyzr attempts to fetch an entity using the protocol declaration `ICSI/1.1` instead of `HTTP/1.1`. A protocol-parsing proxy will likely reject this request as non-conformant.

Invalid Host Field (646,000 clients): Before Netalyzr's release, CERT VU 435052 [9] described how some in-path proxies would interpret the `Host` HTTP header and attempt to contact the listed host rather than forward the request to the intended address. We check for this vulnerability by fetching from our server with an alternate `Host` header of `www.google.com`.

Caching and Transcoding (619,000 clients): Netalyzr twice attempts to fetch an image URL from the server using a direct request that bypasses any local browser caching. Our server tracks first versus second requests, originally returning a particular 67kB image but for the second request returning an alternate version of the image. This process then repeats three more times, each time with different cache-control headers. If the client receives identical images for subsequent requests, we can deduce the presence of caching; altered images indicate transcoding. A more recent addition includes uploading the results of any transcoded images for further analysis.

Filetype Filtering (627,000 clients): Netalyzr attempts to fetch three different filetypes (`.mp3`, `.exe`, and `.torrent`), each representing a type of content that some network use policies may prohibit, and thus attempt to block with proxies.

EICAR Test Virus Filtering (296,000 clients): The initial Netalyzr release checked for the ability to receive the EICAR [5] test "virus," a benign program that antivirus programs recognize for testing purposes. We removed this test after receiving complaints about security software blocking all subsequent connections.

For similar reasons we do *not* include censorship-triggering tests. While technically straightforward to implement, we cannot rule out the possibility that such a test could result in harm to Netalyzr users who might be accused of accessing forbidden content.

4   Fingerprinting and Classifying Proxies

Using the Netalyzr results we just described, we set out to establish a methodology for fingerprinting the detected proxies and, in a subsequent stage, classify them into different categories of functionality.

Some of our tests naturally suggest a proxy's purpose, such as in the case of our caching analysis. We combined information gathered from our measurements with a manual, iterative rule-building approach in which we establish a set of detectors for specific proxy fingerprints. In each iteration, we identified the most prevalent proxy fingerprints and used them to infer the manufacturer and/or proxy model. Sometimes this task proved easy (such as when proxies inject a banner header, e.g., X-BlueCoat-Via); other times it required online searches and studying product whitepapers. Security and login gateways that block our requests generally present a page explaining their presence, while removal of whitespace suggests a transcoding proxy attempting to save bandwidth. Injected content or changes to the 404 error page also provide handy clues, as the injected URLs either directly disclose the company involved or help us track down the responsible parties in discussion forums or blogs.

In total, our resulting detectors comprise 70 generic rules for policy blockers (such as 'Blocked' or 'Denied' keywords) and 29 rules for individual content changes that alter received content.

5   Identified Proxies

Our analysis identified eight categories of web proxies. We sketch each in decreasing order of prevalence, and then discuss "dark proxies" that did not introduce any modifications that we could detect, and apparent country-wide proxies.

Antivirus (6% of clients): even though we removed the EICAR test due to collateral damage, triggering antivirus systems remains the most prevalent type of proxy for tested sessions. We also see indications of end-user security software through header changes validated by web searches. For example, Fortinet software uses a local proxy that adds an X-FCCKV2 header to HTTP requests (210 clients). Note that we do not consider antivirus-blocking alone as an indicator of a proxy for other measurements; we only count sessions in which the HTTP connections exhibit evidence of proxying.

Caches (2.3% of clients): HTTP caches represent the second-most frequent proxy type. These systems attempt to reduce an ISP's upstream bandwidth by returning locally cached content instead of fetching it from origin servers. Since web clients possess their own cache, this only saves bandwidth on popular content.

Security and Censor Proxies (0.55% of clients): We detect two popular models of security proxies through the Via headers they inject. 1,156 clients indicate an IronPort/Cisco Web Security Appliance; 631 clients indicate a McAfee Web Gateway. Both proxies attempt to prevent attacks against web clients.

Similarly, the BlueCoat web filter, evident in 1,993 clients, can act as a security gateway (filtering dangerous content), an employee web-surfing censor, and/or a login gateway. This proxy inserts a X-BlueCoat-Via header in traffic to the server, while changes to the reply traffic consists of just a capitalization change in the `Connection` header and header reordering.

Finally, we received a session run by a volunteer behind a McAfee Smartfilter (operating as a censor) deployed in a Middle Eastern country. This proxy added a `Via: Webcat-Skein` request header and reordered and changed the capitalization on the `Connection`, `Host`, and `Cookie` headers, yet induced no reply header changes. We see 87 clients with this fingerprint.

Transcoding (0.54% of clients): While caches save upstream bandwidth, transcoding [7,8] conserves downstream bandwidth by compressing data into a more compact form. We observe three different transformations, usually applied in combination. The first consists of altered content encoding, replacing an uncompressed response with a gzip-compressed response. We observe 0.5% of clients that gzip-compress our HTTP 404 response or `.exe` file.

The second case, observed in 0.5% of tested clients, reflected proxies removing whitespace in the HTML content returned by our server. These transformations preserve HTML semantics (assuming that no HTML consumer relies on newlines in the rendering process). A common behavior is to compress the `.exe` file but newline-strip the HTML.

Finally, we also detect image transcoding that replaces our 67kB image with a smaller version. We observe 0.2% of tested clients with such modifications, usually preserving reasonable quality: most transcoding resulted in images greater than 22 kB (74.3%). The most compressed replacement consisted of a 5 kB image.

404 Rewriters (0.11% of clients): "Error traffic monetization" involves ISPs attempting to leverage protocol errors as a source of revenue by masking or augmenting the error delivery in order to include advertising [17]. While this controversial practice most commonly involves DNS NXDOMAIN errors, at least one company, Barefruit, also offers monetization of HTTP error traffic. This system requires the use of "a proxy device or DPI system to intercept returning HTTP errors" that the device replaces with a redirection to an advertisement-laden page.

We observe two ISPs, Mediacom (398 clients) and Bresnan(17 clients), that employ HTTP error monetization. The injected content looks identical except for the URL structure in the contained link, suggesting that both ISPs use a common provider for the 404-redirection, though the URLs differ in structure, which may reflect the ISPs working with different vendors for the landing page that offers up the ads. We also observed a bug in the injector: many sessions include the injected JavaScript snippet at the end of the response *headers*, as the injector did not insert an additional line break to separate the header from the injected body.

The DNS and WHOIS information for the Bresnan servers suggests that Xerocole operates the monetization, while Mediacom redirects to Infospace servers. In both cases these companies also provide DNS error monetization for these ISPs, suggesting either the ISPs or the monetization services use a common equipment vendor. Mediacom appears to have discontinued this technique after a public backlash in August 2012 [3]. According to our data, Bresnan appears to have never fully deployed this system, as we see indications of its use only among a small fraction of its users.

By leveraging Netalyzr's ability to query the local network for UPnP-enabled gateway devices and identify gateway device vendors [4], we can expand the analysis to proxying gateway devices. We observe that instances of the Linksys WRT110 contain 404-monetization (139 clients). This system redirects the user to http://websearch.linksys.com and does not appear to be part of the initial firmware, as devices with a manufacturer URL of http://www.linksys.com do not perform 404-monetization, while many (but not all) with a manufacturer URL of http://www.linksysbycisco.com do. This injector simply replaces the initial payload of the HTTP 404 response packet with a redirection, while keeping subsequent content intact. (Indeed, we observed a case where both Mediacom's injector (which injects a script but doesn't change the error code) and the Linksys injector operated on the same response!)

Login Gateways (0.075% of clients): Most login proxies operate within the private side of a NAT, enabling them to authorize connections based on a client's pre-NAT address. Login proxies that reside outside of a NAT, however, require some other means to track which clients the proxy has authorized. Some of these NAT-exterior proxies set a global "authorized" cookie for their own domain. When a new page request arrives from the browser, the login proxy first redirects to the authorization domain, checks for the cookie, and if present redirects the browser back to the original page, setting a cookie within the domain of the original page, whose presence flags subsequent requests to be passed through unmodified. Other configurations simply require that all requests go through a manually configured proxy. We observe 433 clients where our HTTP request encounters blocking by such a proxy.

Content Injectors (0.055% of clients): A comparatively rare class of proxies injects JavaScript or other content into HTML documents. The most common such injector, BitDefender (an antivirus solution seen for 318 clients), did not appear in the earlier survey of Reis et al. [13]. We also observed 58 clients containing an injection of "xpopup.js", part of the CA Personal Firewall popup-blocking suite running on client systems, and 11 clients showing evidence of Sunbelt Popup Killer, a dated (early-to-mid 2000s) anti-popup technology. Reis et al. likewise observed the latter two in their 2008 study [13]. Other injectors in our dataset include the privacy filter Privoxy, a VPN system by AnchorFree (here injecting advertisements), and Bluecoat and Comodo TrustConnect security products.

Three advertising injectors that operate on free hotspot connections appear in our dataset: Meraki toolbar,[2] Ovation Networks, and Icomera. These injectors insert a reference to a JavaScript routine that creates an advertisement-laden information bar on each page. We also observed an Indian ISP using Streamride to inject advertisements into all HTTP connections (injectors typically trigger only selectively [13]).

Some transcoding proxies also inject scripts. For example, we recorded a session by a **vodafone.de** customer that, in addition to stripping whitespace, injected a script ups/ytchunk.js into multiple pages. Web reports provide other mentions of such behavior, such as T-Mobile in the UK injecting a script bmi-int-js/bmi.js.

Finally, we also observed an injector in SouthWest Airline's in-flight WiFi service. The injected toolbar conveys both flight information and branding, operating in a manner similar to the advertising injectors without third-party advertisements.

---

[2] Meraki's HTTP headers include:
```
X-cool-jobs-contact: jobs+proxyball@meraki.com
```

All of the above injectors can cause page loading/rendering problems. A common problem consists of injection-bearing web pages cached by the client that later can no longer retrieve uncached injected scripts (particularly those originally served from private or unallocated IP addresses). The host of Vodafone's injected scripts, for example, resides at 1.2.3.50, part of a reserved address block.

Spyware Proxies (0.036% clients): The OSSProxy.exe local proxy, part of the MarketScore software package (and considered spyware by Symantec) inserts an X-OSSProxy header with the software version.

Dark Proxies. For 8% of all clients in our dataset, we could detect the presence of a proxy via the non-responsive server test, changes to the HTTP headers, or diverging client addresses, but we could not identify any modifications due to the proxy. The first of these proved the most significant: prior to including a non-responsive server test in Netalyzr, 7% of clients show evidence of a dark proxy, while after adding the test this percentage rose to 12%. If we consider those measurements that included the non-responsive server test, but exclude measurements for which the proxy quickly responded to the initial SYN ($\leq$ 5 ms), the proportion of dark proxy clients is still 9%, indicating the likely presence of an in-network proxy on the far side of any NAT. Thus, the majority of these "dark proxies" reside internal to the network rather than at end systems.

Observations of dark proxies could reflect several possibilities. In settings with a login proxy (particularly hotspots), the user may have already authenticated to the login process prior to running Netalyzr, so the proxy at that point only relays content. Caches or transcoders that our tests do not trigger would likewise appear "dark" (although we expect to trigger these proxies as we provide numerous opportunities for them to cache and transcode data), as would proxies that enforce censorship or corporate policies that our probes did not trigger.[3] In a previous interaction with a Netalyzr user, we identified a workplace environment that uses proxies that only manifest in our measurements due to changes in the capitalization of the Connection header. In addition, we directly experienced one setting (the US National Science Foundation's internal network) that contains a proxy visible only via the non-responsive server and SYN-ACK traceroute tests, which locate the proxy in the same network. In both cases, the proxies' purpose was confirmed by visiting "forbidden" sites.

For the dark proxy clients where the connections arrived at the server from the same IP address as non-HTTP traffic, and for which we possess SYN-ACK traceroute results (1,345 clients), we attempted to determine the proxy's location via the traceroute data. We examined the last hop before the ACK-responding system in the traceroutes for both 80/tcp and for a non-standard port (1947/tcp). We considered these different if the last hop showed a different IP address; or, if one or both of the traceroutes failed to report the last hop, the hop count differed. Of the clients measured, 13% had a different traceroute for the two ports, suggesting that the proxy resides in the public network rather than at or inside any NAT.

Finally, regarding the possibility of dark proxies reflecting censorship proxies, we note some suggestive geography relating to the 197 clients that only manifested altered capitalization of the Connection header. When geolocalizing the IP addresses of

---

[3] For our purposes, whether such systems block "bad ideas" or "malicious content", from a network viewpoint they appear identical unless triggered.

these sessions (using MaxMind's GeoLite database), 113 resided in the United States (out of 147,000 total US clients), 20 in Kuwait (out of 223 clients), and 12 in Iran (out of 196 clients).

Country-Level Proxies. Our data also show evidence in some cases of potential country-level proxying, where most or all of a nation's traffic passes through proxies. We examined all countries containing $\geq$ 50 distinct clients. Of these, the five with the highest prevalence of proxies are Bahrain (95%), Singapore (85%), Lebanon (79%), the United Arab Emirates (62%), and Thailand (48%).

Bahrain: While almost all Bahraini clients exhibited proxying, far fewer (42%) exhibited caching. The proxying very likely reflects censorship, as 86% of clients that successfully performed the customized HTTP fetch detected BlueCoat in the network, which has been previously linked to censorship in the Middle East [12].

Singapore: Again, a significantly lower percentage (26%) of clients manifest caching. Although we were unable to identify a common product by name, we noted that many Singapore clients reside behind a proxy that only adds an X-Forwarded-For header.

Lebanon: We suspect that the proxies we detect in Lebanon represent censors, as only 29% manifest caching. A common motif (51% of clients) is the addition of a Cache-Control header (even though almost no sessions actually exhibit caching), perhaps a Via header, and downcasing the Connection header on requests.

United Arab Emirates: Unlike the previous countries, the UAE manifests a higher degree of caching (41%), but 39% of clients also evince use of BlueCoat.

Thailand: Thailand shows a low degree of caching (17% of clients). There are also two somewhat common products, one (15% of clients) downcases all request headers, while the other (11%) adds a Via header.

Kenya: A single traceroute measurement to a client in Kenya indicates an apparent backbone-level cache. In the measurement session, an HTTP traceroute from our server to the client terminates after 82.178.159.110 rather than continuing to the next hop taken by a non-HTTP traceroute, 196.207.31.146. AS-level information for these addresses indicates that they bridge the borders of Kenya and Oman.

6   Conclusion

Web proxies affect a significant fraction of Internet connections. Netalyzr's rich proxy-detection suite highlights proxies in 14% of the clients from which we have collected measurements to date—a significant increase from our 2010 result of 8%, which we attribute primarily to the significantly enhanced resolution of Netalyzr's proxy detection capabilities.

In addition to detecting the presence of proxies, we can often infer their of including caching, transcoding, login gateways, 404-rewriting, several types of content injection, and local antivirus and spyware functionality. For those we cannot identify, we can still identify the network location as either at/within a NAT near the browser, or further upstream in the network. We can also detect and locate (but not classify) censorship proxies that terminate our HTTP connections.

At the country level, we find that Bahrain, Singapore, Lebanon, the United Arab Emirates, and Thailand all extensively manifest the use of proxies, with rates from 48% to 95%. Many of these do not appear to provide caching functionality, leaving nation-wide censorship as a likely explanation.

References

1. Aase, N., Crandall, J., Diaz, A., Knockel, J., Molinero, J.O., Saia, J., Wallach, D., Zhu, T.: Whiskey, Weed, and Wukan on the World Wide Web: On Measuring Censors' Resources and Motivations. In: Proc. USENIX FOCI, Bellevue, WA, USA (August 2012)
2. Auger, R.: Easy method for detecting caching proxies (February 2011), http://www.cgisecurity.com/2011/02/ easy-method-for-detecting-caching-proxies.html
3. CmdrTaco. Mediacom using DPI to Hijack Searches, 404 errors, http://yro.slashdot.org/story/11/04/27/137210/ mediacom-using-dpi-to-hijack-searches-404-errors
4. DiCioccio, L., Teixeira, R., May, M., Kreibich, C.: Probe and Pray: Using UPnP for Home Network Measurements. In: Taft, N., Ricciato, F. (eds.) PAM 2012. LNCS, vol. 7192, pp. 96–105. Springer, Heidelberg (2012)
5. EICAR Anti-Malware Test File, http://www.eicar.org/86-0-Intended-use.html
6. Fielding, R., Gettys, J., Mogul, J., Frystyk, H., Masinter, L., Leach, P., Berners-Lee, T.: Hypertext Transfer Protocol – HTTP/1.1. RFC 2616, IETF (June 1999)
7. Fox, A., Goldberg, I., Gribble, S.D., Lee, D.C., Polito, A., Brewer, E.A.: Experience With Top Gun Wingman, A Proxy-Based Graphical Web Browser for the USR PalmPilot. In: Proc. Middleware (1998)
8. Fox, A., Gribble, S.D., Brewer, E.A., Amir, E.: Adapting to Network and Client Variability via On-Demand Dynamic Distillation. In: Proc. ASPLOS-VII (October 1996)
9. Giobbi, R.: CERT Vulnerability Note VU 435052: Intercepting proxy servers may incorrectly rely on HTTP headers to make connections (February 2009)
10. Huang, L.S., Chen, E.Y., Barth, A., Rescorla, E., Jackson, C.: Talking to yourself for fun and profit. In: Proceedings of the Web 2.0 Security & Privacy (W2SP) Workshop (2011)
11. Kreibich, C., Weaver, N., Nechaev, B., Paxson, V.: Netalyzr: Illuminating The Edge Network. In: Proc. ACM IMC, Melbourne, Australia (November 2010)
12. Citizen Lab. Planet Blue Coat: Mapping Global Censorship and Surveillance Tools, https://citizenlab.org/2013/01/planet-blue-coat-mapping- global-censorship-and-surveillance-tools/
13. Reis, C., Gribble, S.D., Kohno, T., Weaver, N.C.: Detecting In-Flight Page Changes with Web Tripwires. In: Proc. USENIX NSDI (2008)
14. Sfakianakis, A., Athanasopoulos, E., Ioannidis, S.: Inferring Mechanics of Web Censorship Around the World. In: CensMon: A Web Censorship Monitor (August 2011)
15. Somerville, M.: Mobile operators altering (and breaking) web content, http://www.mysociety.org/2011/08/11/ mobile--operators--breaking--content/
16. Verkamp, J., Gupta, M.: Inferring Mechanics of Web Censorship Around the World. In: Proc. USENIX FOCI, Bellevue, WA, USA (August 2012)
17. Weaver, N., Kreibich, C., Paxson, V.: Redirecting DNS for Ads and Profit. In: Proc. USENIX FOCI, San Francisco, CA, USA (August 2011)
18. Wikipedia. Proxy server (June 2012), http://en.wikipedia.org/wiki/Http_proxy#Detection

Towards an Automated Investigation of the Impact of BGP Routing Changes on Network Delay Variations*

Massimo Rimondini, Claudio Squarcella, and Giuseppe Di Battista

Roma Tre University, Rome
{rimondin,squarcel,gdb}@dia.uniroma3.it

Abstract. Understanding fluctuations in network performance is important as many applications, including streaming, conferencing, gaming, and financial transactions, rely on timely delivery of data. Awareness of the effect of routing changes on network delays is key to this understanding, but research in this area is often based on empirical observations that cannot be easily extended to everyday network scenarios.

We study the relationship between BGP routing changes and round-trip times (RTTs), bringing several contributions: 1) an automated methodology that exploits state-of-the-art statistical methods to determine if a routing change caused a significant RTT variation; 2) an application of our methodology on massive RIPE RIS and RIPE Atlas data sets, showing its effectiveness in the wild (for example, at least 72.5% of the unique routing changes were consistently associated with an RTT increase – or decrease – in all their occurrences); 3) various a-posteriori analyses leading to interesting findings for several practical applications.

1 Introduction and State of the Art

Strict performance requirements characterize an ever-growing base of Internet services. Keeping certain performance levels is not only critical for the satisfaction of Service Level Agreements (SLAs), but also important to ensure that the user-perceived quality is always high. Lots of applications, including streaming, conferencing, gaming, and financial transactions, rely on steady performance levels. However, it is a matter of fact that performance fluctuations may occur, depending on several factors like bandwidth, congestion, and routing changes.

In this paper we focus on understanding the relationship between variations of network performance, measured in terms of round-trip times (RTTs), and inter-domain routing changes, computed by the Border Gateway Protocol (BGP). We concentrate on RTTs because they are the most commonly available measurement, ICMP requests are unlikely to be filtered out, and latency is nowadays regarded as an important performance indicator. Similarly, we consider BGP routing changes because their impact is significant, as stated in [10].

---

* Supported by EU FP7 Project "Leone: From Global Measurements to Local Management", grant no. 317647, and by MIUR project AMANDA, prot. 2012C4E3KT_001.

M. Faloutsos and A. Kuzmanovic (Eds.): PAM 2014, LNCS 8362, pp. 193–203, 2014.

We bring the following contributions: 1) a matching methodology to determine whether a routing change caused a significant variation of the RTT, with two key novel aspects: it exploits state-of-the-art statistical methods and it can compute the matching automatically; 2) an experimental verification of the effectiveness of our matching methodology in the wild, performed on publicly available data sets (BGP updates from the RIPE Routing Information Service and RTT measurements from the RIPE Atlas project [1]); 3) a set of a-posteriori analyses based on the results of our matching methodology, which lead to interesting findings for several practical applications.

An augmented awareness of performance fluctuations is of course an added value brought about by our methodology. However, we envision several other applications. For example, learning that BGP routing changes recorded by certain vantage points affect more significantly the RTT towards a certain destination can motivate usage of those vantage points to predict the impact of future routing changes and drive traffic engineering decisions. In principle, placement of a delay-sensitive service can also benefit from knowing that routing changes observed at certain network locations are more likely to affect its reachability. Discovering that certain routing changes affect RTTs towards apparently unrelated destinations can help network administrators in troubleshooting tasks.

In a pioneering contribution [10], the impact of routing changes on RTTs has been confirmed and shown to be non-negligible. Interesting arguments in that paper strongly motivate our study: most delay variations are indeed caused by routing changes rather than congestion, and interdomain routing changes are those that impact most on the average delay variation. However, the problem of automatically associating RTT variations with BGP path changes is not encompassed. In [3], [13,14] the authors study transient network performance degradations due to routing convergence periods, while we concentrate on RTT values during stable routing states. A framework for the simultaneous visualization of BGP and RTT data is presented in [4] but, since the focus of the paper is on the graphical metaphor, the two kinds of data are correlated with a rather simple technique that is intended to only support the demonstration of a prototype visualization tool. Other contributions exploit statistical tools for the analysis of trends in network data. In [8,9] the authors detect the impact of network upgrades by using statistical rule mining and network configuration information to identify meaningful patterns in performance changes. A recent work [12] applies change detection algorithms to compute network coordinates, i.e., metrics that help predict the network delay between pairs of hosts, in a realistic environment.

The rest of the paper is organized as follows. In Section 2 we describe our methodology to match BGP routing changes and significant RTT variations. In Section 3 we apply the methodology to search for BGP-RTT correlations in the wild, using data from RIPE RIS and RIPE Atlas. In Section 4 we introduce various analyses based on the results of our matching methodology. Conclusions and future work are discussed in Section 5. Some of the approaches and analyses presented in this paper are described more extensively in [11].

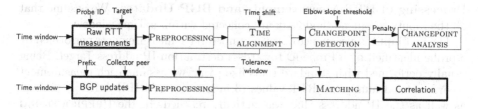

Fig. 1. Main steps in our matching methodology. Thick-border boxes are inputs and outputs. Thin-border boxes are operations. Arrows indicate data flows. Tunable parameters are represented without a box.

2   Matching BGP Routing Changes with RTT Variations

Reference Scenario and Methodology Overview. In the rest of the paper we assume that the inputs to our methodology are collected in the following scenario. We consider an Autonomous System (AS) A that is connected to several other ASes by means of BGP border routers. A subset of these routers, called *Collector Peers* (CPs), forwards all the computed interdomain routes to a central BGP collector that in turn stores them. AS A also comprises *probes* that periodically run standard tools (e.g., ping, traceroute) to measure RTTs (and, possibly, IP routing paths) towards a fixed set of *targets* that are external to AS A: the results of these *measurements* are stored as well. When leaving AS A, traffic from a probe to a target traverses a border router that may or may not be a CP. If it is, a correlation necessarily exists between the measurements performed by the probe and the BGP updates received by the border router for a prefix comprising the target. If it is not, a correlation may still exist because the BGP updates recorded by other CPs for the same prefix may also influence the behavior of the traversed border router. Our goal is to find such correlations, using CPs and probes available in the AS under consideration as vantage points.

The main steps of our matching methodology are in Fig. 1. The methodology takes as input RTT measurements from a set of probes and BGP updates from a set of CPs. These two data sets are very different in nature: RTTs are recorded on a periodical basis and are subject to lots of fluctuations, whereas BGP updates may arrive in bursts and usually involve a limited number of different routing paths. To fill this gap, and to clean up the inputs, we apply several preprocessing steps. We then account for a possible time difference between the two data sets and use a state-of-the-art statistical method to detect significant variations in RTT values. The output of the methodology is an estimate of how much BGP routing changes have an observable impact on RTT values. No additional information (e.g., network topology) is required to apply our methodology. Although we are unable to observe routing changes happening on the reverse path from the target to the probe and RTT measurements may be affected by some biases (probe clock synchronization, presence of load balancers, etc.), our methodology is still able to produce significant results.

Processing of RTT Measurements and BGP Updates. We assume that all the inputs to our methodology are collected within a Time window.

The first input is a sequence of timestamped RTT measurements performed by a probe identified by a Probe ID towards a destination IP address Target. Being usually performed with standard tools like `ping`, we assume each measurement records a fixed number of RTT values (3 in the case of RIPE Atlas [1] probes) as well as the IP address that was actually reached. In the PREPROCESSING step we discard measurements that recorded fewer RTT values than expected or reached an unintended IP address. To better isolate the effect of propagation and transmission delays, which exhibit low variability and depend mostly on the length of routing paths and on the physical distance of devices (see, e.g., [5]), we only consider the minimum RTT value in each measurement. RTT timestamps are then shifted by a fixed Time shift in the TIME ALIGNMENT step, in order to compensate offsets between the clocks of the probes and those of the CPs, and to consider possible delays in the propagation of BGP routing changes (depending, e.g., on the relative position of probes and CPs or on the MRAI timer).

The second input is a sequence of timestamped BGP routing updates observed by a Collector peer for a specific Prefix. Each update describes how, according to BGP, traffic should be routed from the CP to the range of IP addresses falling within Prefix: for this reason, an update carries at least an AS-level path (possibly empty in the case of a withdrawal). During the PREPROCESSING step we retain only BGP routing changes that are eligible for further analysis, based on the outcome of the TIME ALIGNMENT step: of all the BGP updates happening between two consecutive RTT measurements we only retain the most recent one; if the two measurements are separated by a time lapse longer than a Tolerance window, all the BGP updates in between are discarded. Note that the Tolerance window should always be longer than the period of RTT measurements. In this way we get rid of routing changes that can not be "seen" in RTT measurements, preventing any improper deductions on them.

Detection of Significant Delay Variations. A remarkable challenge in our methodology is that RTT values are highly variable: in the not-so-extreme case when every value is representative of an RTT variation, any BGP routing change could in principle be matched with an RTT measurement that is close in time.

To avoid this, in the CHANGEPOINT DETECTION step we seek for time instants at which the mean values of RTT measurements change persistently. We exploit a technique called Pruned Exact Linear Time (PELT) [7], one of the most recent contributions in the field of *changepoint analysis* statistical methods (for a survey, see [2]). PELT uses an efficient algorithm to detect mean and variance shifts in time series data. The precision of the analysis can be tuned by an input parameter called *penalty*: using low values considers volatile shifts as valid changes,

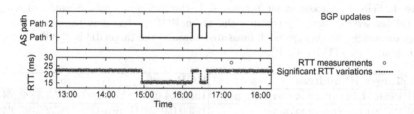

Fig. 2. BGP path changes (upper plot) and associated significant RTT variations detected by PELT in RTT values (respectively, dashed line and dots in the lower plot)

whereas using high values only detects shifts that affect a considerable portion of the input. Simpler methods like moving average would fail in equally detecting long-lasting small changes as well as short-lasting significant ones with as high precision as PELT did in our experiments. We processed RTT measurements with PELT and verified that increasing the penalty results in a hyperbolic-like decay in the number of detected changepoints (see [11]).

Choosing the "right" penalty value is not easy and depends on the nature of the input data: too high penalties may result in a coarse detection of changepoints, while too low penalties may result in interpreting noise as legitimate variations. We adopt a rule called *elbow method* (see, e.g. [6]), traditionally used in statistics: starting from a base value p_0, we run the PELT algorithm for increasing penalties p_i, $i > 0$, and stop when the ratio $-\frac{chpt_i - chpt_{i-1}}{p_i - p_{i-1}}$ between the decrease in the count of detected changepoints $chpt_i$ and the increase of the penalty falls below an Elbow slope threshold: the highest tried penalty value is selected as optimal, because further increasing it would discard too many potentially relevant changepoints. Since PELT operates on values only and does not consider timestamps, to transform input RTT values into a step-wise function we associate each changepoint with the timestamp of the RTT value that caused it. A sample of the result of the application of PELT is in Fig. 2 (lower plot).

Matching and Correlation. In the MATCHING step we look for a correspondence between routing changes and RTT variations. For each BGP update with timestamp t, we consider a time window starting at t and as wide as the Tolerance window parameter. We associate RTT changepoints falling within this window with the current BGP update. To mitigate the imprecisions of PELT, we discard changepoints corresponding to negligible RTT variations (less than 1 ms). A BGP update is marked as "correlated" if there is at least one RTT changepoint associated with it (see Fig. 2, where route flaps in the upper plot are matched with RTT changes in the lower one). To produce an overall Correlation estimate, we define the *correlation factor* as the fraction of preprocessed BGP updates marked as correlated.

Table 1. Selected measurement targets. α is the percentage of AS paths of length ≤ 5 (global average length) towards the given BGP prefix. β is the percentage of probes for which the average RTT measured towards the target IP is ≤ 300ms (value recommended by ITU for VoIP).

ID	Target IP address	BGP prefix	α	β
1001	193.0.14.129 (`k.root-servers.net`)	193.0.14.0/24 (Anycast)	87.5%	99.5%
1003	193.0.0.193 (`ns.ripe.net`)	193.0.0.0/21 (Unicast)	87.2%	97.3%
1004	192.5.5.241 (`f.root-servers.net`)	192.5.5.0/24 (Anycast)	57.8%	100%
1005	192.36.148.17 (`i.root-servers.net`)	192.36.148.0/24 (Anycast)	55.5%	99.1%

3   Experimental Results

Data Sets. In order to apply the methodology in Section 2 to real-world data sets, we considered BGP data collected by hundreds of worldwide spread CPs managed by the RIPE Routing Information Service (RIS) and RTT data collected by thousands of probes deployed within the RIPE Atlas project [1]. Several other projects (e.g., University of Oregon Route Views, CAIDA Archipelago) collect similar data sets: we selected the RIPE projects because, being run by the same organization, they are likely to gather data from ASes where both probes and CPs are available, in accordance with the scenario described in Section 2. As of January 2013 there are 55 such ASes, hosting 126 CPs and 200 probes.

We fixed the Time window to a 2-year period from January 2011 to December 2012, keeping it intentionally large to show the potential of our methodology in finding interesting correlations even in massive amounts of data. For all the 23 targets available in this window, we downloaded: (a) BGP updates and table dumps collected by all available CPs; (b) RTT measurements (performed every 4 minutes) and traceroute measurements (performed every 20 minutes) collected by all available Atlas probes (we used traceroutes in further analyses: see Section 4). Considering that for many targets the amount of measurement information was too small to identify a significant set of RTT changepoints, we restricted the application of our methodology to the targets in Table 1. Since these targets are name servers mostly advertised as anycast BGP prefixes, they may exhibit less RTT fluctuations than other more localized targets: although this made interesting correlations harder to find, experimental results show that our methodology was able to effectively cope with this additional challenge.

Parameter Tuning and Correlation. After processing the downloaded data as explained in Section 2, we searched for an assignment of the tunable parameters in Fig. 1 that could maximize distinction between poorly correlated and well-correlated information. Although we supervised many steps of this search, the obtained parameter values fit all the Targets and Prefixes we considered, eliminating the need to repeat it. At first we arbitrarily fixed the Time shift, the Elbow slope threshold, and the Tolerance window, picked a single Target and Prefix, and applied the matching methodology to compute one correlation factor

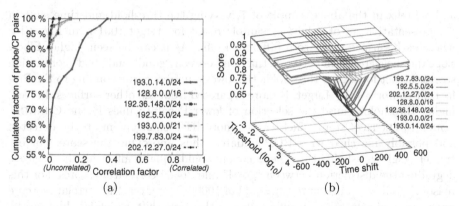

Fig. 3. (a) CDFs of the correlation factor for fixed Target ID 1001 and varying Prefixes, relative to the total number of probe/CP pairs. The Elbow slope threshold was fixed to 0.001, the Time shift to 0, and the Tolerance window to 5 minutes. (b) Correlation score for Target 1001 for varying Elbow slope threshold and Time shift. Each surface is relative to a Prefix. The arrow indicates a choice of parameters that maximizes the difference between "good" (low) and "bad" (high) correlation scores.

for all the data collected by each pair consisting of a Collector peer that recorded BGP updates affecting Prefix and a Probe in the same AS that measured RTTs towards Target. To compare "good" correlations with "bad" ones, we kept the Target fixed and recomputed the correlation factors for a sample of 7 randomly chosen Prefixes, including one that comprises the Target. For each Prefix we plotted the Cumulative Distribution Function (CDF) of the values of the correlation factor, relative to the total number of probe/CP pairs. Fig. 3(a) shows such CDFs for Target 193.0.14.129. To compare factors for different Prefixes, in the figure we only considered CPs that recorded BGP updates for all the 7 Prefixes. As expected, correlation factors with Prefix 193.0.14.0/24, which comprises the Target, are higher (the CDF is shifted to the right), whereas the trends of CDF curves for other correlations are much steeper and similar to each other.

Based on this observation, which recurred in all our experiments, we introduced a more aggregate measure, called *correlation score*, which characterizes the relationship between a set of RTT measurements towards a Target and a set of BGP routing changes for a Prefix, regardless of the specific probe and CP. Considering the CDF of correlation factors for all the probe/CP pairs corresponding to the Target and Prefix of interest, the correlation score is computed as the area of the portion of the CDF plot that is under the curve. Note that a lower correlation score indicates a better correlation (the smaller the area under the CDF, the higher the correlation factors). For example, the correlation score for Prefix 193.0.14.0/24 in Fig. 3(a) is 0.95 (better), whereas correlation scores for other prefixes are all higher than 0.99 (worse).

After introducing the correlation score, we could assess the impact of the Elbow slope threshold and of the Time shift on the computed correlation values. We computed the correlation score for each combination of a Target from Table 1 and a Prefix in the above sample of 7, varying the threshold and time shift in a representative set of values. A sample result for Target 1001 is in Fig. 3(b), where each surface refers to a different Prefix. As it can be seen, higher Elbow slope thresholds result in better distinction between "good" and "bad" correlation scores: in fact for higher thresholds the lowest surface, corresponding to the Prefix that comprises the Target, is more separated from the other surfaces. Indeed, higher thresholds cause the selection of lower Penalty values in the CHANGE-POINT DETECTION step, which causes more RTT changepoints to be detected and possibly matched with BGP updates, thus improving the score. For extremely high thresholds this phenomenon would equally affect all the Prefixes, degrading the distinction between "good" and "bad" correlation scores. For this reason, we chose a maximum threshold of 10000. Moreover, the correlation score improves significantly for specific values of the Time shift, which is a hint on the time offset between RTT measurements and BGP updates.

From the results conveyed by plots like the one in Fig. 3(b) we could determine that picking an Elbow slope threshold equal to 10000 and a Time shift equal to 60 seconds results in an optimal separation between "good" and "bad" correlation scores for all the Targets and Prefixes we considered. Considering the rate of RTT measurements (one every 4 minutes), as well as occasional irregularities in the measurement period, we fixed the Tolerance window at 5 minutes.

4   Analyses Based on Matched BGP-RTT Data

We now discuss a few analyses based on the outcome of our matching methodology, which unveil interesting aspects of the input data sets and support potential applications of our study. Additional details and results can be found in [11].

Statistical Analyses. We performed various statistical analyses on the matchings between BGP changes and RTT variations, with results reported in Table 2.

Let a *path-change* be any occurrence of a transition from an AS path P_1 to an AS path P_2 recorded by a Collector peer and matched with an RTT variation seen by a Probe in the same AS. We first checked whether, in all its occurrences for a given probe/CP pair, a single path-change was always consistently matched with an increase (or decrease) of the RTT: for the majority ($\geq 72.5\%$) of the path-changes we collected, we found this to be true for all probe/CP pairs. At least half of the other path-changes were consistently matched with an RTT change in at least 70% of their occurrences. We then considered *path-change-pairs*, consisting of a path-change from P_1 to P_2 and the reversed path-change from P_2 to P_1, both seen by the same probe/CP pair. For a good fraction ($\geq 43.3\%$) of path-change-pairs, a path-change and its reversed counterpart corresponded, in all their occurrences, to opposite variations of the RTT. We then found that at least 57.4% of the path-changes that increased (decreased) the AS path length were consistently matched, in all their occurrences, with an RTT increase (decrease).

Next, we switched to more quantitative analyses of RTT variations. We inspected the predictability of the effect of a path-change by computing the average ($\overline{\Delta RTT}$) and standard deviation ($\sigma_{\Delta RTT}$) of the RTT variations associated

Table 2. Results of our statistical analyses for the Targets listed in Table 1

	1001	1003	1004	1005
path-changes with consistent $\text{sign}(\Delta RTT)$	87.5%	78.6%	72.5%	86.4%
pc-pairs with $\text{sign}(\Delta RTT_{P_1 \to P_2}) = -\text{sign}(\Delta RTT_{P_2 \to P_1})$	64.8%	52.1%	43.3%	68.8%
path-changes with $\text{sign}(\Delta pathlen) = \text{sign}(\Delta RTT)$	76.4%	57.4%	64%	80.6%
path-changes with $\sigma_{\Delta RTT} / \overline{\Delta RTT} < 0.25$	73.6%	75.5%	95.5%	93.1%

with all the occurrences of the path-change for a probe/CP pair. For most path-changes ($\geq 73.6\%$) the ratio $\sigma_{\Delta RTT} / \overline{\Delta RTT}$ was below 0.25, i.e., the same routing change resulted in fairly similar RTT variations. We also inspected whether the position of the first modified AS in a path-change influenced the extent of RTT variations. With the exception of Target 1001, we found that changes happening close to the AS hosting the probe corresponded to larger average RTT variations, whereas changes happening far in the AS path were less impactful.

Comparison with Traceroute Data. As specified in Section 3, we also collected traceroute measurements from the RIPE Atlas probes, which we used to perform a preliminary validation of the results of our matching methodology. We considered a single probe/CP pair, a specific Target, and the Prefix comprising it. First of all, we mapped to ASes the IP addresses reported by traceroutes. Then, we shifted traceroute timestamps by the Time shift value found in Section 3, and matched them with BGP updates collected by the selected CP for Prefix: similarly to the MATCHING step in our methodology, we marked each BGP update as "correlated" if it corresponded to a change in the traceroute path.

Instead of directly comparing AS-level traceroute paths with BGP paths, we checked whether the correlation between BGP and RTT data was reflected by the one between BGP and traceroute data. The results of this check, detailed in [11], give useful insights. The majority of probe/CP pairs with high correlation factor also exhibit a high percentage of BGP updates correlated with traceroute path changes (although predictable, this observation further validated the results of our methodology). Also, for most probe/CP pairs with low correlation factor, the percentage of BGP updates correlated with traceroutes is close to zero: that is, for poorly correlated BGP and RTT data there is no evidence of correlation even with traceroute data.

Further Analyses and Applications. There are a few other analyses that can be performed based on the results of our methodology. We provide here a few examples, which also support various practical applications. First of all, it is possible to single out *equivalence classes* of CPs and probes that exhibit a highly correlated behavior. CPs in a class are therefore best candidates to understand, motivate, and, possibly, predict, delay variations recorded by probes in the same class, a useful piece of information for traffic engineering decisions. Moreover, quantifying the influence that routing updates for a Prefix recorded by different CPs had on the delays towards a Target falling in that Prefix could help determine the network locations where routing changes are less likely to affect the reachability of a delay-sensitive service. In addition, the presence of a correlation between routing updates for a Prefix and delays towards a Target not comprised in this Prefix can be evidence of a network problem and aid troubleshooting.

5   Conclusions and Future Work

In this paper we describe a methodology to automatically analyze the impact of BGP routing changes on network delays. We prove its effectiveness using publicly available data and propose some interesting analyses based on its outcome.

Lots of facets of our study deserve further investigation. Extending the analysis to different data sources (e.g., CAIDA's Archipelago), vantage points, and targets can further validate the effectiveness of our technique. RTT variations could be analyzed with different statistical methods, in order to extract further useful information on network behavior from noise, gaps, or complex patterns in the data. Further, we want to improve our analysis by studying the impact of intradomain routing changes even on one-way performance indicators, in a controlled scenario where routing events are triggered on purpose. We also envision an extension of the analyses illustrated in Section 4.

References

1. RIPE Atlas, http://atlas.ripe.net/ – RIPE RIS, http://ris.ripe.net/
2. Basseville, M., Nikiforov, I.: Detection of Abrupt Changes: Theory and Application. Prentice-Hall, Inc. (1993)
3. Chuah, C.N., Bhattacharyya, S., Diot, C.: Measuring I-BGP updates and their impact on traffic. Tech. Rep. TR02-ATL-051099, Sprint ATL (2002)
4. Da Lozzo, G., Di Battista, G., Squarcella, C.: Visual discovery of the correlation between BGP routing and round-trip delay active measurements. Computing, 1–11 (2013)
5. Hernandez, A., Magana, E.: One-way delay measurement and characterization. In: Proc. ICNS (2007)
6. Ketchen, D., Shook, C.: The application of cluster analysis in strategic management research: an analysis and critique. Strategic Mgmt. Journal 17(6), 441–458 (1996)
7. Killick, R., Fearnhead, P., Eckley, I.: Optimal detection of changepoints with a linear computational cost. Jour. Amer. Stat. Assoc. 107(500), 1590–1598 (2012)
8. Mahimkar, A., Ge, Z., Wang, J., Yates, J., Zhang, Y., Emmons, J., Huntley, B., Stockert, M.: Rapid detection of maintenance induced changes in service performance. In: Proc. CoNEXT (2011)
9. Mahimkar, A., Song, H., Ge, Z., Shaikh, A., Wang, J., Yates, J., Zhang, Y., Emmons, J.: Detecting the performance impact of upgrades in large operational networks. In: Proc. SIGCOMM (2010)
10. Pucha, H., Zhang, Y., Mao, Z., Hu, Y.: Understanding network delay changes caused by routing events. In: Proc. SIGMETRICS (2007)

11. Rimondini, M., Di Battista, G., Squarcella, C.: From BGP to RTT and beyond: Matching BGP routing changes and network delay variations with an eye on traceroute paths, Technical Report arXiv:1309.0632 (2013)
12. Tsamoura, E., Gounaris, A.: Incorporating change detection in network coordinate systems for large data transfers. In: Proc. PCI (2013)
13. Wang, F., Mao, Z.M., Wang, J., Gao, L., Bush, R.: A measurement study on the impact of routing events on end-to-end internet path performance. SIGCOMM Comput. Commun. Rev. 36(4), 375–386 (2006)
14. Zhang, Y., Mao, Z., Wang, J.: A framework for measuring and predicting the impact of routing changes. In: Proc. INFOCOM (2007)

Peering at the Internet's Frontier:
A First Look at ISP Interconnectivity in Africa

Arpit Gupta[1], Matt Calder[2], Nick Feamster[1],
Marshini Chetty[3,4], Enrico Calandro[4], and Ethan Katz-Bassett[2]

[1] Georgia Tech
[2] University of Southern California
[3] University of Maryland
[4] Research ICT Africa

Abstract. In developing regions, the performance to commonly visited destinations is dominated by the network latency, which in turn depends on the connectivity from ISPs in these regions to the locations that host popular sites and content. We take a first look at ISP interconnectivity between various regions in Africa and discover many circuitous Internet paths that should remain local often detour through Europe. We investigate the causes of circuitous Internet paths and evaluate the benefits of increased peering and better cache proxy placement for reducing latency to popular Internet sites.

1   Introduction

An Internet user's experience depends on having reliable paths that offer good performance to the set of sites that a user commonly visits. In the developed world, we have grown accustomed to rich peering and interconnection between a variety of ISPs, ranging from access networks to content providers. In developing regions, however, the story is more nuanced. The servers that host popular content (*e.g.*, Facebook, Google) may be distant, sometimes even on a different continent. Even when an Internet destination or content *is* nearby, a user's path to that destination may be circuitous, if two ISPs do not connect directly. For example, a user's path between South Africa and Kenya might "detour" through Europe if the African ISPs do not directly connect with one another. These pathologies can significantly degrade Internet performance and can affect decisions about how and where to place Internet content and services. For example, a content provider might deploy a cache in a particular ISP in one region, expecting to serve a large group of users in that region. Yet, if many Internet paths to that ISP from nearby users are circuitous, the cache will provide limited benefit to local users.

In this paper, we characterize the nature of interdomain Internet connectivity in Africa, focusing in particular on the connectivity at two major local Internet exchange points in Africa, JINX in Johannesburg and KIXP in Nairobi. To construct a view of Internet paths between various destinations in Africa, we perform continual traceroute measurements from BISmark routers in South Africa to the Measurement Lab servers deployed in South Africa, Kenya, and Tunisia. We use these traceroutes to explore the extent to which Internet paths that would otherwise remain local ultimately take a circuitous path through a remote exchange point (typically in Europe). We then use more

M. Faloutsos and A. Kuzmanovic (Eds.): PAM 2014, LNCS 8362, pp. 204–213, 2014.

detailed BGP routing information from RouteViews, Packet Clearing House (PCH), and Hurricane Electric, as well as information from PeeringDB and the IXP websites, to help explain *why* these Internet paths are circuitous.

We also quantify whether better peering or more extensive placement of caching proxies (or both) can reduce latency to popular services. We perform a trace-driven emulation to recommend specific steps for improving the performance of specific services in Africa. For example, we observe that the deployment of a Google cache node in a particular ISP will provide no benefit to Internet users in other local ISPs *unless* that ISP makes specific peering arrangements with ISPs hosting cache nodes. Based on this observation, we study how certain "surgical" peering arrangements within Africa could improve Internet performance by short-circuiting longer routes via European IXPs. Specifically, we study the following two questions:

- *What is the nature of interdomain Internet paths between locations in Africa? (Section 3)* We characterize interdomain peering between various ISPs in Africa. We measure the presence of local ISPs at various African IXPs, and the extent to which ISPs (or groups of ISPs) choose to interconnect at these exchanges. We find that 66.8% of the paths between residential access links and Google cache nodes in Africa leave the continent. Many circuitous paths result from the fact that local ISPs are often not present at local exchanges, and, when they are, they often do not peer with one another.
- *What can be done to reduce latency to Internet services in Africa? (Section 4)* We explore how both additional peering relationships and proxy cache server deployments could improve the performance of specific services for users in Africa by short-circuiting circuitous paths.

To facilitate follow-on work in this area, we have released the measurement and analysis code for the results in this study [6].

2   Measurements

To measure latency between endpoints and infer peering relationships at IXPs, we rely on 2 datasets: (1) BGP routing tables from RouteViews, PCH, and Hurricane Electric; (2) periodic traceroutes from BISmark routers deployed across South Africa to globally deployed Measurement Lab servers, IXP participants, and Google cache server deployments across Africa.

Caveats and limitations. Our data has several caveats. First, many of the Internet paths that we measure are either to or from locations in one country, South Africa. Thus, our measurements may not reflect the nature of paths in other African countries. We are expanding the deployment across other countries in Africa, and we hope that this study will encourage others to study similar phenomena. Second, peering in Africa is rapidly evolving, and the characteristics we observe from our current measurements will certainly change. Our study provides a snapshot of the current state of peering in parts of Africa and an evaluation of the benefits of improved peering.

2.1   Interdomain Routes: BGP Routing Tables

We also use several sources of BGP routing tables: RouteViews, PCH, and Hurricane Electric. We used the BGP AS path attribute in the routing tables to infer peering relationships between ASes at each IXP. Each of these data sets provides a complementary view into the connectivity between ASes in Africa. In the case of RouteViews and PCH, an AS will peer with a route server at each of these collection points, providing routes to all of its customer ASes, but not to its peers. Most of the ASes at each IXP do not provide routes to RouteViews or PCH, making it difficult to determine the complete set of peering relationships at an IXP. To gain a more complete picture of peering relationships at each IXP, we crawled the Hurricane Electric web portal. This portal allows us to see many additional inter-AS relationships that are not visible in other data sets. If two ASes are (1) adjacent in any AS path that we observe and (2) both present at an IXP, we assume that a peering relationship exists at that IXP. Unfortunately, none of these datasets allow us to see peering links between customer ASes in these BGP feeds, so our view of peering is still limited. To augment these measurements, we use traceroute measurements from BISmark nodes, as described below.

2.2   Router-Level Paths: BISmark Routers

BISmark (Broadband Internet Service Benchmark) is the combination of OpenWrt-based custom firmware and user-space packages [9]; we deploy the software on home gateway routers immediately downstream of the residential broadband access link. BISmark runs on any OpenWrt-capable device, but we have primarily deployed the software on the NetGear WNDR 3700 and 3800. Because the router is always on and connected directly to the provider, we can perform continuous measurements. The BISmark router deployment in South Africa provides the primary vantage points from access networks for this study. We deployed 17 BISmark routers across 7 ISPs and all 9 provinces in South Africa (Figure 1). We performed regular measurements from these BISmark routers to nine global Measurement Lab servers (Figure 1), including three locations in Africa: Tunis, Johannesburg, and Nairobi. We perform traceroutes between the BISmark nodes and the Measurement Lab servers in both directions every thirty minutes using Paris traceroute. These traceroutes expose sequence of ASes that these paths traverse. We use the latency information in each traceroute hop for clues as to when an Internet path may have left Africa (given the scale of these latency values, the coarse-grained latency measurements are sufficient to make such inferences) and the latency in the last hop of the traceroute to estimate the latency to the corresponding M-Lab server.

We use the BISmark vantage points to send traceroute probes to all the IXP participants to infer the peering relationships at these IXPs. If a router at the IXP appears in the path, we conclude that the peering link is present at the IXP. We discarded measurements if the traceroute had missing hop information at a transition between two ASes, since such missing data would prevent us from determining if an additional AS was present between the two that we observed. These measurements revealed 40 additional links at JINX and 14 additional links at KIXP. In cases where an IXP participant hosts a BISmark router, this additional visibility is significant. For example, in the case of AS36874 (Cybersmart), which hosts two BISmark routers, we can verify 15 out of 20 visible peering links using these additional measurements.

Table 1. The ISPs that host BISmark routers in South Africa

ISP	ASN	Routers
MTN Business Solutions	16637	6
Telkom-Internet	37457	3
Internet Solutions	3741	3
Cybersmart	36874	2
SAIX-NET	5713	1
DPBOL	11845	1
MWEB	10474	1

Fig. 1. The South African BISmark nodes continuously measure latency to nine global Measurement Lab servers

In 2012–2013, Google dramatically expanded its infrastructure for supporting search, adding 1,200 new sites across 850 ASes, which more than doubled the number of countries in which it has a presence [3]. Using data from previous work [3], we identify the 31 Google cache sites in South Africa and Kenya as of early September 2013. From each BISmark router in South Africa, we issue periodic traceroutes to each of these 31 sites, as well as sites in London and Amsterdam. In South Africa, we perform traceroutes to the following ASes that also host Google cache servers: TENET, TICSA, IS, MWEB, Google, MTNNS, and Cell C. In Kenya, we perform traceroutes to the following ASes that host Google cache servers: SafariCom, KENET, AccessKenya, JTL, and Wananchi. Three Google sites are hosted in ASes that also contain BISmark routers: IS, SAIX, and MWEB. Two other sites that contain BISmark routers, Cybersmart and DataPro, have SAIX as a provider.

3   A First Look at ISP Interconnectivity in Africa

We first explore the prevalence of high-latency paths, as measured from the BISmark routers in South Africa to the global M-Lab server destinations (Section 3.1); we explore the nature of these paths in both directions. We then explore the *causes* of these circuitous paths (Section 3.2). Based on our findings, the subsequent sections make recommendations for improving performance to Internet services in Africa.

3.1   High-Latency Paths

Figure 3a shows the distribution of median network latencies observed from the BISmark routers in South Africa to various M-Lab servers around the world. We define the *latency penalty* as the ratio of the observed median latencies to the best-case propagation delay between South Africa and that city (determined by speed-of-light propagation). Figure 3b shows the latency penalties observed for each destination. For both figures, the cities are shown in increasing order of the geographic distance from South Africa. Due to the nature of peering relationships, the increase in latency does not correlate with geographic distance. For example, even though South Africa is closer geographically to Porto Allegre, Brazil than it is to London, latencies to Porto Allegre

208   A. Gupta et al.

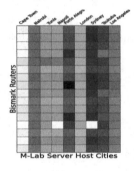

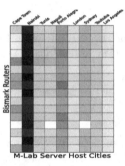

(a) Absolute latencies

(b) Latencies normalized by geographic distance

Fig. 2. The 31 Google sites in sub-Saharan Africa

Fig. 3. Latency between BISmark routers and M-Lab servers in various cities. Cities are ordered by increasing distance from South Africa. Darker pixels represent larger values.

are higher, since the path between South Africa and Brazil traverses the London Internet Exchange (LINX). Similar pathologies are evident to other destinations, such as Nairobi, which is geographically close to South Africa but whose paths to South Africa traverse the LINX.

We find that ASes in Africa often do not peer with each other anywhere on the continent. As a result, many Internet paths "detour" through Europe. In the next section, we further explore the extent and causes of these high-latency circuitous paths.

3.2 The Cause of High Latency: Circuitous Paths

We define a *circuitous path* as one that traverses a geographic location that is far from the path created by taking the geographically shortest path between two endpoints. There are two common reasons for circuitous paths: (1) the ASes that provide connectivity along the Internet path between two endpoints are not physically present in a local Internet exchange point (IXP) that is close to the geographic shortest path; or (2) the ASes that provide connectivity are present at a geographically proximal IXP but do not have business relationships with one another or do not prefer that route.

The presence of a local IXP facilitates local peering between multiple ISPs and prevents local traffic from leaving the region. The existence of a local IXP is not enough to guarantee a low-latency path: local ISPs must also choose to connect at the local IXPs. When local ISPs do not connect at a local IXP, the resulting paths can be circuitous. For example, Liquid Telecom (AS 30844) connects at JINX and has a presence in Nairobi [8], but does not peer at KIXP. As a result, users in South Africa must reach must reach many Kenyan networks via LINX in London, significantly increasing the latency of these paths.

Observation: Local IXPs are often not present on local Internet paths. We analyzed the traceroutes between BISmark routers in South Africa and Measurement Lab server locations in Tunisia, Kenya, and South Africa to quantify prevalence of different IXPs

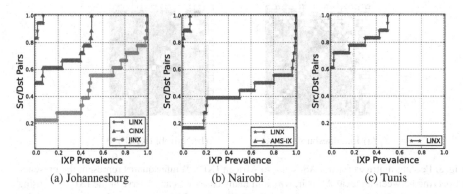

(a) Johannesburg   (b) Nairobi   (c) Tunis

Fig. 4. Distribution of IXP prevalence for the paths from BISmark nodes in South Africa to M-Lab servers in three different cities

along Internet paths between end points within Africa. We confirmed that the routers at the IXPs responded to our traceroute probes; we used these responses to identify an IXP's presence on a particular path. We define *IXP prevalence*, which quantifies the pervasiveness of an IXP for various routing paths between the two end hosts. For a pair of end hosts with N observed routing paths, IXP prevalence for the IXP I, P_I, is defined as: $P_I = \sum_{i=1}^{N} x_i P_i, \forall x_i \in \{0, 1\}$, where P_i is the prevalence of the ith routing path and $x_i = 1$ indicates IXP I is present for this route.

Local IXPs in South Africa keep local traffic within South Africa. In contrast, local IXPs are much less prevalent along paths between South Africa and other African countries. Figure 4 shows the distribution of IXP prevalence for paths between BISmark routers in South Africa and the three Measurement Lab locations in Africa. Figure 4a shows the IXP prevalence distribution for the Johannesburg M-Lab server; because most BISmark routers are located in South Africa, we observe most of the traffic to Johannesburg traverses IXPs in Johannesburg (JINX) and Cape Town (CINX). Figure 4b, on the other hand, shows a completely different story for paths between the BISmark routers in South Africa and the M-Lab server in Nairobi. The results show a lack of peering at local IXPs and we also did not observe any private peering. Interestingly, KIXP is not at all prevalent for these paths. Figure 4c shows that paths to the M-Lab server in Tunis do not traverse local IXPs in either Tunisia or South Africa.

Cause #1: ISPs do not connect to local IXPs. Sometimes, local ISPs do not connect at the local IXP at all. For example, we observed that Liquid Telecom (AS 30844) connects at JINX and has a fiber presence in Nairobi [8], but for some reason decides not to peer at KIXP, thus causing users in South Africa to take circuitous paths to destinations in Kenya. ISPs in Africa often prefer to interconnect at European exchange points such as LINX because of economy of scale. Most ISPs they need to peer with are present at LINX, not at the local exchanges, so connectivity at LINX is a requirement. Because African ISPs typically all connect at LINX anyhow, connecting at local IXPs simply represents an additional cost with limited additional benefit. Further, the absence of IP traffic between African countries, such as between South Africa and Kenya, reduces

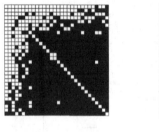   

(a) Johannesburg (JINX)   (b) Nairobi (KIXP)

Fig. 5. Peering matrices for the ASes at two African IXPs. White squares represent the presence of peering between an local AS pair, which in many cases we can observe at the IXP itself using traceroute data. Black squares represent pairs of ASes for which we do not observe peering.

the incentive of ISPs to connect locally. Deploying a cache server in one country to serve the users in another might increase traffic local to the African continent, but such a scenario introduces a catch-22: A service provider such as Google cannot improve performance for South African users by deploying a cache server in Kenya (or vice versa) until the local interconnectivity improves.

Cause #2: ISPs are present at the local IXP, but do not peer. In other cases, ISPs may be present at the same local IXP but may choose not to peer with one another. To study this phenomenon, we analyzed the *peering matrix* of several IXPs, which shows the IXP participants that peer with one another. We constructed peering matrices for the major IXPs in South Africa and Kenya (JINX and KIXP, respectively) using methods from previous work [2, 7]. We used both PeeringDB and the website of each IXP to enumerate the IXP participants. We then analyzed the BGP routing tables as described in Section 2.1 to infer peering relationships at each IXP.

Figure 5 shows the peering matrices for JINX and KIXP. We mapped 51 and 27 ASes for JINX and KIXP, respectively, but the figure includes only the ASes for which we could confirm at least one peering link for these peering matrices (30 ASes at JINX and 22 ASes at KIXP). Figure 5 assumes that if we observe a peering in any path between local ASes that the peering exists at the local IXP, even when we do not always directly observe the peering at the IXP itself. Our data sometimes prevents us from verifying the precise location of the peering link. When we use BGP AS paths, we cannot locate the peering link; we can only observe the existence of peering. In the case of our traceroute measurements, occasionally we see a direct peering without address space from the IXP, but such an observation does not mean a peering at the IXP does not exist. Peering may exist at the IXP but be numbered from one of the peer AS's address ranges, or the path through the IXP may be less preferred than another local private peering. We assumed that a relationship between two local ASes implies a peering relationship at the corresponding local IXP. Note that inferring peering links at an IXP is a hard problem [2] and even after combining multiple data sources, we were not able to infer all the peering links at these IXPs.

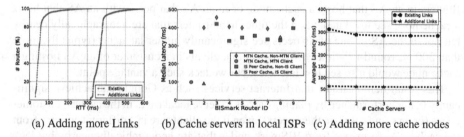

| (a) Adding more Links | (b) Cache servers in local ISPs | (c) Adding more cache nodes |

Fig. 6. Performance benefits associated with adding additional peering links, placing caching servers in local ISPs, and adding more cache nodes in a region

Figure 5 suggests that the peering matrices at each of these IXPs may be sparse. Even when local ISPs are present at an IXP, they do not always peer with one another. When local ISPs do not peer with one another at these exchanges, paths between the local ISPs may be circuitous. Specific examples at KIXP are telling: AS 36914 (KENET) is present at KIXP but we only observed its peering with Ubuntunet and Jamii Telecom. Thus, most paths between KENET and South Africa take a circuitous path through LINX, even though several transit providers at KIXP have direct peering relationships with providers in South Africa (*e.g.*, AS 12556, Internet Solutions, and AS 16637, MTN, are both present at KIXP but do not peer with KENET).

4   Reducing Latencies to Popular Internet Sites and Services

We now evaluate the expected performance improvements that clients in Africa would experience as a result of increased peering at major local ISPs. We also evaluate the relative benefits of adding links versus deploying additional local cache nodes for improving the performance of distributed services using the recent Google cache expansion.

4.1   Add More Peering Links

We quantify the performance benefits of increasing peering at local IXPs to avoid circuitous routes between local ASes. We assume that any circuitous path to Europe could be avoided if the path includes two ASes in Africa that are both present at either JINX or KIXP. In these cases, we replace the delay associated with traversing a path through Europe with the propagation delay between JINX and KIXP, which is about 30 milliseconds. Figure 6a shows the distribution of existing latencies between South Africa and KIXP, and how that distribution would change if these circuitous paths could be avoided. Adding peering links between the ASes that are already present at these local exchanges can significantly improve performance.

4.2   Add More Local Caches

Figure 6b shows the median latencies (from measurements issued every ten minutes over three days) from BISmark routers in South Africa to two Google cache nodes, one in Kenya hosted by a peer of Internet Solutions, and one in Uganda hosted by MTN. Routers in an AS that hosts a cache node or in an AS that peers with an AS that hosts a cache node see low latency; on the other hand routers that are geographically nearby but not in the AS or one of its peers see significantly higher latencies (typically, more than 300 ms round-trip times). We expect that clients in a customer of an AS hosting a cache node would also see low latencies, but we lack such a vantage point.

This result demonstrates that Internet services such as Google can achieve significantly better performance by placing caches to serve local users in the caches' customer cones (or, in some cases, in their peers), even if the clients are in a different country from the caches. Performance from BISmark nodes that are geographically nearby but lack direct paths typically leave the continent and must traverse exchange points in Europe (*e.g.*, LINX). Even when direct paths do exist, the performance benefits may depend on cache placement, since caches typically serve only over customer links and not to providers and peers. Thus, in the absence of adequate interconnectivity, adding cache servers may not improve latency performance for local users who are outside the customer cone of any Google cache. If, on the other hand, a service provider adds caches *and* peers with local ISPs, latencies for local users can improve significantly, even if the service provider places only a single cache in a local ISP. Figure 6c shows the effects of adding additional Google cache nodes in Kenya (which we simulated by taking the minimum latency between a client among k Google cache nodes in Kenya), with and without additional local peering links. This result suggests that content providers should encourage local ISPs to connect at local exchanges, which might ultimately reduce the number of cache server deployments required to achieve a particular level of service.

5   Related Work

A recent study on "boomerang routing" [5] observed that many paths between ISPs in Canada take indirect paths through the United States. We observe similar phenomena for Internet paths that are located in Africa, with the exception that the boomerang is to Europe, as opposed to the United States (and the concern is performance, as opposed to security). Other recent work has studied the internal anatomy and interconnectivity of IXPs [1, 2] but do not share our focus on performance or connectivity in Africa. Other work has highlighted the importance of Internet exchange points for the development of Internet connectivity [4]. Policy work has highlighted the importance of self-organization to improve the efficiency of peering at IXPs in developing-world contexts [10], a behavior that we believe will become increasingly important as peering and interconnection increases in Africa in the coming years.

6   Conclusion

We have taken a first look at Internet paths between locations in Africa, focusing on paths between South Africa, Kenya, and Tunisia. Although this initial study does not represent connectivity across an entire continent, it highlights specific phenomena that deserve attention and further study. First, a significant fraction of local Internet paths in

Africa detour through Europe, resulting in latency penalties of several hundred milliseconds. For example, 66.8% of paths between BISmark routers and Google cache servers in Africa leave the continent. (Latency penalties to other global regions such as South America are also high.) Second, we find that local ISPs are often either (1) not present at the local exchanges; or (2) do not peer with one another at the local exchanges.

ISPs may or may not connect at specific IXPs or peer with one another at a given local IXP for many reasons. These reasons may be economic and political as much as technical, and this issue deserves further study. In contrast to ISPs in developed regions, ISPs in Africa must attain "backhaul" connectivity to large, distant IXPs in Europe, where they can achieve economies of scale with connectivity to other ISPs. Once an ISP connects to Internet destinations via Europe, it has less incentive to connect to local IXPs, which impose additional cost but no significant gains, particularly for ISPs where much traffic is remote. Some disincentives for local peering may relate to the absence of large volumes of traffic between local ISPs, yet we expect that the continued expansion of cache nodes into these regions (*e.g.*, from Google) may change this dynamic. In turn, the deployment of any single cache node may garner much more significant performance benefits in the presence of richer local peering arrangements. As more cache nodes are deployed and more traffic *could* remain local, the peering ecosystem may rapidly evolve to include more local peering links.

Acknowledgments. This work was partially supported by NSF Awards CNS-1059350 and CNS-1162088, and a Google Focused Research Award.

References

1. Ager, B., Chatzis, N., Feldmann, A., Sarrar, N., Uhlig, S., Willinger, W.: Anatomy of a Large European IXP. In: Proc. ACM SIGCOMM (2012)
2. Augustin, B., Krishnamurthy, B., Willinger, W.: IXPs: Mapped? In: Proceedings of the 9th ACM SIGCOMM Internet Measurement Conference, IMC 2009, pp. 336–349. ACM, New York (2009)
3. Calder, M., Fan, X., Hu, Z., Katz-Bassett, E., Heidemann, J., Govindan, R.: Mapping the Expansion of Google's Serving Infrastructure. In: Proceedings of the ACM Internet Measurement Conference, IMC 2013 (October 2013)
4. Chatzis, N., Smaragdakis, G., Feldmann, A.: On the importance of Internet eXchange Points for Today's Internet Ecosystem. CoRR, abs/1307.5264 (2013)
5. Clement, A., Obar, J.: Internet Boomerang Routing: Surveillance, Privacy and Network Sovereignty in a North American Context (2013)
6. Github: Peering-Africa, https://github.com/agupta13/Peering-Africa
7. He, Y., Siganos, G., Faloutsos, M., Krishnamurthy, S.: Lord of the links: a framework for discovering missing links in the internet topology. IEEE/ACM Trans. Netw. 17(2), 391–404 (2009)
8. Liquid Telecom Fiber, http://www.liquidtelecom.com/fibre/fibre-map
9. Sundaresan, S., de Donato, W., Feamster, N., Teixeira, R., Crawford, S., Pescapè, A.: Measuring home broadband performance. Commun. ACM 55(11), 100–109 (2012)
10. Weller, D., Woodcock, B.: Internet traffic exchange: Market developments and policy challenges. Technical report. OECD Publishing (2012)

Assessing DNS Vulnerability to Record Injection[*]

Kyle Schomp[1], Tom Callahan[1], Michael Rabinovich[1], and Mark Allman[2]

[1] Case Western Reserve University, Cleveland, OH, USA
[2] International Computer Science Institute, Berkeley, CA, USA

Abstract. The Domain Name System (DNS) is a critical component of the Internet infrastructure as it maps human-readable names to IP addresses. Injecting
fraudulent mappings allows an attacker to divert users from intended destinations
to those of an attacker's choosing. In this paper, we measure the Internet's vulnerability to DNS record injection attacks—including a new attack we uncover.
We find that record injection vulnerabilities are fairly common—even years after
some of them were first uncovered.

Keywords: Domain Name System (DNS), Measurement, Security, Cache
Poisoning.

1 Introduction

The Domain Name System (DNS) is a critical component of the Internet infrastructure. DNS maps human-readable hostnames (e.g., "amazon.com") to IP addresses and
is involved to some degree in most Internet transactions. Given the foundational role
of DNS in today's Internet, DNS security has a profound effect on the overall security,
trust, and operability of the network. In particular, substituting an authoritative mapping with a fraudulent record allows an attacker to divert user access to nefarious hosts
with implications ranging from replacing the original content and phishing attacks to
installing malware on client hosts. In this paper, we measure the prevalence of DNS
vulnerabilities to attacks designed to substitute the authoritative mapping. Collectively,
these attacks are known as "record injection" attacks. We consider known attacks and a
new vulnerability we uncover, as well as the extent of the adoption of suggested best-
practice defenses.

Fraudulent hostname-to-IP address mappings originate in two places: (i) a component in the hostname resolution machinery (e.g., a local DNS resolver) or (ii) a man-in-
the-middle that can monitor DNS transactions and either change or inject responses. A
variant of the first is a cache poisoning attack whereby an attacker populates the cache
of a DNS resolver with an illegitimate record, which the resolver then uses to satisfy
subsequent requests for the given hostname.

Cache poisoning attacks generally rely on open DNS resolvers that will act upon
DNS requests from arbitrary Internet hosts. Open resolvers have long been a known
security issue. However, the prevalence of such resolvers is increasing—from 15M in
2010 [11] to 30M in 2013 [14]. While not all open resolvers are vulnerable, their increasing numbers provide a larger attack surface that we must understand. Moreover, as

---

[*] Work supported in part by NSF grants CNS-0831821, CNS-1213157 and CNS-1237265.

M. Faloutsos and A. Kuzmanovic (Eds.): PAM 2014, LNCS 8362, pp. 214–223, 2014.

we discuss below, open resolvers often give attackers a vector to attack closed resolvers, which further weakens the overall system.

The Internet engineering community has spent considerable energy fortifying DNS with DNSSEC [1] which cryptographically protects the integrity of the authoritative bindings set by the holder of a name. While DNSSEC is the long-term security strategy for the DNS, deployment is currently low—with only about 1% of the resolvers validating DNSSEC records [6,9]. Given the low DNSSEC deployment, understanding the security landscape of DNS without DNSSEC remains of critical importance.

Unfortunately, assessing the extent of security threats within the DNS infrastructure is anything but straightforward. The path a DNS transaction takes through a maze of intermediate resolvers is often both complex and hidden from external view. This paper develops techniques to attribute vulnerabilities to various actors in this infrastructure. Our key observations are: (i) that some closed resolvers are still vulnerable to cache poisoning, (ii) while vulnerability mitigations exist, deployment is not ubiquitous, and (iii) 7–9% of home networks are vulnerable to a simple new cache poisoning attack we uncover. Our general finding is that DNS security soft spots are not rare—even for vulnerabilities that have been known for years. Finally, note that our datasets are available for community use [13].

2   Terminology and Methodology

The architecture of the client-side DNS resolution infrastructure varies across providers—which we discuss in depth in companion work [14]. Here we provide a short overview of our terminology. Generally, client systems do not query authoritative DNS servers ("ADNS") directly, but rather rely on a recursive resolver, which we denote "RDNS", to handle these interactions and return the final address mapping. An RDNS may optionally leverage additional RDNS servers in the lookup process. We denote open resolvers that will answer arbitrary requests as "ODNS". We often find that ODNS resolvers do not perform recursive lookup themselves, but rather simply forward requests to an RDNS. We denote a forwarding ODNS as an "FDNS". The RDNS querying our ADNS for an FDNS is an indirect RDNS, which we denote "$RDNS_i$".

Our basic methodology for studying the vulnerability of the client-side DNS infrastructure is to probe the Internet in search of ODNS resolvers, similar to previous efforts [5,14]. We register a domain and deploy an ADNS for this domain.[1] We then use approximately 100 PlanetLab [3] nodes to randomly scan the IP address space with DNS requests for various hostnames within our domain. We embed the IP address of the target of our scan in the hostname request. Therefore, the queries arriving at our ADNS illuminate the set of ODNS servers. Additionally, the ADNS can use the source IP address to discover the set of RDNS resolvers. Given these two pieces of information, we can distinguish between ODNS resolvers that are themselves performing recursive lookup from those that are merely forwarding the requests to another resolver—i.e., the set of FDNS servers. Table 1 provides information about the datasets we discover and

---

[1] Note, unless otherwise stated, we always work within our own unused namespace as to not interfere with users' normal activities.

Table 1. Collected Datasets

Scan	Begin	Dur. (Days)	# ODNS	# RDNS
S_1	2/29/12	17	1.09M	69.5K
S_2	3/1/13	11	40.5K	5.3K
S_3	7/19/13	12	2.31M	86.1K

Table 2. RDNS Characteristics

Observation	RDNS	
	No.	%
Total	69K	100%
Unclassified	12K	18%
Classified	57K	82%
Complex Trans. ID Seq.	57K	100%
Var. Ephemeral Port	48K	84%
0x20 Encoding	195	0.3%

utilize in the remainder of the paper. While the general methodology we sketch here applies to all our experiments, the specifics vary across experiments as we study different aspects of the infrastructure. The specifics are given in the relevant sections below.

Note, we return to methodological issues in § 8. In particular, we use the techniques we develop in the paper to address two specific issues. First, we aim to understand whether the ODNS servers we find are actually in operational use by real users. Second, since we do not probe the entire Internet address space, we seek to understand if our sample is representative of the broader Internet.

3   Kaminsky's Attack

Kaminsky [10] describes a DNS cache poisoning attack which leverages the connectionless nature of typical UDP-based DNS requests to insert an NS record[2] into the victim's cache. The Kaminsky attack proceeds with the attacker A sending a large number of requests for hostnames within a domain to be poisoned, $P.com$, to a victim RDNS V in the form of queries for $random\_string.P.com$. A legitimate response to such requests must (i) be from the ADNS for $P.com$, (ii) be directed to the correct ephemeral UDP port number (the source port listed in the request message), (iii) contain the query string from the request and (iv) use the transaction ID assigned in the request. However, A knows the query string and can readily determine and spoof the IP address of the ADNS—leaving only checks (ii) and (iv) as protection against illegitimate responses. By sending a large number of requests with different query strings, A can then use brute force guessing of port numbers and transaction IDs in forged replies until a reply is accepted by V.

Mitigating the Kaminsky attack involves increasing the amount of entropy in DNS requests such that the average cost of mounting a successful attack is prohibitively high. Resolvers can increase entropy by randomizing both the DNS transaction ID and the ephemeral port number. While randomizing only the DNS transaction ID is insufficient protection, randomizing both values is an effective strategy [10]. Another technique to increasing entropy is "0x20 encoding" [4] in which the RDNS randomly changes the capitalization throughout query strings. Authoritative servers should be case insensitive

---

[2] An NS record contains the hostname of the ADNS for all hostnames within a particular domain. For instance, Google has an NS record that indicates the authoritative source for the binding of "news.google.com" to an IP address.

when resolving the query yet retain the capitalization in their response [12]. Hence, checking that the capitalization in the request and response matches is another way to decrease an attacker's likelihood of forming an acceptable response.

To understand the vulnerability to the Kaminsky attack we assess the adoption of the strategies for enhancing entropy by sending multiple requests for unique hostnames to each ODNS. Then, in our S_1 dataset, we check successive queries from a single RDNS at our ADNS for variation in the ephemeral port selection, DNS transaction ID, and for the use of 0x20 encoding. Table 2 shows our results. First, our dataset does not contain enough requests,[3] to accurately characterize 12K (or 18%) of the RDNS resolvers. For the remainder, we find that nearly all RDNS resolvers employ a complex (presumably random) method for selecting DNS transaction IDs.[4] Further, 84% of the classified RDNS resolvers use some variation in their ephemeral port selection. That means 9K RDNS servers *use a static ephemeral port on all transactions*! Per the discussion above, both the ephemeral port and the transaction ID values must be random to thwart attacks and therefore roughly 16% of classified RDNS servers are vulnerable to the Kaminsky attack. Furthermore, we observe RDNS resolvers using static source ports in 37% of the autonomous systems in our dataset, which illuminates the breadth of the issue. Additionally, we find that 0x20 encoding is in use by roughly 0.3% of RDNS resolvers—showing that resolvers are generally not using this strategy for increasing the entropy of requests.[5] These results are nearly identical when only considering the $RDNS_i$ subset of RDNS resolvers that we know to serve FDNS clients.

Finally, we note that the use of *RDNS pools* (e.g., [7, 14]) serves to mitigate the Kaminsky attack as well. Regardless of the IP address the attacker uses as entry point into the pool, the IP address used to communicate with the ADNS is chosen according to an algorithm unknown to the attacker. Therefore, to launch a Kaminsky attack against an RDNS pool, the attacker must either target every RDNS in the pool simultaneously, know how the pool distributes requests internally, or guess the destination IP address.

4 Bailiwick Rules Violations

Bailiwick rules prevent malicious ADNS servers from inserting fraudulent records into resolvers' caches [2]. Under this attack, a legitimate response from $X.com$ also includes an "additional answers" section that supplies arbitrary unrelated bindings—e.g., for $www.Y.com$. To potentially save time later, a susceptible resolver adds $www.Y.com$ to its cache. During our S_1 scan, we test for this vulnerability by returning legitimate responses from our domain that also include information for a non-existent google.com subdomain.[6] We then query the ODNS for the google.com subdomain and determine

---

[3] We require at least ten transactions for the results in this paper, but in other experiments we find the insights are not sensitive to the exact threshold.

[4] We conclude that resolvers do not use static, incrementing, or decrementing transactions IDs by observing a high standard deviation in the transaction ID sequence.

[5] Our results may be a lower bound on the adoption of 0x20 encoding as at least one major RDNS pool—Google Public DNS [8]—uses 0x20 encoding on a white-listed set of domains. Unfortunately, we have no information on the prevalence of white-listing.

[6] This will not interfere with regular Google traffic as the hostnames involved are not in use.

whether the response includes our poisoned result or an error message from Google indicating a non-existent domain.

Preventing this attack can be accomplished through the implementation of bailiwick rules—such as checking that any records in the "additional answers" section belong to the domain owned by the responding ADNS. In the most simplistic attack, we find 675 cases where client-side DNS infrastructure readily caches a DNS response for a mapping we provide for a bogus google.com subdomain. Furthermore, we observe 231 cases where the resolvers cache any additional record from a response to an MX query (these are queries for the mail server for the domain in question) and 203 cases where the resolver caches any additional CNAME-type record. Overall, there are a total of 749 cases where we find a resolver falling prey to at least one of these record injection attacks. While a relatively small number, these RDNS resolvers are completely exposed to crude poisoning by malicious ADNS servers, with no guessing involved.

5   Preplay Attack

The Kaminsky attack requires an attacker to forge an acceptable DNS response. However, in the course of our investigation we determined that FDNS servers were vulnerable to a previously unknown injection attack. While FDNS servers do not themselves recursively look up mappings, they often do have caches of previous lookups. The FDNS servers populate these caches with the responses from upstream RDNS resolvers. In some cases we find that FDNS servers fail to validate the DNS responses. This leaves these FDNS servers vulnerable to the crudest form of cache injection: a "preplay" attack whereby an attacker sends a request to a victim FDNS and then, before the legitimate response comes back, the attacker answers the request with a fraudulent response. The FDNS will then forward the fake response to the originator and cache the result. An FDNS that (i) forwards requests with a new random ephemeral port number and DNS transaction ID and (ii) verifies these and the upstream RDNS' IP address on returning responses would be protected against the preplay attack. Such protections would reduce an attacker to guessing a variety of values in the short amount of time before the legitimate response from the RDNS arrives. However, we find a non-trivial number of FDNS servers simply forward on the packets received and/or do not verify the values on DNS responses. This leaves the door open for a crude attack whereby an attacker does not have to guess these values, but can just use those from the original request.

To assess the extent of this vulnerability during our S_2 and S_3 experiments, we send a request for a hostname within our domain to each ODNS and immediately issue a fraudulent response containing IP address X. On the other hand, our ADNS responds to these requests with a binding to IP address Y. The probing host issues a subsequent request and determines which IP address is in the ODNS' cache.

In its most primitive form, the preplay attack does not involve spoofing or guessing to make the fraudulent response appear legitimate—we use the ephemeral port number and DNS transaction ID from the original request. Additionally, we use the probing machine's genuine IP address. We use variants of this attack that attempt to leverage information arriving at the ADNS (e.g., the RDNS server's IP address) to craft DNS responses that look more legitimate. However, to date our variants do not point to higher vulnerability rates. Finally, while we use the DNS default port 53 as the ephemeral port in the results herein, using a random ephemeral port number shows similar results.

We first test the preplay attack during the S_2 scan. Unlike our other scans which were performed from PlanetLab nodes, the S_2 scan leverages a single node in a residential network.[7] For each ODNS we attempt each attack variant three times to reduce any impact from packet loss. Of the roughly 41K ODNS servers we test, we find 3.5K (or 8.6%) to be vulnerable to the preplay attack. Therefore, we conclude that ODNS servers are failing to take three simple measures to thwart this attack: (i) use a new and random DNS transaction ID, (ii) verify that the source IP address in DNS responses matches the IP address of the upstream RDNS, and (iii) verify the destination port number on responses. The latter is particularly intriguing as it suggests these devices are not running a traditional protocol stack in which packets arriving on an unbound port number are dropped. Given we find no increase in the success rate with our attempts at spoofing, we return to PlanetLab with the S_3 scan to assess the vulnerability at a larger scale. Of the 2.3M ODNS servers we test, we find 170K (or 7.3%) to be vulnerable to the preplay attack.

6   DNS Message Rewriting

We now examine DNS record modification by network operators. Depending on one's perspective this may or may not be considered a security issue. However, we believe that responses deviating from the authoritative intent are at least worth understanding.

NXDOMAIN Rewriting: A DNS request for a non-existent name evokes a response with the "NXDOMAIN" return code. Previous anecdotal observations indicate that such responses are prone to interception and replacement with valid addresses by some ISPs and DNS providers. This practice is generally attempting to monetize the unfulfilled request (e.g., by trying to sell the domain or sending a user to a similar page in an attempt to meet their intent). In our S_1 experiment, we send a request to each ODNS that causes our ADNS to return an NXDOMAIN message. We find that roughly 258K (23.7%) of ODNS servers are subject to NXDOMAIN rewriting as we receive an address in response to our invalid query, which is close to previous measurements [15][8] To understand who may be responsible for rewriting, we analyze the set of RDNS resolvers on the path of rewritten messages. We determine an RDNS is a probable rewriter if more than half the open resolvers served by the RDNS experience rewriting. We find over 100 ISPs/DNS providers that we suspect of performing rewriting by default, including Qwest/Centurylink, OpenDNS, Frontier, Rogers, Airtel, RoadRunner, and TE Data.

Search Engine Hijacking: Previous work shows several ISPs alter DNS responses from major search engines in an effort to place a proxy between the user and the search results [15–17]. This allows the ISPs to monetize users' searching (e.g., by placing ads

---

[7] Due to some of our (unreported) tests using spoofed addresses (against PlanetLab's AUP).

[8] As a methodological note, one must be careful in selecting query strings. For instance, we initially misclassified OpenDNS as not performing rewriting because our queries began with dotted-quad IP addresses—a pattern OpenDNS excludes from its rewriting process. A second pass with a different query string correctly classifies OpenDNS as a rewriter. Thus, our findings are conservative due to other potential edge cases.

on the results). Since our strategy allows us to assess ISPs' RDNS resolvers, we investigate this behavior and find no evidence the practice is now in widespread use. Still, we find 18 smaller regional ISPs that appear to rewrite DNS responses for google.com.

7 Implications

Duration of Record Injection: The injection attacks we discuss above can only be successful when part of the DNS infrastructure caches a fraudulent record and then returns that record in response to a normal user request. An assessment of the caches of FDNS and RDNS resolvers [14] finds (i) little evidence of cache evictions based on capacity limits and (ii) that records with long TTLs—which can be set in injected records—stay in the cache for at least one day in 60% of the $RDNS_i$ resolvers and 50% of the FDNS servers. This shows the impact of record injection can be long-lived.

Indirect Attacks: It is not enough for RDNS resolvers to act on requests only from authorized devices as these devices are in turn commonly globally accessible and open RDNS resolvers to indirect attacks. The large and growing set—doubling to over 30M in the last three years—of open resolvers [14] represents an attack vector to otherwise inaccessible RDNS resolvers. For instance, we find that 62% of the RDNS resolvers in the S_1 dataset do not answer external queries and yet we are still able to probe these servers. Further, using ODNS servers to indirectly attack other portions of the DNS ecosystem provides a layer of obfuscation that helps attackers escape attribution.

Phantom DNS Records: A class of denial-of-service attacks relies on placing a large DNS record in a cache (at an RDNS, say) and then spoofing requests that will cause the record to be sent to some victim. This can both hide the actual origin of the attack, as well as amplify (in volume) an attackers traffic by using records that are larger than requests. To date this requires attackers to register a domain and serve large records to insert them into the various caches or find an ADNS that is already serving large records. However, using record injection techniques, an attacker does not need to be bound to any centralized infrastructure. In fact, any domain could be readily inserted in the cache and then used in a subsequent attack. This leaves less of a paper trail that can potentially trace back to an attacker. The preplay attack allows such record injection into millions of devices with trivial effort.

8 Context

We now return to contextual issues surrounding our measurements, as sketched in § 2. **Are Open Resolvers Used?** We first turn to the question of whether ODNS servers in fact serve users or are active, yet unused artifacts. This bears directly on whether the preplay attack represents a real problem. First, in companion work we use several criteria—including scraping any present HTTP content on the ODNS, consulting blacklists of residential hosts and observing UDP protocol behavior—to determine that "78% [of ODNS servers] are likely residential networking devices" [14]. Using the same criteria against the FDNS servers in the S_3 scan, we find that 91% of the FDNS servers that are vulnerable to the preplay attack are likely residential network devices. While this result does not speak directly to use, our experience is that these devices act as DNS forwarders for devices within homes and therefore we believe this suggests actual use.

Additionally, we seek to test directly for evidence that the FDNS servers we probe are in use by some client population. We start by gathering round-trip time (RTT) samples for each FDNS and the corresponding RDNS. For the FDNS we use the preplay attack to measure the RTT by taking the time between sending a fraudulent response to the FDNS and receiving the response back from the FDNS at our client. Measuring the RTT to the RDNS is more complicated. The process starts with the client requesting some name N from our ADNS. The ADNS responds with some CNAME N', which the RDNS then resolves and our ADNS returns a random address A. The mapping between N and A then returns to the FDNS and ultimately our client. The client then issues a request for N'—which will presumably be in the RDNS' cache, but given the primitive nature of preplay-vulnerable FDNS devices not in the FDNS' cache. The response for N' will be A when the RDNS answers the request from the cache.

After we obtain RTTs for both FDNS and RDNS, we seek to understand whether popular web site names are in the FDNS cache as a proxy for whether the FDNS is in use by a population of users. We therefore issue DNS requests for the Alexa[9] top 1,000 web sites and time the responses.[10] Given unreliable TTL reporting by FDNS servers [14], we determine that a given hostname is in the FDNS cache using the time required to resolve the name. Since we expect individual FDNS to have diurnal variation, we perform the lookups on each FDNS every 4 hours for one day. Our own queries will populate the FDNS cache and therefore we must exercise care with subsequent probes lest we wrongly conclude users employ the FDNS when it is our own probes we observe. We mitigate this issue in two ways. First, we probe all names with an authoritative TTL of 4 hours or more only once, accounting for 415 names. Second, we inject records into FDNS cache from our ADNS with the same TTLs as the remaining 1,585 records in our corpus (all of which are less than 4 hours). At each 4 hour interval we check our own records and if the FDNS incorrectly returns a record that had an initial TTL of x we exclude all but the initial query for popular names with an initial TTL of at least x.

We determine that a given hostname is in the FDNS cache if the time required to resolve the name during our S_3 scan does not exceed the median FDNS RTT. Figure 1 shows the distribution of the fraction of FDNS servers that hold a given number of records in their cache. The "All" line shows the distribution for all preplay-vulnerable FDNS servers. We find 81% of the FDNS servers have at least one popular name in their cache at some point during the experiment. However, the distribution also shows that over 30% of the FDNS servers have at least 100 hostnames in the cache. This seems unlikely and we believe these represent cases where our heuristic is not properly delineating between the FDNS and RDNS cache. Therefore, in an effort to better delineate the FDNS and RDNS caches we plot the subset of FDNS servers where the maximum FDNS RTT is at least 10 msec less than the minimum RDNS RTT, which we denote as "Far from RDNS". This subset encompasses 8.4K FDNS servers and we do see the tail

---

[9] www.alexa.com

[10] Note, we augment the list of sites by prepending each web site name from Alexa with "www"—which is not included in the list—and we therefore probe for 2,000 names.

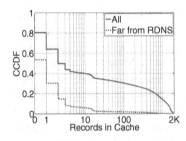

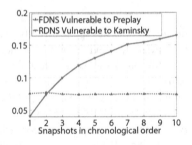

Fig. 1. Distribution of popular websites in FDNS server caches

Fig. 2. Vulnerability frequency at snapshots during discovery

of the distribution fall away. Within this subset, 53% of the FDNS servers are in use. Additionally, we examine the subset of FDNS servers that are accessible for our entire 24 hour experiment. In this subset, we find more in-use FDNS servers—90% of all FDNS servers and 68% of FDNS servers that are far from their corresponding RDNS resolver. We exclude the 24 hour lines from the graph for readability.

Note, our heuristic provides a lower bound on the number of in-use FDNS servers since we only measure a fraction of the 24 hour period. Indeed, the median TTL for the popular names is 10 minutes. Assuming the median TTL, an FDNS that enforces the TTL and an FDNS available for 24 hours, our strategy provides a one-hour window into the FDNS' cache—or, just over 4% of the day. Further, our extensive probing of the FDNS' cache may actually overflow the cache thus pushing out records added via use. Therefore, we believe that many of the FDNS servers that do not show as in use are in fact in use, but that short TTLs and our coarse and extensive probing conspire to hide the use. Our general conclusion is that the FDNS servers we find are in fact in use by people during their normal browsing.

Representativeness: Finally, we return to the issue of representativeness of our results as mentioned in § 2. Since our scans do not encompass the entire Internet our insights could be skewed by our scanning methodology. To check this we divide our scans into ten chronological slices and derive the cumulative vulnerability rate at each slice for the Kaminsky and preplay attacks. The slices are equal in size in terms of the number of vulnerable RDNS servers and vulnerable ODNS servers for the Kaminsky and preplay vulnerabilities, respectively. The cumulative vulnerability rate should plateau once the dataset is typical of the broader population. Figure 2 shows the cumulative vulnerability rate across the ten slices for both attacks. The FDNS vulnerability rate reaches steady state immediately, illustrating that we are in fact capturing a representative sample of FDNS servers with random sampling of IP addresses—which is not surprising.

On the other hand, the figure shows that for the Kaminsky attack, the vulnerability rate increases as the scan progresses, indicating that the RDNS resolvers we discover at the beginning of the scan are *less* vulnerable to the Kaminsky attack than those we discover later in the scan. While we choose ODNS servers at random, we only indirectly discover RDNS resolvers. In particular, the probability of discovering an RDNS resolver is directly proportional to the size of the FDNS population that it serves. Thus, as the scan proceeds the discovery rate decreases and we find smaller scale RDNS resolvers. We believe these results sum to indicate that busier RDNS servers are better maintained and less vulnerable to the Kaminsky attack. The plot also indicates that our estimate of the Kaminsky vulnerability rate is a lower bound.

9 Conclusion

In this study, we assess the susceptibility of the client-side DNS infrastructure to record injection attacks. We find that many open resolvers are still vulnerable to record injection. Further, these devices provide a back door to attack shared DNS infrastructure. Through active probing, we assess the extent of known record injection threats and the deployment of known protective techniques. We further uncover and measure a new attack vector—the preplay attack. We find 7–9% of the open DNS resolvers are vulnerable to the preplay attack and 16% of recursive DNS servers are vulnerable to the Kaminsky attack. Therefore, we conclude that the client-side DNS ecosystem is nontrivially vulnerable to record injection attacks.

References

1. Arends, R., Austein, R., Larson, M., Massey, D., Rose, S.: DNS Security Introduction and Requirements. RFC 4033 (2005)
2. Bernstein, D.: http://cr.yp.to/djbdns/notes.html
3. Chun, B., Culler, D., Roscoe, T., Bavier, A., Peterson, L., Wawrzoniak, M., Bowman, M.: PlanetLab: An Overlay Testbed for Broad-Coverage Services. ACM CCR 33(3) (2003)
4. Dagon, D., Antonakakis, M., Vixie, P., Jinmei, T., Lee, W.: Increased DNS Forgery Resistance Through 0x20-bit Encoding: Security via Leet Queries. ACM CCS (2008)
5. Dagon, D., Provos, N., Lee, C., Lee, W.: Corrupted DNS Resolution Paths: The Rise of a Malicious Resolution Authority. In: NDSS (2008)
6. Fujiwara, K.: Number of Possible DNSSEC Validators Seen at jp. In: DNS-OARC Workshop (2012)
7. Google Public DNS. Performance Benefits, https://developers.google.com/speed/public-dns/docs/performance
8. Google Public DNS. Security Benefits, https://developers.google.com/speed/public-dns/docs/security
9. Gudmundsson, O., Crocker, S.: Observing DNSSEC Validation in the Wild. In: Workshop on Securing and Trusting Internet Names, SATIN (2011)
10. Kaminsky, D.: Black Ops 2008: It's the End of the Cache As We Know It. In: Black Hat USA (2008)
11. Leonard, D., Loguinov, D.: Demystifying Service Discovery: Implementing an Internet-Wide Scanner. In: ACM Internet Measurement Conference (2010)
12. Mockapetris, P.: Domain Names Implementation and Specification. RFC 1035 (1987)
13. Schomp, K., Callahan, T., Rabinovich, M., Allman, M.: Client-Side DNS Infrastructure Datasets, http://dns-scans.eecs.cwru.edu/
14. Schomp, K., Callahan, T., Rabinovich, M., Allman, M.: On Measuring the Client-Side DNS Infrastructure. In: ACM Internet Measurement Conference (2013)
15. Weaver, N., Kreibich, C., Nechaev, B., Paxson, V.: Implications of Netalyzr's DNS Measurements. In: Workshop on Securing and Trusting Internet Names (SATIN) (2011)
16. Weaver, N., Kreibich, C., Paxson, V.: Redirecting DNS for Ads and Profit. In: Workshop on Free and Open Comm. on the Internet (2011)
17. Zhang, C., Huang, C., Ross, K., Maltz, D., Li, J.: Inflight Modifications of Content: Who Are The Culprits? In: LEET (2011)

How Vulnerable Are Unprotected Machines on the Internet?

Yuanyuan Grace Zeng[1], David Coffey[2], and John Viega[1]

[1] SilverSky
{yzeng,jviega}@silversky.com
[2] McAfee, Inc.
david_coffey@mcafee.com

Abstract. How vulnerable are unprotected machines on the Internet? Utilizing Amazon's Elastic Compute Cloud (EC2) service and our own VMware ESXi server, we launched and monitored 18 Windows machines (Windows 2008, XP and 7) without anti-virus or firewall protection at two distinct locations on the Internet—in the cloud and on-premise. Some machines ran a wide-open configuration with all ports open and services emulated, while others had a out-of-the-box configuration with default ports and services. After launching, all machines received port scans within minutes and vulnerability probes within a couple of hours. Although all machines with wide-open configurations attracted exploitations within a day, machines with out-of-the-box configurations observed very few vulnerability exploitations regardless of their locations. From our months-long experiment we found that: a) attackers are constantly searching for victims; b) the more opening ports/listening services a machine has, the more risks it is exposed to; c) brute-force logins are the most common type of attack; d) exploitations targeting vulnerabilities of software or operating systems are not widely observed.

1 Introduction

The Internet is a playground for opportunistic attackers. Thousands of threats are circulating around the Internet. Most computers today are protected by firewalls, IDS/IPS and anti-virus (AV) tools. But what happens in the worst-case scenario when they do not have any protection? Previous experiments on "Time-to-Live-on-the-Network" [5] and "Survival Time" [11] of Windows machines were conducted quite a few years ago with test machines running old Windows operating systems. The Internet Storm Center of SANS made the "Four-Minute Windows Survival Time" [10] claim in 2008 and was especially criticized for using a Windows XP RTM or SP1 version in the test.

Since the time of these initial time-to-live studies, the Internet threat environment has become deadlier. Meanwhile, the Windows operating systems have become more secure. But in the past five years, we failed to see any study on attacks towards unprotected machines running current operating systems. To close this gap, we wanted to investigate how well an unprotected machine with a current operating system does in today's threat environment. Left to its own devices, how soon will it be probed and attacked? And what is the most prevalent attack targeting the unprotected machine?

M. Faloutsos and A. Kuzmanovic (Eds.): PAM 2014, LNCS 8362, pp. 224–234, 2014.
© Springer International Publishing Switzerland 2014

We are interested in testing unprotected machines at two places on the Internet: one is in the cloud and the other is on-premise connecting directly to a DSL line. We would like to study the in-cloud scenario because enterprises are increasingly turning to the cloud for various business purposes. Also, since Windows operating systems account for more than 80% market share [3], we would like to focus our study on the most widely-used Windows operating systems. To the best of our knowledge, this is the first experiment carried out on Windows 2008 and Windows 7 machines. Unlike previous experiments that only captured the elapsed time for a machine to get infected, our experiment kept track of different stages of a malware infection process. We measured the time elapsed starting with the initial deployment of the test machine to the first occurrence of all following events: port scan, vulnerability probe, and exploitation. Based on detailed traffic and event logs captured, we were able to conduct a thorough analysis on the scan/probe/exploitation activities.

2   Related Work

Besides the aforementioned empirical time-to-live studies on Windows machines, there are other areas of research related to our work. One such area is vulnerability assessment. Ten *et al.* [13] proposed a framework to quantify and evaluate the vulnerabilities of SCADA systems at multiple levels. Hartung *et al.* [6] demonstrated the ease of compromising a sensor node and tampering its data, and suggested a few countermeasures to improve a sensor's security posture. McQueen *et al.* [7] created a time-to-compromise model for a system component that is visible to an attacker, taking into account known and visible vulnerabilities, and attacker skill level. Another relevant topic is the analysis on the Internet-wide malware propagation. Moore *et al.* [8] conducted a case study on the infamous Code-Red worm at the global level, detailing the spread of this worm and the properties of the infected machines. Shannon *et al.* [12] monitored the outbreak of Witty worm through a network telescope and reported findings such as the scanning rate, the infection duration as well as the number of victims over a period of time. Moore *et al.* [9] studied the use of public search engines to locate vulnerable servers and found that as an alternative to vulnerability scanning this approach was widely used in compromising web servers to host malware and phishing sites.

3   Experiment Design

3.1   Scope of the Experiment

Usually, a machine gets infected through either of the two ways: user-involved infection or vulnerability exploitation. A user-involved infection requires a user to take certain actions such as clicking a link or downloading and executing a file. An infection via vulnerability exploitation normally gets its way into the machine silently without a user's awareness. Our experiment only considers the vulnerability exploitation scenario with no user in the loop. Every Windows machine in our experiment meets the following requirements:

- Each machine is connected to the Internet with a unique public IP address.
- All incoming traffic (TCP, UDP and ICMP) is allowed by a network-based firewall.

- The in-host Windows firewall is disabled and no anti-virus (AV) is installed.
- Wireshark captures all network traffic; Regshot [4] monitors Registry changes and Windows event logs keep track of system-wide activities such as logins/logouts and application status changes. Those logs together are used to decompose probes and attacks.

3.2   Experiment Set-Up

Our experiment spanned two periods of time: February to April and August to October of 2012. We set up and collected data from 18 machines in total at two locations—the Amazon's Elastic Compute Cloud (EC2) and a VMware ESXi server on-premise.

In-Cloud Experiment. We ran 15 machines in Amazon's EC2 environment with two configuration profiles: "wide-open" and "out-of-the-box". In the wide-open scenario, a machine opens all ports and emulates all possible services. This way the machine can attract as many malicious attempts as possible. In the out-of-the-box scenario, a machine runs only with default open ports and services. This scenario gives us a baseline of how many malicious attempts an unprotected machine might encounter.

Windows is by far the most popular operating system on the Internet. Its server versions are generally exposed to more risks than home/professional versions. Our tests were carried out on Windows Server 2008 R1 SP2 and R2 SP1. As mentioned earlier, we disabled all firewall and anti-virus programs and configured the security policies so that Amazon allowed all incoming connections to those machines. To create the wide-open scenario, we installed a low-interactive honeypot named HoneyBot [1] and changed several services to avoid interference. After the configuration was complete, we took a snapshot of the instance and created an AMI (Amazon Machine Image) for later use. We launched ten instances on EC2 using the same AMI and made sure that they were hosted in different geographical zones and were allocated different IP addresses. For the out-of-the-box scenario, we made a clean install of Windows Server 2008 and did not install any programs other than Wireshark and Regshot. By default, common ports such as 135 (RPC), 139 (NetBIOS), 445 (SMB) and 3389 (RDP) were open. We ran five such instances on EC2.

On-Premise Experiment. To create a testbed, we installed a VMware ESXi 5.0 server and connected it to a DSL line at our office location in North Carolina. This time we wanted to test out non-server Windows OS versions. Since OS platform statistics [3] showed that Windows 7 and Windows XP accounted for a majority of Windows operating systems being used (55% and 25% in August 2012), we created three virtual machines on the ESXi server: one running Windows 7 Professional SP1 and two running Windows XP Professional SP2. Their default open ports included 135 (RPC), 139 (NetBIOS), 445 (SMB) and 3389 (RDP). We later opened port 21 (FTP), 25 (SMTP), 80 (HTTP), 443 (HTTPS), 1433/1434 (MSSQL) on those Windows XP machines. Each virtual machine was assigned a unique public IP and we ran port scans to confirm that machines were indeed reachable from the Internet. Other configurations were the same as the in-cloud machines.

4   Experiment Results

4.1   In-Cloud Experiment

Scan, Probe, and Exploitation Times of Occurrence. Malware infections follow a predictable pattern. Using a port scan, an attacker tests whether a port on a target machine is open. If so, a vulnerability probe gathers more information about a listening service, such as the version of the service to identify specific vulnerabilities; and an exploitation delivers malicious payloads to finally compromise the machine. In the wide-open scenario, after launching, on average it took about 23.4 minutes to see the first port scan, and 56.4 minutes to see the first vulnerability probe (the exact number for each server shown in Figure 1). Probes hit well-known ports such as 22 (SSH), 23 (Telnet), 25 (SMTP), 80 (HTTP), 445 (SMB), 1080 (SOCKS Proxy), 1433 (Microsoft SQL Server) and 3389 (RDP). Looking at each server (honeypot) individually, we found that honeypots 1, 7, 8 and 9, which were hosted in the same zone on EC2, waited longer to see the first port scans and probes. We surmised that the IP space of that zone was new and not yet explored by attackers. With respect to exploitation time windows, we observed that almost all first exploitation attempts came in within 24 hours, with the average time being 18.6 hours (Figure 2). We captured exploitation attempts on port 445 (SMB), 1434 (Microsoft SQL Monitor), 2967 (Symantec AV) and 12147 (Symantec Alert Management System 2). Almost all exploitations during our months-long experiment were known threats. This is expected because the HoneyBot program was able to emulate many known vulnerabilities to attract attacks. Interestingly, exploits targeting five to even ten years old vulnerabilities were still floating around. For example, the attack at port 1434 was the Slammer worm dating back to 2003, and the stack overflow vulnerability at port 2967 was disclosed in 2006.

In the out-of-the-box scenario, it took an average of 13 minutes for the first port scan to arrive (Figure 3). Port scans hit ports such as 8080 (HTTP) and 1433 (Microsoft SQL Server). The first vulnerability probe arrived within 3 hours on average (Figure 3); all probes were login attempts to the Samba share (445) or via RDP (3389). We monitored the servers for a few weeks, but failed to see any exploitation attempts mainly due to the limited number of open ports (services).

Top Targeted Ports. In the wide-open scenario, all ports were open on each test machine. We analyzed the traffic to see which ports were targeted most often. Table 1 plots the top 10 ports ordered by the percentage of total traffic each port accounts for. As shown, 1080 (SOCKS) was the most targeted port. The SOCKS protocol is used to tunnel traffic through firewalls from inside to outside, but it is often misconfigured. Attackers take advantage of misconfigured SOCKS services to tunnel their attack traffic inward and mask the origin of their traffic—that's why this port attracted so many hits. Port 1433, the Microsoft SQL Server listener, also received much attack traffic. Port 25 (SMTP) was also popular. Spammers who look for open relays frequently probe this port. Many of the other top ports were related to the HTTP service, such as 80, 8000, 8080 and 8888. In the out-of-the-box scenario, we can see that (also in Table 1) more than 60% of traffic went to port 445 and 3389 which were open by default. Other common ports such as 1433, 80, 4899 and 1080, though not open, also received numerous scans.

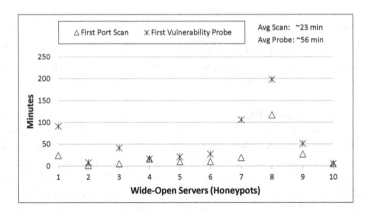

Fig. 1. Scan and Probe Times of Occurrence on Wide-Open Servers (in minutes)

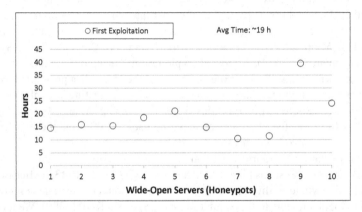

Fig. 2. Exploitation Attempt Times of Occurrence on Wide-Open Servers (in hours)

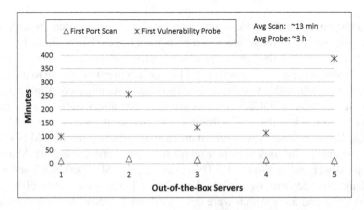

Fig. 3. Scan and Probe Times of Occurrence on Out-of-the-Box Servers (in minutes)

Login Attempts. In our experiment, we observed a huge number of login attempts. Almost all of them were failures according to Windows security event logs. Every test machine, on average, received over 1,000 login requests daily either through port 445/139 (SMB/NetBIOS) or port 3389 (RDP). SMB (Server Message Block) is an application layer protocol that is mainly used for file sharing on Windows systems. It can run directly over TCP port 445 or run in the session layer via port 139 over TCP. RDP (Remote Desktop Protocol) provides remote desktop connections for Windows. We looked at failed login attempts at port 3389 on our test machines. As it turned out, multiple offending IPs tested out the same dictionary of usernames. Table 2 demonstrates this set of usernames. In particular, the username *administrator*—the default administrative account name—was brute-forced the most. Examining the SMB login attempts,

Table 1. Top 10 Targeted Ports

Wide-Open		Out-of-the-Box	
Port	% of Conn	Port	% of Conn
1080 SOCKS	15.50%	445 SMB	32.26%
445 SMB	10.94%	3389 RDP	28.85%
1433 MSSQL	8.03%	38856	6.07%
3389 RDP	6.29%	139 NetBIOS	2.81%
80 HTTP	6.01%	1433 MSSQL	2.48%
110 POP3	3.18%	22292	1.73%
22 SSH	2.93%	80 HTTP	1.58%
25 SMTP	2.91%	4899 Radmin	1.13%
139 NetBIOS	2.83%	27977	0.93%
8000 HTTP	1.76%	1080 SOCKS	0.90%

Table 2. Brute-Forced Usernames

Usernames			
1	administrator	root	test2
123	aspnet	server	test3
a	backup	sql	user
actuser	console	support	user1
adm	david	support_388945a0	user2
admin	guest	sys	user3
admin1	john	test	user4
admin2	owner	test1	user5

we observed that attackers tried several administrator name variations such as *admin*, *administrator* and *db2admin*. All of those attempts failed except for a few anonymous (guest) logons. Anonymous logins do not require a username or password to connect to the SMB server. This is an optional feature of SMB and should generally be disabled. Anonymous logins may pose a security risk to the system because a remote attacker could launch exploits to gain user privileges or even control of the affected system.

Exploitations. In our experiment, we found that most exploitations attempted on our wide-open machines were not new attacks. There was one interesting attack we would like to highlight—an attack on port 12147 where Symantec's Alert Management System 2 (AMS2) service listens. AMS2 is a component of multiple Symantec products including Symantec AntiVirus Corporate Edition and Symantec Endpoint Protection. AMS2 has multiple known vulnerabilities. For example, in 2009 a remote-code-execution vulnerability of AMS2 allowed attackers to execute arbitrary commands by sending a crafted packet. Our honeypot captured one such packet—the attacker attempted to get a remote shell to create a VBScript in the target machine. We extracted and reorganized the exploit packet payload and found that the main purpose of the script was to download an executable named *winnew.exe* from the attacker, save it as *installer.exe* to the *C:* drive, and then run it. With the remote command shell, the attacker was able to do whatever he wanted to the target machine. Our honeypots also captured similar exploits targeting the same vulnerability, but with different payloads.

Table 3. Summary Statistics

Machine	Total Time	1st Port Scan	1st Probe	# of Compromises	# of Connections Daily	# of Offending IPs Daily
Win XP Pro SP2	14 days	50m	1h51m	1	453	69
Win XP Pro SP2	7 days	6m	1h37m	1	2372	54
Win 7 Pro SP1	29 days	3m	2h41m	0	618	45

4.2   On-Premise Experiment

Scan, Probe, and Exploitation Times of Occurrence. In the on-premise experiment, Table 3 shows the summary statistics of the three virtual machines (Two Windows XP and one Windows 7) on an ESXi server. They were connected to a DSL line in our office location. They all received port scans within an hour, probes within a couple of hours, though only the two XP machines were eventually compromised by attackers. The average numbers of inbound connections on daily basis were different from one machine to another. Apparently, some offending IPs behaved more aggressively than others, which we will show later.

Top Targeted Ports. As far as top targeted ports are concerned (Table 4), Windows XP and Windows 7 machines shared a similar set of targeted ports such as 1433, 3389, 445 and 139. The MSSQL port 1433 was disproportionally targeted due to the Microsoft SQL server installed on the XP machines. Note that many ports in the top list were never open in our experiment—attackers made constant requests to them simply because most likely services running on those ports had vulnerabilities. Thus, it is important for network administrators and IT security staff to secure those services at first.

Top Offending IPs. Table 5 lists the top 5 offending IPs along with targeted ports per IP and the number of connections initiated. The observation is that, as opposed to scanning all/multiple ports on a machine, the attacker normally focused on one particular port

Table 4. Top 10 Targeted Ports

Windows XP		Windows 7	
Port	% of Conn	Port	% of Conn
1433 MSSQL	36.58%	139 NetBIOS	53.56%
3389 RDP	8.88%	445 SMB	23.10%
445 SMB	1.62%	3389 RDP	13.87%
5900 VNC	1.53%	1433 MSSQL	1.58%
139 NetBIOS	0.59%	5900 VNC	1.55%
25 SMTP	0.40%	22 SSH	0.76%
22 SSH	0.31%	23 Telnet	0.48%
4899 Radmin	0.22%	4899 Radmin	0.45%
110 POP	0.22%	8080 HTTP	0.45%
80 HTTP	0.19%	51595 UDP	0.41%

Table 5. Top 10 Offending IPs with Targeted Ports

Windows XP		Windows 7	
IP/Port	# of Conn	IP/Port	# of Conn
64.31.*.*	**6988**	**80.90.*.***	**5663**
1433	6988	*139*	2790
218.65.*.*	**1987**	*445*	2873
3389	1987	**184.154.*.***	**4628**
199.36.*.*	**1360**	*137*	2
1433	1360	*139*	4626
117.41.*.*	**1050**	**122.199.*.***	**1463**
1433	1050	*3389*	1463
159.226.*.*	**912**	**205.210.*.***	**682**
1433	912	*135*	1
		139	454
		445	227
		200.91.*.*	**623**
		135	1
		139	310
		445	312

(service). For example, the top one offending IP to XP machines initiated thousands of connections only to the MSSQL port 1433, whereas the top offending IP to the Windows 7 machine persistently reached out to SMB port 445/139. Apparently, brute-forced login attempts accounted for a majority of the incoming connections.

Top Countries. We used MaxMind's GeoIP database [2] to map source offending IPs to geographic locations. As shown in Figure 4, the top three countries remained the same for XP and 7 machines. The top one country is China, accounting for over one third of total malicious traffic. United States is at the second place and followed by Korea. We need to point out that the location of an offending IP does not necessarily

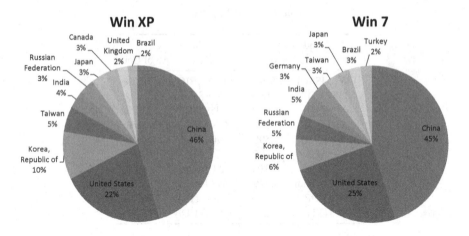

Fig. 4. Top 10 Countries of Attacks

reflect where the attacker is because an attacker can remotely control compromised machines all over the world.

Compromises. As mentioned earlier, the Windows 7 machine stayed strong throughout the experiment, whereas the two Windows XP machines fell victim and were eventually under attackers' control. How did the compromises take place? Long story short: both were due to weak passwords as opposed to OS/software vulnerability exploitations. We will walk through them one by one.

Compromise I: The compromise of one XP machine was attributed to a Microsoft SQL Server brute-force attack. The intruder successfully broke the 'sa' account password ("password1") within 9 hours of service startup, and then enabled the *xpcmd_shell*, an extended stored procedure, to issue commands directly to the Windows command shell. With this privileged access, the machine was in the intruder's hand. The victim machine subsequently started FTP sessions with its command server and downloaded and exe-cuted multiple Trojan payloads. Instructed by the command server, the machine made numerous connection attempts to an online gaming site.

Compromise II: The compromise of another XP machine also resulted from a weak password ("tryout") of the Administrator login account. The intruder launched thou-sands of RDP sessions and finally made a right guess. It was about two days between our machine going online and being compromised. From the pcap traces, we could tell that the original intruder did not hold the machine for his own use. It seems that the compromised machine was given (or even sold) to someone else. Though the break-in method is a standard one, how the victim machine was used is noteworthy. There was no system change or file modification on the machine. We caught the wrongdoer at the scene the moment he was fabricating his eHarmony profile on the compromised machine. His IP was from Nigeria and there was a picture of an Italian actor on the desk-top. Looking at the browsing history we found that this person had visited quite a few online dating sites to create new profiles and browse other peoples' pages—he logged on to this machine solely for this purpose. Given all the information, very likely, this is the starting point of an online dating scam. Why did he use someone else's machine to do so? Normally, web sites can track users by IP addresses and people conducting malicious activities are afraid of getting caught if using their own computers.

5   Conclusion and Future Work

In this paper, we presented our experiment on monitoring 18 unprotected Windows machines at two Internet locations: in the cloud and on-premise. Our key findings are:

- *Every machine on the Internet is scanned within minutes after connecting.* It does not matter whether a machine connecting to the Internet opens ports or not—any machine will be scanned within several minutes. This is not surprising because attackers don't know whether a port is open unless they scan it.
- *More open ports means more vulnerability probes.* The elapsed time between the machine startup and the arrival of vulnerability probes depends on the specific services that are running. The more listening services a machine has, the sooner it will be probed, and the more risks it will be exposed to.
- *More vulnerabilities means more exploitation attempts.* It is rare that attackers send exploitations blindly without first knowing that their targets are vulnerable. On the other hand, if unprotected machines have holes, chances are good that attackers will find them and attempt to exploit them. How long it takes depends on the vulnerabilities a machine has.
- *Brute-force logins are the most common type of attack.* We observed that brute-force login attempts were much more frequent than vulnerability probes or exploitations. On each machine, we captured dictionary attacks at port 445 (SMB) and 3389 (RDP), attempting thousands of username/password combinations. Most attempts targeted accounts with administrator privileges. Weak or default passwords can be easily broken and provide the best entry point.
- *Vulnerability exploitations without users' interaction are possible but not widely observed.* Even though every wide-open machine (all ports open and services emulated) received at least one vulnerability exploitation within hours, we saw very few exploitations on out-of-the-box machines. Generally speaking, exploitations coming directly from the Internet and targeting vulnerabilities of operating systems or applications are less prevalent nowadays—most exploitations are delivered at the client-side and require users' involvement such as opening a file or clicking a link.

As future work, we plan to broaden the scope of the experiment. We would like to 1) increase the number of test machines; 2) add other operating systems such as OS X and Linux; 3) deploy machines at more locations such as home and campus networks. We expect to run this experiment on an ongoing basis and regularly report our findings.

References

1. Honeybot, http://www.atomicsoftwaresolutions.com/honeybot.php
2. Maxmind geoip database,
   http://www.maxmind.com/en/geolocation_landing

3. Os platform statistics, `http://www.w3schools.com/browsers/browsers_os.asp`
4. Regshot, `http://sourceforge.net/projects/regshot/`
5. Avantgarde: Time to live on the network. Tech. rep. (2004)
6. Hartung, C., Balasalle, J., Han, R.: Node compromise in sensor networks: The need for secure systems. Department of Computer Science University of Colorado at Boulder (2005)
7. McQueen, M.A., Boyer, W.F., Flynn, M.A., Beitel, G.A.: Time-to-compromise model for cyber risk reduction estimation. Quality of Protection, 49–64 (2006)
8. Moore, D., Shannon, C.: Code-red: a case study on the spread and victims of an internet worm. In: 2nd ACM SIGCOMM Workshop on Internet Measurment, pp. 273–284 (2002)
9. Moore, T., Clayton, R.: Evil searching: Compromise and recompromise of internet hosts for phishing. In: Dingledine, R., Golle, P. (eds.) FC 2009. LNCS, vol. 5628, pp. 256–272. Springer, Heidelberg (2009)
10. SANS: Four-minute windows survival time, `http://isc.sans.edu/diary.html?storyid=4721`
11. SANS: Survival time, `http://isc.sans.edu/survivaltime.html`
12. Shannon, C., Moore, D.: The spread of the witty worm. IEEE Security & Privacy 2(4), 46–50 (2004)
13. Ten, C.W., Liu, C.C., Manimaran, G.: Vulnerability assessment of cybersecurity for scada systems. IEEE Transactions on Power Systems 23(4), 1836–1846 (2008)

A Closer Look at Third-Party OSN Applications: Are They Leaking Your Personal Information?

Abdelberi Chaabane[1], Yuan Ding[2], Ratan Dey[2],
Mohamed Ali Kaafar[1,3], and Keith W. Ross[2]

[1] INRIA, France
[2] Polytechnic Institute of NYU, USA
[3] NICTA, Australia

Abstract. We examine third-party Online Social Network (OSN) applications for two major OSNs: Facebook and RenRen. These third-party applications typically gather, from the OSN, user personal information. We develop a measurement platform to study the interaction between OSN applications and fourth parties. We use this platform to study the behavior of 997 Facebook applications and 377 RenRen applications. We find that the Facebook and RenRen applications interact with hundreds of different fourth-party tracking entities. More worrisome, 22% of Facebook applications and 69% of RenRen applications provide users' personal information to one or more fourth-party tracking entities.

1 Introduction

OSN user profiles represent a rich source of personal information, including demographic information, users' interests and their social relations. Privacy threats resulting from this direct exposure of personal information have been widely publicized and researched. Third-party OSN applications are tremendously popular with some apps being actively used by more than 100 million users in Facebook. Besides, with apps potentially having access to users' personal information, through access permissions, they introduce an alternative avenue for privacy leakage. With the users' personal information being exposed outside of the OSN sphere, the privacy risk becomes even higher.

We examine third-party OSN applications for two major OSNs: Facebook and RenRen. These third-party applications typically gather, from the OSN, user personal information, such as user ID, user name, gender, list of friends, email address, and so on. Third-party applications also typically interact with "fourth parties," such as ad networks, data brokers, and analytics services. According to Facebook's Terms of Service, third-party applications are prohibited from sharing users' personal information, collected from Facebook, with such fourth parties. We develop a measurement platform to study the interaction between OSN applications and fourth parties.

We use this platform to analyze the behavior of 997 Facebook applications and 377 applications in RenRen. We observe that 98% of the Facebook applications gather users' basic information including full name, hometown and friend list,

M. Faloutsos and A. Kuzmanovic (Eds.): PAM 2014, LNCS 8362, pp. 235–246, 2014.

and that 75% of apps collect the users' email addresses. We also find that the Facebook and RenRen applications interact with hundreds of different fourth-party tracking entities. More worrisome, 22% of the Facebook applications and 69% of the RenRen applications provide users' personal information to one or more fourth-party tracking entities.

1.1 Related Research

Krishnamurthy and Wills examined privacy leakage that can occur from OSNs directly to external entities [5,6]. Chaabane et al. evaluated the tracking capabilities of the OSNs in [1]. However, to our knowledge, this is the first paper to explore indirect privacy leakage to external entities via third-party applications. Another line of related research has analyzed the permission systems in third-party applications. Chia et al. showed that community ratings are not reliable and that most applications request more permissions than needed [2]. Frank et al. extended this work, showing that Facebook permissions follow a predefined pattern and that malicious applications deviate from it [4]. Finally, Xia et al. proposed *Tessellation* [9] a framework to correlate user identity – using various OSN identifiers extracted from the social network traffic – to its online behavior. Our approach is complementary as it shows that OSN identifiers can be also extracted from other sources (i.e., traffic between third party applications and external entities). None of these works examine the flow of personal information from the third-party apps to fourth-party entities.

2 Background

This section introduces the general concepts behind third-party applications for both Facebook and RenRen networks. For concreteness, we discuss these concepts in the context of Facebook, and point out how RenRen differs at the end of this section.

As shown in Figure 1, while logged into the OSN, the user selects an app, which brings the user to a web page that includes a "canvas" served by Facebook, the application (in an iframe) served by the publisher's server, and possibly some advertisements served by ad networks. If it is the user's first visit, Facebook displays a dialog frame which asks the user for permissions to access information in the user's profile (step 1). This dialog frame indicates the particular set of permissions the application is requesting. The application can, for example, request permission for "basic info" [1], which includes user name, profile picture, gender, user ID (account number), and user networks. Applications also have access to friend lists and any other information users choose to make public (e.g., interests and notes). In order to access additional attributes, or to publish content to Facebook on behalf of the user, the application needs additional permissions.

The user's browser then contacts Facebook seeking an *access token*, which is used to query Facebook servers to fetch the user's information (steps 2 and

---

[1] https://developers.facebook.com/docs/graph-api/reference/user/

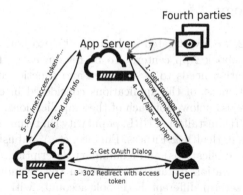

Fig. 1. An overview of the Facebook application architecture

3). The token is transmitted to the publisher's server (step 4), which queries Facebook for user information (steps 5 and 6). Once the server obtains the user information, it may load all or some of that information in the HTML (for example, using JavaScript) provided to the user's browser.

OSN applications typically further interact with "fourth parties" such as ad networks, data brokers, and analytics services. Different techniques can be used to contact these external entities, among which include using an iframe (e.g., loading an ad) and Javascript (e.g., sending data to an analytics service). Observe that when these entities are contacted, the referrer field is automatically filled with the current page (i.e. application main page) URI. Our focus in this paper is on these external entities and whether the personal information obtained by the user's browser is transferred to the external entities.

From an architectural point of view, RenRen has the same conceptual features and operation as Facebook with a few minor exceptions. In particular, RenRen has only three permissions: (i) access personal information and friend relations, (ii) access timeline information (e.g., posts, shared content) and (iii) allowing the app to post on behalf of the user. The first permission is granted by default to all applications.

Privacy Issues: Third party applications naturally give rise to several privacy issues. First, the application code is hosted on the publisher's own servers and are out of Facebook's control. This inherently prevents Facebook from monitoring and/or controlling the application's behavior, and impedes any proactive measures to block malicious activities. Second, as user information is transferred out of Facebook servers, user information usage and dissemination is out of the user's control. Finally, privacy control for third-party apps are very limited due to the coarse-grain granularity of permissions, and as such it is debatable whether this is in accordance with the "principle of minimal privilege" which states that only minimum privileges should be granted to fulfil the task.

3   Methodology

In December 2012, we investigated each of the 997 working applications listed on the official Facebook App center.[2] To be referenced by the Facebook App center, the application needs to be reviewed and sanctioned by the Facebook staff.[3] As a result, most of the applications considered in our study are very popular, as we discuss below. For each of these applications, we first obtain the application name, ID, installation URL, popularity (in terms of number of users), category (e.g., game, Health & Fitness, Finance, etc.), publisher (which was not available for a few applications) and a summary description. We then automate the process of application installation based on the Selenium WebDriver.[4] In particular, using several different Facebook accounts with distinctly different user profiles, we install and accept the requested permissions for each of the 997 applications. To monitor the application behavior, we use a modified version of a Firefox plug-in [7], allowing us to record all the HTTP and HTTPS traffic. Similarly, we investigated each of the 377 working applications listed on the RenRen App center.

3.1   Limitations of the Methodology

In our experimental methodology, we aim to measure and characterize third-party applications in a semi-controlled environment. We note, however, that our tested applications are all gathered from the official App center and as such do not represent the totality of the OSN third-party application ecosystem, since there are many other applications that do not belong to the App Center. For the privacy leakage analysis, our methodology only examines traffic originating from the user browser; any information leakage that might happen outside this channel (e.g., communication between the application servers and external entities) are not identified. Therefore, the extent of privacy leakage quantified un this paper serves as a *lower bound*.

3.2   Basic Characteristics of Applications

Our main interest centers on the applications' interactions with external fourth-party servers and resulting privacy leakages. To this end, it is useful to first understand the basic characteristics of the Facebook and RenRen applications under investigation. Specifically, in this subsection, we examine the popularity of the applications, the applications' publishing companies, and the permissions the applications request.

Application Popularity: Figure 2a shows the cumulative distribution for the popularity of our tested Facebook and RenRen applications. We observe that

---

[2] https://www.facebook.com/appcenter/
[3] https://developers.facebook.com/docs/appcenter/guidelines/
[4] http://seleniumhq.org/

both distributions exhibit a similar shape with 60% of the Facebook and RenRen applications having more than 100 thousands users and 10 thousands users, respectively. Importantly, the most popular applications have more than 100 million users in Facebook and more than 10 million in RenRen. This shows the potential of third-party applications to collect large volumes of user data.

Table 1. Most frequent app companies for Facebook (997 apps)

6waves	2.35%
Zynga	1.66%
Playdom	1.37%
Peak Games	1.17%
Kingnet	1.07%
Electronic Arts	1.07%
MindJolt	0.98%

Table 2. Most frequently requested permissions for Facebook (997 apps)

User basic information	98%
Personal email address	74.5%
Publish Action	59.6%
Access user's birthday	33.6%
Publish stream	20.5%
Access user's likes	12.25%
Access user's location	9.8%

Application Companies: We were able to collect the publisher's company name for 845 applications. Table 1 shows the top seven publishers among the applications considered. These top seven companies only cover 10% of the applications; furthermore, there are 536 different publishers for the 997 tested applications. From a data retention perspective, this suggests that user data is more likely to be scattered among multiple entities, further reducing the user's control over its data.

Permissions: Table 2 shows the most frequently requested permissions. As expected a large fraction of applications request permission to obtain the basic information, which as mentioned previously, encompasses not only the user name but also all information the user makes public in the public profile. Requests for access to email information is also very frequent (75%). Sensitive information such as user' birthday and hometown seems to be less requested with 33% and 10% respectively.

4   Interaction with External Entities

Now we turn our attention to the interaction between the third-party application running in the browser and external entities. Since most, if not all, of the functionalities are very similar in Facebook and RenRen networks, we mainly discuss features of the Facebook network. However, the figures show our results for both OSNs.

HTTP Connections. For an application to function properly in Facebook, the user browser has to contact three main domains: the Facebook login page at `facebook.com` to exchange credentials, the Facebook content server at `fbcdn.net` to extract user data (e.g., the user's photo) and the application's main server. For each of our tested applications, we capture the traffic exchanged

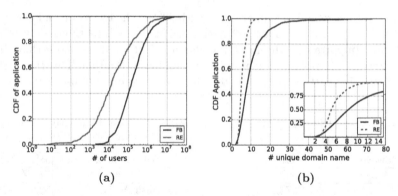

Fig. 2. (a) Application popularity, (b) Number of contacted servers for each application

between the browser and the external entities, and extract the external domains with which the application communicates. Figure 2b shows the CDF of the number of unique contacted domains per application for both Facebook and RenRen OSNs. Surprisingly, more than 75% of the Facebook applications exchange traffic with at least six different domains, and for almost 10% of the tested applications the number of unique domains exceeds 20.

The RenRen network exhibits a slightly different behavior with 70% of the tested applications contacting less than 6 servers. The maximum number of domains contacted by RenRen applications is four times smaller than in Facebook. This suggests that the tracking eco-system in RenRen is less complex and includes a smaller number of entities.

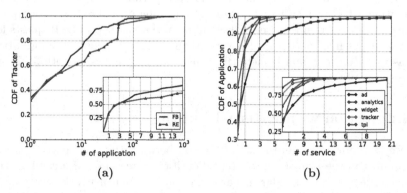

Fig. 3. (a) Tracker distribution for third-party apps (b) Distribution of tracker categories

Tracker distribution. Many of these external entities are "trackers," including ad networks and analytics services, which are contacted when the user visits the application webpage. To identify the tracker domains, we use lists provided by Ghostery, AdBlock and the Microsoft Tracking Protection List (TPL) to compile a set of 10,292 tracking domains. The total number of trackers identified within our set of Facebook and RenRen applications is 410 and 126, respectively. Their distributions are shown in Figure 3a. These results show that for Facebook (respectively, RenRen), 39% (respectively, 37%) of the tracking domains are employed by a single application. The tail of the CDF also shows that a few trackers are employed by a large number of applications, with less than 5% of the trackers in both Facebook and RenRen tracking more than 100 different applications. The top 3 of the observed trackers is composed of Google Analytics (with 613 tracked applications), smartadserver (416 applications) and Turn.com (344 apps).

Tracker Categories. We now further classify the set of identified trackers into five categories: ad networks (e.g., Google Adsense) referred to as Ad; analytical services (e.g., Google analytics) referred to as analytics; online service plug-ins (e.g., Twitter connect) referred to as widgets; ad-network tracking services as special tracking features (e.g., DoubleClick Floodlight), which are referred to as trackers. Finally, we also consider the trackers not belonging to these classes but included in the Microsoft Tracking Protection List (Scorecard Research) and refer to these as tpl.

Figure 3b shows the cumulative distribution of the trackers according to their different categories (only for Facebook). As expected, we observe that more than 70% of the applications use analytics services. Notably, Google analytics is employed by 60% of the applications, far ahead of all other analytics services. Note that 84% of the applications use a single analytics service, and only 2% of use more than 3 different analytics services.

More than 60% of the tested applications did not use a known "ad network", which puts in question the revenue model of these applications. There are numerous ways for a Facebook application to generate revenue: inserting ads from a particular ad-network (which is the case for 40% of our tested applications); by monetizing the "pay more, play more" scheme which allows the users to buy virtual credits; by selling private advertising space (e.g., through the Facebook exchange protocol FBX); or selling user data, although this is officially not compliant with the application development agreement. We highlight that the high proportion of applications not relying on ad-network revenue is surprising, which merits further investigation.

The sharp slope of the ad CDF curve shows that a large fraction of the applications that use ad-networks tend to include a variety of different networks; in particular, 10% of the applications embed at least 5 different ad-networks. Other types of trackers are less popular and most of them are employed by a single application.

5   Personal Information Leakage

In this section we present a methodology to detect potential privacy leakage from Facebook and RenRen apps to fourth parties. We then employ this methodology to quantify the amount of privacy leakage.

```
GET /api/.../?s=USERID&g=male&lc=US&f=1...
Host: api.geo.kontagent.net
```

```
GET /__utm.gif?..&utmhn=iframe.
onlinesoccermnager.nl&utmul=en-us
&...& utmhid=110829611
&utmp=userName, ProfilePicture,email
,Network First/LastName, USERID
Host: www.google-analytics.com
```

Domain	Leaking	Total
kontagent.net	60	66
ajax.googleapis.com	38	480
google-analytics.com	36	624
6waves.com	18	30
socialpointgames.com	13	16
mindjolt.com	9	10
disney.com	8	9
adobe.com	6	183

Figure 4 & Table 2. Left: (top) Information leakage to Kontagent, (down) Information leakage to Google Analytics – Right: Number of leaking Facebook apps vs. total number apps contacting this domain

5.1 Methodology

Our methodology is as follows. First, we create multiple user accounts with distinctly different profiles (i.e., attribute values). For each of these accounts, we then automatically install and run the apps and record the network traffic. We then examine, for each app and user pair, whether the HTTP requests are transferring user information to fourth parties. For instance, to assess whether a user's gender is leaked, we check all requests that transfer the string "male" for a male user and "female" for a female user. While this approach allows us to automatically search for personal data leakages, encrypted or encoded data are not detected as we only use string matching. We further checked the API documentation of known services (e.g., kontagent and Google analytics) to assess the meaning of parameters observed in the traffic.[5]

5.2 Data Leakage Classification

The process of leaking information to external entities can be categorized into two types: *intentional* and *unintentional*.

Intentional information leakage. In this scenario, the app developer intentionally transmits user information to external entities (usually analytic services) by embedding user data into the HTTP request. The total number of Facebook apps that are leaking user info intentionally is 183. In the following, we study two representative examples:

Kontagent. This company presents its business as helping customers "derive insights from app data in ways beyond traditional analytics." Kontagent provides detailed statistics about app usage. To achieve this, the app sends a set of user

---

[5] For instance, Kontagent is using a parameter g=m for transmitting the gender (male).

attributes to Kontagent; the API specification[6] provides a set of functions for transferring user data, among which are year of birth, country of origin, or friend count. Note also that the API allows the transfer of any other type of data as an associative array. Figure 4 shows how user ID, gender and location are transferred to Kontagent.

Google Analytics. As with Kontagent, some developers are using Google Analytics to generate statistics about app usage. To do so, they embed user data inside the request to Google Analytics. This data can then be used (in Google dashboard) to derive statistics. Figure 4 shows how data is transferred.

Unintentional data leakage. A website may unintentionally leak personal information to a third party in a Request URI or referrer. Krishnamurthy et al. [6] examined this problem for 120 popular websites and found that 48% leaked a user identifier. We consider user information to be leaked unintentionally if it is transferred through the referrer. In fact, the referrer is automatically filled by the browser; thus data leakage through it is generally the result of poor data sanitisation. The total number of applications leaking info through the referrer field is 79.

5.3   Statistics

Table 4 shows the number of applications that leak various user attributes. More than 18% of apps transmit user ID to an external entity. While this information seems harmless, in fact querying Facebook Graph API[7] with the User ID allows the external entity to gather all public information about the user (i.e., username, full name, link to Facebook profile, hometown, gender, and so on). Moreover, as the user ID is unique, it can be used to track a user across different apps. Finally, there is substantial evidence that user ID (and username) can be used to (re)identify a user [8]. We observe that 1% of apps are transmitting age to an external entity; this attribute is considered highly sensitive and only few users disclose it publicly [3]. Finally, the low value for country and city (only two apps are leaking this info) can be explained by two facts: First, some apps are using IP-geo location to identify the user location.[8] Second, Facebook provides a more coarse grained attribute that determines the user language (e.g., fr_FR). In a second step, we analyzed how many attributes are leaked per application. Table 5 shows that 220 applications (22%) leak at least one attribute, 48 leak at least 2 attributes and 14 more than 2.

The question remains: To whom is this data being transferred? Table 2 answers this question. From a domain perspective, three main categories are sharing data gathering in the top 10 domains: analytics services (e.g., Kontagent), social app companies (e.g., 6waves) and entertainment companies (e.g., disney).

---

[6] https://github.com/whydna/Kontagent-API---ActionScript3-Wrapper
[7] http://goo.gl/KlOL8
[8] Facebook is using IP-Geo location in its ad platform to determine user location.

Table 2 shows that analytics services are way ahead of the others for data gathering. However, there is a significant distinction between them. Kontagent's main goal is to draw statistics from social apps and as such is inherently dependent on the user data that the app is leaking. This can clearly be seen by the large proportion of apps that are using Kontagent and are leaking user information (60 apps out of 66). On the other hand, the Google service is not expressly designed to derive statistics about social apps but is instead adapted to this task. Not surprisingly, a relatively smaller percentage of applications using a Google service are leaking user information.

Social app companies are ranked second (6waves, socialpointgames and mindjolt). This can be explained by the app publishing process. For instance, 6waves is the company behind the Astro Garden app. However, this app is not hosted under the 6waves domain but rather under `redspell.ru`. As such, 6waves is considered an external entity as it is not the app main page. To centralize data gathering, this company sends back user data to the main corporate server (e.g., 6waves.com) which explains the data leakage. Note that using this process, companies like 6waves can track users across multiple applications. Finally, entertainment companies such as Disney and Adobe are ranked third.

Disney is gathering data in a systematic way which is shown by the high number of apps that are leaking data (8 out 9). As such, Disney is collecting data from different (affiliated) apps and collecting the data in a centralized way. Adobe, on the other hand, is receiving the user information unintentionally. This claim is confirmed by the small number of apps that are leaking data (6 out of 183). In most cases, the information is transmitted to Adobe in the referrer when loading the Flash player.

5.4   RenRen Leakage

At a first glance, RenRen apps appear to be privacy preserving as no user data is transferred to fourth parties. However, a deeper look shows that the situation is much worse than for Facebook. Recall from Section 2 that the app receives an *access token* from the OSN operator, and this token is then used to query the OSN for the user data. Our measurements reveal that 69% of RenRen tested apps are transmitting this token to external entities. This behavior represents a major privacy breach as external entities "inherit" the app privileges and can therefore query RenRen on behalf of the user. Table 3 shows the top external domains receiving the access token. In contrast with Facebook, the leaked information is sent to both Chinese and US tracking companies.

6   Discussion and Conclusion

Several third party applications are leaking user information to "fourth" party entities such as trackers and advertisers. This behavior affects both Facebook and RenRen with varying severity. 22% of tested Facebook applications are transmitting at least one attribute to an external entity with user ID being the most

Table 3. Number of leaking Ren-Ren apps vs. total Number apps contacting this domain

scorecardresearch.com	170	377
sinaapp.com	61	64
google-analytics.com	38	51
doubleclick.net	36	51
baidu.com	23	69
linezing.com	12	13
friendoc.net	10	10

Table 4. Information leaked by Facebook apps

Info	# App
user ID	181
Name	17
Gender	72
Country	2
City	2
Age	10

Table 5. Number of attributes leaked per application

# leaked attribute	# Apps
One or more	220
2 or more	48
3 or more	14
More than 3	0

prominent (18%). While in 183 applications the user information is intentionally transmitted to fourth parties (e.g., through an API call), some leakages are the result of a poor data sanitization and hence can be considered unintentional. In the other hand, RenRensuffers from a major privacy breach caused by the leakage of the *access token* in 69% of the tested apps. These tokens can be used by trackers and advertisers to impersonate the app and query RenRen on behalf of the user.

While user information is transmitted to several entities, some major players might represent a bigger risk. For instance, Google is able to track 60% of Facebook applications and receives some user information from 8% of them. In RenRen, the situation is even worse, as 45% of tested apps transmit the full user profile to a single tracker (`scorecardresearch.com`). Hence, a single social networking app might lead to users being tracked across multiple websites with their real identity. Web tracking in combination with personal information from social networks represents a serious privacy violation that shifts the tracking from a virtual tracking (i.e., the user is virtual) to a real "physical" tracking (i.e., based on user personal information).

Acknowledgements. Thanks to Alan Mislove for shepherding this manuscript and the anonymous reviewers for their valuable feedback. This research was funded by French ANR project PFlower.

References

1. Chaabane, A., Kaafar, M.A., Boreli, R.: Big friend is watching you: Analyzing online social networks tracking capabilities. In: WOSN (2012)
2. Chia, P.H., Yamamoto, Y., Asokan, N.: Is this app safe?: A large scale study on application permissions and risk signals. In: WWW (2012)
3. Dey, R., Jelveh, Z., Ross, K.: Facebook users have become much more private: A large-scale study. In: PERCOM Workshops (2012)
4. Frank, M., Dong, B., Porter Felt, A., Song, D.: Mining permission request patterns from Android and Facebook applications. In: ICDM (2012)

5. Krishnamurthy, B., Wills, C.E.: Characterizing privacy in online social networks. In: WOSN (2008)
6. Krishnamurthy, B., Wills, C.E.: On the leakage of personally identifiable information via online social networks. In: WOSN (2009)
7. Mayer, J.R., Mitchell, J.C.: Third-party web tracking: Policy and technology. In: S&P (2012)
8. Perito, D., Castelluccia, C., Kaafar, M.A., Manils, P.: How unique and traceable are usernames? In: Fischer-Hübner, S., Hopper, N. (eds.) PETS 2011. LNCS, vol. 6794, pp. 1–17. Springer, Heidelberg (2011)
9. Xia, N., Song, H., Liao, Y., Iliofotou, M., Nucci, A., Zhang, Z., Kuzmanovic, A.: Mosaic: Quantifying privacy leakage in mobile networks. In: SIGCOMM (2013)

On the Effectiveness of Traffic Analysis against Anonymity Networks Using Flow Records

Sambuddho Chakravarty[1], Marco V. Barbera[2], Georgios Portokalidis[3],
Michalis Polychronakis[1], and Angelos D. Keromytis[1]

[1] Columbia University, NY, USA
{sc2516,mikepo,angelos}@cs.columbia.edu
[2] Sapienza Universita Di Roma, Rome, Italy
barbera@di.uniroma1.it
[3] Stevens Institute of Technology, NJ, USA
gportoka@stevens.edu

Abstract. We investigate the feasibility of mounting a de-anonymization attack against Tor and similar low-latency anonymous communication systems by using NetFlow records. Previous research has shown that adversaries with the ability to eavesdrop in real time at a few internet exchange points can effectively monitor a significant part of the network paths from Tor nodes to destination servers. However, the capacity of current networks makes packet-level monitoring at such a scale quite challenging. We hypothesize that adversaries could use less accurate but readily available monitoring facilities, such as Cisco's NetFlow, to mount large-scale traffic analysis attacks. In this paper, we assess the feasibility and effectiveness of traffic analysis attacks against Tor using NetFlow data. We present an active traffic analysis technique based on perturbing the characteristics of user traffic at the server side, and observing a similar perturbation at the client side through statistical correlation. We evaluate the accuracy of our method using both in-lab testing and data gathered from a public Tor relay serving hundreds of users. Our method revealed the actual sources of anonymous traffic with 100% accuracy for the in-lab tests, and achieved an overall accuracy of 81.6% for the real-world experiments with a false positive rate of 5.5%.

1 Introduction

Anonymous communication networks hide the actual source (or destination) address of internet traffic, preventing the server (or client) and other entities along the network from determining the actual identities of the communicating parties. Among others [2, 3], Tor [8] is probably the most widely used low-latency anonymity network. To offer acceptable quality of service, Tor and similar systems try to preserve packet interarrival times. Unfortunately, this makes them vulnerable to traffic analysis attacks [5, 11, 13, 17, 20, 21], whereby an adversary with access to traffic from/to entry and exit nodes, can correlate seemingly unrelated traffic flows and reveal the actual endpoints.

As Tor nodes are scattered around the globe and the nodes of circuits are selected at random, mounting a traffic analysis attack, in practice, would require a powerful adversary with the ability to monitor traffic at a multitude of autonomous systems (AS).

M. Faloutsos and A. Kuzmanovic (Eds.): PAM 2014, LNCS 8362, pp. 247–257, 2014.

Murdoch and Zieliński, however, showed that monitoring traffic at a few major internet exchange (IX) points could enable traffic analysis attacks against a significant part of the Tor network [18]. Furthermore, Feamster et al. [12], and later Edman et al. [10], showed that even a single AS may observe a large fraction of entry and exit-node traffic—a single AS could monitor over 22% of randomly generated Tor circuits. Recently, Johnson et al. [15], extended this study and observed, through simulation, that compromised high bandwidth Tor relays and IX operators, observing both entry and exit traffic, could de-anonymize 80% of random Tor circuits.

Packet-level traffic monitoring at this scale requires the installation of passive monitoring sensors capable of processing tens or hundreds of Gbit/s traffic. Although not impossible, setting up a passive monitoring infrastructure at such a scale is challenging in terms of cost, logistics, and effort. An attractive alternative for adversaries would be to use the readily available, albeit less accurate, traffic monitoring functionality built into the routers of major IXs and ASs, such as Cisco's NetFlow. Murdoch and Zieliński showed through simulation that traffic analysis using sampled NetFlow data is possible, provided there are adequate samples. Still, there have been no prior efforts to explore the various practical aspects of mounting traffic analysis attacks using NetFlow data.

As a step towards filling this gap, in this paper we study the feasibility and effectiveness of traffic analysis attacks using NetFlow data, and present a practical active traffic analysis attack against Tor. Our approach is based on identifying pattern similarities in the traffic flows entering and leaving the Tor network, using statistical correlation. To alleviate the uncertainty due to the coarse-grained nature of NetFlow data, our attack relies on a server under the control of the adversary that introduces deterministic perturbations to the traffic of anonymous visitors. Among all client-to-entry-node flows, the actual victim flow can be distinguished due to its high correlation with the respective exit-node-to-server flow, as both carry the induced traffic perturbation pattern.

We evaluated the effectiveness of our traffic analysis attack in a controlled lab environment, as well as using public Tor relays. In the in-lab environment, our method revealed the actual sources of anonymous traffic with 100% accuracy. When evaluating our attack with traffic going through public Tor relays, our method detected the actual source in 81.6% of the cases, with a a false positive rate of 5.5% and false negative rate of 12.7%. Due to the sensitivity of the correlation process, especially for flows with sparse samples, we couple correlation with heuristics to filter out flows that are unlikely to correspond to a victim, thus reducing false positives.

2   Related Work

Tor [8] safeguards the anonymity of internet users by relaying TCP streams through a network of overlay nodes, run by volunteers. It typically hides the identity (IP address) of the initiator of a connection, although the opposite is also possible through the use of *hidden services*. Murdoch and Danezis [17] developed the first practical traffic analysis attack against Tor. Their technique involved a corrupt server and a client that buildt one-hop circuits via candidate relays to determine relays participating in a circuit. Hopper et al. [13] used this method, along with one-way circuit latency and the Vivaldi network coordinate system, to determine the possible source of anonymous traffic.

In 2009, however, Evans et al. [11] demonstrated that Murdoch and Danezis' method was not accurate, due to an increase in the number of relays and the large volume of Tor traffic. They proposed a modification to amplify the traffic by loops in circuits.

Previously, we proposed a method for performing traffic analysis using remote network bandwidth estimation tools to identify the Tor relays and network routers involved in Tor circuits [7]. Our method assumed that the adversaries were in a position to perturb the victim traffic by colluding with the server, and are in control of various network vantage points, from where they can remotely observe variations in network bandwidth. Mittal et al. [16] demonstrated a modified version of the Murdoch and Danezis' attack that relies on path bandwidth variation.

In 2007, Murdoch et al. [18] proposed the use of NetFlow data from routers in IXes to perform traffic analysis attacks against traffic entering and leaving the Tor network. They discovered that there is a small number of IXes that can potentially observe a large part of Tor traffic, and allow the use of existing facilities, such as Cisco NetFlow, to mount traffic analysis attacks. They proposed a traffic and attack model that receives as input NetFlow traffic gathered from monitoring a Tor relay. They described, through simulations, how varying the number of flows, bandwidth, and end-to-end delay, affects the accuracy of determining the source of anonymous traffic. In a follow-up work, Johnson et al. [15] recently showed that a small number of compromised Tor relays that advertise high bandwidth and IXes observing both entry end exit traffic, can de-anonymize 80% of various types of Tor circuits within six months.

Previous efforts did not explore the feasibility and effectiveness of using a facility such as NetFlow to determine the source of anonymous traffic from a practical perspective. Our work attempts to assess the possibilities of accurately de-anonymizing Tor users using NetFlow data by implementing and experimentally evaluating a traffic analysis attack in realistic settings.

3   Approach

Threat Model and Attack Methodology: The goal of the attacker is to determine the network identity (i.e., public IP address) of a client using Tor to access a server. We assume the attacker can observe NetFlow traffic records on routers at or near Tor relays. In our model, the attacker deliberately injects a traffic variation pattern on one side of a victim Tor connection, which travels via the relays to the peer. The easiest way for the attacker to achieve this is by controlling the server; the attacker would then serve sufficient content volume (e.g., a large volume of "invisible" HTML content) and inject traffic perturbation patterns in the connection between the Tor exit node and the server. We also assume that attackers can select specific anonymous connections they are interested in (e.g., those that correspond to a particular user identity in the server). Alternatively, attackers could de-anonymize all clients accessing the server; our current work demonstrates de-anonymization of a single client at a time. Simultaneous anonymization of multiple clients (with or without correlation between client identities and anonymous sessions) is left for future work. A powerful adversary could monitor a large part of the relays participating in the Tor network, one of which with high probability would correspond to the entry node of the targeted user. Alternatively, an

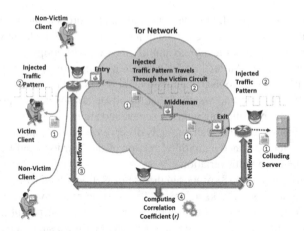

Fig. 1. NetFlow-based traffic analysis against Tor: The client is forced to download a file from the server ①, while the server induces a characteristic traffic pattern ②. After the connection is terminated, the adversary obtains flow data corresponding to the server-to-exit and entry-to-client traffic ③, and computes their correlation coefficient ④.

attacker could follow a more focused approach by employing existing techniques [7, 16] to identify the actual relays used by the victim's circuit, and only monitor those.

In a second, related scenario, the attacker is a malicious Tor client seeking to identify a Tor hidden server. In this case, the attacker injects a traffic perturbation pattern and observes it between the hidden server and its entry node, against using the Net-Flow records to perform the correlation. Note that the attacker need not actually control one end of a Tor circuit. For example, the attacker could inject a pattern in a chosen anonymous connection between the server and an exit node, without the server knowing about it. This scenario introduces additional complexity in terms of victim selection, especially when the connections between the Tor exit node and the server are encrypted. We defer further study of this scenario to future work.

As shown in Figure 1, after the transfer ends, the adversary obtains the flow records of all the client-to-entry-node connections that were monitored (from one or more entry nodes), and computes their correlation with the given exit-node-to-server flow. Various factors, such as flow cache eviction timeout values and the inherently bursty nature of traffic (especially web traffic), commonly result in an inadequate number of flow samples than what is ideally required for computing the correlation coefficient. The longer the duration of the fingerprinted transfer, the higher the chances that enough flow samples will be gathered. In our experiments, we assume that the victim downloads a large file (in the order of tens of megabytes), generating sustained traffic for a duration of about 5–7 minutes. Depending on the capabilities of the involved routers, the same accuracy could be achieved using shorter data transfers.

Implementation: In our prototype, the server fluctuates a client's traffic using Linux Traffic Controller [14]. We explored two different kinds of traffic perturbation patterns. The first was a simple "square wave" pattern, achieved by repeatedly fluctuating the victim's transfer rate between two values. The second a was more complex "step" pattern, achieved by repeatedly switching between several predetermined bandwidth values. These different perturbations help evaluate our attack accuracy through both simple and complex injected traffic patterns.

For our initial in-lab experiments, flow records were generated and captured using the open source tools ipt_netflow [4] and flow-tools [1], respectively. In such a controlled environment, free of congestion and external interference, our approach achieved 100% success in determining the source of anonymous connections (more details for this experiment are included in our technical report [6]).

In the experiments presented in this paper, we obtained data from a public Tor relay serving hundreds of Tor clients. The flow records for the server-to-exit traffic were generated and captured using the aforementioned flow tools. The flow records for the entry-to-client traffic were generated first using the flow tools, running on the same host as the entry node, and later by our institutional edge router. For the latter, the flow data from the router was often sparse due to aggressive sampling. Multiple intervals were typically aggregated into a single flow record. This generally happens due to the combination of flow expiration timeout values and the router's network load. As such aggregation is not deterministic, it is difficult to divide a large interval into smaller ones without knowing the ordinate values of the aggregated intervals. Since correlation analysis requires the two time series to have the throughput values taken at the same points, we devised the following strategy to align the time points.

Flow records are arranged as time intervals with the bytes transferred in each of them [6]. To correctly align the time points, we first take the intervals of all server-to-exit records and divide them into steps of one second. We then consider the starting and ending times of every entry-to-client flow record and attempt to align them with the one-second steps of the server-to-exit flow. For every successfully aligned time point, we assume the corresponding entry-to-client (and respective server-to-exit) throughput value to be the average throughput of the entry-to-client (and respective server-to-exit) interval that covers this time point, obtained by dividing the total bytes transferred in the corresponding interval by the length of that interval. Unaligned time points are ignored. Finally, we compute the correlation of throughput values of the two aligned sets.

4   Experimental Evaluation

To evaluate our attack using data obtained from public Tor relays we used the set-up shown in Figure 1. Victim clients were hosted on three different PlanetLab locations: Texas (US), Leuven (Belgium) and Corfu (Greece). The clients communicated via Tor circuits through our relay to a server under our control in Spain.

Flow Collection using NetFlow Tools: In our first set of experiments, the flow records were obtained from the server and the entry node using the open source flow generation and capture tools mentioned in the previous section. We configured the active and inactive timers to 5 seconds each. This resulted in a uniform view of the traffic with an adequate number of samples for accurately computing correlation. The first experiment involved the server injecting a "square-wave" like traffic pattern having an amplitude

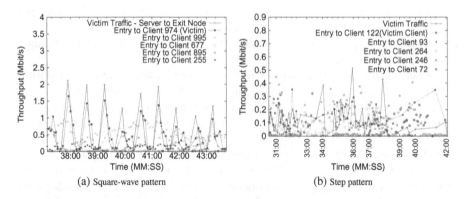

Fig. 2. A victim flow with a server-induced "square-wave" (a) and "step" (b) pattern. The remaining points correspond to the non-victim flows with the four highest correlation coefficients.

of roughly 2 Mbit/s, achieved by switching the server-to-exit traffic bandwidth between 2 Mbit/s and 30 Kbit/s, every 20 seconds. Figure 2(a) shows sample traffic throughput variations for five flows, from one such experiment. These five flows are the ones with the highest correlation to the server-to-exit flow (solid line) that carries the injected traffic pattern. The victim flow had the highest correlation coefficient of 0.83 (among 1100 other clients), while the second-highest correlation, for to a non-victim client, was 0.17.

We repeated similar experiments with the server injecting a more complex "step" like pattern, achieved by switching the server-to-exit traffic throughput between roughly 1 Mbit/s, 50 Kbit/s, 300 Kbit/s and 100 Kbit/s, every 20 seconds. This pattern was again repeated several times. Figure 2(b) shows one such sample where the server injected the "step" like pattern. The victim flow had the highest correlation coefficient of 0.84 (among 874 other clients), while the second-highest correlation, corresponding to a non-victim client, was 0.25. In general, we observe higher correlation of the server-to-exit and the victim traffic, when the server injects the "step" like pattern.

These experiments were repeated 90 times (15 times for each traffic pattern, for each of the three client location). The average correlation between the server-to-exit and entry-to-victim traffic statistics (corresponding to the flows that were most correlated to the flow carrying the traffic pattern) was higher than the average correlation to the non-victim client statistics, as shown in Figures 3(a) and 3(b). We were able to correctly identify the victim in 76 out of the 90 tests. The average correlation of the injected pattern for the victim traffic was lower than those for in-lab tests. This happens because the traffic pattern is distorted when it leaves the Tor entry node and proceeds towards the victim, reducing the victim's correlation coefficient.

We also found four instances where the correlation of the injected traffic pattern with the victim client traffic was lower compared to some other non-victim clients' traffic. Such false positives are primarily a combined effect of the background network congestion and routing in Tor relays, which attempts to equally distribute the available bandwidth among all circuits. To deal with such inaccuracies, we also computed the average throughput of the clients' traffic (over the duration of the experiment), and subtracted it from the average throughput of the server-to-exit traffic. For the victim traffic,

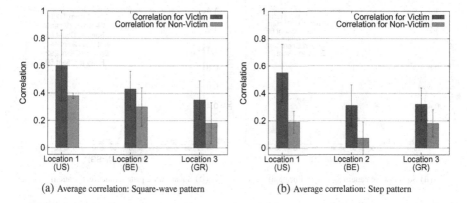

(a) Average correlation: Square-wave pattern   (b) Average correlation: Step pattern

Fig. 3. (a) Average Pearson's Correlation between server injected "square-wave" like pattern and the victim and non-victim flows for the different planetlab client locations. (b) Average Pearson's Correlation between server injected "step" pattern and the victim and non-victim flows for the different planetlab client locations.

this difference is often amongst the smallest. This difference between the victim traffic and server-to-exit traffic can be used to filter out flows that could lead to inaccurate correlation coefficients arising from an inadequate number of flow samples. We used this observation in the experiments that involved sparse data from Cisco routers, to remove flows where the average throughput was not comparable to that of the victim's.

Flow Collection from Cisco Router: To evaluate the attack effectiveness when using data from our institutional edge router, we used the same experimental set-up that we used to test our attack using data obtained from open source packages. However, the entry-node-to-client traffic statistics were gathered from our institutional router. The router was configured with an active and inactive timeouts of 60 and 15 seconds respectively. We configured the NetFlow packages on the server with the same values. But, from our initial experience, we realized that the data obtained from the router was sparse and non-uniformly aligned, compared to the flow records from server-to-exit. We thus applied our rectification strategy (described previously) to align the flows. The rectified flow values were then directly used as input to the correlation coefficient formula.

These experiments were essentially the same as those described in the previous subsection. The first experiment involved the server injecting a "square-wave" like traffic pattern with an amplitude of about 1 Mbit/s. However, here the server switched the throughput every 30 seconds, instead of 20 seconds, enabling us to capture adequate (≥ 10) samples for computing the correlation coefficient[1]. Figure 4(a) presents a sample bandwidth variation pattern for the server-to-exit traffic and the entry-node-to-client traffic. It shows server-to-exit traffic with more data points and fewer entry-to-client points. Figure 4(b) presents the same data pattern after it has been rectified.

As mentioned previously, we eliminated flows whose average of the traffic throughput was not comparable to that of the server-to-exit throughput variation. We computed

---

[1] This was done solely to compensate for the lack of samples obtained when the experiments ran for a shorter duration of 20 seconds (as previously).

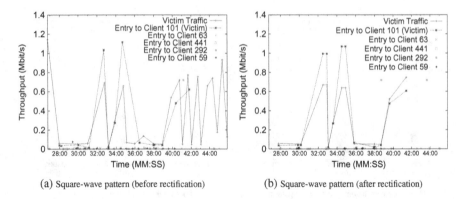

(a) Square-wave pattern (before rectification)   (b) Square-wave pattern (after rectification)

Fig. 4. (a) Server induced "square-wave" pattern of amplitude 1 Mbit/s along with other non-victim flows from the entry-to-victim and non-victim hosts having the four highest correlation co-efficient. Victim location: Texas, US. (b) Flows in Figure 4(a) adjusted and corrected using our rectification strategy.

the difference between average throughput for the server-to-exit and the entry-to-client traffic (for all clients). From our experience, for the victim traffic, the difference was within 120 Kbit/s. We removed flows where this difference was over 120 Kbit/s.

These experiments were also repeated with the server injecting a "step" like pattern, achieved by switching the traffic between 1 Mbit/s, 50 Kbit/s, 300 Kbit/s and 100 Kbit/s, every 30 seconds. The average correlation between the server-to-exit and entry-to-client traffic statistics was higher than the average correlation to the non-victim client statistics. These can be seen in Figures 5(a) and 5(b). We correctly identified the victim flow in 71 out of the 90 trials (success rate of 78.9%). There were six false positives in our measurements, where non-victim clients showed highest correlation to the server-to-exit traffic. In these false positive, the number of sample intervals for the entry-to-client traffic were less than half the number of sample intervals corresponding to the server-to-exit traffic. These fewer sample intervals resulted in correlation representing an inaccurate relationship. In 13 of the remaining cases we were not able to correctly select the victim either because the correlation coefficient was statistically not significant (< 0.2), or the victim flow was filtered out as its average throughput varied from the the the average server-to-exit throughput by more than 120 Kbit/s.

Monitoring multiple Tor relays: Finally, we evaluated our attack in a scenario involving an additional relay. We launched a second relay in our institution. The purpose of this second Tor relay was to judge the effectiveness of our attack in the presence more clients. The two relays together served about 1500 clients. This scenario indicates what to expect when an adversary monitors multiple relays.

Our experiments involved injecting the "step" like pattern, described above. These experiments were repeated 24 times, 8 times for to each of the victim client location. We observed higher average correlation between server-to-exit and entry to victim client traffic, compared to non-victim clients' traffic. We were able to correctly identify the victim client in 14 out of the 24 trials (success rate 58.3%). There were three false positives, where the correlation of the server-to-exit traffic was higher to a non-victim than

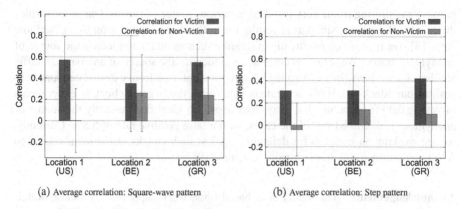

(a) Average correlation: Square-wave pattern   (b) Average correlation: Step pattern

Fig. 5. (a)Average Pearson's Correlation between server injected "square-wave" pattern and the victim and non-victim flows, for the different planetlab client locations. (b) Average Pearson's Correlation between server injected "step" like pattern and the victim and non-victim flows, for the different planetlab client locations.

to the victim. The remaining seven were false negatives, where the correlation coefficient was not statistically significant (< 0.2). The false negatives were primarily a result of the few sample points obtained during the experiment, which were further reduced by our flow alignment method. This loss of information decreases the correlation of the server-to-exit and entry-to-victim client traffic.

5 Limitations

Our attack is very accurate in an in-lab set-up with symmetric network paths and capacities (having low congestion and no uncontrolled disturbances). However, in tests with public Tor relays, the overall correlation between server-to-exit and entry-to-victim traffic is decreased due to congestion and Tor's traffic scheduling, which distort the injected traffic pattern. In experiments involving data from the institutional Cisco router, such effects were quite pronounced. Moreover, the were fewer sample intervals compared to the data obtained from Linux NetFlow packages. This was due to flow aggregation, and lead to to flow records with unequal lengths, not evenly spaced. To counter such effects, we devised an approximation strategy, described in Section 3. Such approximations decrease the overall correlation of server-to-exit with entry-to-victim traffic, since the process eliminates data points from flow intervals that cannot be correctly rectified. This resulted in false positives in our measurements. Although not very precise, these results are indicative of the capabilities of more powerful adversaries. A powerful adversary could launch a *sybil* attack [9] by running many high-bandwidth Tor nodes to attract a large fraction of Tor traffic. Such relay operators, equipped with flow capture tools, would not require access to network routers for flow records.

6 Conclusion

We have demonstrated the practical feasibility of carrying out traffic analysis attacks using statistical correlation of traffic measurements obtained from NetFlow, a popular network monitoring framework installed in various router platforms. Our work verifies the results of previous simulation results for traffic de-anonymization using NetFlow data [18]. We focused on practically evaluating such an attack to identify the source of anonymous traffic. We relied on correlation to identify the source of anonymous traffic amidst various flows. In a controlled lab environment, free from external network congestion, our attack was 100% accurate in identifying the targeted client. In experiments involving data from public Tor relays, our approach identified correctly the source of anonymous traffic in 81.6% of the cases, with a false positive rate of 5.5%. Currently, we are working on methods for defending against such attacks, using ideas related to selective dummy traffic transmissions schemes [19].

Acknowledgements. This material is based upon work supported by (while author Keromytis was serving at) the National Science Foundation. Any opinion, findings, and conclusions or recommendations expressed in this material are those of the author(s) and do not necessarily reflect the views of the National Science Foundation.

References

[1] Flow Tools Package, http://freecode.com/projects/flow-tools
[2] I2P Anonymous Network, http://www.i2p2.de/
[3] Java Anonymization Proxy, http://anon.inf.tu-dresden.de/
[4] Netflow iptables module, http://sourceforge.net/projects/ipt-netflow/
[5] Bauer, K., McCoy, D., Grunwald, D., Kohno, T., Sicker, D.: Low-resource routing attacks against tor. In: Proceedings of the 2007 ACM Workshop on Privacy in Electronic Society (WPES), pp. 11–20 (2007)
[6] Chakravarty, S., Barbera, M.V., Portokalidis, G., Polychronakis, M., Keromytis, A.D.: On the Effectiveness of Traffic Analysis Against Anonymity Networks Using Flow Records. Computer Science Department Technical Report (CUCS Tech Report) CUCS-019-13, Columbia University (July 2013)
[7] Chakravarty, S., Stavrou, A., Keromytis, A.D.: Traffic analysis against low-latency anonymity networks using available bandwidth estimation. In: Gritzalis, D., Preneel, B., Theoharidou, M. (eds.) ESORICS 2010. LNCS, vol. 6345, pp. 249–267. Springer, Heidelberg (2010)
[8] Dingledine, R., Mathewson, N., Syverson, P.: Tor: The Second-Generation Onion Router. In: Proceedings of the 13th USENIX Security Symposium, pp. 303–319 (August 2004)
[9] Douceur, J.R.: The sybil attack. In: Druschel, P., Kaashoek, M.F., Rowstron, A. (eds.) IPTPS 2002. LNCS, vol. 2429, pp. 251–260. Springer, Heidelberg (2002)
[10] Edman, M., Syverson, P.F.: AS-awareness in Tor path selection. In: Al-Shaer, E., Jha, S., Keromytis, A.D. (eds.) Proceedings of the 2009 ACM Conference on Computer and Communications Security, CCS 2009, pp. 380–389. ACM (November 2009)
[11] Evans, N., Dingledine, R., Grothoff, C.: A Practical Congestion Attack on Tor Using Long Paths. In: Proceedings of the 18th USENIX Security Symposium (USENIX Security), pp. 33–50 (August 2009)
[12] Feamster, N., Dingledine, R.: Location Diversity in Anonymity Networks. In: Proceedings of the ACM Workshop on Privacy in the Electronic Society (WPES), pp. 66–76 (October 2004)

[13] Hopper, N., Vasserman, E.Y., Chan-Tin, E.: How Much Anonymity does Network Latency Leak? In: Proceedings of ACM Conference on Computer and Communications Security (CCS), pp. 82–91 (October 2007)

[14] Hubert, B., Graf, T., Maxwell, G., Mook, R., Oosterhout, M., Schroeder, P., Spaans, J., Larroy, P.: Linux Advanced Routing and Traffic Control HOWTO

[15] Johnson, A., Wacek, C., Jansen, R., Sherr, M., Syverson, P.: Users get routed: Traffic correlation on tor by realisitic adversaries. In: Proceedings of the 20th ACM Conference on Computer and Communications Security, CCS 2013 (November 2013)

[16] Mittal, P., Khurshid, A., Juen, J., Caesar, M., Borisov, N.: Stealthy traffic analysis of low-latency anonymous communication using throughput fingerprinting. In: Proceedings of the 18th ACM Conference on Computer and Communications Security, CCS 2011, pp. 215–226. ACM, New York (2011)

[17] Murdoch, S.J., Danezis, G.: Low-Cost Traffic Analysis of Tor. In: Proceedings of IEEE Symposium on Security and Privacy, pp. 183–195 (May 2005)

[18] Murdoch, S.J., Zieliński, P.: Sampled traffic analysis by internet-exchange-level adversaries. In: Borisov, N., Golle, P. (eds.) PET 2007. LNCS, vol. 4776, pp. 167–183. Springer, Heidelberg (2007)

[19] Shmatikov, V., Wang, M.-H.: Timing analysis in low-latency mix networks: Attacks and defenses. In: Gollmann, D., Meier, J., Sabelfeld, A. (eds.) ESORICS 2006. LNCS, vol. 4189, pp. 18–33. Springer, Heidelberg (2006)

[20] Wright, M.K., Adler, M., Levine, B.N., Shields, C.: An analysis of the degradation of anonymous protocols. In: Proceedings of the Network and Distributed Security Symposium, NDSS (2002)

[21] Fu, X., Ling, Z.: One cell is enough to break tor's anonymity. In: Proceedings of Black Hat Technical Security Conference, pp. 578–589 (February 2009)

Scaling Bandwidth Estimation to High Speed Networks

Qianwen Yin, Jasleen Kaur, and F. Donelson Smith

University of North Carolina at Chapel Hill

Abstract. Existing bandwidth estimation tools fail to perform well at gigabit and higher network speeds. In this paper we study several sources of noise that must be overcome by these tools in high-speed envrionments and propose strategies for addressing them. We evaluate our Linux implementation on 1 and 10Gbps testbed networks, showing that our strategies help significantly in scaling bandwidth estimation to high-speed networks.

1 Introduction

Bandwidth estimation tools perform well on 100Mbps networks [1–3], but they fail to do so at gigabit and higher speeds. This is because very small inter-packet gaps(less than 12 microseconds) are needed for probing for higher bandwidth– they are more susceptible to being disturbed by small-scale buffering at shared resources. In this paper, we study the impact of buffering-related noise on high-speed networks, namely, receiver-side interrupt coalescence and small-scale burstiness in cross traffic. We then propose strategies to address them.[1] We evaluate our strategies using a Linux implementation in a lab testbed with 1 and 10 Gbps links. We find that our new mechanisms help significantly in scaling bandwidth estimation to high-speed networks.

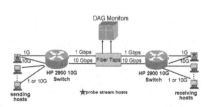

Fig. 1. Lab Testbed Configuration

2 Experimental Methodology

Laboratory Testbed. We use the dedicated network illustrated in Fig 1. The switch-to-switch path in the core of the topology can be either 1Gbps or 10Gbps. We focus on the latter here. High-end hosts are used to estimate avail-bw with 10Gbps Ethernet adapters. The network includes additional 12 pairs of hosts to generate cross traffic sharing the switch-to-switch link. Endace DAG monitoring NICs are attached to the fiber links between two switches, providing line-rate capture of all frames with nanosecond precision timestamps.

---

[1] We use the probing framework used by PathChirp[4] for the experimental study.

M. Faloutsos and A. Kuzmanovic (Eds.): PAM 2014, LNCS 8362, pp. 258–261, 2014.
© Springer International Publishing Switzerland 2014

With a locally-modified SURGE program, we generate average 4Gbps cross traffic on the 10Gbps link simulating synthetic and highly dynamic web traffic. A complete trace was obtained from DAG to compute *ground truth avail-bw.*

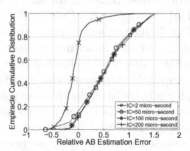

Probe Stream Structure. We use the similar probe stream structure as pathChirp. Each probe stream probes for 10 rates. Each rate is 20% higher than the previous one. [1, 5] show that using mutliple packets per rate for PathChirp leads to more robust estimation. Thus by default, we send 16 packets at each rate.

Fig. 2. AB Estimation Error

Accurate Send-gap Creation. To ensure that inter-packet gaps are created accurately, we design a Qdisc scheduler as a kernel module for creating send-gaps with errors smaller than 1 microsecond. The scheduler sits between the bottom of IP and the NIC device driver. Inter-packet gaps are precisely enforced by inserting appropriately sized PAUSE frames which will be discarded by the first inbound switch.

Receiver-side Timestamping. Existing tools timestamp packets for measuring receiver gaps at the application layer. To record software timestamps with the best-possible accuracy, we implement a kernel module attached as an ingress Qdisc to the adapter sitting between the device driver and the bottom of IP.

3   Interrupt Coalescence at Receivers

The Issue We first study how much effect the receiver latencies have on the software timestamps by comparing the receiver-logged gaps with the corresponders computed from DAG trace taken between the switches (these gaps are evaluated within 1 micro-second difference from those obtained via hardware timestamps at the receiver NIC). For interrupt coalesce, we use interrupt latency(IC) as default, 2, 50, 100, and 200 microseconds respectively. We find

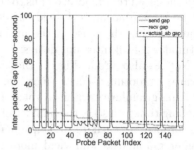

Fig. 3. Sample Stream: Spikes, Dips

that:(i) in all cases except 2-microsecond IC, the receiver-logged gaps follow a bimodal distribution, with one peak at "infeasibly-small" and the other peak close to IC value; and (ii)overestimation occurs to over 90% probe streams and the relative estimation error can be up to 160%(Fig 2)!

Solutions: Spike Removal, Exponential Smoothing, Probe Time Scale
Fig 3 illustrates a typical probe stream with default interrupt coalesce setting, where alternate spikes-and-dips pattern completely dominates the structure. Applying pathChirp algorithm in this stream results in 19Gbps *avail-bw* –the maximum probing rate used by this stream. This is because the receive gaps are never consistently larger than the send gaps for any lower probing rate.

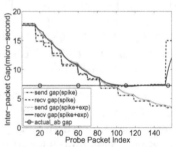

Fig. 4. Spike Removal & Smoothing

The spikes-and-dips pattern can be explained well. For efficiency, arriving packets are held in the NIC buffers and processed in a batch after several have arrived–the first in a batch would experience a large preceding gap, whereas all subsequent observe fairly small gaps. While such batching does destroy the actual receive gaps, do the *average* inter-packet gaps observed within a batch somewhat preserve the intended probe-stream structure? To under-

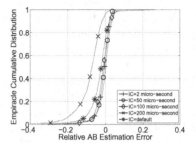

Fig. 5. Impact of IC Configuration

stand this, we identify the start and end for each buffered batch, and replace all observations in the interval with that mean gap observed in that interval. Fig 4 shows the result of applying this process to the same probe stream—we find that such a buffering-aware averaging mechanism indeed preserves lots of information about the intended probe-stream.

For robustness, we further use exponential smoothing across all observations, and then feed the smoothed gaps to the bandwidth estimation logic. The example probe stream accurately yields *avail-bw* of 10 Gbps on doing so. Fig 5 shows that reducing the noise in the measured receive gaps produces more accurate estimates for all interrupt delays.

Notice also from Fig 4 that spike-aware smoothing does not preserve probing granularity within a spike. Larger probing timescales(i.e. the number of packets probed at each rate) helps maintain higher granularity and yield more robust estimation, which is shown in Fig 6 by increasing probing timescale from 16 to 32, 64 and 128 packets/rate.

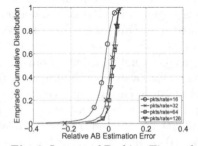

Fig. 6. Impact of Probing Timescale

4   Cross Traffic Burstiness

We then repeat the experiments in Section 3, but this time with the bursty cross-traffic described in Section 2 sharing the 10 Gbps bottleneck link. The relative estimation error without our mechanisim ranges from 150% to 350%. In contrast, Fig 7 shows the much improved estimation with spike removal and exponential smoothing.

5   Conclusion

In this paper, we identify the noise caused by bursty cross traffic and buffering latencies at receiver side that must be overcome by bandwidth estimation tools on high-speed links. In our controlled testbed we demonstrate that current tools fail to scale to 1Gbps networks. We then present

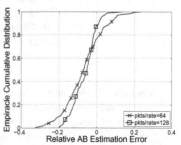

Fig. 7. Impact of Bursty Cross Traffic

techniques to address these issues: spike removal, exponential smoothing and increasing probing timescale. We evaluate our Linux implementation in a 10Gbps testbed using highly-variable cross traffic, showing that our techniques significantly help in scaling bandwidth estimation to high-speed networks. As a future work, we will improve our spike-removal algorithm to deal with all types of batching-related noise. And we plan to conduct intensive experiments over multi-hop high-speed networks and on wide-area 100G ESnet testbed.

References

1. Shriram, et al.: Empirical evaluations of techniques for measuring available bandwidth. In: IEEE INFOCOM 2007 (2007)
2. Shriram, A., Murray, M., Hyun, Y., Brownlee, N., Broido, A., Fomenkov, M., Claffy, K.: Comparison of public end-to-end bandwidth estimation tools on high-speed links. In: Dovrolis, C. (ed.) PAM 2005. LNCS, vol. 3431, pp. 306–320. Springer, Heidelberg (2005)
3. Strauss, et al.: A measurement study of available bandwidth estimation tools. In: ACM SIGCOMM on Internet measurement 2003 (2003)
4. Ribeiro, et al.: pathchirp: Efficient available bandwidth estimation for network paths. In: PAM 2003 (2003)
5. Kang, Loguinov: Characterizing tight-link bandwidth of multi-hop paths using probing response curves. In: IWQoS (2010)

Scalable Accurate Consolidation
of Passively Measured Statistical Data

Silvia Colabrese[1], Dario Rossi[1], and Marco Mellia[2]

[1] Telecom ParisTech, Paris, France
{silvia.colabrese,dario.rossi}@enst.fr
[2] Politecnico di Torino, Torino, Italy
marco.mellia@polito.it

Abstract. Passive probes continuously collect a significant amount of traffic volume, and autonomously generate statistics on a large number of metrics. A common statistical output of passive probe is represented by probability mass functions (pmf). The need for consolidation of several pmfs arises in two contexts, namely: (i) whenever a central point collects and aggregates measurement of multiple disjoint vantage points, and (ii) whenever a local measurement processed at a single vantage point needs to be distributed over multiple cores of the same physical probe, in order to cope with growing link capacity. Taking an experimental approach, we study both cases assessing the impact of different consolidation strategies, obtaining general design and tuning guidelines.

1 Introduction

This paper focuses on consolidation of multiple statistics, and especially of distribution quantiles, gathered from passive probes. We briefly mention two completely orthogonal scenarios where this need arises. First, in the case of multiple vantage points, consolidation of data coming from multiple sources yields a more statistically representative population sample. Second, in the case of a single vantage point, it may be necessary to split traffic processing over multiple independent cores to avoid CPU bottlenecks.

These two scenarios appear to be rather different at first sight. In the former case, the number of vantage points can vary between a handful to many different collection points, each of which gathers traffic mixture with likely different characteristics. In the latter case, processing can be split among a handful of cores in a CPU (possibly more for GPU-based architectures), each of which is processing a random sample of the incoming traffic.

Yet, on a closer look these diverse scenarios translate into similar constraints. In the case of multiple vantage points, the first and foremost constraint is represented by the amount of data that is required for the consolidation – transferring the least possible amount of data is hence desirable. In the case of parallel processing at a single vantage point, the constraint is instead represented by processing power – to limit the computational overhead tied to the consolidation process, elaborating the least possible amount of data is hence desirable.

Hence, we argue that a single flexible methodology could fit both purposes, which we address in this paper.

M. Faloutsos and A. Kuzmanovic (Eds.): PAM 2014, LNCS 8362, pp. 262–264, 2014.

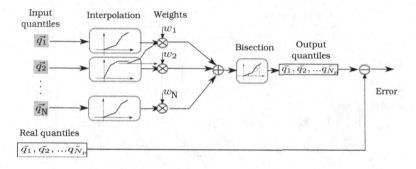

Fig. 1. Synopsis of the experimental workflow

2   Methodology

While from computational complexity or network overhead viewpoints, reducing the amount of data to be processed and transferred would be desirable, this however clearly tradeoffs with accuracy: in this paper, we focus on this tradeoff.

While our aim is to obtain general design and tuning guidelines, our experiments are based on a specific instance of metrics gathered through the Tstat measurement tool, a passive flow-level monitor that we developed over the last years [4]. For each flow, Tstat tracks over 100 metrics (see [2] for more details), that are used to build standard fixed-width histograms. Percentiles of the distribution are then evaluated with linear interpolation, and stored in Round Robin Databases (RRD).

Our methodology is as in Fig. 1. Input blocks (shaded gray) are quantiles vectors q_i gathered from multiple (local or remote) probes, which are processed to gather consolidated quantile vectors as output to the process. We *interpolate* input quantile vector to get a cumulative distribution function (CDF). We consider two interpolation strategies, namely: a *Linear (L)* and a *Monotonic Spline (S)* strategy (in the latter case, we ensure monotonicity using the Piecewise Cubic Hermite Interpolating Polynomial [5]).

These interpolated functions are weighted by the amount of traffic they represent (weights can be computed in terms of flows, packets or bytes), and added to get the total CDF. Finally, as output of our workflow, we obtain the consolidated $\overline{q}_i$ deciles vector from the total CDF with the bisection method. Finally, the consolidated continuous output is compared to the real quantiles $\tilde{q}_i$ of the aggregated distribution, obtained from running Tstat on the aggregated traces. In what follows, we evaluate the accuracy of the overall workflow by assessing the relative error $(\overline{q}_i - \tilde{q}_i)/\tilde{q}_i$.

As ouput, we limitedly consider *deciles* of the distribution. However, our methodology exploits input quantiles to reconstruct the distributions and operate over CDFs, so that in principle input and output sets do not need to be homogeneous. We thus argue that CDF interpolation can benefit of a larger number of samples (i.e., knots in Spline terms), providing a more accurate description for the intermediate consolidation process. As such, we consider two cases: a *Single (S)* case, where *deciles* are both input and output, and a *Double (D)* case where we additionally use intermediate quantiles (i.e., 5th, 15th, 25th to 95th) as input to the process.

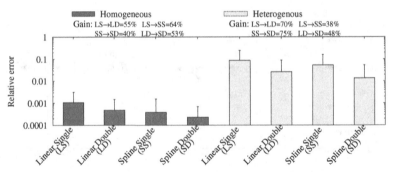

Fig. 2. Error in the consolidation process

3 Experiments

We use several traces, some of which are publicly available. Vantage points pertain to different network environments (e.g., Campus [1, 3] and ISP networks [6]), countries (e.g., EU [3,6] and Australia [1]) and have been collected over a period of over 8 years.

We compactly represent consolidation errors in Fig. 2 (meand and stdev bars over all metrics and quantiles), indicating with *homogeneous* and *heterogeneous* the case of multiple local and distributed vantage points respectively. We further annotate the picture with relative accuracy gain with respect to different consolidation strategies. Shortly, (i) consolidation error is practically negligible for local processes (median error is about 0.1% and maximum 1%), but large for heterogeneous probes (median 1%, maximum 30%, and possibly >100% for naïve strategies); (ii) the use of intermediate quantiles (e.g., 5th, 15th, and so on), is desirable as it significantly improves accuracy (up to 75% in the case of multiple vantage points); (iii) interpolation via Splines is preferable, as it yields to an accuracy gain over Linear interpolation of 40% in our dataset.

Acknowledgement. This work has been carried out at LINCS http://www. lincs.fr and funded by the FP7 mPlane project (grant agreement no. 318627).

References

1. Auckland traces, http://www.wand.net.nz/
2. Tstat homepage, http://tstat.tlc.polito.it
3. Unibs traces, http://www.ing.unibs.it/ntw/tools/traces/
4. Finamore, A., Mellia, M., Meo, M., Munafo, M., Rossi, D.: Experiences of internet traffic monitoring with tstat. IEEE Network (2011)
5. Fritsch, F.N., Carlson, R.E.: Monotone piecewise cubic interpolation. SIAM Journal on Numerical Analysis 17(2), 238–246 (1980)
6. Tammaro, D., Valenti, S., Rossi, D., Pescape, A.: Exploiting packet sampling measurements for traffic characterization and classification. In: Wiley IJNM, pp. 451–476 (2012)

A Needle in the Haystack - Delay Based User Identification in Cellular Networks*

Marco V. Barbera, Simone Bronzini, Alessandro Mei, and Vasile C. Perta

Sapienza University, Rome, Italy
{barbera,bronzini,perta,mei}@di.uniroma1.it

Abstract. In this work, we discuss a technique for identifying users in cellular networks that exploits the effect that RRC state machine transitions have on the measured round-trip time of mobile devices. Our preliminary experiments performed in a controlled environment, show that it is possible to leverage popular real-time messaging apps, such as Facebook, WhatsApp and Viber, to trigger an observable delay pattern on a user's device, and use it to identify the device.

Keywords: Cellular Networks, Security, Privacy.

1 Introduction

With respect to broadband fixed networks, cellular networks are very constrained in terms of both energy and radio resources available to each mobile device. To balance between efficiency and user experience, mobile devices (referred to as "user equipment" by the standard) are assigned radio resources depending on the volume of data they send or receive from the network. This process is regulated by means of transitions in a Radio Resource Control (RRC) state machine that is associated to each device. RRC states are typically CELL_IDLE, CELL_FACH, and CELL_DCH, corresponding to no, low, or full radio resources respectively. Promotions from lower to higher resource states are not immediate. Rather, they introduce an observable extra delay (*i.e.*, 1 or 2 seconds) to packets sent to a mobile device that has not recently used network resources (*e.g.*, is in the CELL_IDLE state). Because of this, round-trip times are sufficient to remotely characterise the RRC state machine used by devices in a target cellular network, as recently shown by Qian *et al.* [3]. In this work we verify whether round-trip time variations due to RRC state machine transitions, in conjunction with network activity triggered by mobile push notifications, may, in principle, allow to remotely identify the IP address of users of popular mobile messaging apps. This could represent a potential threat to mobile users, as it would permit an adversary to perform focused attacks on a specific set of devices, such as the stealth-spam-attack discussed by Peng *et al.* [2]. More in general, this is another example of attack exploiting the unique characteristics of mobile networks and devices [1,5,4].

---

* This work has been partially supported by a Google Faculty Research Grant 2013.

M. Faloutsos and A. Kuzmanovic (Eds.): PAM 2014, LNCS 8362, pp. 265–267, 2014.

2   Identifying Mobile Devices from RTT Variations

In our model, an adversary produces some network traffic on the target user device (*e.g.,* using a sequence of instant messages), which triggers RRC state transitions on the device and induce some observable pattern on the round-trip times towards it. At the same time, the adversary looks for similar delay patterns towards all, or a subset of, the devices of the mobile network operator. This results in a set of candidate IPs IP_range that is reduced in size by iteratively applying the same procedure multiple times. To produce traffic on the user's device, we propose the use of real-time messaging apps such as Google Talk, or near real-time apps such as Facebook Messenger, Viber, and Whatsapp. In fact, to improve the detection accuracy, messages to the user's device should be delivered within a short time after they have been sent, assuming the user is online. Note that it is not necessary for the adversary to be socially very close to the target user. For instance, both WhatsApp and Viber allow messages to be sent to any user, given her mobile phone number. To measure round-trip times, the adversary has to be able to directly reach the target user device from a vantage point. This is possible if the cellular network assigns public, reachable IP addresses to the devices, or, if device-to-device probing is allowed between devices with a private IP address. This has been recently estimated to be the case for around 50% of the cellular networks [4]. The initial IP_range can be set to the whole set of IPs of the cellular network carrier, if no extra information on the target user is known. If the user's coarse-grained location is known, to speed up the process, the set can instead be restricted by mapping IP addresses of mobile devices to a given geographical area using the method proposed by Qian *et al.* [4].

3   Evaluation

To test the effectiveness of our detection methodology, we used as a target device a Samsung Galaxy S Plus attached to a popular Italian cellular network. During th test, the device was left idle, under stable network conditions and signal strength. The device was assigned an IP in a /19 subnet, which we used as the initial IP_range set. The adversary, a Linux host attached to our university's network, continuously probed the round-trip times (RTTs) towards the IP_range set by means of low-rate ping packets sent every 10 seconds. The probing rate has to be chosen in such a way that ping packets alone cannot keep the devices' state-machines at a high-power state (*i.e.,* CELL_DCH). If a too-high rate is used, then all the devices IP_range would roughly show the same low-delay pattern, thus making detection impossible. To trigger periods of network traffic on the target's user device pattern we alternated a 3 minutes interval where no data is sent to the device, with a 2 minutes interval where the RRC machine state of the device is kept on CELL_DCH by means of, *e.g.,* Facebook, WhatsApp, or Viber instant messages. To restrict IP_range to the set of possible IPs of the target device, the adversary looks for devices whose RTT suddenly drops by at least α milliseconds after the message sequence has been sent. These corresponded to the devices that, during the probing period, switched from a low-power state to a higher-power state (*e.g.,* CELL_IDLE $\rightarrow$ CELL_DCH). This is exemplified in Figure 1, where it can also be observed how network

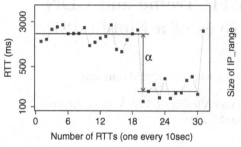

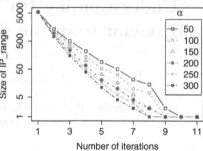

Fig. 1. Sudden drop in the RTT when the target device passes from CELL_IDLE to CELL_DCH

Fig. 2. Convergence of the algorithm with different values of α (in ms). Each iteration lasts 5 minutes.

delays are at least an order of magnitude lower than delays produced by RRC state transitions. In Figure 2 we show how the IP_range set shrinks by iteratively applying our detection methodology with different values of α. Interestingly, with just one iteration, the IP_range candidate set shrinks by around the 90% almost independently on the α parameter used. This is probably because many devices in the initial IP_range set are in CELL_IDLE state. Discarding these devices is very easy, as they always yield very high RTTs. After some iterations, the percentage of devices that is discarded each time slowly decreases, while the parameter α has a higher impact. In this case, increasing the threshold α helps taking into account only the strong delay variations given by actual RRC machine state transitions. Overall, we were able to correctly guess the IP of the target user's device in a few iterations (around 8 in the example). Detecting the user's device IP address with this level of accuracy may take more time when starting with a larger IP_range set. However, depending on the scenario, the number of iterations could be reduced by terminating the search when the IP_range set becomes smaller than a certain threshold. For instance, to save bandwidth resources in a spam attack [2], an adversary could be satisfied with just a small enough set of possible IPs of the target user's device.

References

1. Lee, P.P., Bu, T., Woo, T.: On the detection of signaling DoS attacks on 3G wireless networks. In: INFOCOM. IEEE (2007)
2. Peng, C., Li, C.Y., Tu, G.H., Lu, S., Zhang, L.: Mobile data charging: new attacks and countermeasures. In: CCS. ACM (2012)
3. Qian, F., Wang, Z., Gerber, A., Mao, Z.M., Sen, S., Spatscheck, O.: Characterizing radio resource allocation for 3G networks. In: IMC. ACM (2010)
4. Qian, Z., Wang, Z., Xu, Q., Mao, Z.M., Zhang, M., Wang, Y.M.: You can run, but you cant hide: Exposing network location for targeted DoS attacks in cellular networks. In: NDSS (2012)
5. Traynor, P., Lin, M., Ongtang, M., Rao, V., Jaeger, T., McDaniel, P., La Porta, T.: On cellular botnets: measuring the impact of malicious devices on a cellular network core. In: CCS. ACM (2009)

Understanding HTTP Traffic and CDN Behavior from the Eyes of a Mobile ISP⋆

Pedro Casas, Pierdomenico Fiadino, and Arian Bär

Telecommunications Research Center Vienna - FTW, Vienna, Austria
surname@ftw.at

Abstract. Today's Internet is dominated by HTTP services and Content Delivery Networks (CDNs). Popular web services like Facebook and YouTube are hosted by highly distributed CDNs like Akamai and Google. Understanding this new complex Internet scenario is paramount for network operators, to control the traffic on their networks and to improve the quality experienced by their customers, specially when something goes wrong. This paper studies the most popular HTTP services and their underlying hosting networks, through the analysis of a full week of HTTP traffic traces collected at an operational mobile network.

Keywords: HTTP Traffic, Content Delivery Networks, Mobile Networks.

1 Introduction

Today's Internet is shaped by the success of large services running on top of HTTP. HTTP is currently the dominating content delivery protocol, accounting for more than 75% of the residential customers traffic [1]. HTTP-based services such as YouTube and Facebook are forcing the Internet to shift the content as close as possible to the users. The very last few years have seen an astonishing development in Content Delivery Networks (CDNs) technology, and nowadays Internet content is delivered by large CDNs like Akamai or Google.

This paper studies the dynamics of the top Internet services running on HTTP. Using a full week of HTTP traffic traces collected at the mobile broadband network of a major European ISP, we study the associations between services and the hosting organizations providing the content. The dataset consists of more than half a billion HTTP flows. For each flow, the dataset contains the contacted URL, the server IP address, the total bytes exchanged with this server IP, the duration of the flow, and a timestamp. The dataset includes the organization/AS owning the server IP hosting the content, extracted from the MaxMind databases[1]. The services running on top of the HTTP flows are classified using HTTPTag [6]. HTTPTag is an on-line HTTP classification system based on pattern matching, applied to the requested URL.

⋆ This work has been performed in the framework of the EU-IP project mPlane, funded by the European Commission under the grant 318627.

[1] MaxMIND GeoIP databases, http://www.maxmind.com

M. Faloutsos and A. Kuzmanovic (Eds.): PAM 2014, LNCS 8362, pp. 268–271, 2014.

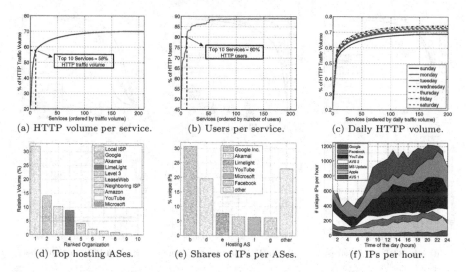

(a) HTTP volume per service.   (b) Users per service.   (c) Daily HTTP volume.

(d) Top hosting ASes.   (e) Shares of IPs per ASes.   (f) IPs per hour.

Fig. 1. (up) HTTP traffic classification using HTTPTag. (down) IPs and top ASes hosting the top services on a single day.

The study and characterization of the Internet traffic hosted and delivered by the top content providers and CDNs has gained important momentum in the last few years [2–4]. In the specific case of HTTP traffic, classification and analysis has been the focus of many recent studies [1,5–7].

2 HTTP Services, CDNs, and Content Providers

Figs. 1(a) and 1(b) depict the distribution of HTTP traffic volume and number of users covered by HTTPTag on a normal day. HTTPTag classifies more than 70% of the total HTTP traffic volume caused by almost 90% of the web users in the studied network. The top-10-volume services account for almost 60% of the overall HTTP traffic, and the 10 most popular services are accessed by about 80% of the users. Fig. 1(c) shows the HTTP volume labeled by HTTPTag on the studied dataset. The list of top-volume services include YouTube, Facebook, Google Search, Apple Store and iTunes, two Adult Video Streaming services (AVS 1 and AVS 2), and Windows Update.

These services are hosted by multiple ASes. Fig. 1(d) depicts the fraction of HTTP traffic volume hosted by the top ASes and CDNs. The local ISP ASes host more than 30% of the total traffic, evidencing the large usage of content caching. Google hosts the lion share of YouTube, whereas Akamai hosts contents such as Facebook static files, Apple Store/iTunes, and Windows updates among others. Figs. 1(e) and 1(f) depict the share and daily number of unique server IPs hosting the top services. Google and Akamai are the most distributed orgs. in terms of server IPs. The change in the number of IPs being used by Google Search, Facebook, and YouTube is impressive, going from about 250 IPs per service at 5 am to up to 1200 in the case of Google Search.

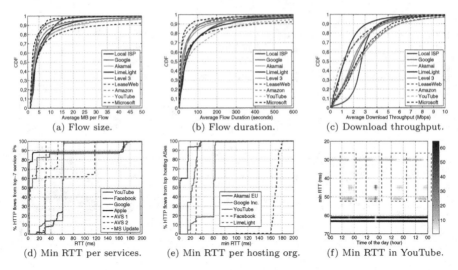

(a) Flow size.   (b) Flow duration.   (c) Download throughput.

(d) Min RTT per services.   (e) Min RTT per hosting org.   (f) Min RTT in YouTube.

Fig. 2. (up) Characterization of the flows served by different organizations. (down) Distribution and variation of min RTT per service and per hosting organization.

3   Content Location and Performance

We study now the characteristics of the flows provisioned by each organization, focusing only on the largest flows, bigger than 1 MB. Figs. 2(a) and 2(b) depict the distribution of the average flow size and duration for some of the top organizations hosting content. Flows provided by LeaseWeb and Akamai are the biggest in terms of volume and duration, and specially LeaseWeb delivers very big and long flows. In terms of throughput, Fig. 2(c) depicts the average download throughput distribution; flows cached at the local ISP are served the fastest, with an average download throughput of about 2.7 Mbps, followed by Akamai, Amazon, and Microsoft.

To conclude, we analyze the location of the servers hosting the content. We consider the min Round Trip Time (RTT) to the hosting servers as a measure of the servers distance from the vantage point. Figs. 2(d) and 2(e) depict the min RTT values per service and per hosting organization. A large fraction of the Facebook, Apple, and Windows Update flows come from servers probably located in the same city of the vantage point, as min RTT values are below 5ms. These three services are largely provided by Akamai. The AVS 2 service seems to be mainly served from two locations in Europe (min RTT ≈ 30ms), perfectly matching the results for Limelight (the hosting CDN). Fig. 2(f) depicts the hourly evolution of the min RTT for YouTube flows during 4 consecutive days. Each column depicts the CDF of the min RTT. Most of the flows are delivered from the two Google locations depicted in Fig. 2(b) at 61ms and 63ms. Markedly min RTT shifts occur every day at exactly the same time slots, suggesting the usage of time/load-based server selection policies by Google.

References

1. Maier, G., Feldmann, A., Paxson, V., Allman, M.: On Dominant Characteristics of Residential Broadband Internet Traffic. In: IMC (2009)
2. Gehlen, V., Finamore, A., Mellia, M., Munafò, M.M.: Uncovering the Big Players of the Web. In: Pescapè, A., Salgarelli, L., Dimitropoulos, X. (eds.) TMA 2012. LNCS, vol. 7189, pp. 15–28. Springer, Heidelberg (2012)
3. Krishnan, R., Madhyastha, H., Srinivasan, S., Jain, S., Krishnamurthy, A., Anderson, T., Gao, J.: Moving Beyond End-to-End Path Information to Optimize CDN Performance. In: IMC (2009)
4. Nygren, E., Sitaraman, R., Sun, J.: The Akamai Network: A Platform for High-Performance Internet Applications. SIGOPS 44(3) (2010)
5. Erman, J., Gerber, A., Sen, S.: HTTP in the Home: It is not just about PCs. ACM CCR 41(1) (2011)
6. Fiadino, P., Bär, A., Casas, P.: HTTPTag: A Flexible On-line HTTP Classification System for Operational 3G Networks. In: INFOCOM (2013)
7. Schneider, F., Ager, B., Maier, G., Feldmann, A., Uhlig, S.: Pitfalls in HTTP Traffic Measurements and Analysis. In: Taft, N., Ricciato, F. (eds.) PAM 2012. LNCS, vol. 7192, pp. 242–251. Springer, Heidelberg (2012)

On Understanding User Interests through Heterogeneous Data Sources

Samamon Khemmarat[1], Sabyasachi Saha[2], Han Hee Song[2],
Mario Baldi[2], and Lixin Gao[1]

[1] University of Massachusetts Amherst, MA, USA
[2] Narus Inc., CA, USA

Abstract. User interests can be learned from multiple sources, each of them presenting only partial facets. We propose an approach to merge user information from disparate data sources to enable a more complete, enriched view of user interests. Using our approach, we show that merging different sources results in three times of more interest categories in user profiles than with each single source and that merged profiles can capture much more common interests among a group of users, which is key to group profiling.

1 Introduction

User interest profiles allow businesses and service providers to customize their services and products to better suit users' needs and likings. User "footprints" left in cyberspace, spread across different services, contain a large amount of information about them. While many research works focused on joining user data across various services of the same type (*e.g.*, online social networks) [2], aggregating users' interests at various social networks or websites can only capture a very specialized, partial view of the user, the persona that user wants the world to see. A more comprehensive user profile can be captured by combining user information from different types of services. However, it is not trivial to do so because of each service having its own representation of user data. In the last few years, Internet users are increasingly interactive and form groups with shared interests (*e.g.*, meetup.com, Google Hangouts, etc.). Understanding the common interests of groups of users allows services to be tailored to groups [3]. However, such group profiling requires finding commonality in information from different users, which needs to be done at a semantic level.

The goal of this research work is to represent user interests as they can be learned from different data sources in a single format that can be easily explained, compared, and combined. We propose a generalized method that flexibly joins user interests from heterogeneous sources of data. Using the proposed approach, we create user profiles from two representative data sets, online social network (OSN) profiles and web browsing traces collected from a Cellular Service Provider (CSP) and combine them. We show that our approach (i) can create a richer user profile from heterogeneous information sources, and (ii) can create more effective group profile by finding more common interests among users, compared to using a single information source.

M. Faloutsos and A. Kuzmanovic (Eds.): PAM 2014, LNCS 8362, pp. 272–274, 2014.
© Springer International Publishing Switzerland 2014

2 Reconstructing User Interest

We construct a profile P_{ur} of a user, u, analyzing raw data from a single information source, r. To allow comparing and merging interests across different sources and users (or to group interests of users), interests from each source are mapped on a category hierarchy $\mathcal{H}$. Then we create the unified user profile $\mathcal{P}_u$ combining the interest categories in all P_{ur}. In particular, the process includes the following key steps.

1. Interest Item Extraction. We define an *interest item* as a unit of data that provides information about coherent topics of interests, e.g., a URL requested by a user in browsing activity logs. We built specific parsers and noise filters, for each data source, to extract a set of interest items $\mathcal{I}_u$ for user u.

2. Interest Item Enhancement. In this step we create a vector , V_k, of terms, t_{kj}, that enrich the semantics of each interest item, $i_k \in \mathcal{I}_u$, using additional resources and processes, e.g., using synonyms of words or metadata of URLs. V_k, is used to aid interest item categorization (next step).

3. Interest-to-Category Mapping. Each interest item, i_k, is mapped into an interest category hierarchy $\mathcal{H}$. Using Machine Learning techniques, we categorize i_k to one or few interest categories $\{h_s\}(\in \mathcal{H})$.

4. User Profile Creation. A user's (u) interest profile, P_{ur}, can be created by aggregating all of his interest categories, represented as a single vector of interest categories along with the frequencies $\{(h_s, f_s)\}$ with which interest items map on them. We, then, create the unified user profile $\mathcal{P}_u$ combining all P_{ur} of the user.

3 Experimental Results

Our dataset contains data of 15,428 users. The association between the browsing traces and OSN's ID of a user was done with the Mosaic system [4].The browsing traces, T1 and T2 are 5-day long and were collected from a backbone router of a major CSP in North America. The categories from the ODP directory [1] are used as reference interest categories, to which the extracted interest items from different data sources are mapped to.

For each individual user, we study interest items overlap between profiles. Figure 1 plots quantities of interest categories that overlap between the profiles

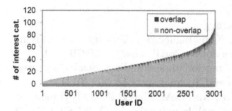

Fig. 1. Overlaps between browsing and OSN profiles

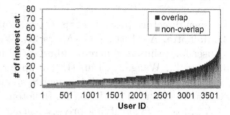

Fig. 2. Overlaps between the browsing profiles from T1 and T2

Table 1. Effectiveness of group profiling

Profile type		10 user group		50 user group	
		grp int	top-1 cov.	grp int	top-1 cov.
Uncat.	Browse	0	0.27	1	0.46
	OSN	0	0.01	0	0.00
Cat.	Browse	4	0.86	5	0.80
	OSN	6	0.92	7	0.93
Cat.& Merged		13	0.97	14	0.96

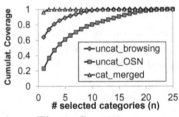

Fig. 3. Group coverage

from the two sources. We contrast this result with Figure 2, which plots the same quantities for two browsing profiles created from two periods of time, T1 and T2. The smaller overlap in Figure 1 suggests that a richer profile can be created by combining data from disparate sources. The average number of interest categories per user increases by up to 3 times when the profiles are combined.

Group Profile. Now, we show the effectiveness of merging profiles when we want to discover interests commonly shared among a group of users, *e.g.*, gathered in a coffee shop. The effectiveness is measured as (i) the number of *group interests*, interests shared by more than 50% of users, and (ii) the fraction of users in the group that have the most popular interest, referred to as *top-1 coverage*. The comparison is performed between three types of profiles, original OSN and browsing profiles with no categorization, categorized OSN and browsing profiles, and merged categorized profiles. We generate 50 groups of 10 and 50 randomly selected users from our dataset. Table 1 shows that using the categorized & merged profiles results in the highest number of group interests as well as the best top-1 coverage. Furthermore, we define *coverage* for a set of categories to be the proportion of users for whom at least one of his interests can be found in the set. In Figure 3 evaluating the number of interest categories required to satisfy users in the group, we observe that the categorized & merged profiles require only two interest categories to satisfy all members, whereas the uncategorized profiles require 25 categories to be picked to cover interests of all members.

With our results, we illustrated that combining interests from multiple sources leads to increased availability of user data and higher utility in profiling a group of users.

References

1. Open directory project, http://www.dmoz.org
2. Malhotra, A., Totti, L.C., Meira Jr., W., Kumaraguru, P., Almeida, V.: Studying user footprints in different online social networks. CoRR, abs/1301.6870 (2013)
3. Tang, L., Wang, X., Liu, H.: Group profiling for understanding social structures. ACM Transactions on Intelligent Systems and Technology 3(1), 15 (2011)
4. Xia, N., Song, H.H., Liao, Y., Iliofotou, M., Nucci, A., Zhang, Z.-L., Kuzmanovic, A.: Mosaic: Quantifying privacy leakage in mobile networks. In: ACM SIGCOMM (2013)

Nightlights: Entropy-Based Metrics
for Classifying Darkspace Traffic Patterns

Tanja Zseby[1], Nevil Brownlee[2,3], Alistair King[3], and kc claffy[3]

[1] Vienna University of Technology, 1240 Vienna, Austria
[2] University of Auckland, Auckland 1010, New Zealand
[3] CAIDA, UC San Diego, CA 92093, USA

An IP darkspace is a globally routed IP address space with no active hosts. All traffic destined to darkspace addresses is unsolicited and often originates from network scanning or attacks. A sudden increases of different types of darkspace traffic can serve as indicator of new vulnerabilities, misconfigurations or large scale attacks. In our analysis we take advantage of the fact that darkspace traffic typically originates from processes that use randomly chosen addresses or ports (e.g. scanning) or target a specific address or port (e.g. DDoS, worm spreading). These behaviors induce a concentration or dispersion in feature distributions of the resulting traffic aggregate and can be distinguished using entropy as a compact representation. Its lightweight, unambiguous, and privacy-compatible character makes entropy a suitable metric that can facilitate early warning capabilities, operational information exchange among network operators, and comparison of analysis results among a network of distributed IP darkspaces.

Using traffic from five months from a large /8 darkspace monitor, we investigate the use of an entropy vector for IP darkspace traffic classification. As reference we perform an in-depth analysis with the tool iatmon [2] to classify the traffic into 15 different traffic types. We then compare our entropy results to the detailed iatmon analysis. We use the approach and the formula presented in [3] to calculate an estimate for Shannon entropy from IP address and port number distributions: $H(X) = -\sum_{i=1}^{N} \frac{n_i}{S} \cdot log_2 \left(\frac{n_i}{S} \right)$, where $i...N$ are the different bins in the frequency distribution (IP addresses or ports). n_i denotes the number of packets that belong to bin i (e.g. all packets with port number 445). X denotes the distribution of a feature (sIP, dIP, $sPort$ or $dPort$), formed by the frequencies $n_1, ...n_N$ of all bins N. S denotes the total number of observations (packets received) in the time interval. In the /8 darkspace we get $N = 2^{24}$ possible destination addresses and therefore $H(dIP)_{max} = 24$.

For each time interval t we compute an entropy vector that contains the four entropy values: $\boldsymbol{H}_t = [H_t(sIP), H_t(dIP), H_t(sPort), H_t(dPort)]$. We expect different changes in the entropy vector ($+\Delta h$ increase, $-\Delta h$ decrease), which provide a unique signature for different darkspace events.

A **multi-source horizontal scan** disperses source IPs and source ports, but concentrates the destination port distribution. $H(dIP)$ dispersion is already close to the maximum (24 bits) in darkspace data, so we expect only small effects on $H(dIP)$ (denoted by $(+\Delta h)$): $\Delta \boldsymbol{H}_t = [+\Delta h, (+\Delta h), +\Delta h, -\Delta h]$. **Backscatter** traffic occurs if victims of a DoS attack are attacked with spoofed source addresses and reply to those spoofed addresses. For backscatter we expect a

M. Faloutsos and A. Kuzmanovic (Eds.): PAM 2014, LNCS 8362, pp. 275–277, 2014.
© Springer International Publishing Switzerland 2014

concentration of the source IP distribution, because a lot of traffic is sent from relatively few (victim) sources. We expect a source port concentration toward the port that was used as destination port to attack the victim machine, whereas destination ports disperses if the attacker used random source ports. Again we expect only a small effect on $H(dIP)$: $\Delta\mathbf{H}_t = [-\Delta h, (+\Delta h), -\Delta h, +\Delta h]$. For a **distributed probe** we expect a source address and source port dispersion, caused by the use of bots or spoofed addresses, and a concentration of destination address and port toward the target: $\Delta\mathbf{H}_t = [+\Delta h, -\Delta h, +\Delta h, -\Delta h]$.

We analyse darkspace traffic from 5 month: Nov 2008 (Conficker outbreak), Jan/Feb 2011 and Jan/Feb 2012. We first classify the traffic into 15 traffic classes using an in-depth analysis with iatmon [2]. The output serves as a baseline against which to evaluate our entropy-based inferences. Then we calculate one entropy vector for each hour interval, using the tool Corsaro[1] and the statistical package R[2]. We then compare the detailed iatmon results with the more lightweight entropy analysis to see if new events follow the expected entropy patterns and thus can be classified based on entropy.

Multi-Source Scans: The detailed iatmon analysis of Nov 2008 data reveals an increase of *TCP horizontal scan* packets, caused by the Conficker outbreak, where hosts began to scan port 445 trying to spread the worm [1]. The outbreak of the new worm is clearly visible in entropy vectors, following the expected entropy pattern for a multi-source scan.

Backscatter is captured effectively by the entropy vector in our experiments. Figure 1 shows the results from Feb 2012 as an example. It shows the entropies (1st and 2nd graph) and the amount of backscatter packets according to iatmon's classification (3rd graph). As expected, if backscatter increases we observe an increase in $H(dPort)$, a decrease in $H(sPort)$ and $H(sIP)$ and no significant changes for $H(dIP)$. Table 1 lists the correlation coefficients between entropy and backscatter traffic. The observations also conform to the expected behavior. While the increase in backscatter traffic does not always affect the overall packet count (last row in table 1), it always shows significant changes in entropy.

Table 1. Correlation coefficients for time series of amount of backscatter (bs) traffic (as seen by iatmon) and entropy (rows 1,2) and bs traffic and packet count (row 3)

corr. coeff.	Jan11	Feb11	Jan12	Feb12	corr. coeff.	Jan11	Feb11	Jan12	Feb12
$bs,H(sIP)$	-0.48	-0.38	-0.37	-0.75	$bs,H(dIP)$	0.14	0.29	0.36	0.44
$bs,H(sPort)$	-0.60	-0.52	-0.58	-0.83	$bs,H(dPort)$	0.69	0.62	0.69	0.91
$bs,pktcount$	0.28	0.39	0.48	0.76					

Large **probing** events are also visible in entropy. The iatmon analysis for Jan 2011 shows a large distributed probe originating from many sources (spoofed and/or bots) directed to a specific IP address and port. The new probe traffic is clearly visible in the entropy statistics (figure 2); the increase in new sources

---

[1] http://www.caida.org/tools/measurement/corsaro/
[2] http://www.r-project.org/

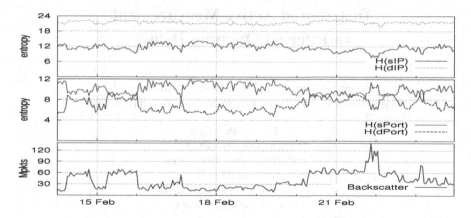

Fig. 1. Entropy correlation with backscatter traffic (February 2012), showing IP address entropies $H(sIP)$, $H(dIP)$ (1st graph), port entropies $H(sPort)$, $H(dPort)$ (2nd graph), amount of backscatter traffic according to iatmon analysis (3rd graph)

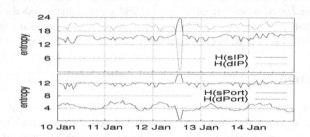

Fig. 2. Entropy during TCP Probe

drives up $H(sIP)$. High concentration of traffic to one address and one port causes $H(dIP)$ and $H(dPort)$ to drop significantly.

Our results show that entropy-based metrics can reveal noteworthy events in IP darkspace. We plan to further investigate the use of entropy to also detect smaller changes or nested events, and evaluate the utility of this method for early warning and privacy-respecting information sharing among darkspace operators.

References

1. Aben, E.: Conficker/Conflicker/Downadup as seen from the UCSD Network Telescope. Technical report, CAIDA (February 2009)
2. Brownlee, N.: One-way traffic monitoring with iatmon. In: Taft, N., Ricciato, F. (eds.) PAM 2012. LNCS, vol. 7192, pp. 179–188. Springer, Heidelberg (2012)
3. Lakhina, A., Crovella, M., Diot, C.: Mining Anomalies Using Traffic Feature Distributions. SIGCOMM Comput. Commun. Rev. 35(4), 217–228 (2005)

Distributed Active Measurement
of Internet Queuing Delays

Pellegrino Casoria[1,3], Dario Rossi[1], Jordan Augé[2],
Marc-Olivier Buob[2], Timur Friedman[2], and Antonio Pescapé[3]

[1] Telecom ParisTech
`first.last@enst.fr`
[2] UPMC Sorbonne Universites
`first.last@lip6.fr`
[3] Universitá di Napoli Federico II
`first.last@unina.it`

Abstract. Despite growing link capacities, over-dimensioned buffers are still causing, in the Internet of the second decade of the third millennium, hosts to suffer from severe queuing delays (or bufferbloat). While maximum bufferbloat possibly exceeds few seconds, it is far less clear how often this maximum is hit in practice. This paper reports on our ongoing work to build a spatial and temporal map of Internet bufferbloat, describing a system based on distributed agents running on PlanetLab that aims at providing a quantitative answer to the above question.

1 Introduction

Given the abundance of active measurement approaches, it may seem at first sight redundant to focus on bufferbloat measurement via active techniques. Yet, this work nicely fit in a gap of the design space explored by the research community.

Our system targets large-scale high-frequency scanning, customized to periodically report very detailed per-host statistics (e.g., percentiles). As individual probes are capable of scanning about 10K hosts in a second, it follows that using 100 PlanetLab nodes we could in principle follow about 1 million hosts every second or, trading space for time, cover the whole Internet in about one hour. Interest of our approach can be summarized as follows.

Due to architectural similarities with scanners [1, 10] and systems based on distributed agents [2, 3], our approach allows to achieve spatial scales larger than [8, 11] (already in this paper) and [4,5] (prospectively). Additionally, our efficient implementation allows much higher scan frequency than [2–5, 8, 11], where the frequency of background latency measurement is typically too sparse to offer an adequate bufferbloat characterization from the user perspective. Finally, in terms of the delay statistics, we avoid to measure *maximum* latency under controlled load as in [8, 9, 11], and rather gather the (typical) delay by continuous host measurement, hence sampling the user load during their *normal* activities.

2 Bufferbloat Scanner Architecture

Building over TopHat [6], we design a distributed architecture for Internet bufferbloat scanning. At the core of our scanner, lay an efficient tool to ping a large amount of hosts

M. Faloutsos and A. Kuzmanovic (Eds.): PAM 2014, LNCS 8362, pp. 278–280, 2014.
© Springer International Publishing Switzerland 2014

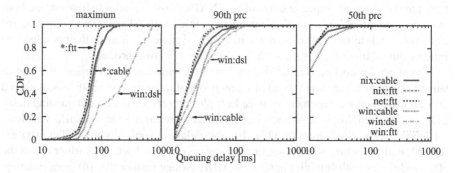

Fig. 1. Validation of the Internet measurement campaign

with the least possible resources. While our tool is far less efficient than the recently released zMap, it is still an order of magnitude faster than the fastest settings of the Nmap Scripting Engine.

We divide measurement periods (of 5 minutes by default), at the beginning of which each measurement server ask for instructions (essentially, a list of destinations/subnets and the sampling frequency, 1 Hz by default). At the end of each measurement period, per-hosts statistics (delay percentiles, etc.) are collected for further post-processing.

For each target, we gauge the queuing delay via ICMP measurements as $q_i = RTT_i - \min_{j \le i} RTT_j$. By ensuring that queuing does not happens at the measurement servers, we can however correctly infer the remote queuing delay. We validate this approach (i) to be very accurate with non-NATted hosts, (ii) to yield a coarse queuing indication (e.g., a binary bufferbloat flag) for NATted hosts.

We notice that the generally measurement are *initiated* by the end-host [4, 5, 8, 9] (SamKnows/BISmark [11] slightly differ in that measurement starts from the HGW). In our case, measurement are instead *targeting* the end-hosts: this is common in large-scale census studies [1, 10] (of which we inherit the scalability property) but has not been explored so far, to the best of our knowledge, for bufferbloat measurements.

3 Measurement Campaign

We report results on a preliminary measurement campaign. We focus on moderate number of hosts $O(10^4)$ on the same ISPs, that we continuously probe at 0.5 Hz frequency from 2 separate PlanetLab nodes for a period of about 8 continuous hours. Overall, we receive replies to 47% of our sent packets, for a total of $O(10^8)$ valid samples – using only two PlanetLab servers, we already achieve a quite significant scale in terms of spatial reach and temporal frequency.

For validation purposes, we infer (i) the access type (AT) of our target hosts by issuing reverse DNS queries, as well as (ii) the remote operating system (OS) through nmap fingerprinting. As for the access type, we expect the breakdown of queuing delay along DSL, FTTH and cable access to yield an intuitive validation of the observed statistics. Additionally, we argue that in case the remote OS is reliably found to be a Windows OS, then queuing delay are representative of non-NATted host statistics (where our methodology is more reliable). Overall, we manage to infer both AT and OS information for 2546 hosts: while this subset is not statistically significant, it nevertheless allows to validate our methodology as it covers the full AT× OS cross-product.

We collect per-host percentiles during 5 minutes windows: Fig. 1 reports the Cumulative Distribution Function (CDF) of a few per-host queuing delay statistics, gathered over all hosts and measurement rounds. Left plot reports the maximum queuing delay CDF: as expected, from the picture clearly emerges that (a) fiber access suffers the lowest delays irrespectively from the OSs, (b) cable delays are only slightly higher, whereas (c) DSL end-hosts may seldom suffer from delays close to 1 sec. We further report the 50th (right) and 90th (middle) percentiles CDF. Notice further that (d) from practical purposes, the 90th percentile is lower than 100 ms under any combination of OS and AT – including end-hosts behind DSL. Moreover, since the *win:cable* and *win:dsl* lines now clearly separate from the others, we infer that the methodology needs to be refined as it likely underestimates bufferbloat delay for NATted hosts – although observation (d) suggests bufferbloat to be a not necessarily frequent problem.

Acknowledgements. This work has been carried out during Pellegrino Casoria internship at LINCS http://www.lincs.fr. The research leading to these results has received funding from the European Union under the FP7 Grant Agreement n. 318627 (Integrated Project "mPlane").

References

1. http://internetcensus2012.bitbucket.org/
2. http://www.caida.org/projects/ark/
3. http://www.netdimes.org/new/
4. Bischof, Z., Otto, J., Sánchez, M., Rula, J., Choffnes, D., Bustamante, F.: Crowdsourcing ISP characterization to the network edge. In: ACM SIGCOMM W-MUST (2011)
5. Bischof, Z.S., Otto, J.S., Bustamante, F.E.: Up, down and around the stack: ISP characterization from network intensive applications. In: ACM SIGCOMM W-MUST (2012)
6. Bourgeau, T., Augé, J., Friedman, T.: Tophat: supporting experiments through measurement infrastructure federation. In: TridentCom (2010)
7. Chirichella, C., Rossi, D.: To the moon and back: are internet bufferbloat delays really that large. In: IEEE INFOCOM Workshop on Traffic Measurement and Analysis, TMA (2013)
8. Jiang, H., Wang, Y., Lee, K., Rhee, I.: Tackling bufferbloat in 3G/4G networks. In: ACM IMC (2012)
9. Kreibich, C., Weaver, N., Nechaev, B., Paxson, V.: Netalyzr: Illuminating the edge network. In: ACM IMC (2010)
10. Leonard, D., Loguinov, D.: Demystifying service discovery: implementing an internet-wide scanner. In: ACM IMC (2010)
11. Sundaresan, S., de Donato, W., Feamster, N., Teixeira, R., Crawford, S., Pescapè, A.: Broadband internet performance: a view from the gateway. In: ACM SIGCOMM (2011)

Author Index